ARINA TANEM

I'm sorry, some of you may be a little embarrassed at the cover illustration for this volume.* But my image of Rurijo is of her being naked (it might be because she gives a strong impression of innocence like a newborn), so I really wanted to draw that. Usually there are no illustrations on the back cover because we have to print the summaries and barcodes there. This illustration was originally an unused folded two-page spread for a title page. I always wanted to use it somehow, so I'm glad it finally got to see the light of day.

Arina Tanemura began her manga career in 1996 when her short stories debuted in *Ribon* magazine. She gained fame with the 1997 publication of *I·O·N*, and ever since her debut Tanemura has been a major force in shojo manga with popular series *Kamikaze Kaito Jeanne*, *Time Stranger Kyoko*, *Full Moon*, and *The Gentlemen's Alliance †*. Both *Kamikaze Kaito Jeanne* and *Full Moon* have been adapted into animated TV series.

*Tanemura Sensei is referring to the Japanese edition.
The illustration can be seen on pages 180 and 181 of this volume.

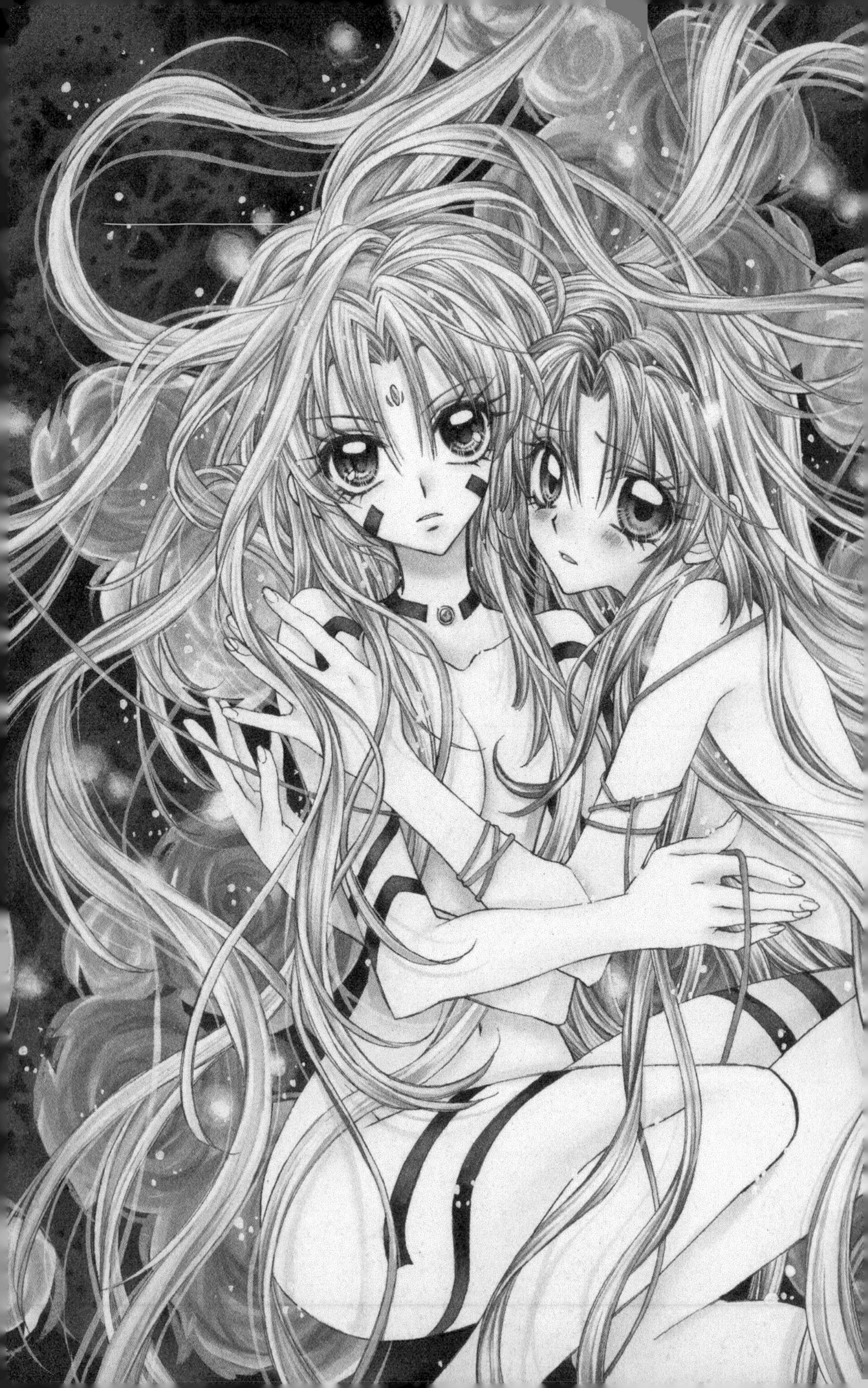

Own the Complete **Arina Tanemura Collection!**

Mistress ★ Fortune

Sakura Hime:
The Legend of Princess Sakura

The Gentlemen's
Alliance †

Short-Tempered
Melancholic and
Other Stories

The Gentlemen's Alliance †:
Arina Tanemura Illustrations

Time Stranger Kyoko

I.O.N.

The Arina Tanemura Collection:
The Art of Full Moon

Full Moon

Sakura Hime: The Legend of Princess Sakura
Volume 5
Shojo Beat Edition

STORY AND ART BY
Arina Tanemura

Translation & Adaptation/Tetsuichiro Miyaki
Touch-up Art & Lettering/Inori Fukuda Trant
Design/Sam Elzway
Editor/Nancy Thistlethwaite

SAKURA-HIME KADEN © 2008 by Arina Tanemura
All rights reserved.
First published in Japan in 2008 by SHUEISHA Inc., Tokyo.
English translation rights arranged by SHUEISHA Inc.

Printed in the U.S.A.

Published by VIZ Media, LLC
P.O. Box 77010
San Francisco, CA 94107

10 9 8 7 6 5 4 3 2 1
First printing, December 2011

www.shojobeat.com   www.viz.com

RURIJO

MAIMAI

ENJU

SHURI

UKYO

Princess Sakura's older brother. He used to be kind, but he has a deep hatred of humans now.

SAKURA HIME
The Legend of Princess Sakura

Story Thus Far

Heian era. Princess Sakura is 14 years old and learns from Byakuya that she is the granddaughter of Princess Kaguya, a princess from the moon. She is the only person able to wield the mystic sword Chizakura that can kill the demon youko. And at the same time, she finds out that her fated soul symbol is "destroy"...

Aoba discovers this and captures Sakura, intending to kill her. Fujimurasaki arrives and Sakura is given orders from the Emperor to officially hunt down a youko.

Sakura travels to Uji where she is told by her lady-in-waiting, Oumi, that the councilor is a traitor. But then Oumi turns into a youko and attacks Sakura...!

The person behind the treachery is a mysterious man named Enju, who is Sakura's brother Kai whom she believed to be dead... He had been tricked by the emperor and held captive in a water chamber. The experience gave him a strong hatred for humans. He stole Sakura away and brought her to Shura Yugenden.

After finding out where Sakura is, Aoba and the others succeed in entering Enju's hideout. But Byakuya is confronted by Maimai who claims, "Being beautiful is the only way I can exist," and overwhelms her in battle...?!

SAKURA HIME
The Legend of Princess Sakura

....

CONTENTS

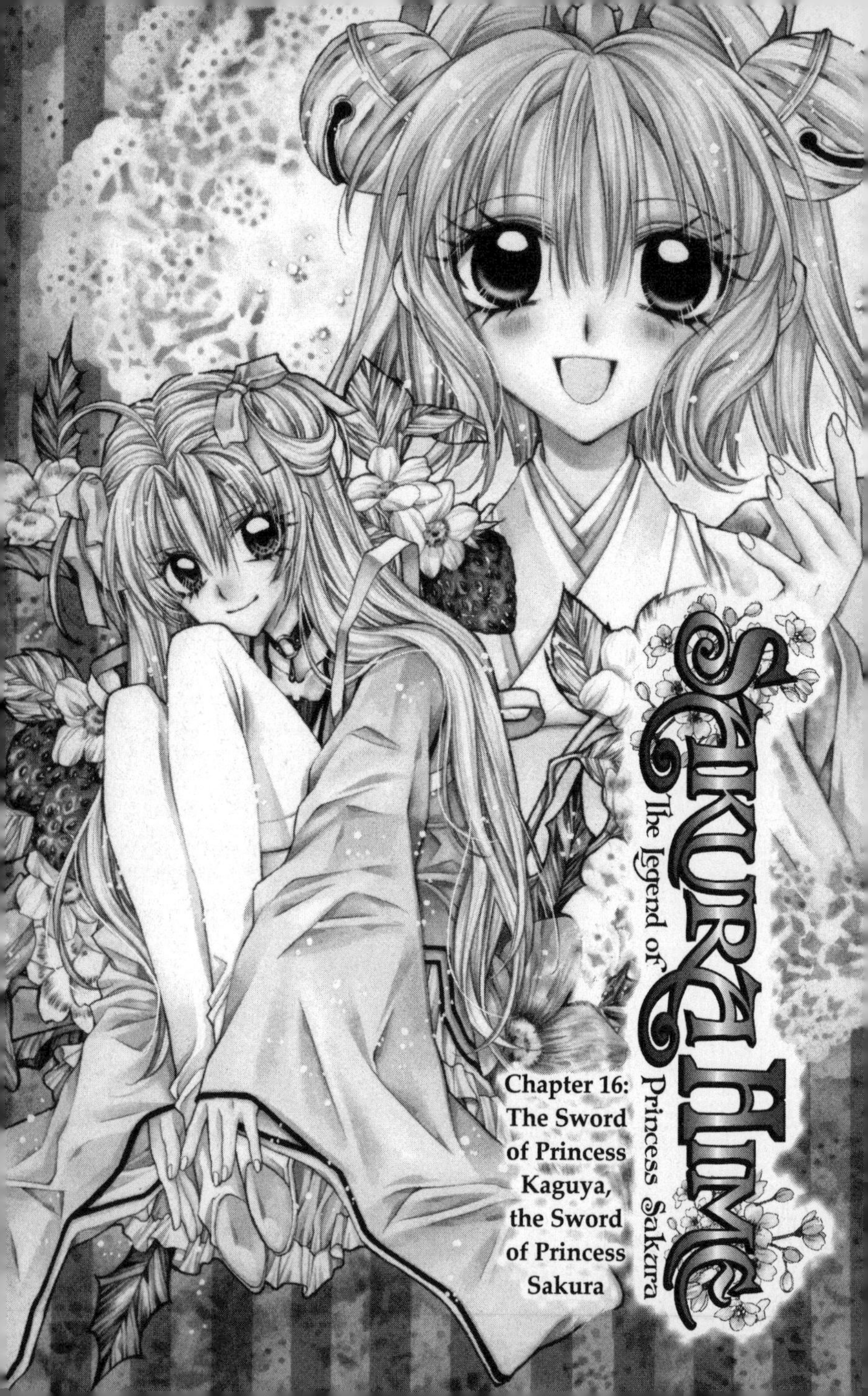
Sakura Hime
The Legend of Princess Sakura
Chapter 16: The Sword of Princess Kaguya, the Sword of Princess Sakura

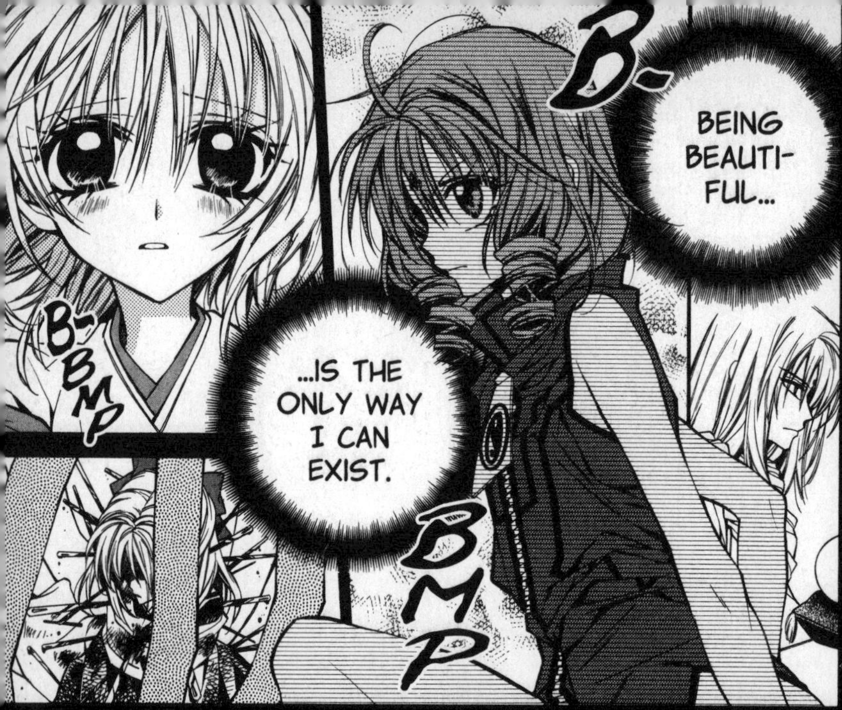
B-
BEING BEAUTI-FUL...
B-BMP
...IS THE ONLY WAY I CAN EXIST.
BMP

Chapter 16: The Sword of Princess Kaguya, the Sword of Princess Sakura

※ I'm giving away the story.

Lead-in Don't ever forget to smile, no matter what the situation is. That is what we promised each other.

This is the climax of the battle between Byakuya and Maimai. I have been looking forward to drawing this scene with Byakuya ever since the series started.

Byakuya's clothes and the shaded areas are similar to Jeanne, an old character of mine, so I was trying hard not to make them look the same. But once the chapter was complete, I was surprised to hear a fan of mine thought she looked like a totally different character by another manga artist. This has happened before actually. (I was worried that people would say Toya looks like Kagura, another character of mine, but they said he was similar to a different character!) (laugh) Not that I really mind, but...

I've gotten a little sidetracked. (Ahem.)

The last scene is Maimai's imagination of "what things might have been like if he had not met Enju and had asked Mai for her hand in marriage."

Starting from this chapter or so, I've started using a G-pen, which is soft-tipped, to do the outlines of the artwork so they're thicker. I've expressed the shadows using lines too, so I wanted to make those lines stand out more. (Before I used 90% Maru-Pen [Mapping Pen] and 10% G-pen. Now I use 90% G-pen and 10% Maru-Pen.)

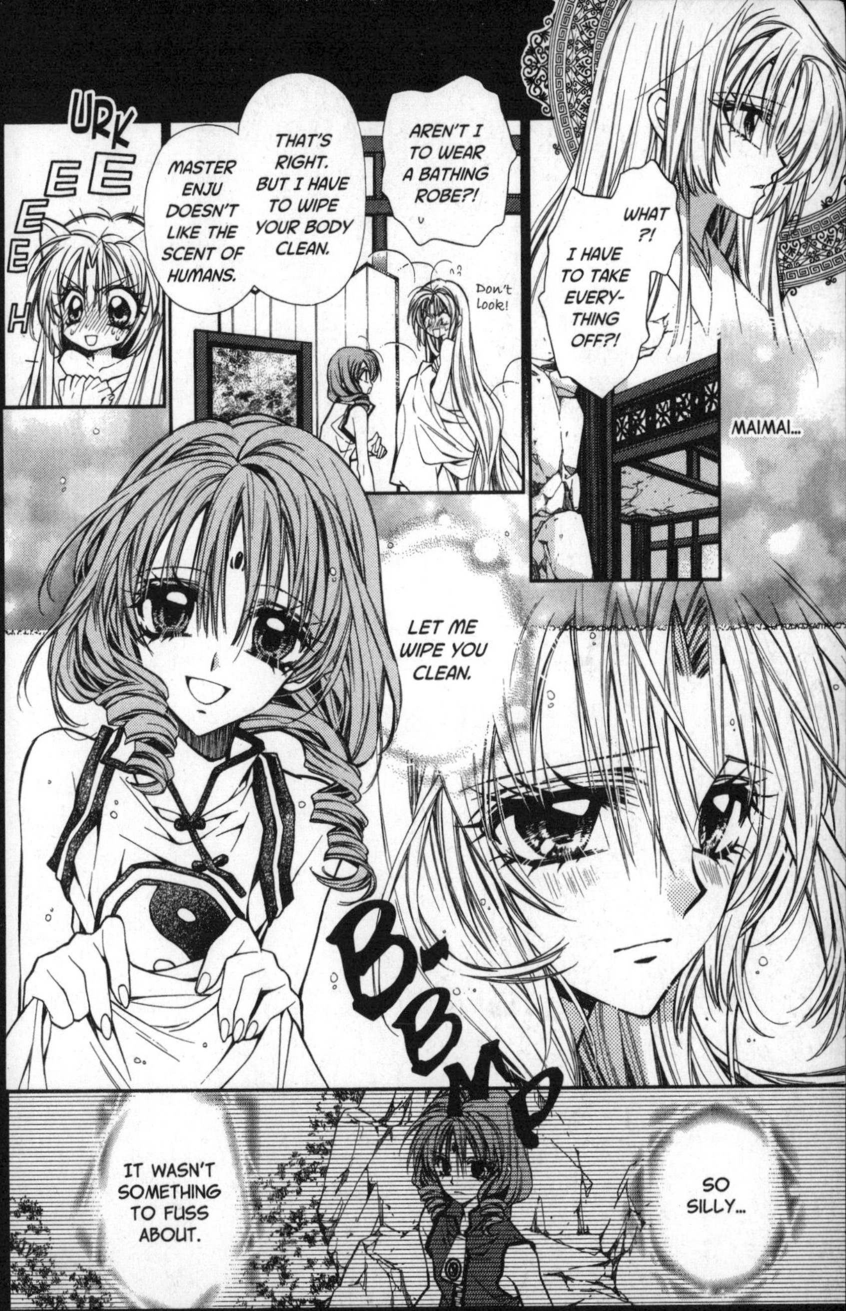
WHAT ?!
I HAVE TO TAKE EVERY-THING OFF?!
AREN'T I TO WEAR A BATHING ROBE?!
Don't look!
THAT'S RIGHT. BUT I HAVE TO WIPE YOUR BODY CLEAN.
MASTER ENJU DOESN'T LIKE THE SCENT OF HUMANS.
URK
EEEEEH
MAIMAI...
LET ME WIPE YOU CLEAN.
B-BMP
SO SILLY...
IT WASN'T SOMETHING TO FUSS ABOUT.

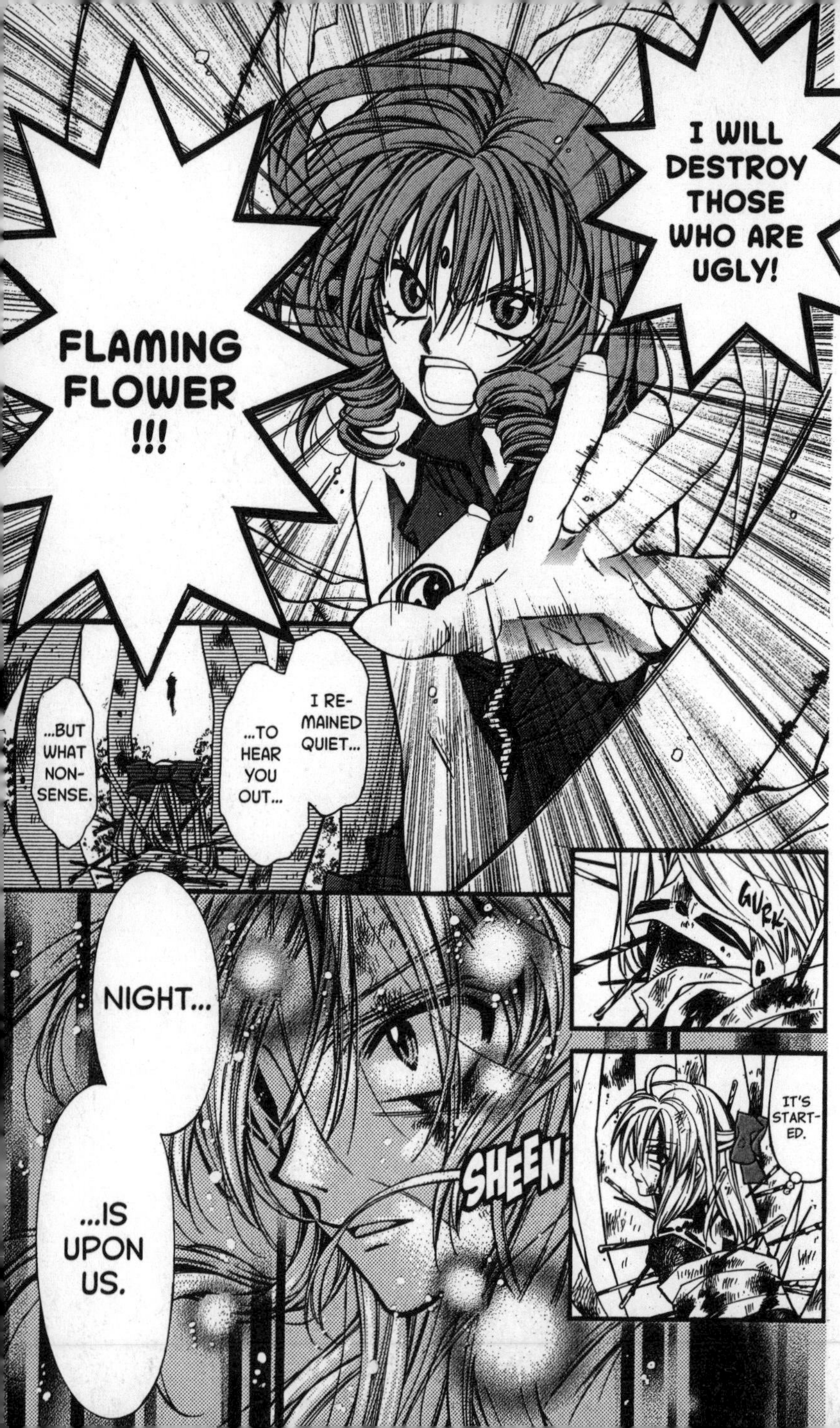
I WILL DESTROY THOSE WHO ARE UGLY!
FLAMING FLOWER !!!
I REMAINED QUIET...
...TO HEAR YOU OUT...
...BUT WHAT NONSENSE.
GURK
IT'S STARTED.
SHEEN
NIGHT...
...IS UPON US.

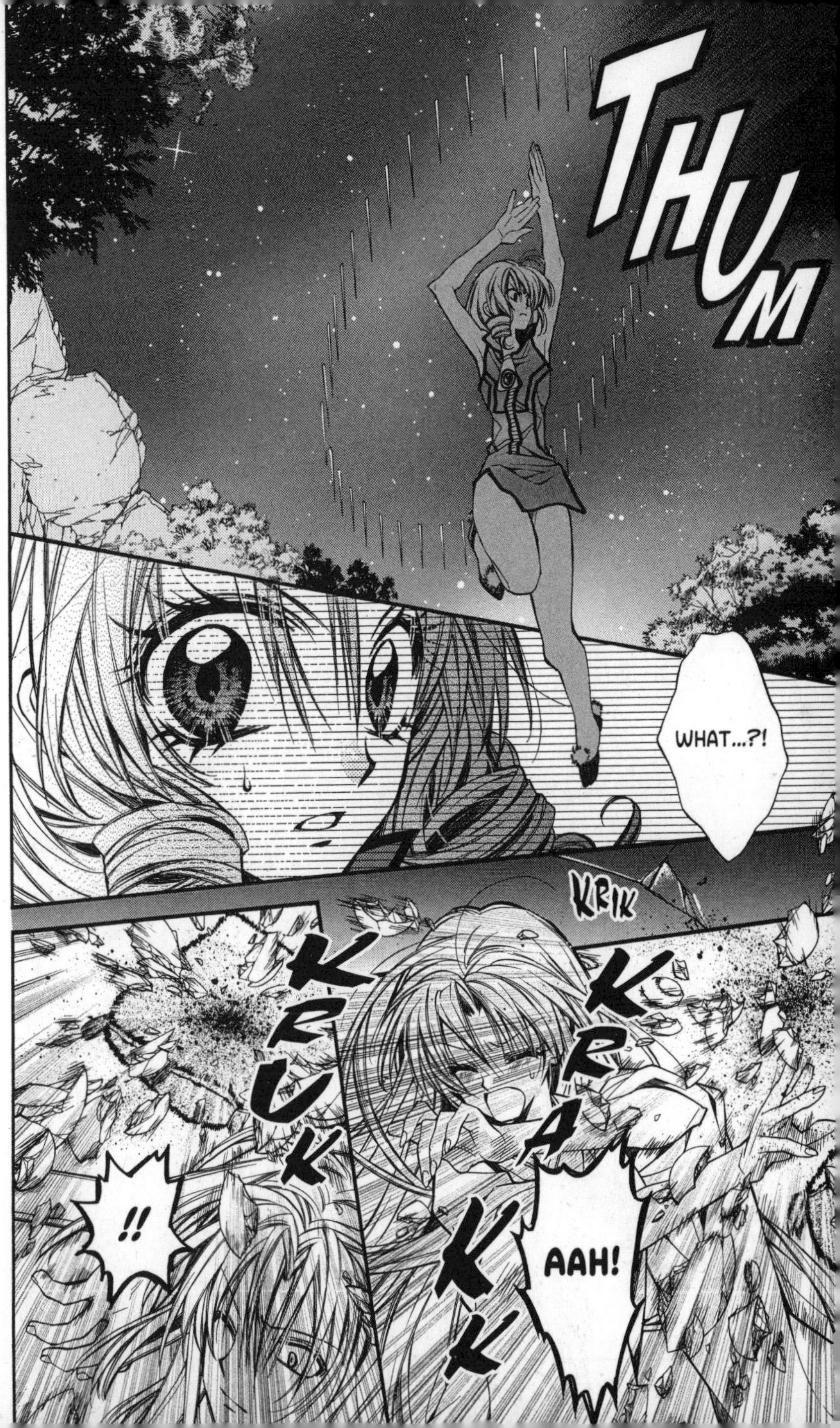
THUM
WHAT...?!
KRIK
KRAKKK
AAH!
KRUK
!!

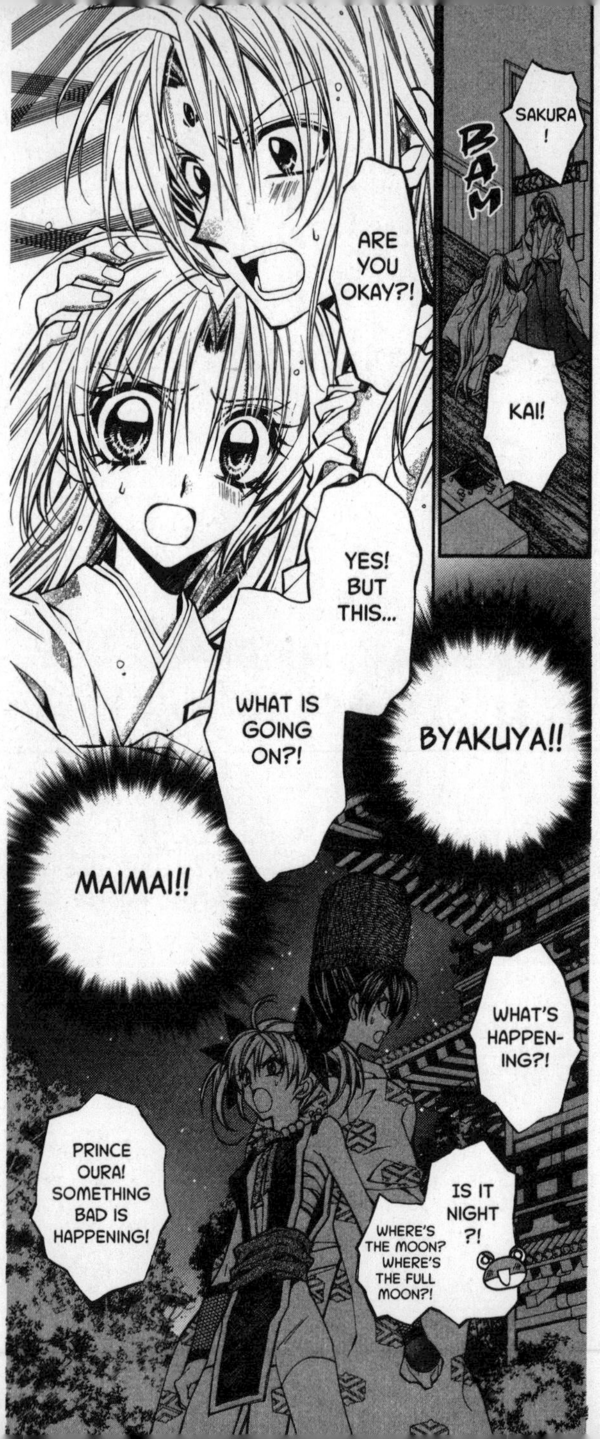
SAKURA!
BAM
KAI!
ARE YOU OKAY?!
YES! BUT THIS...
WHAT IS GOING ON?!
BYAKUYA!!
MAIMAI!!
WHAT'S HAPPEN-ING?!
IS IT NIGHT?!
WHERE'S THE MOON? WHERE'S THE FULL MOON?!
PRINCE OURA! SOMETHING BAD IS HAPPENING!

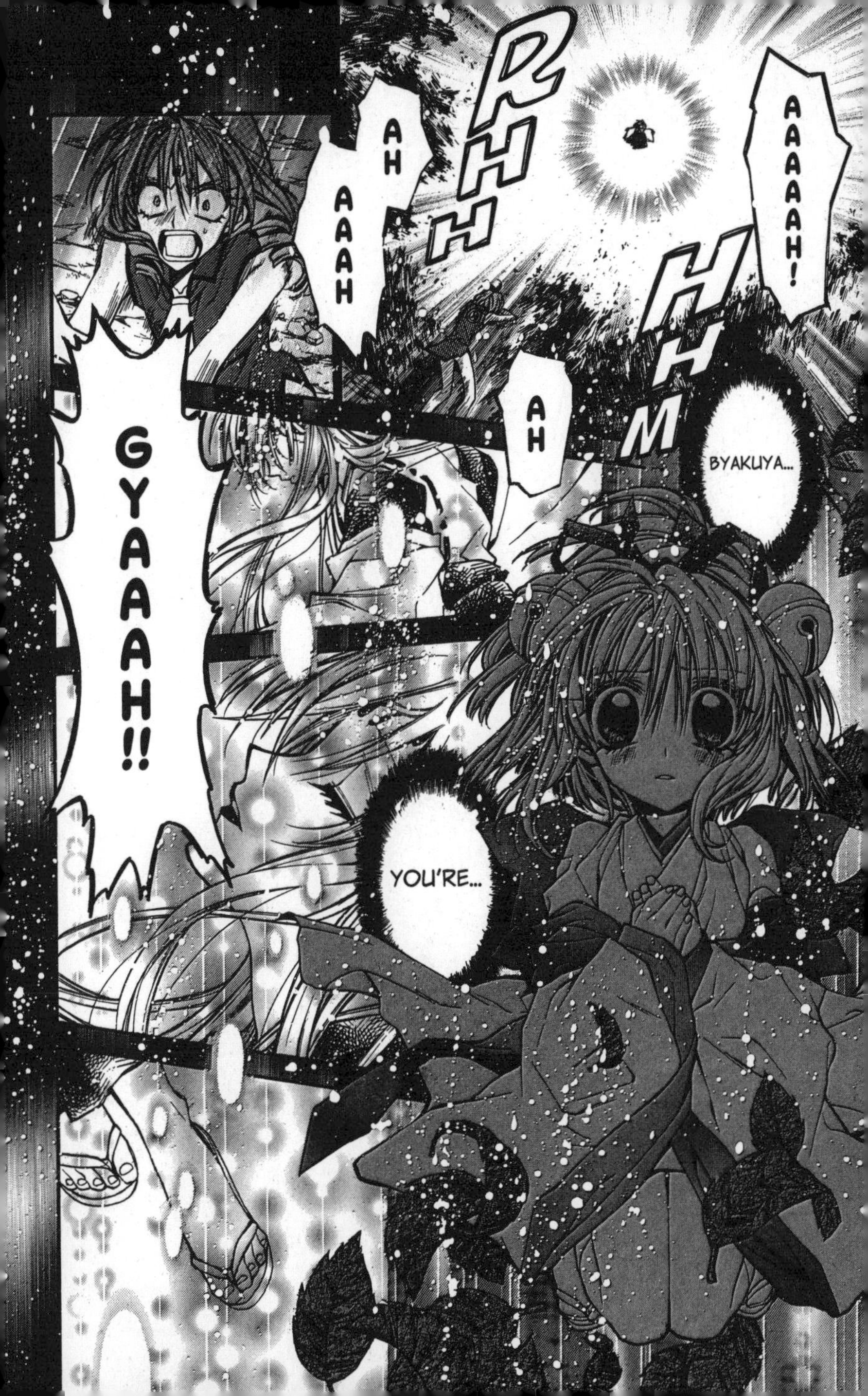

AAAAAAH!
RHHH
HHHM
AH AAAAH
AH
BYAKUYA...
GYAAAAH!!
YOU'RE...

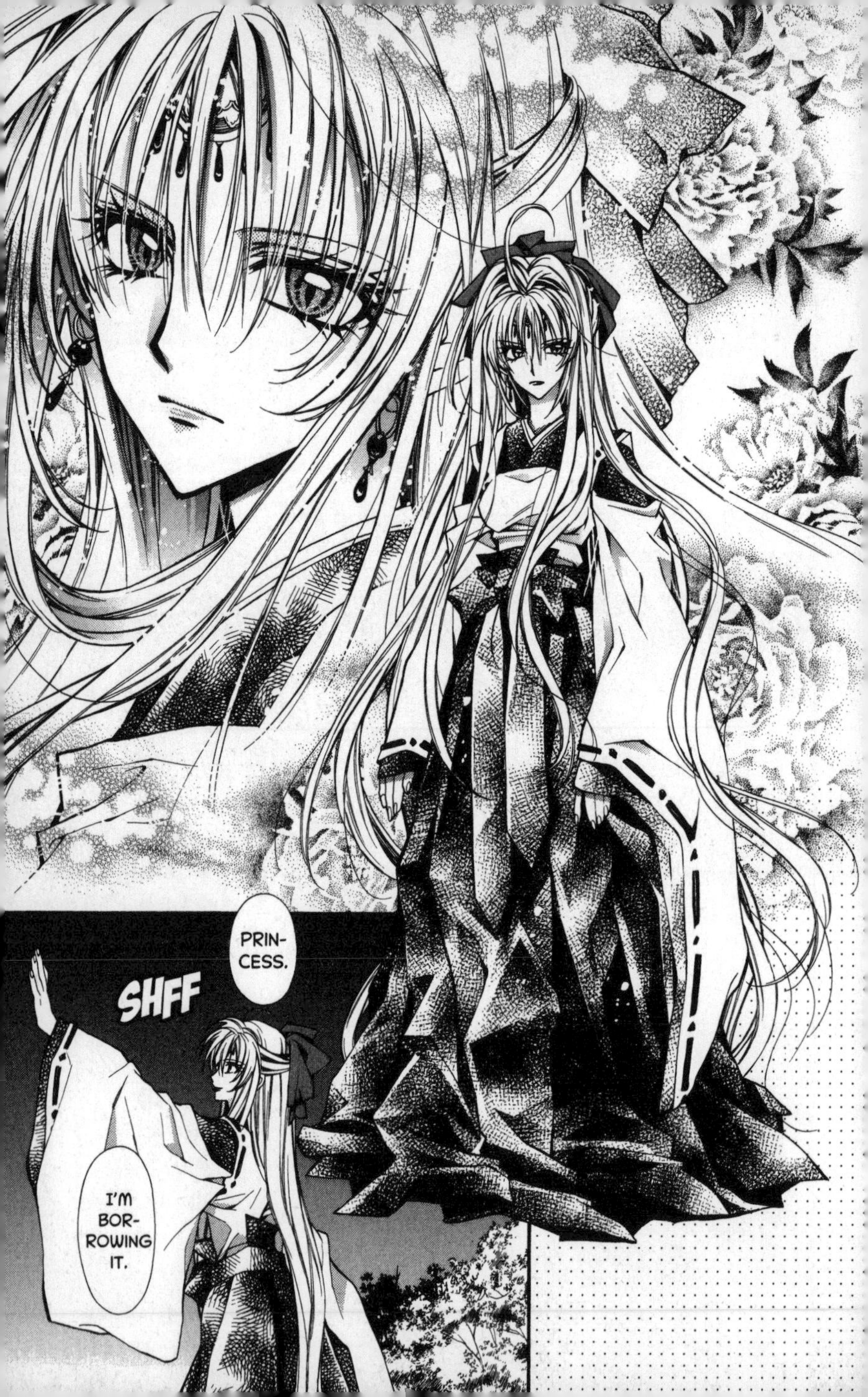
PRIN-CESS.
SHFF
I'M BOR-ROWING IT.

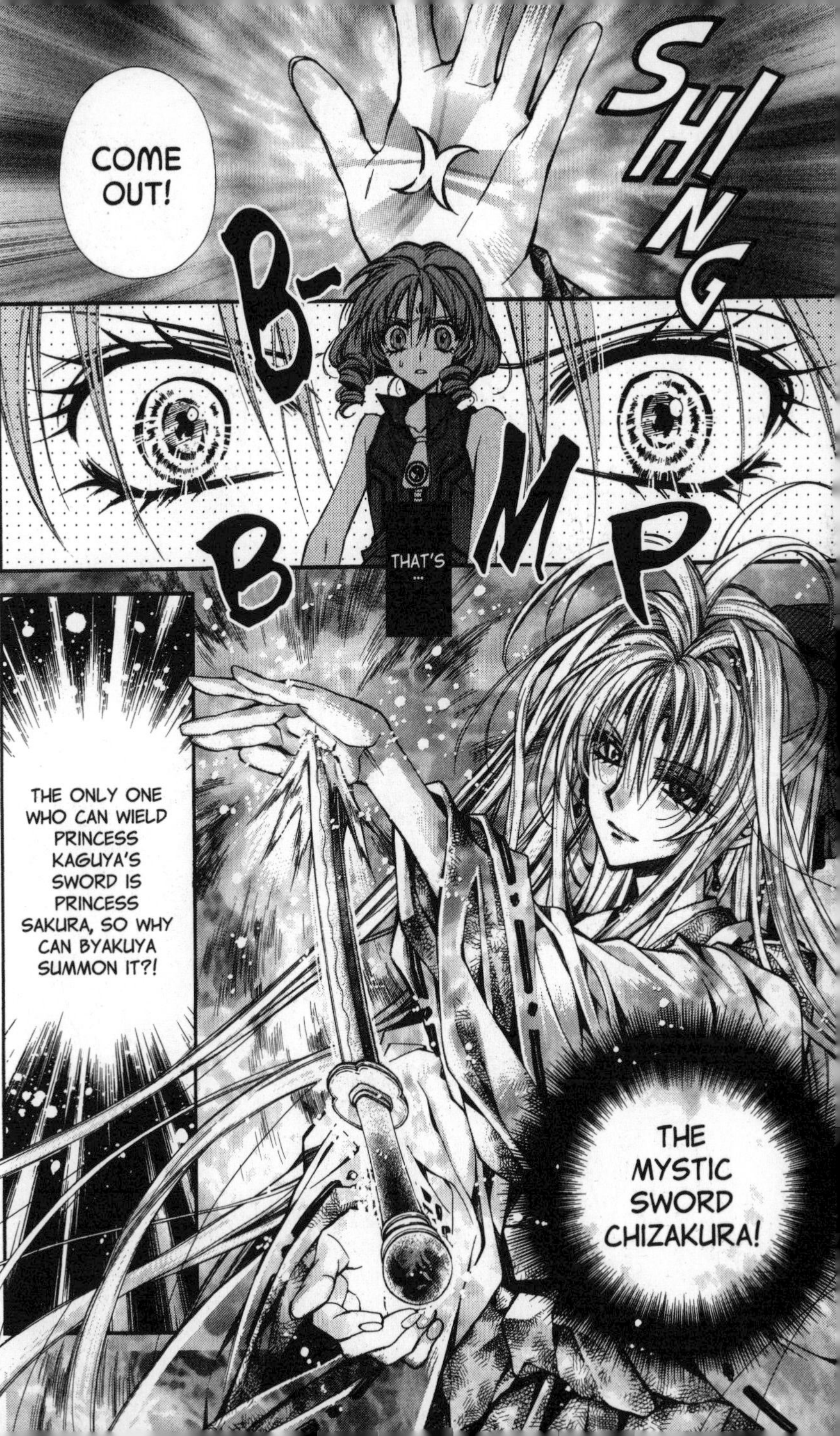
SHING
COME OUT!
B-BMP
THAT'S...
THE MYSTIC SWORD CHIZAKURA!
THE ONLY ONE WHO CAN WIELD PRINCESS KAGUYA'S SWORD IS PRINCESS SAKURA, SO WHY CAN BYAKUYA SUMMON IT?!

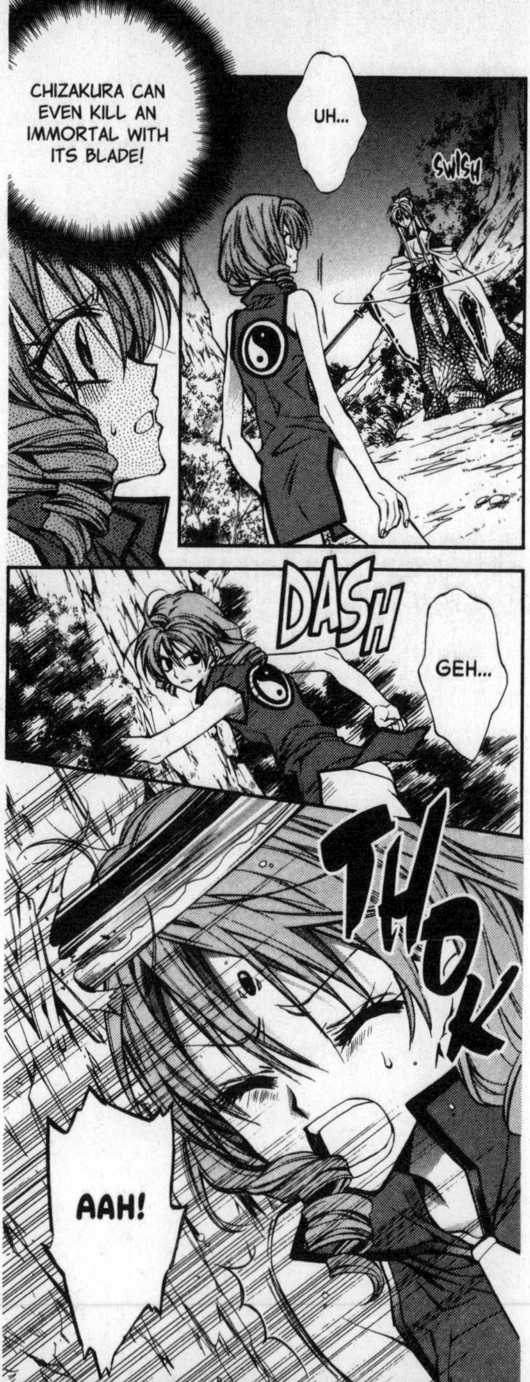
UH...
SWISH
CHIZAKURA CAN EVEN KILL AN IMMORTAL WITH ITS BLADE!
GEH...
DASH
THOK
AAH!

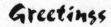

Greetings

Hello, everyone! ✿ Arina Tanemura here. This is volume 5 of *Sakura Hime: The Legend of Princess Sakura.* ♪

I've been leading a very productive life of drawing color illustrations, playing *Monster Hunter*, drawing illustrations, going driving with a friend, drawing illustrations, working on my essay in *Cobalt*, having a party, doing my storyboard...

I've been going to beauty spas too. (But just as I thought... I don't usually have time to go since I'm so busy.)

I've lost 6.6 pounds since I started going, and so far I haven't had any diet rebounds.

I realized I can't really do anything about the cellulite by myself , so I decided to have the professionals do something about it.

I've also made up my mind to not buy any clothes until I've lost weight. (The last time I bought clothes was ten months ago...)

Anyway, let's start.

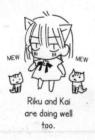

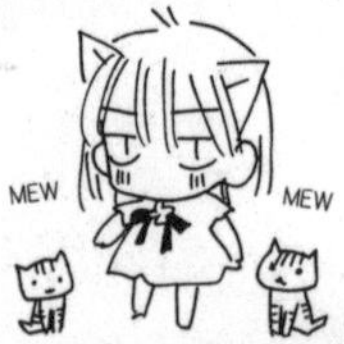
MEW
MEW

Riku and Kai are doing well too.

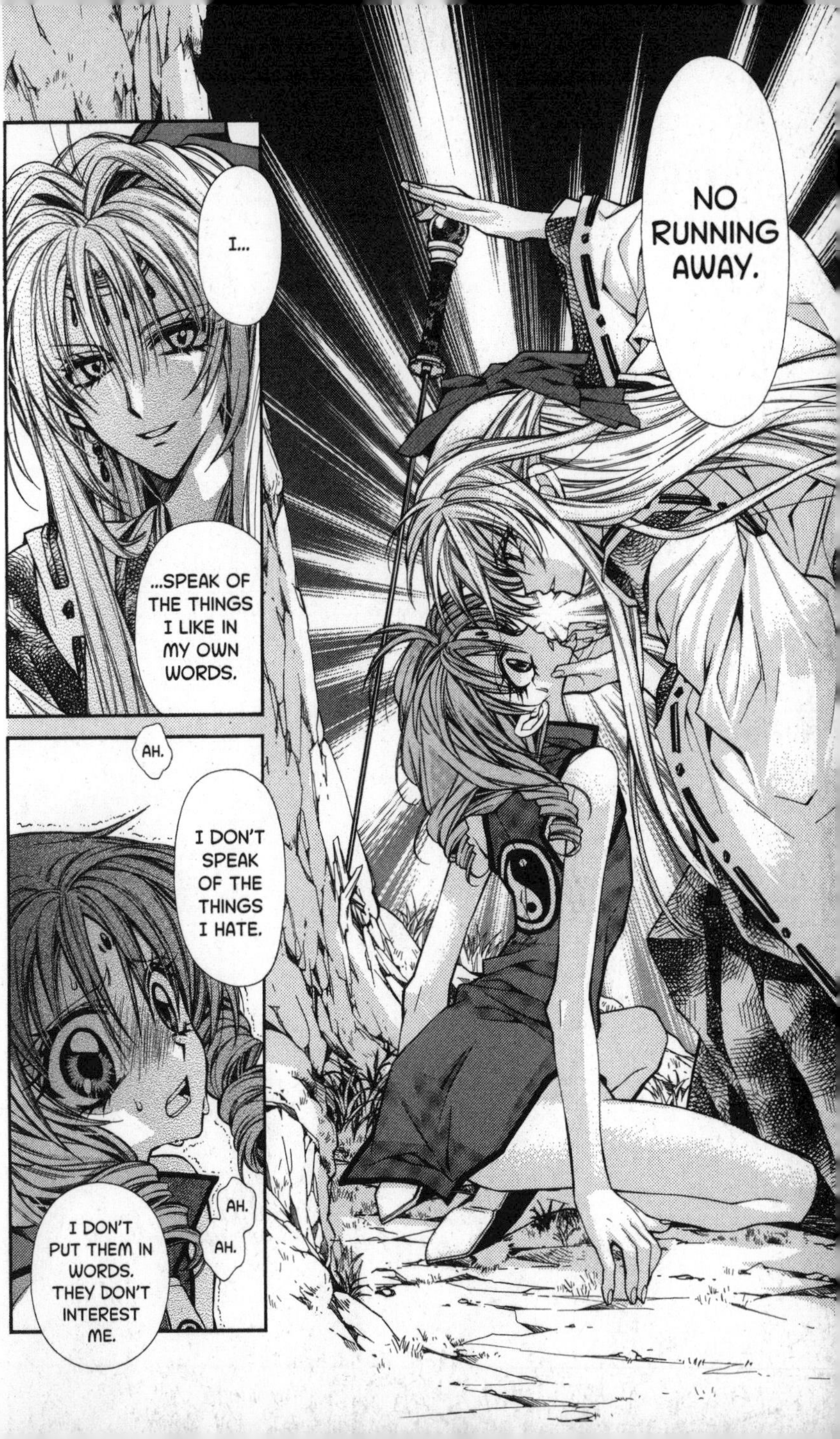
NO RUNNING AWAY.
I...
...SPEAK OF THE THINGS I LIKE IN MY OWN WORDS.
AH.
I DON'T SPEAK OF THE THINGS I HATE.
AH.
AH.
I DON'T PUT THEM IN WORDS. THEY DON'T INTEREST ME.

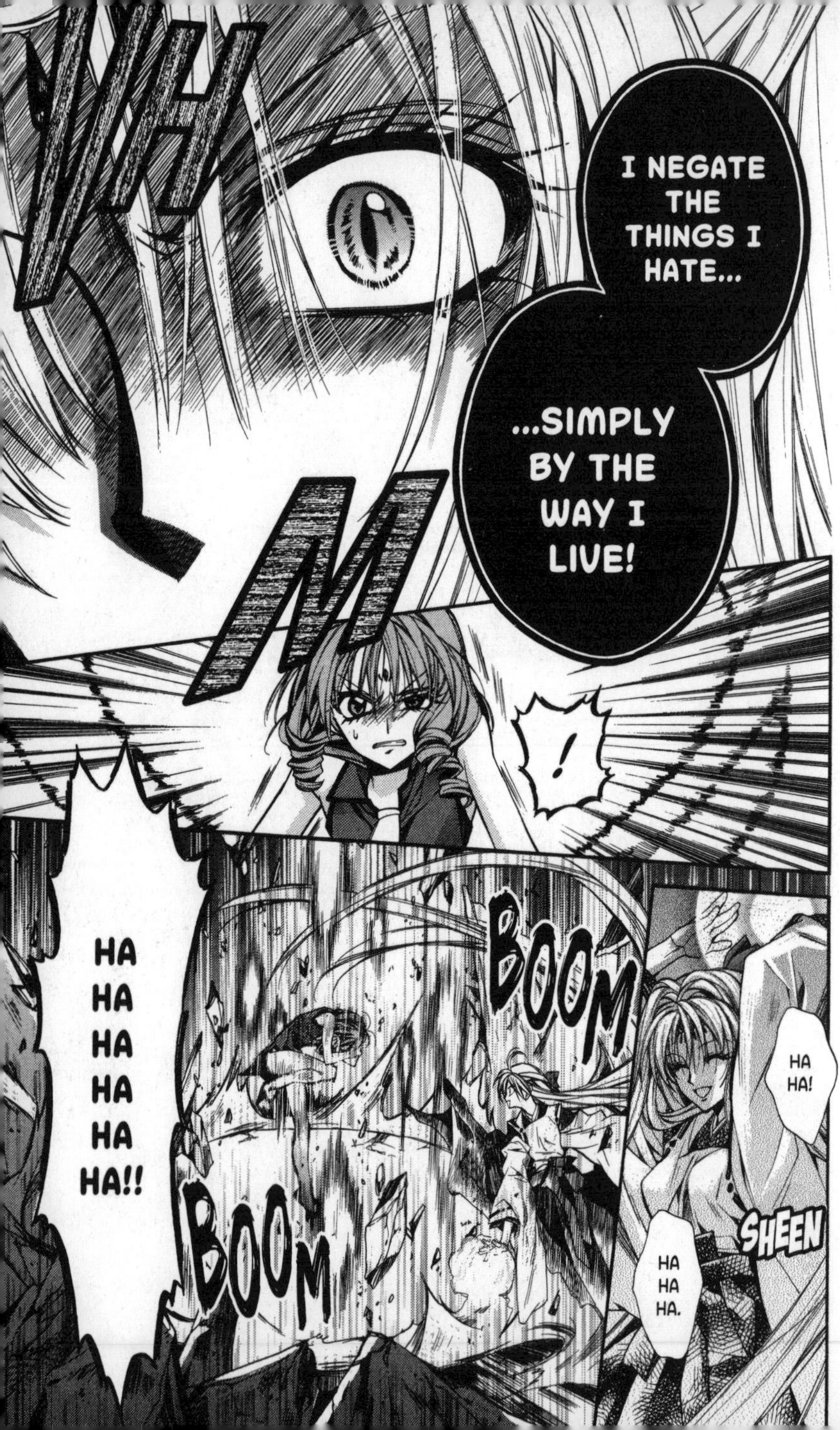
WHM
I NEGATE THE THINGS I HATE...
...SIMPLY BY THE WAY I LIVE!
!
HA HA!
HA HA HA.
SHEEN
BOOM
BOOM
HA HA HA HA HA HA!!

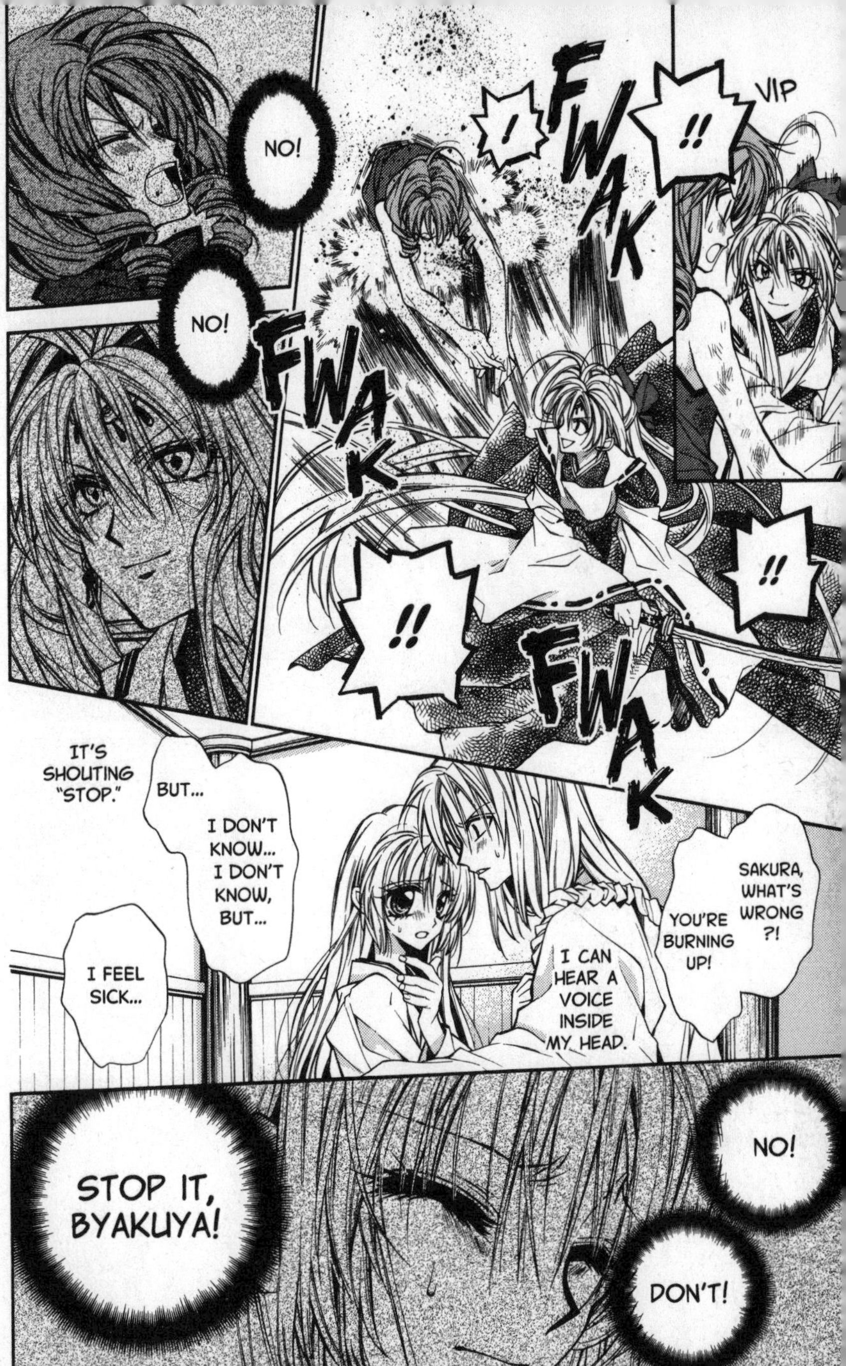
VIP
!!
!
FWAK
FWAK
!!
!!
FWAK
NO!
NO!
SAKURA, WHAT'S WRONG?!
YOU'RE BURNING UP!
I CAN HEAR A VOICE INSIDE MY HEAD.
I DON'T KNOW... I DON'T KNOW, BUT...
IT'S SHOUTING "STOP."
BUT...
I FEEL SICK...
NO!
DON'T!
STOP IT, BYAKUYA!

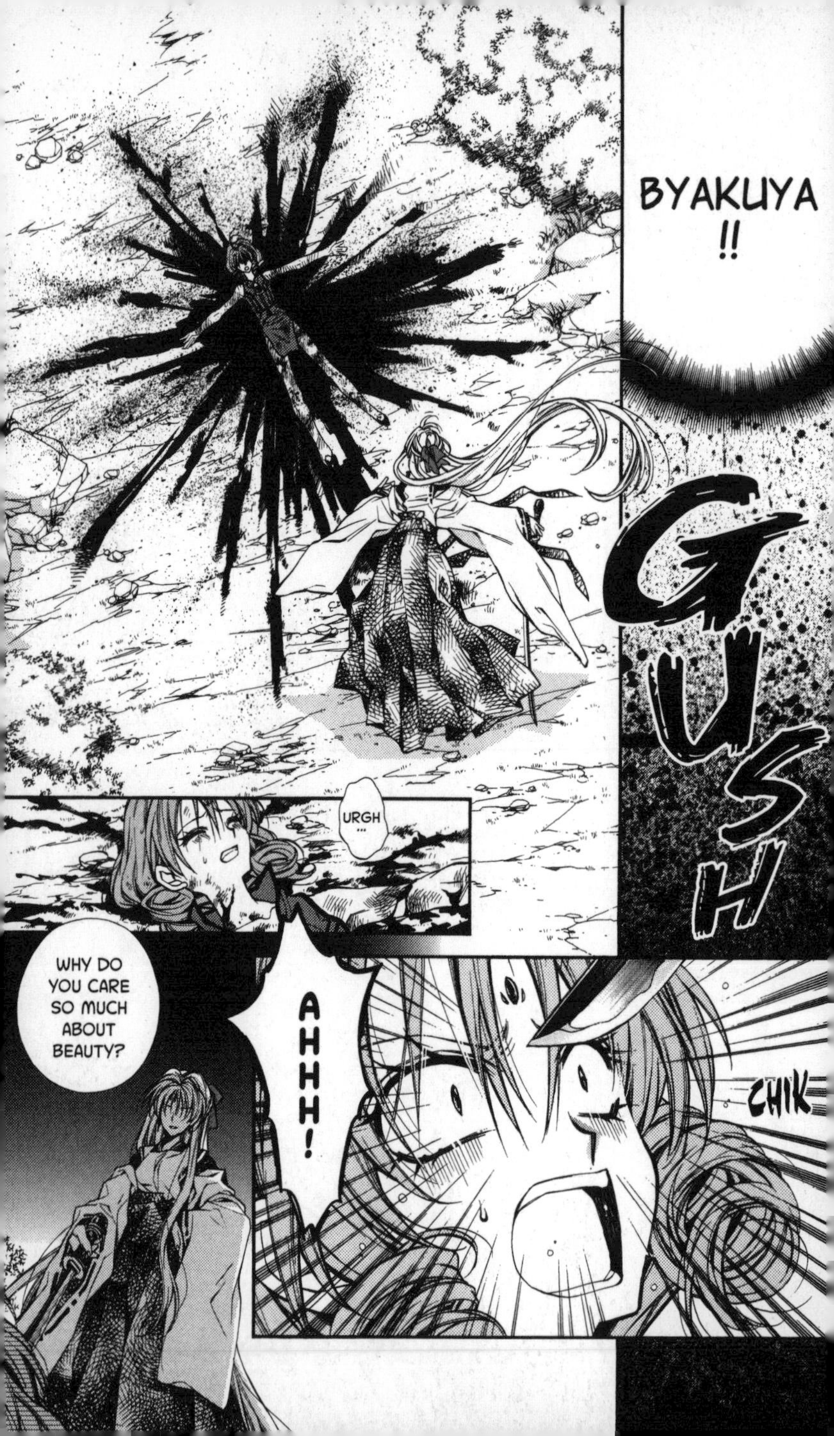
BYAKUYA !!
GUSH
URGH...
CHIK
AHHH!
WHY DO YOU CARE SO MUCH ABOUT BEAUTY?

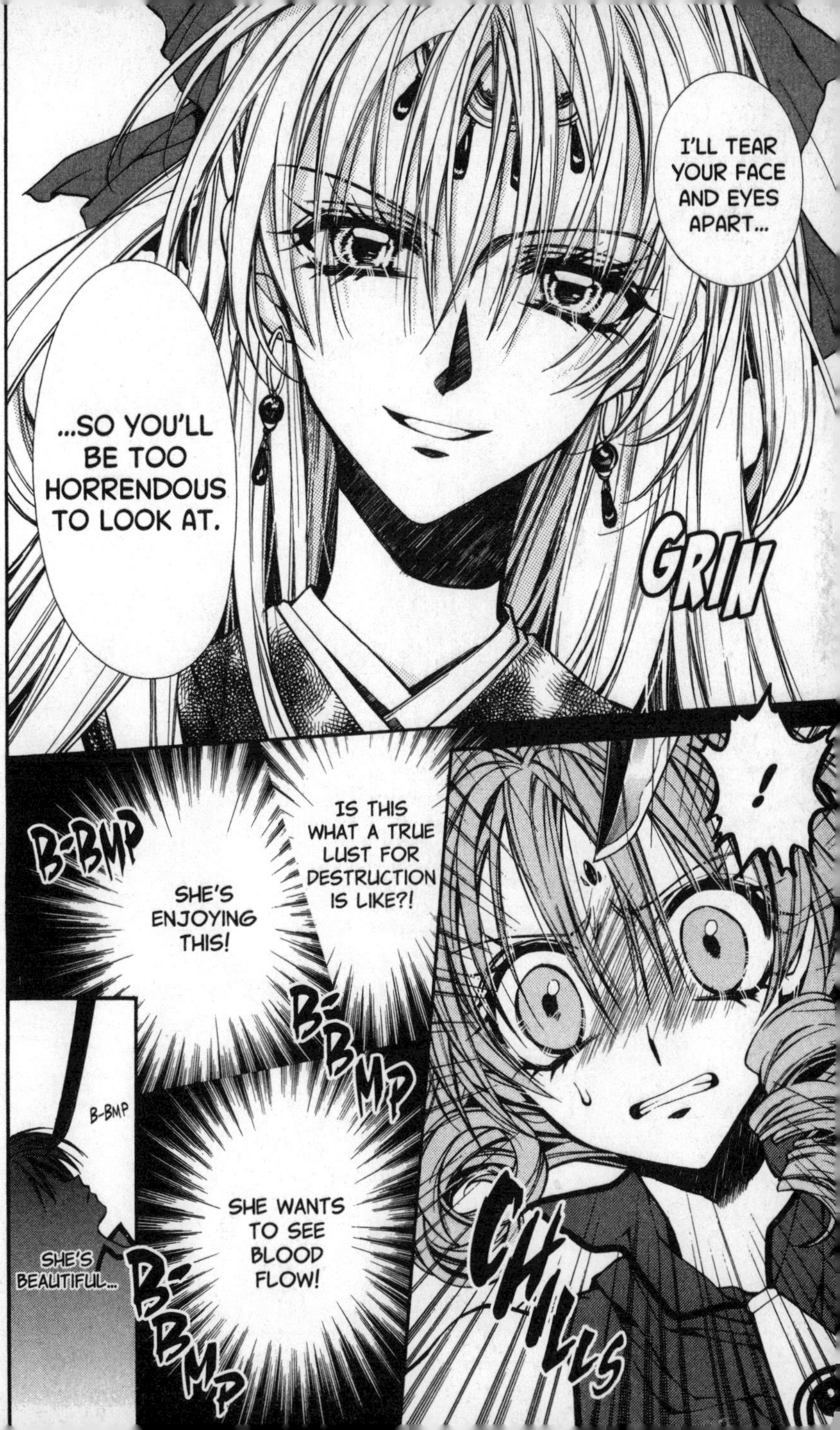
I'LL TEAR YOUR FACE AND EYES APART...
...SO YOU'LL BE TOO HORRENDOUS TO LOOK AT.
GRIN
!
CHILLS
IS THIS WHAT A TRUE LUST FOR DESTRUCTION IS LIKE?!
SHE'S ENJOYING THIS!
B-BMP
B-BMP
B-BMP
SHE WANTS TO SEE BLOOD FLOW!
SHE'S BEAUTIFUL...
B-BMP

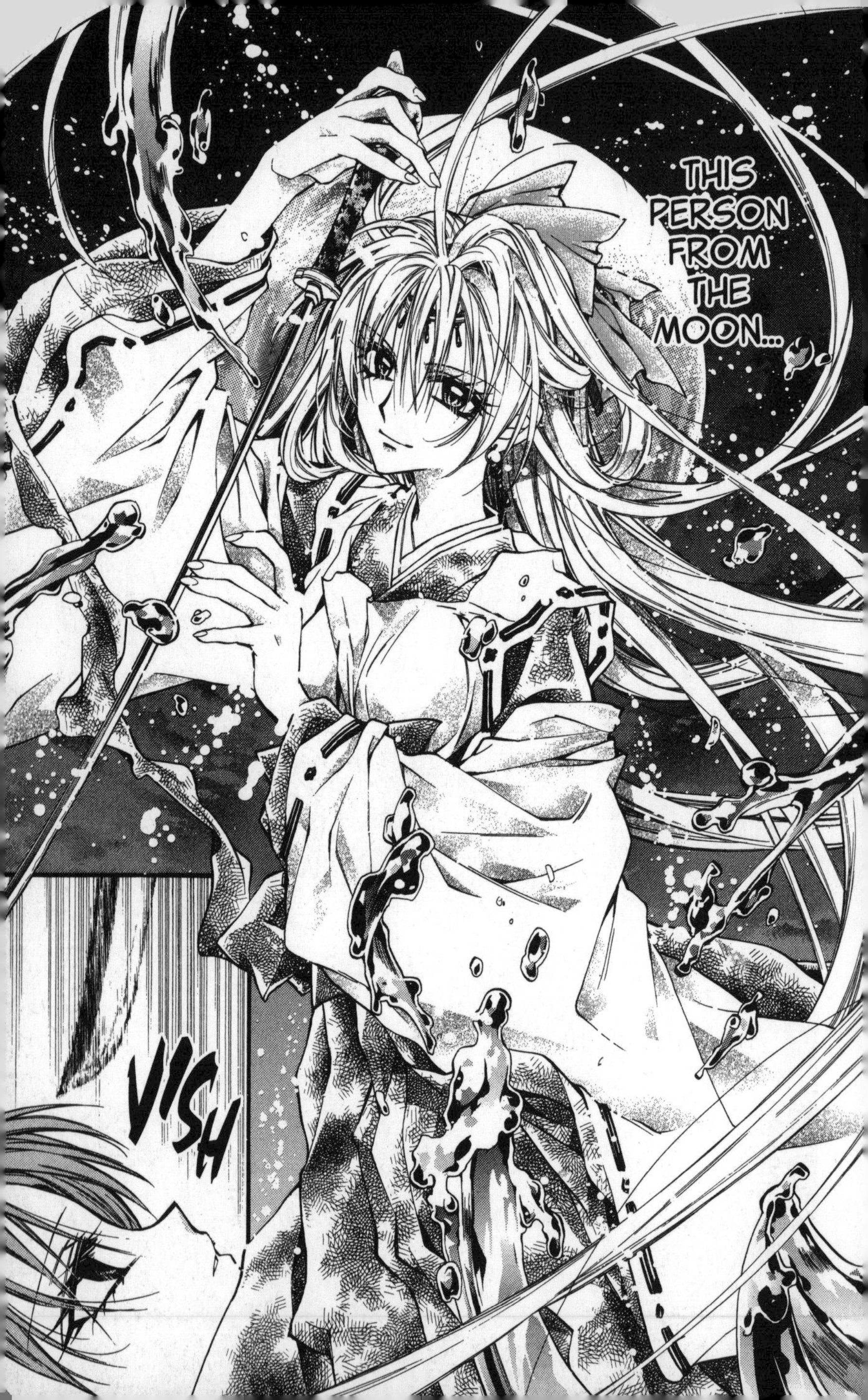
THIS PERSON FROM THE MOON...
VISH

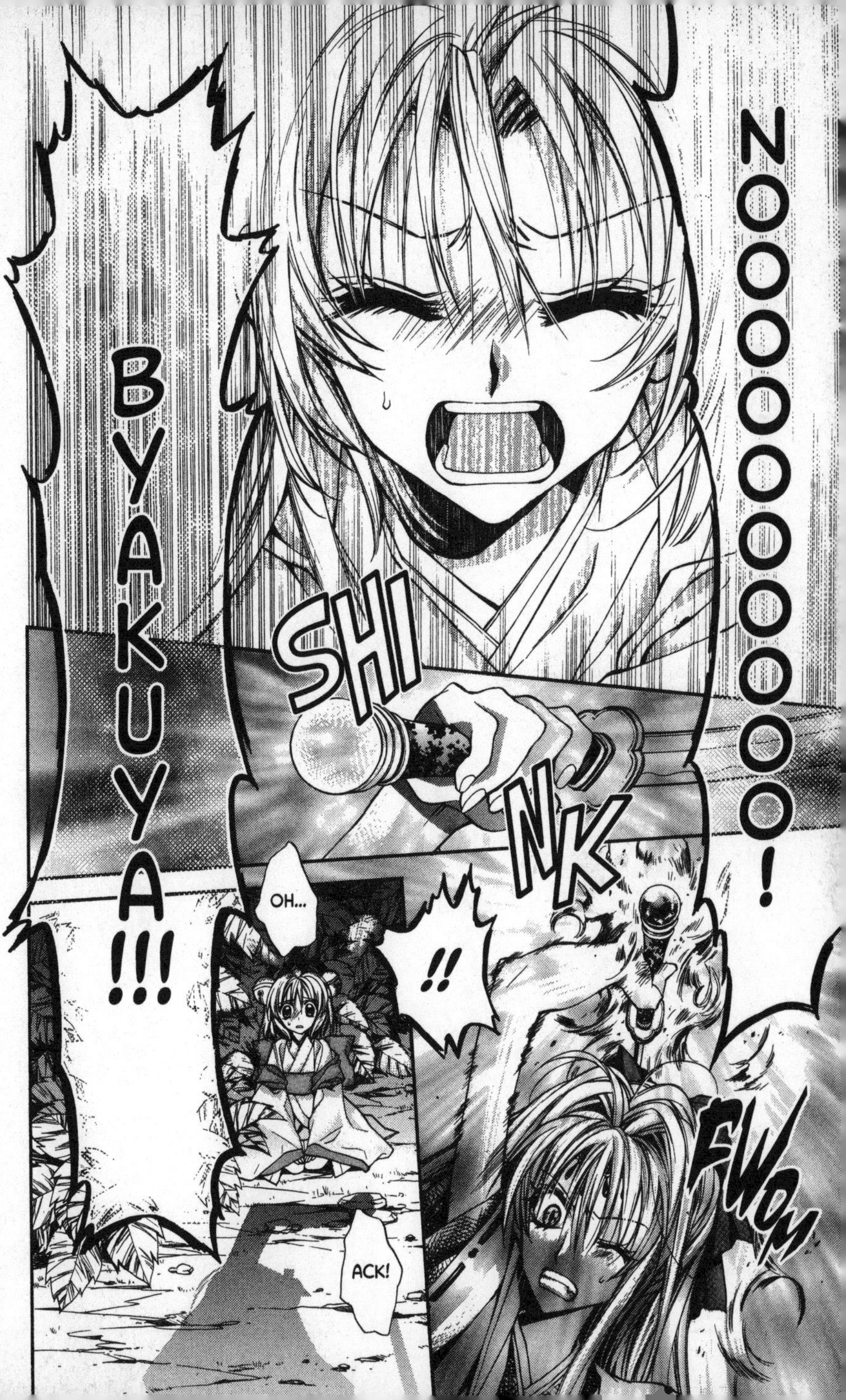
NOOOOOOOOOOO!
BYAKUYA!!!
SHINK
OH...
!!
FWOM
ACK!

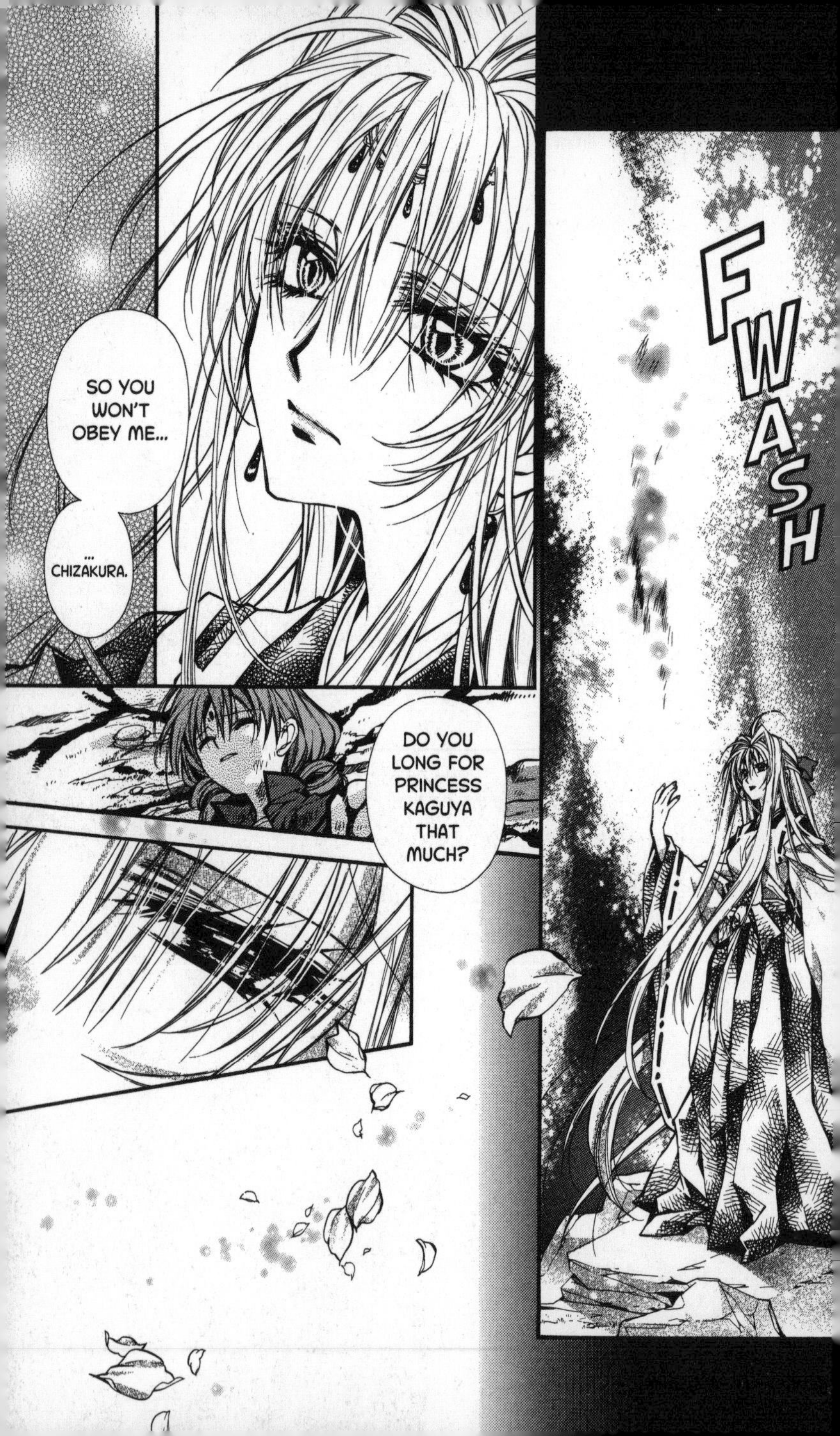
FWASH
SO YOU WON'T OBEY ME...
...CHIZAKURA.
DO YOU LONG FOR PRINCESS KAGUYA THAT MUCH?

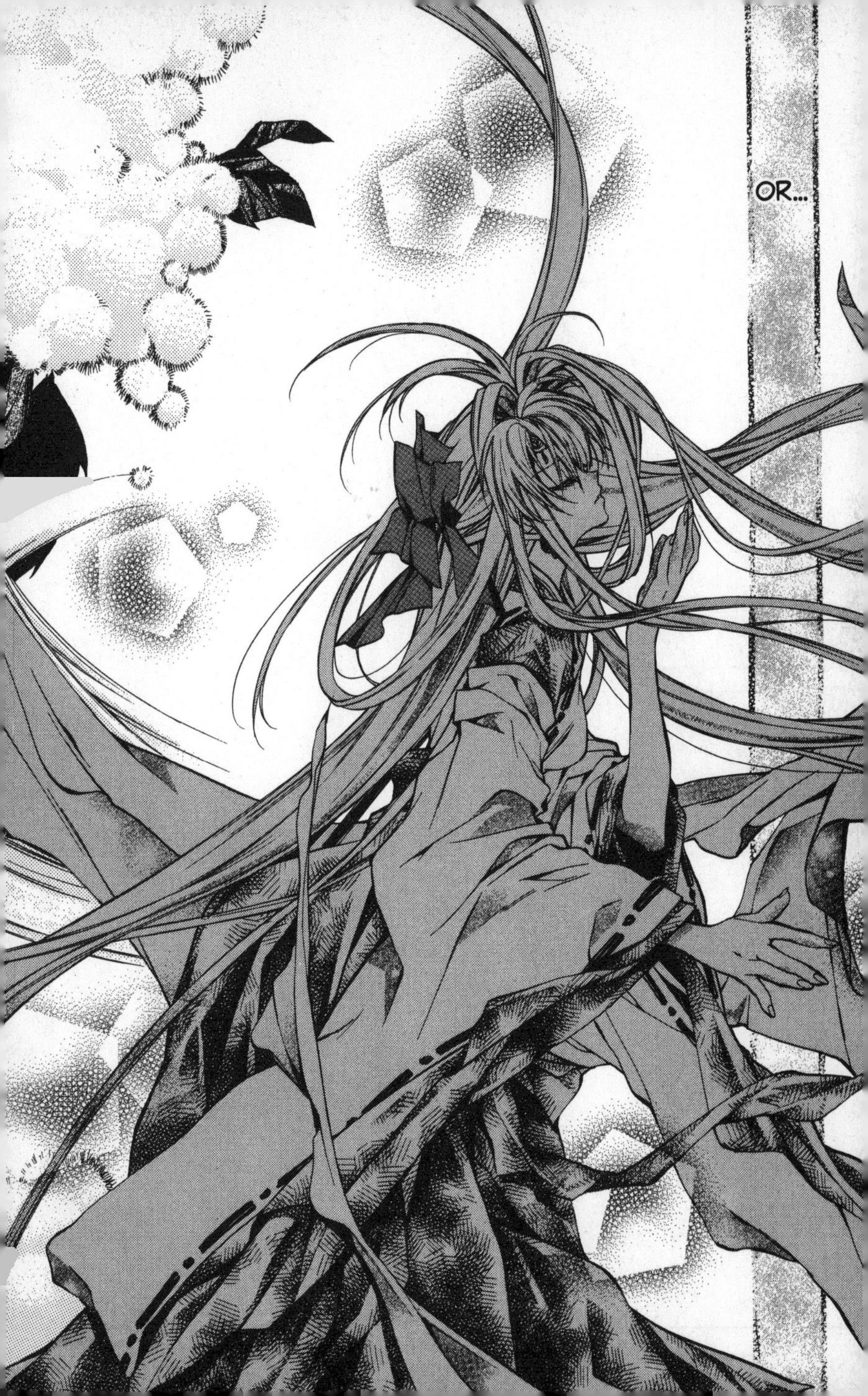
OR...

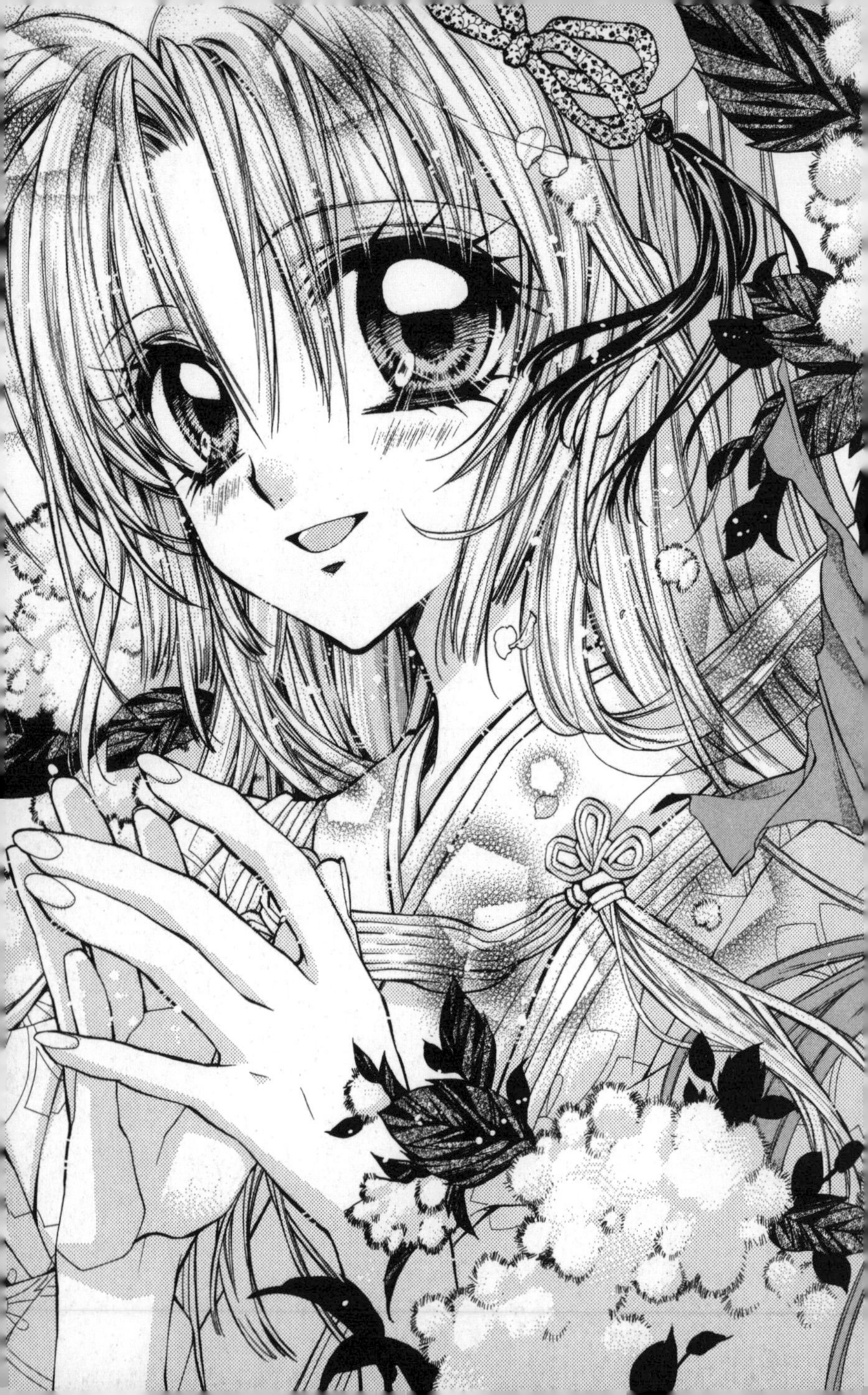

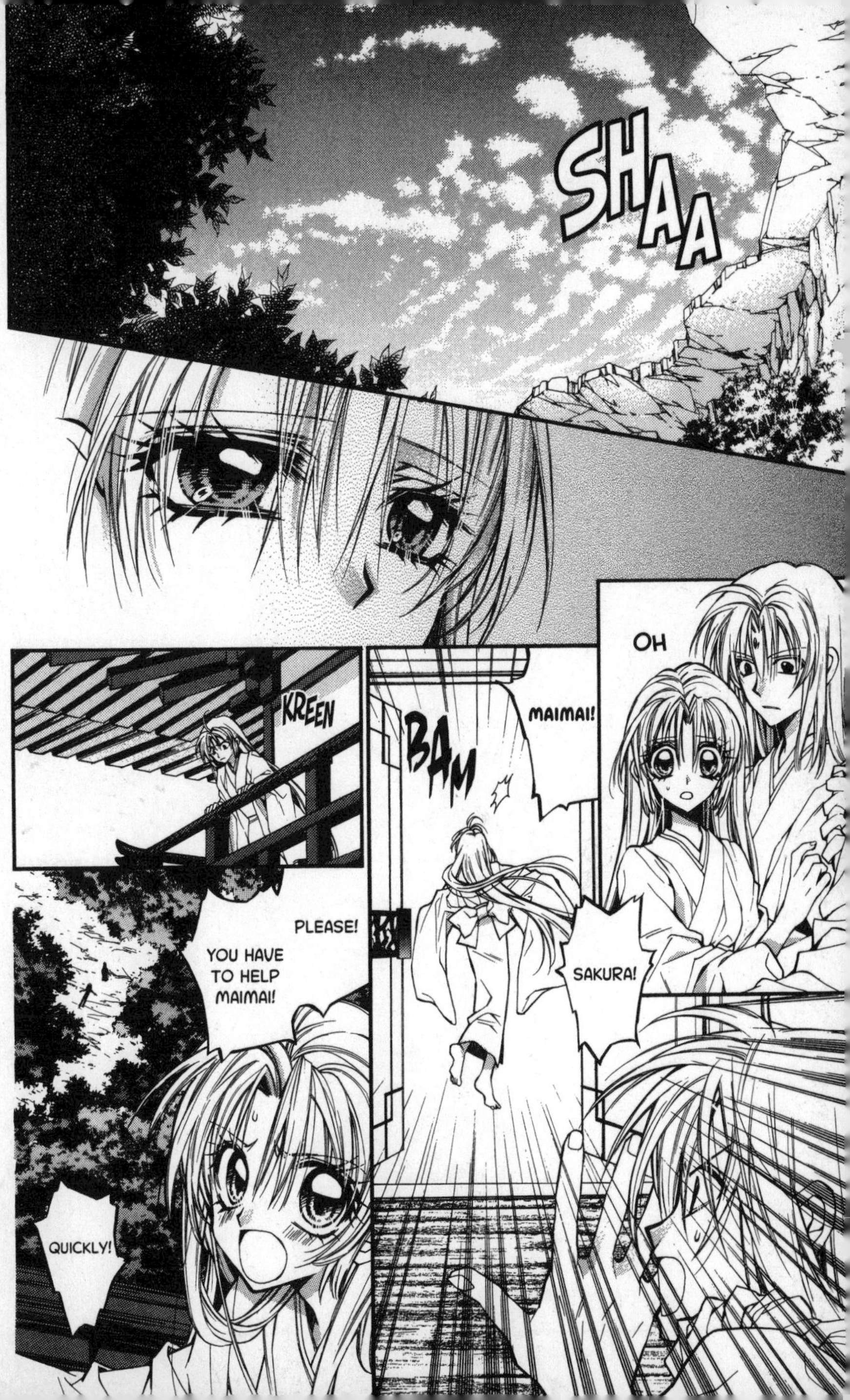
SHAA
OH
SAKURA!
MAIMAI!
BAM
KREEN
PLEASE!
YOU HAVE TO HELP MAIMAI!
QUICKLY!

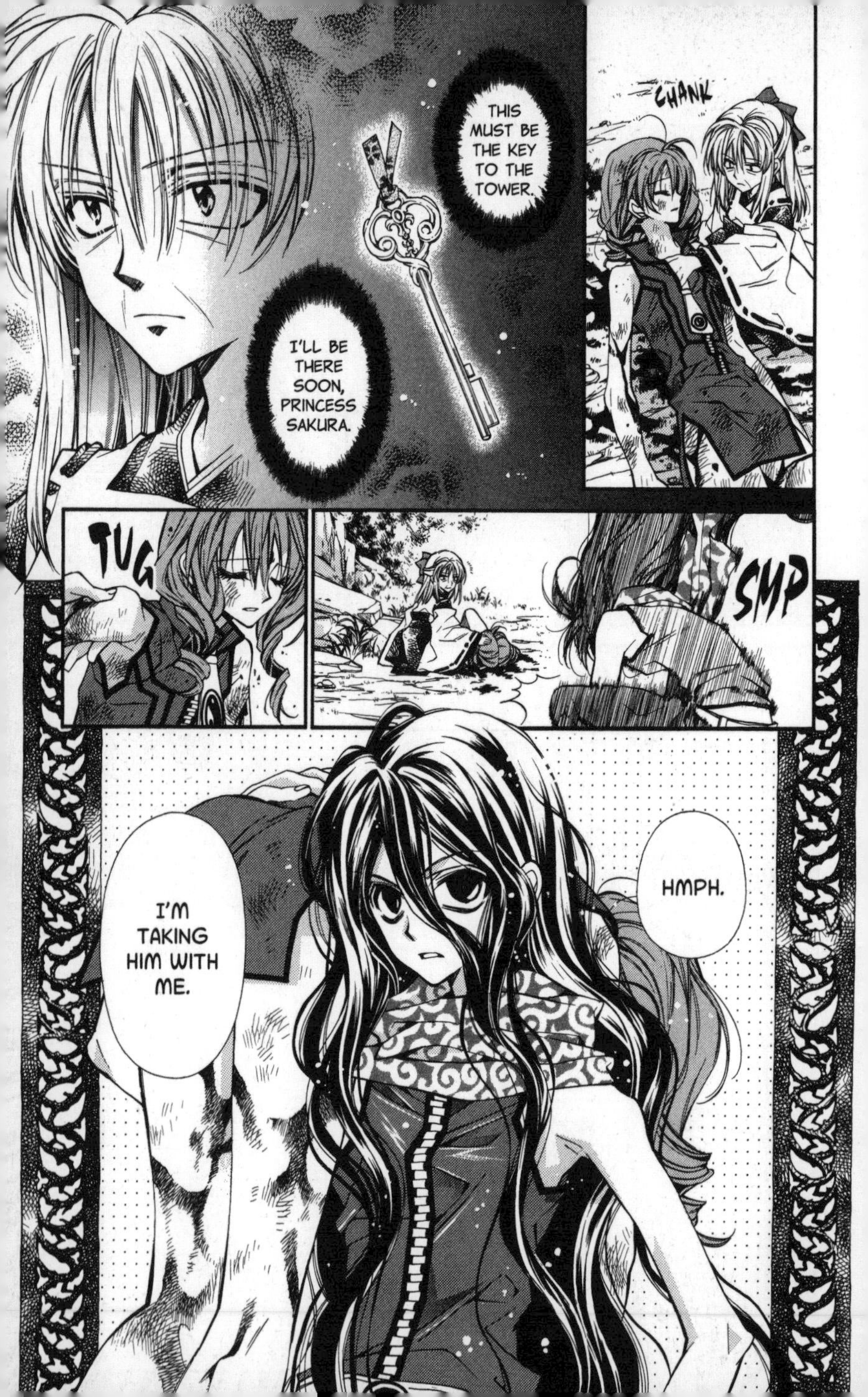
CHANK
THIS MUST BE THE KEY TO THE TOWER.
I'LL BE THERE SOON, PRINCESS SAKURA.
SMP
TUG
HMPH.
I'M TAKING HIM WITH ME.

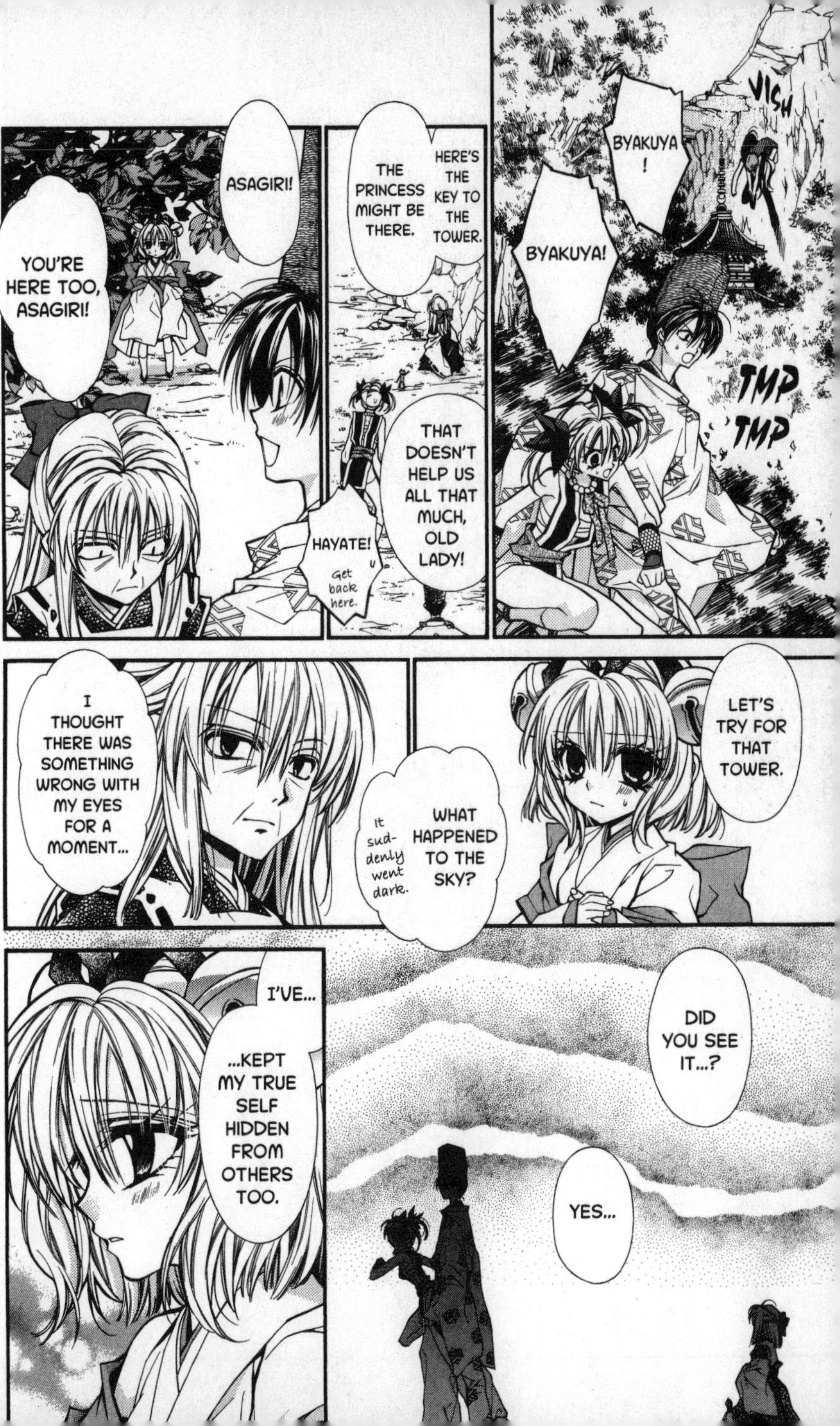
VISH
BYAKUYA!
BYAKUYA!
TMP TMP
HERE'S THE KEY TO THE TOWER.
THE PRINCESS MIGHT BE THERE.
THAT DOESN'T HELP US ALL THAT MUCH, OLD LADY!
HAYATE!
Get back here.
ASAGIRI!
YOU'RE HERE TOO, ASAGIRI!
LET'S TRY FOR THAT TOWER.
WHAT HAPPENED TO THE SKY?
It suddenly went dark.
I THOUGHT THERE WAS SOMETHING WRONG WITH MY EYES FOR A MOMENT...
DID YOU SEE IT...?
YES...
I'VE...
...KEPT MY TRUE SELF HIDDEN FROM OTHERS TOO.

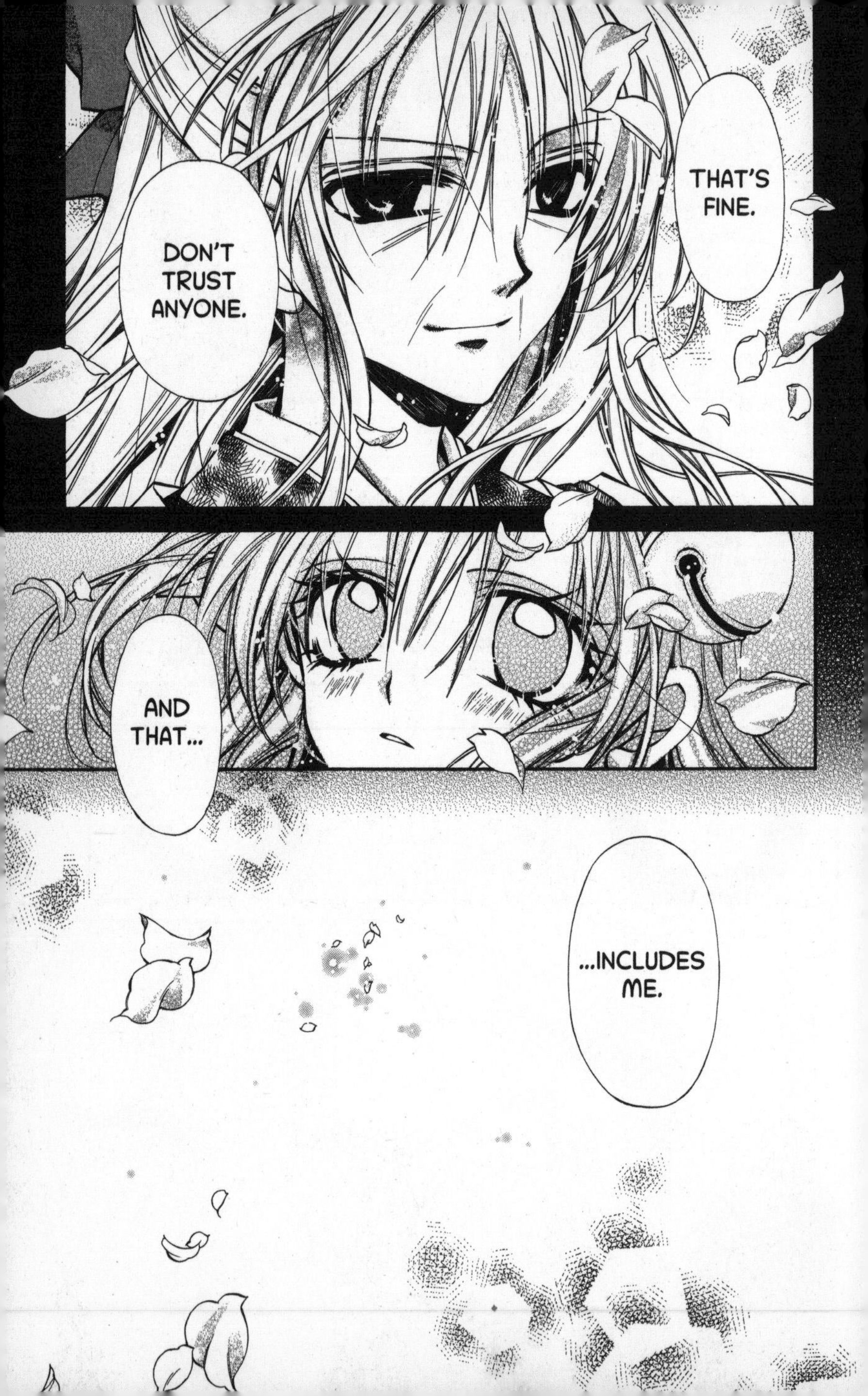
THAT'S FINE.
DON'T TRUST ANYONE.
AND THAT...
...INCLUDES ME.

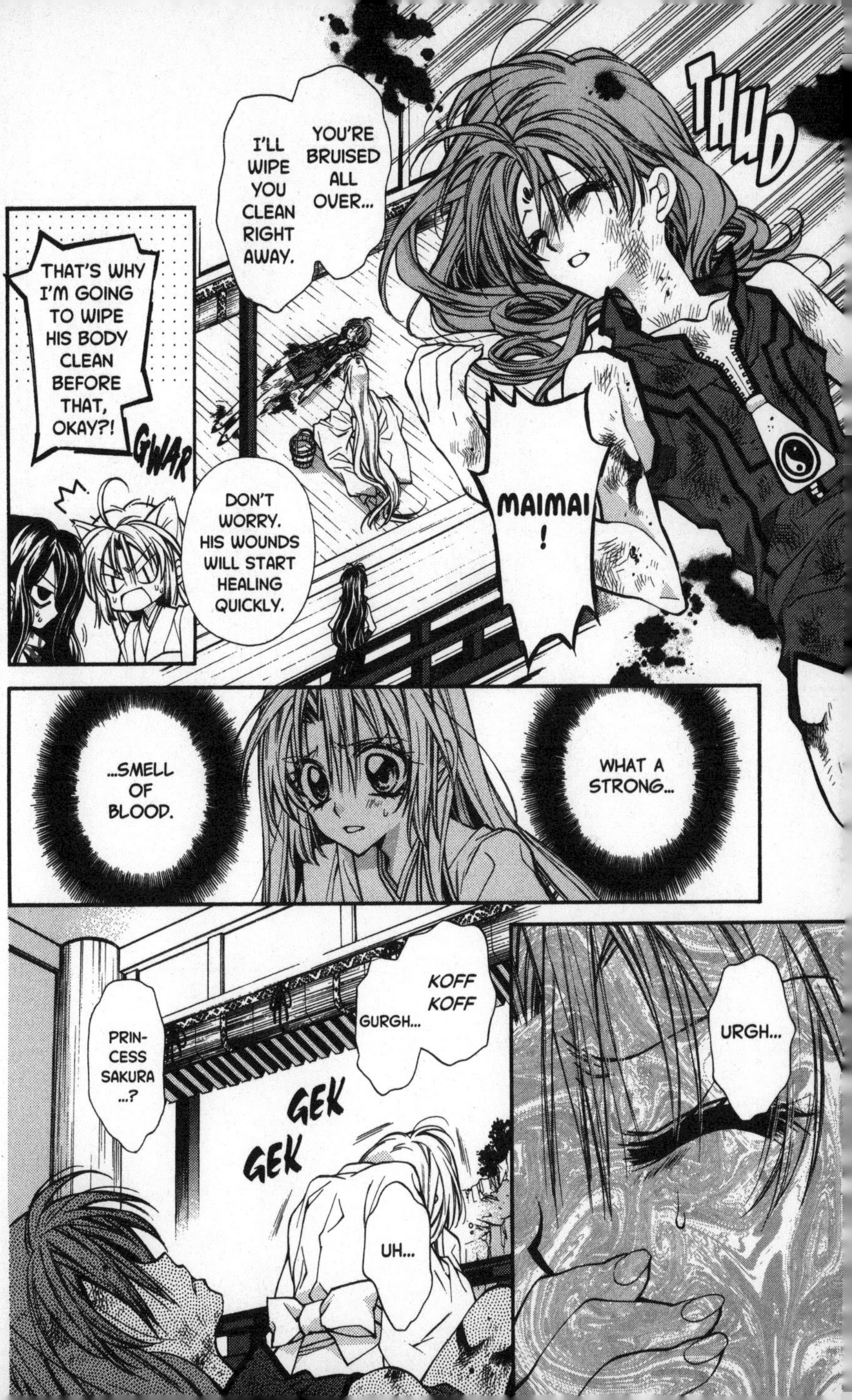

THUD
YOU'RE BRUISED ALL OVER...
I'LL WIPE YOU CLEAN RIGHT AWAY.
MAIMAI!
DON'T WORRY. HIS WOUNDS WILL START HEALING QUICKLY.
THAT'S WHY I'M GOING TO WIPE HIS BODY CLEAN BEFORE THAT, OKAY?!
GWAR
WHAT A STRONG...
...SMELL OF BLOOD.
URGH...
KOFF KOFF
GURGH...
PRIN-CESS SAKURA ...?
GEK GEK
UH...

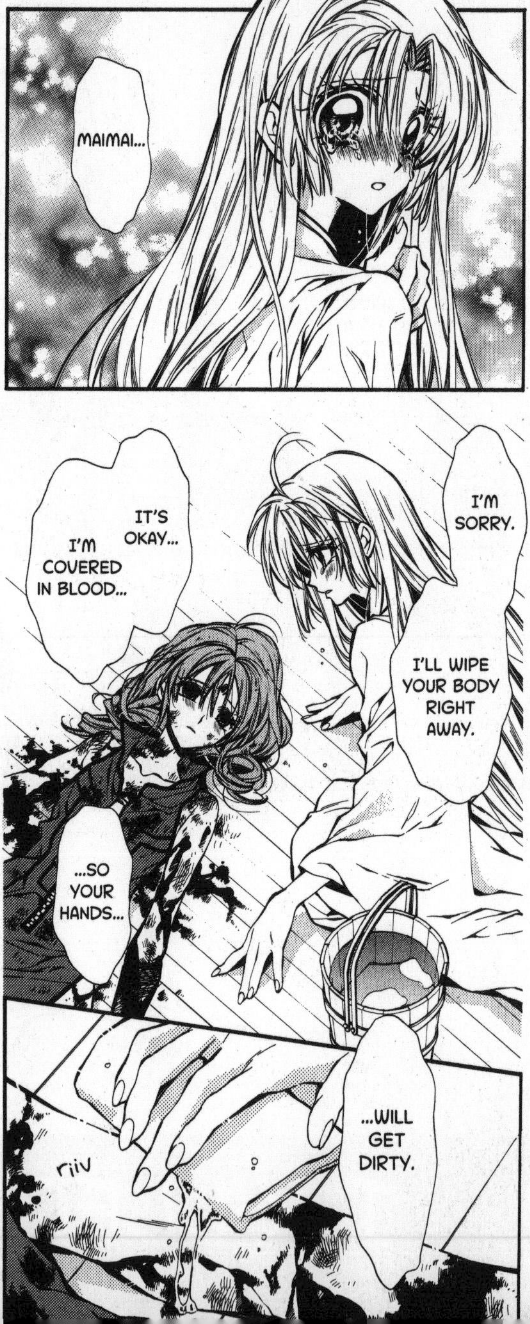
MAIMAI...
I'M SORRY.
I'LL WIPE YOUR BODY RIGHT AWAY.
IT'S OKAY...
I'M COVERED IN BLOOD...
...SO YOUR HANDS...
...WILL GET DIRTY.
riiv

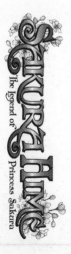

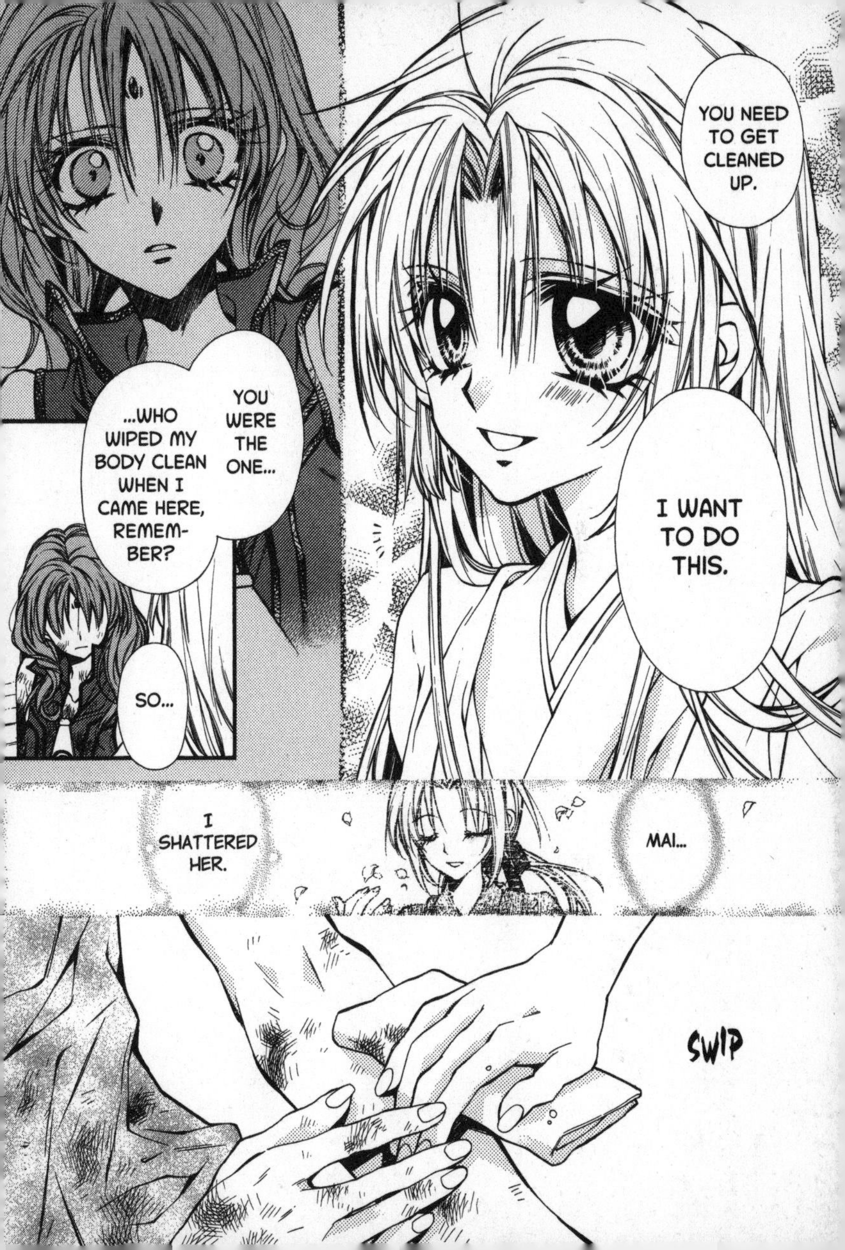
YOU NEED TO GET CLEANED UP.
I WANT TO DO THIS.
YOU WERE THE ONE...
...WHO WIPED MY BODY CLEAN WHEN I CAME HERE, REMEMBER?
SO...
MAI...
I SHATTERED HER.
SWIP

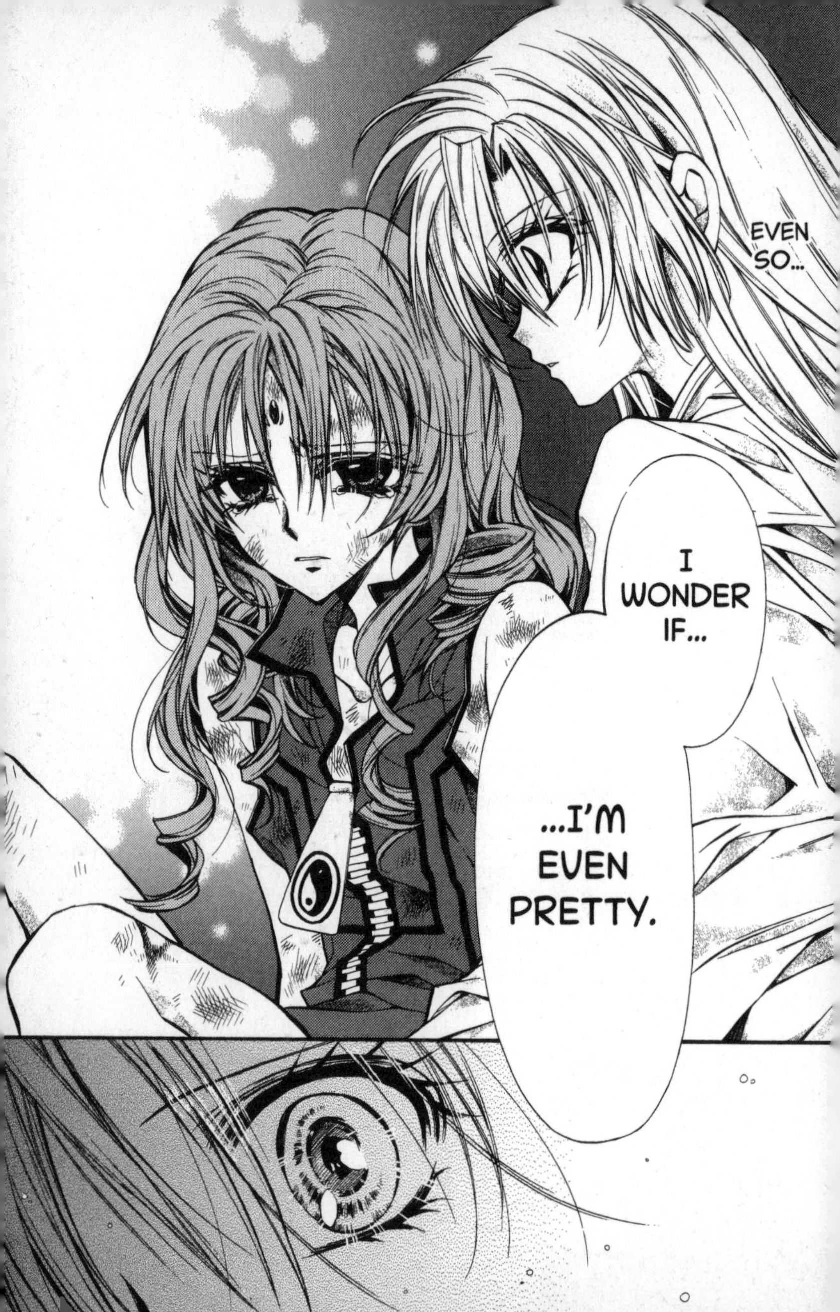
EVEN SO...
I WONDER IF...
...I'M EVEN PRETTY.

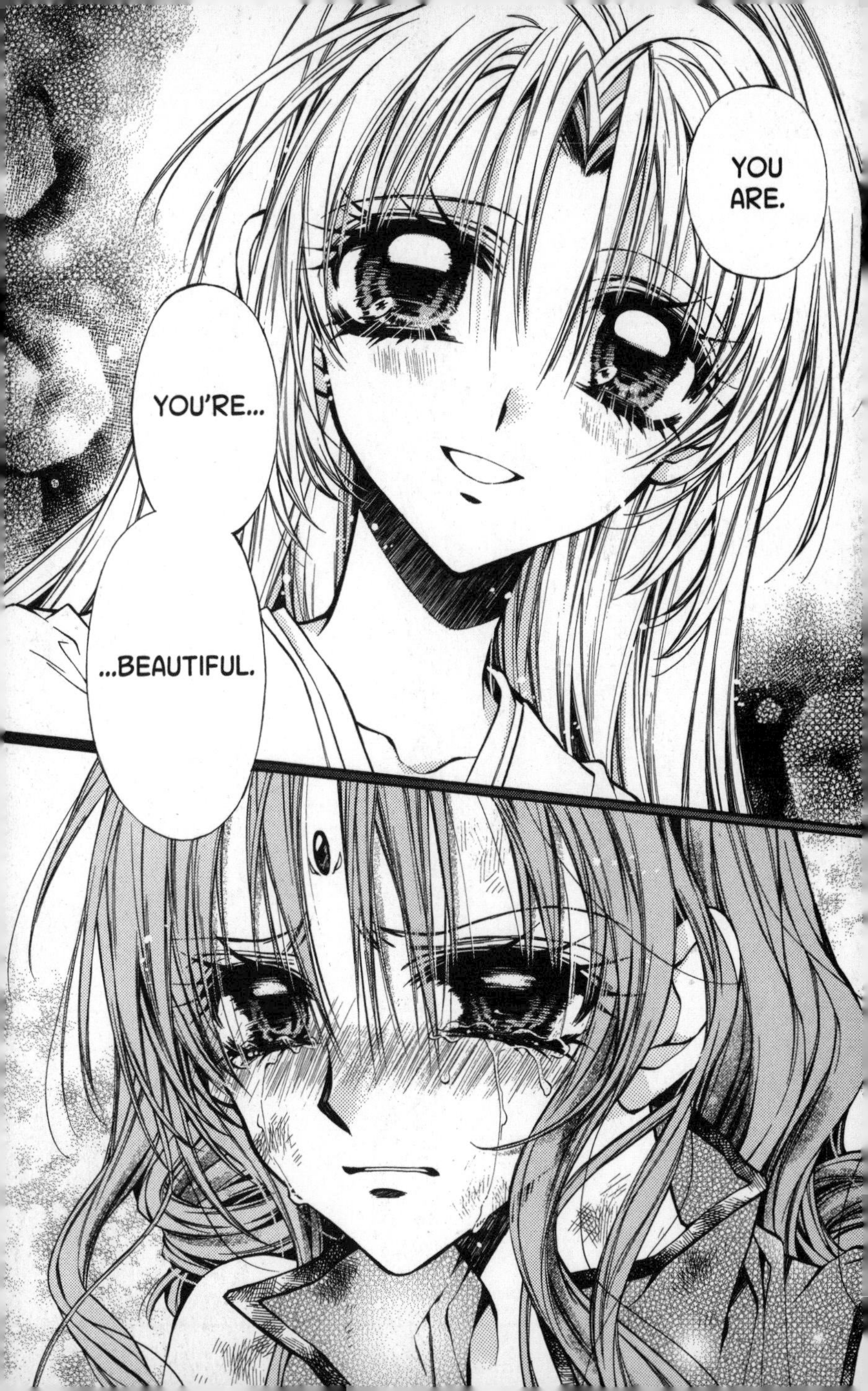
YOU ARE.
YOU'RE...
...BEAUTIFUL.

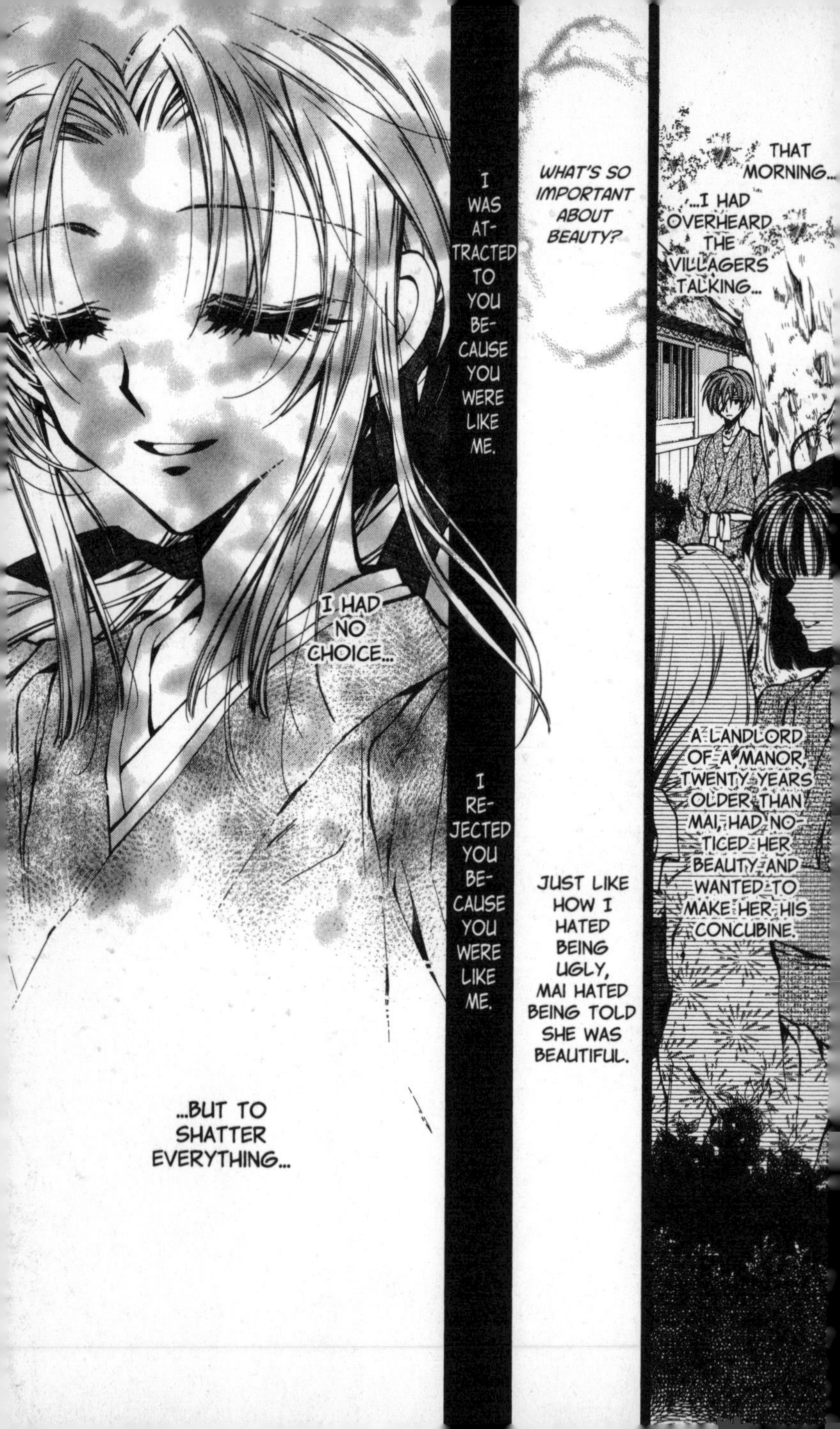
THAT MORNING...
...I HAD OVERHEARD THE VILLAGERS TALKING...
A LANDLORD OF A MANOR, TWENTY YEARS OLDER THAN MAI, HAD NOTICED HER BEAUTY AND WANTED TO MAKE HER HIS CONCUBINE.
WHAT'S SO IMPORTANT ABOUT BEAUTY?
JUST LIKE HOW I HATED BEING UGLY, MAI HATED BEING TOLD SHE WAS BEAUTIFUL.
I WAS ATTRACTED TO YOU BECAUSE YOU WERE LIKE ME.
I REJECTED YOU BECAUSE YOU WERE LIKE ME.
I HAD NO CHOICE...
...BUT TO SHATTER EVERYTHING...

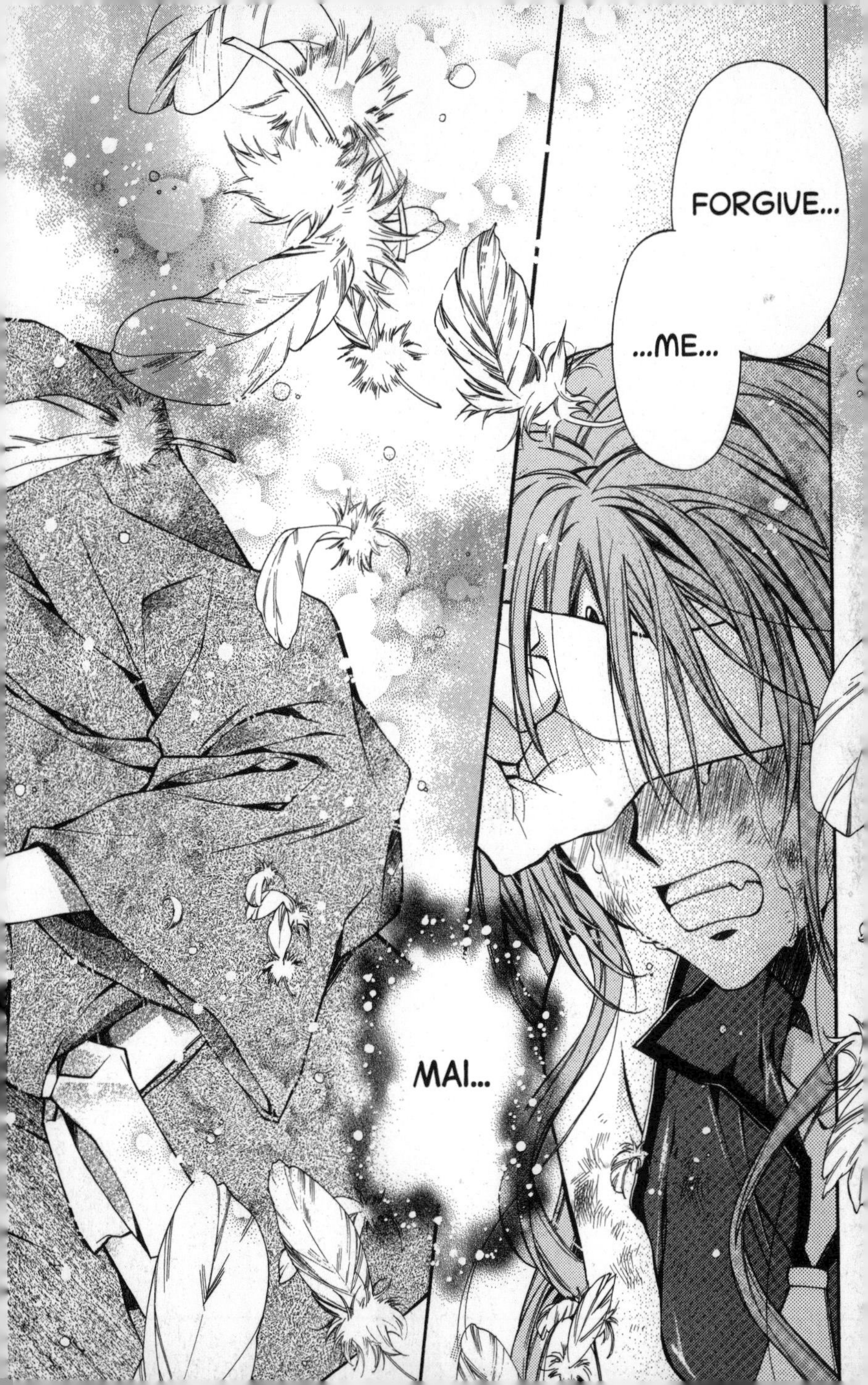
FORGIVE...
...ME...
MAI...

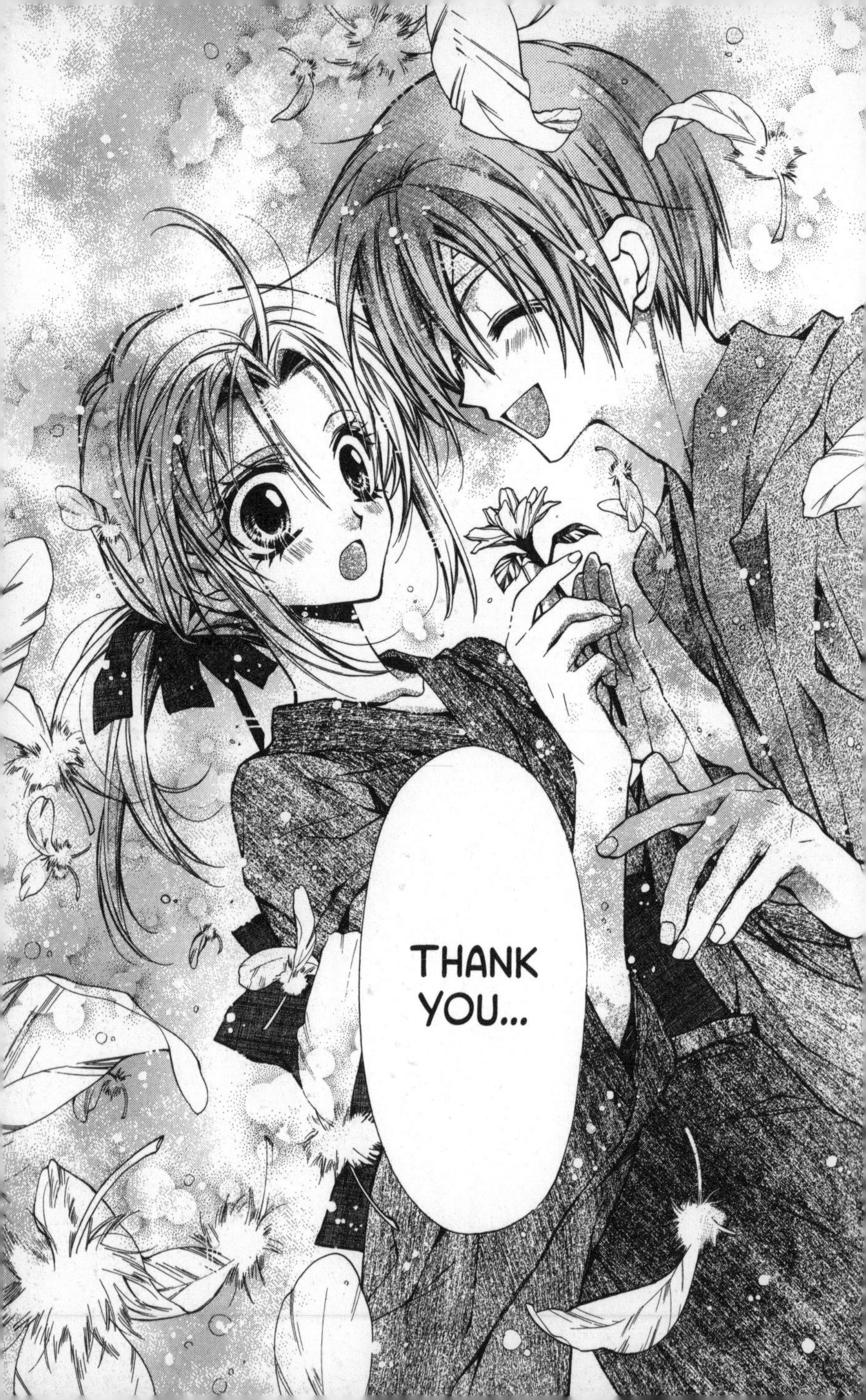
THANK YOU...

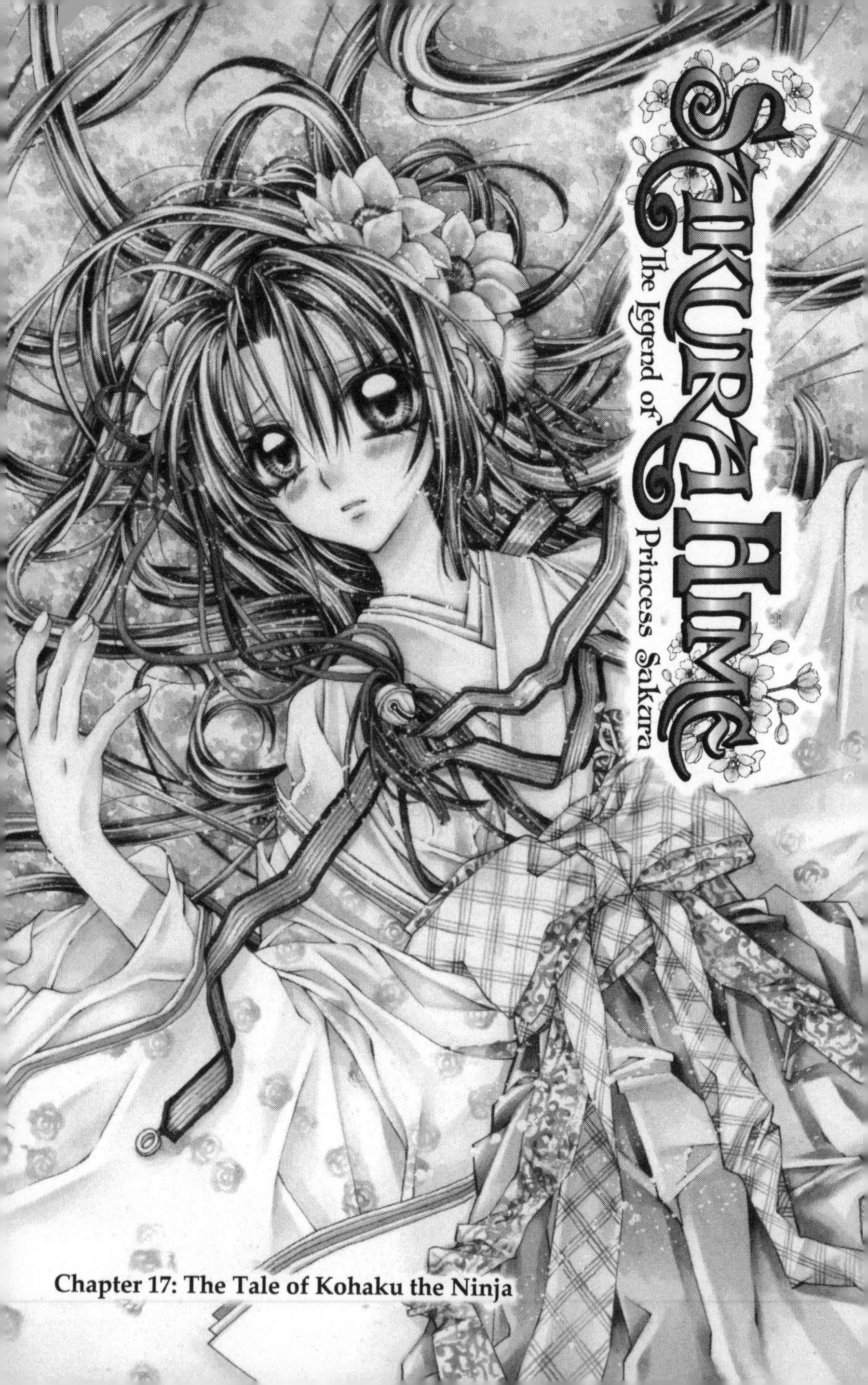
Sakura Hime
The Legend of Princess Sakara

Chapter 17: The Tale of Kohaku the Ninja

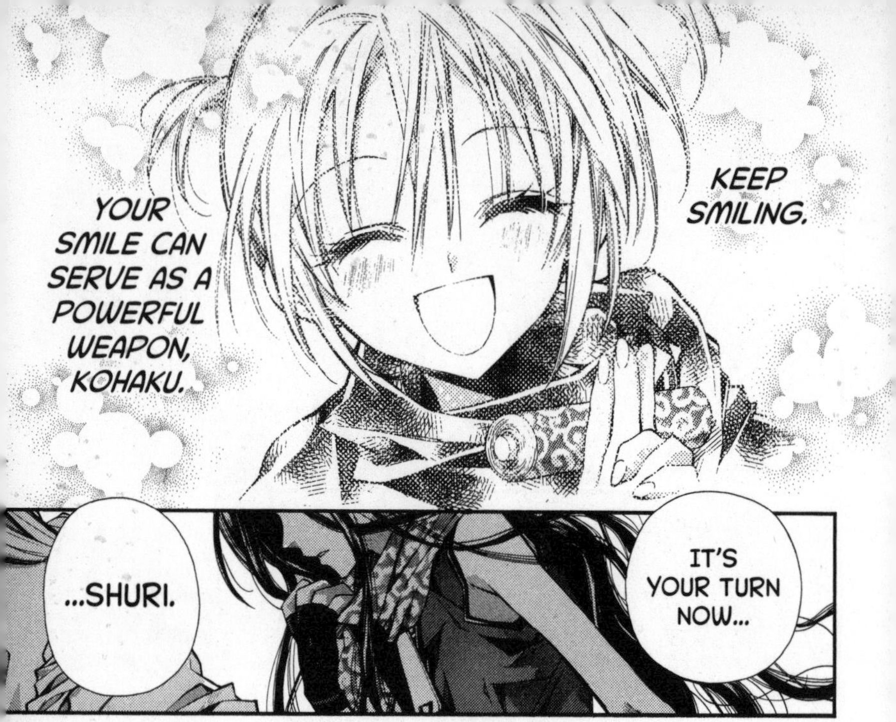
KEEP SMILING.
YOUR SMILE CAN SERVE AS A POWERFUL WEAPON, KOHAKU.
IT'S YOUR TURN NOW...
...SHURI.

Chapter 17: The Tale of Kohaku the Ninja

※ I'm giving away the story. [Lead-in] Do I feel that pain because I love you? Or do I love you because I feel that pain? Which is it?!

Ooh, I had so much fun drawing little Kohaku! And she was easy to draw too... (laugh) She ties her short hair into pigtails.

I always wanted to write about the childhood friends in the ninja village, but I never thought I'd get the chance to do it like this. My editor has told me to take my time on *Sakura Hime*, so the story for this manga develops slower than in my usual series. I was able to create this arc thanks to that. I was surprised how the term "weapon" sounded so ninjalike when Shuri told Kohaku, "Your smile can serve as a powerful weapon." (I know I'm the one who came up with that line, but my hand moves faster than my thoughts when my characters start to move on their own, so it doesn't feel like a line I wrote myself.)

The reason Hayate turned into a frog is because ninja and frogs have been linked since the old days, Ma'am. Kohaku and Hayate's romantic relationship will probably continue to change (probably?) so please watch over them patiently. (They're already starting to move about on their own, so I really can't tell how the story will unfold). >△< ;

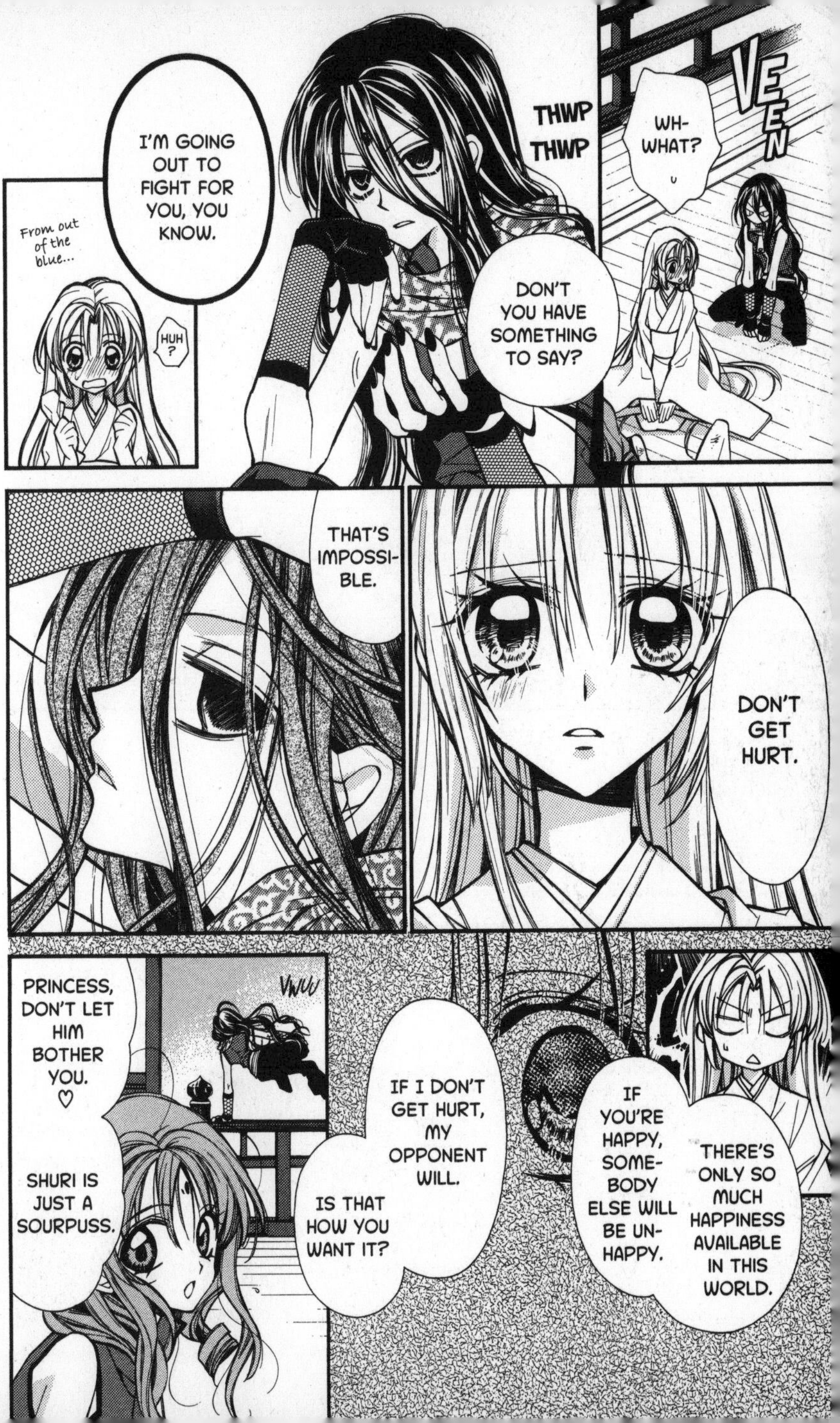
VEEN
WH-WHAT?
THWP THWP
DON'T YOU HAVE SOMETHING TO SAY?
I'M GOING OUT TO FIGHT FOR YOU, YOU KNOW.
From out of the blue...
HUH?
DON'T GET HURT.
THAT'S IMPOSSI-BLE.
THERE'S ONLY SO MUCH HAPPINESS AVAILABLE IN THIS WORLD.
IF YOU'RE HAPPY, SOME-BODY ELSE WILL BE UN-HAPPY.
IF I DON'T GET HURT, MY OPPONENT WILL.
IS THAT HOW YOU WANT IT?
VWUU
PRINCESS, DON'T LET HIM BOTHER YOU. ♡
SHURI IS JUST A SOURPUSS.

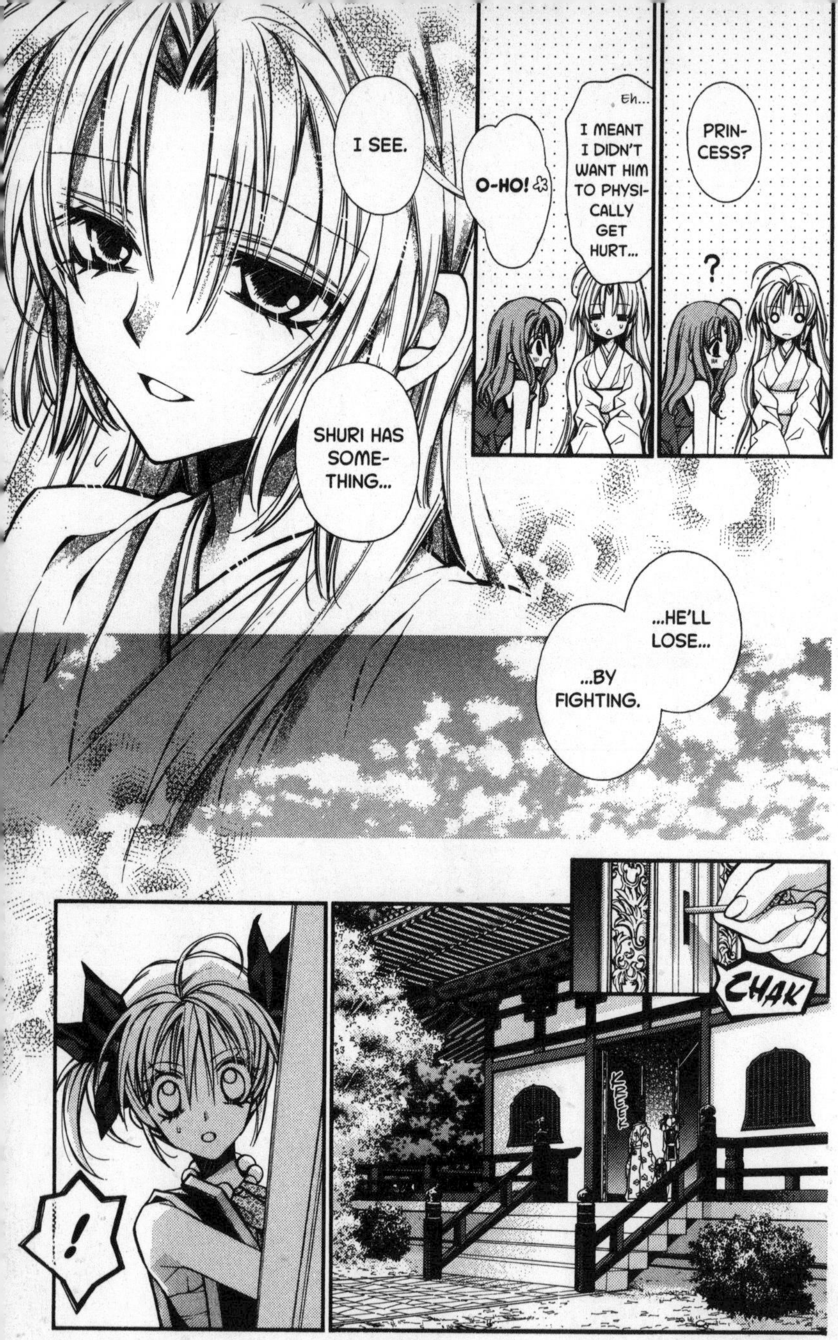
PRIN-CESS?
Eh...
I MEANT I DIDN'T WANT HIM TO PHYSICALLY GET HURT...
O-HO!
I SEE.
SHURI HAS SOMETHING...
...HE'LL LOSE...
...BY FIGHTING.
CHAK
!

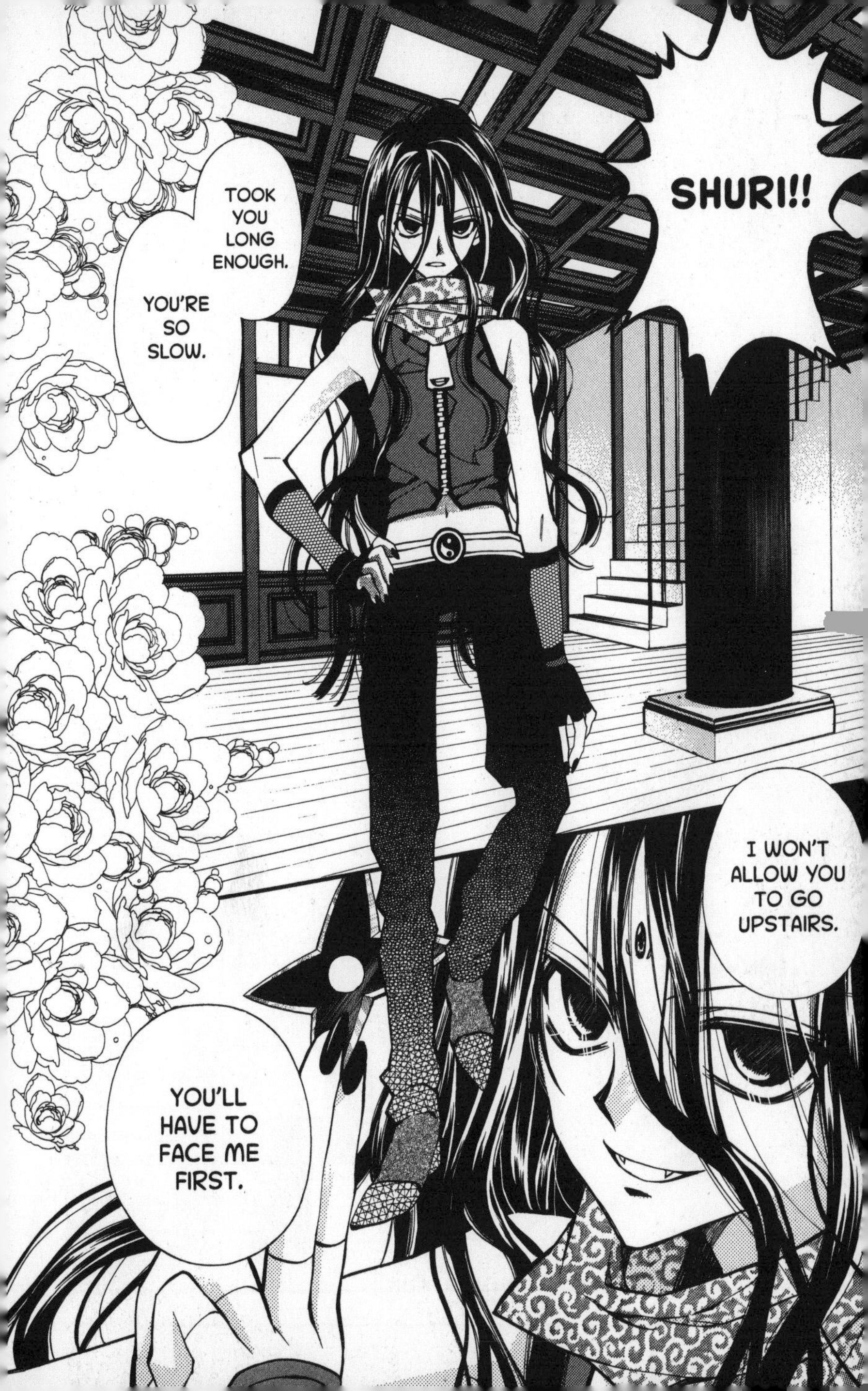
SHURI!!
TOOK YOU LONG ENOUGH.
YOU'RE SO SLOW.
I WON'T ALLOW YOU TO GO UPSTAIRS.
YOU'LL HAVE TO FACE ME FIRST.

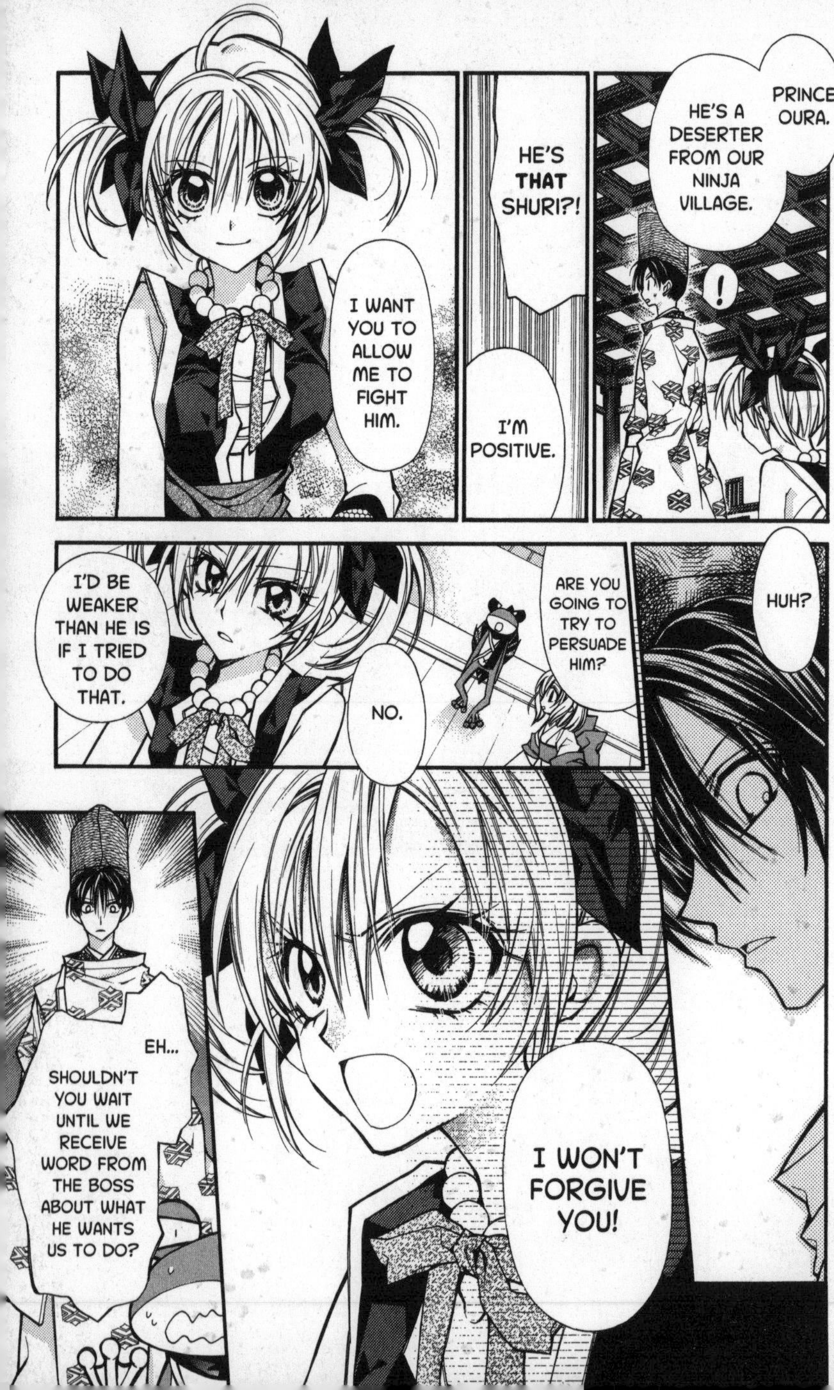
PRINCE OURA.
HE'S A DESERTER FROM OUR NINJA VILLAGE.
!
HE'S THAT SHURI?!
I'M POSITIVE.
I WANT YOU TO ALLOW ME TO FIGHT HIM.
HUH?
ARE YOU GOING TO TRY TO PERSUADE HIM?
NO.
I'D BE WEAKER THAN HE IS IF I TRIED TO DO THAT.
I WON'T FORGIVE YOU!
EH...
SHOULDN'T YOU WAIT UNTIL WE RECEIVE WORD FROM THE BOSS ABOUT WHAT HE WANTS US TO DO?

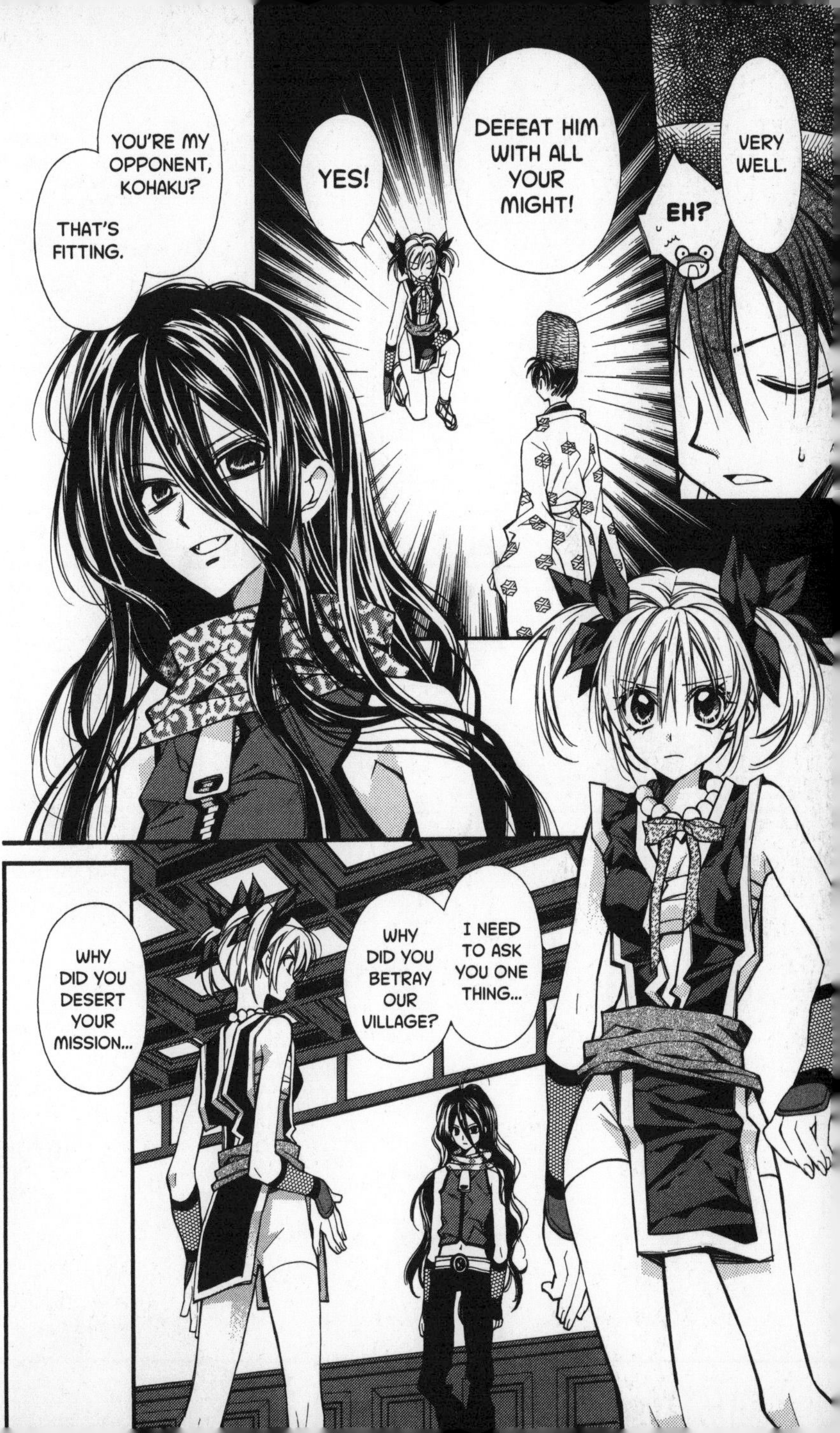
VERY WELL.
EH?
DEFEAT HIM WITH ALL YOUR MIGHT!
YES!
YOU'RE MY OPPONENT, KOHAKU?
THAT'S FITTING.
I NEED TO ASK YOU ONE THING...
WHY DID YOU BETRAY OUR VILLAGE?
WHY DID YOU DESERT YOUR MISSION...

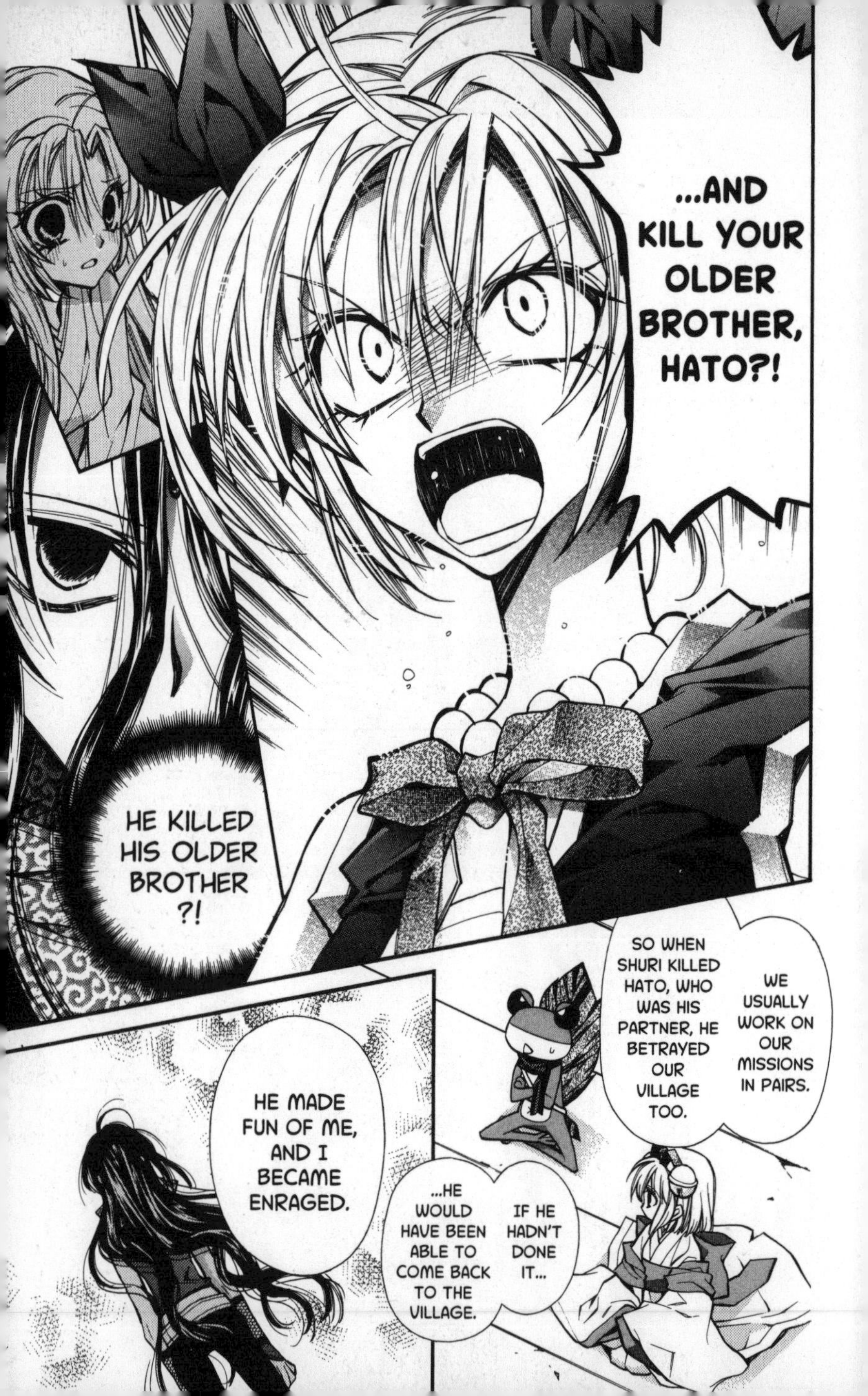
...AND KILL YOUR OLDER BROTHER, HATO?!
HE KILLED HIS OLDER BROTHER ?!
WE USUALLY WORK ON OUR MISSIONS IN PAIRS.
SO WHEN SHURI KILLED HATO, WHO WAS HIS PARTNER, HE BETRAYED OUR VILLAGE TOO.
IF HE HADN'T DONE IT...
...HE WOULD HAVE BEEN ABLE TO COME BACK TO THE VILLAGE.
HE MADE FUN OF ME, AND I BECAME ENRAGED.

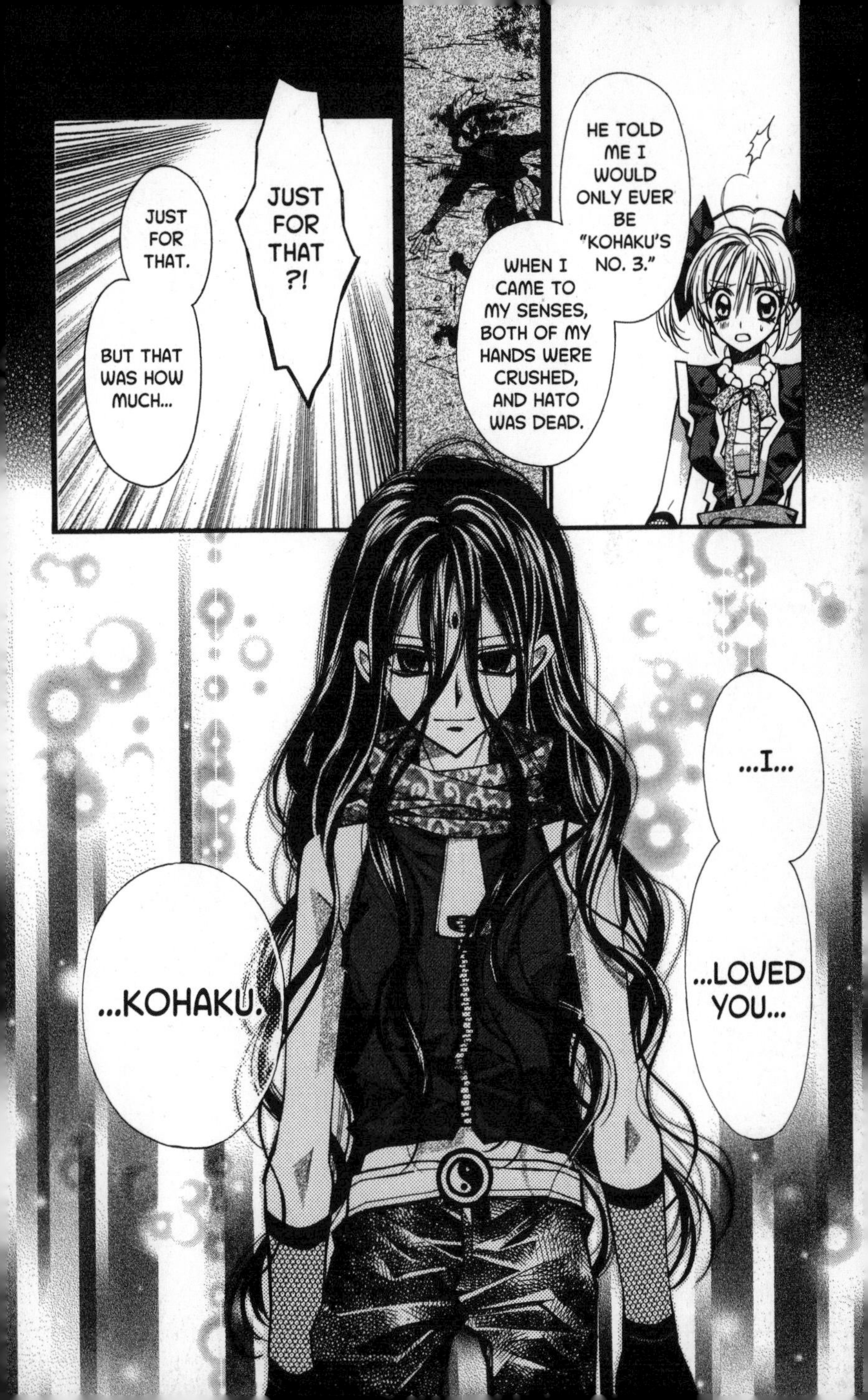
HE TOLD ME I WOULD ONLY EVER BE "KOHAKU'S NO. 3."
WHEN I CAME TO MY SENSES, BOTH OF MY HANDS WERE CRUSHED, AND HATO WAS DEAD.
JUST FOR THAT ?!
JUST FOR THAT.
BUT THAT WAS HOW MUCH...
...I...
...LOVED YOU...
...KOHAKU.

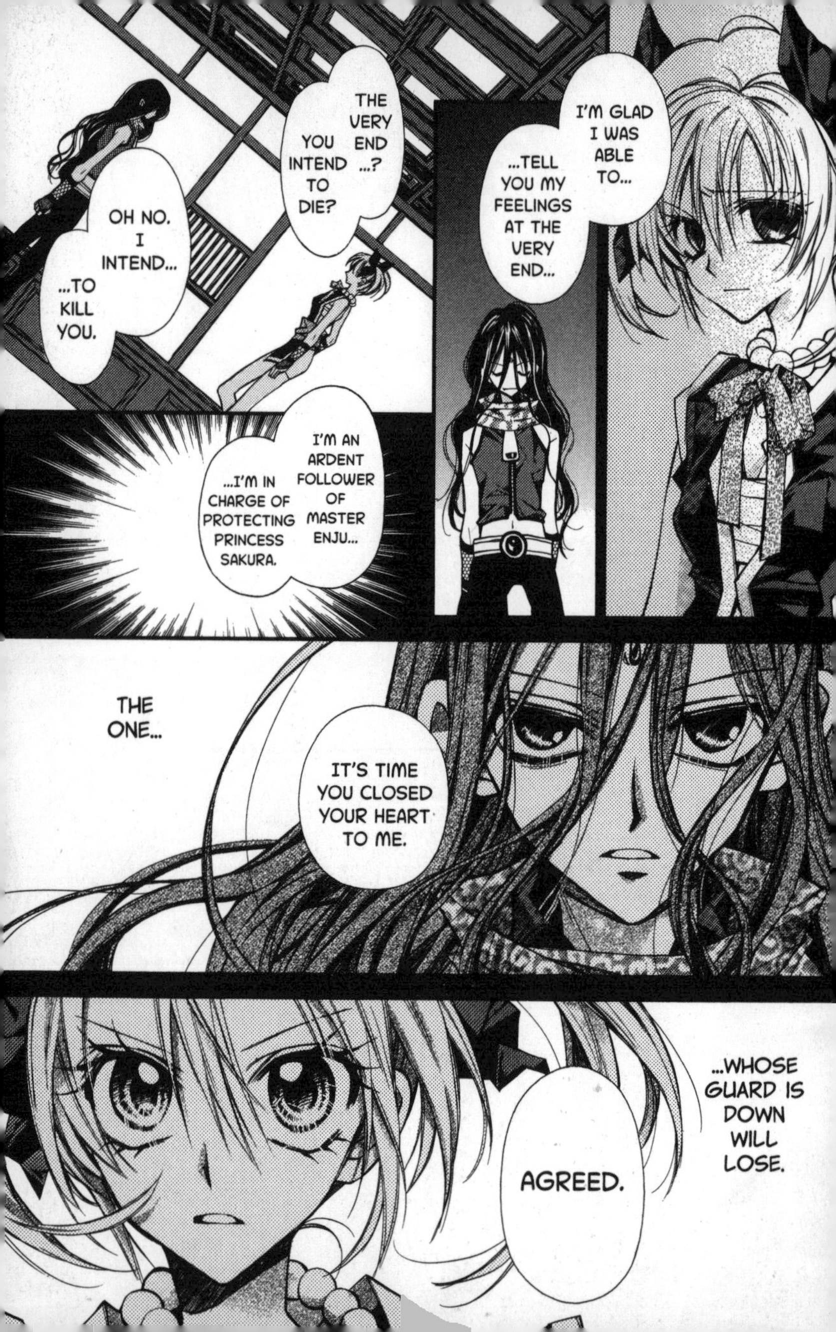

I'M GLAD I WAS ABLE TO...
...TELL YOU MY FEELINGS AT THE VERY END...
THE VERY END ...? YOU INTEND TO DIE?
OH NO. I INTEND...
...TO KILL YOU.
I'M AN ARDENT FOLLOWER OF MASTER ENJU...
...I'M IN CHARGE OF PROTECTING PRINCESS SAKURA.
IT'S TIME YOU CLOSED YOUR HEART TO ME.
THE ONE...
...WHOSE GUARD IS DOWN WILL LOSE.
AGREED.

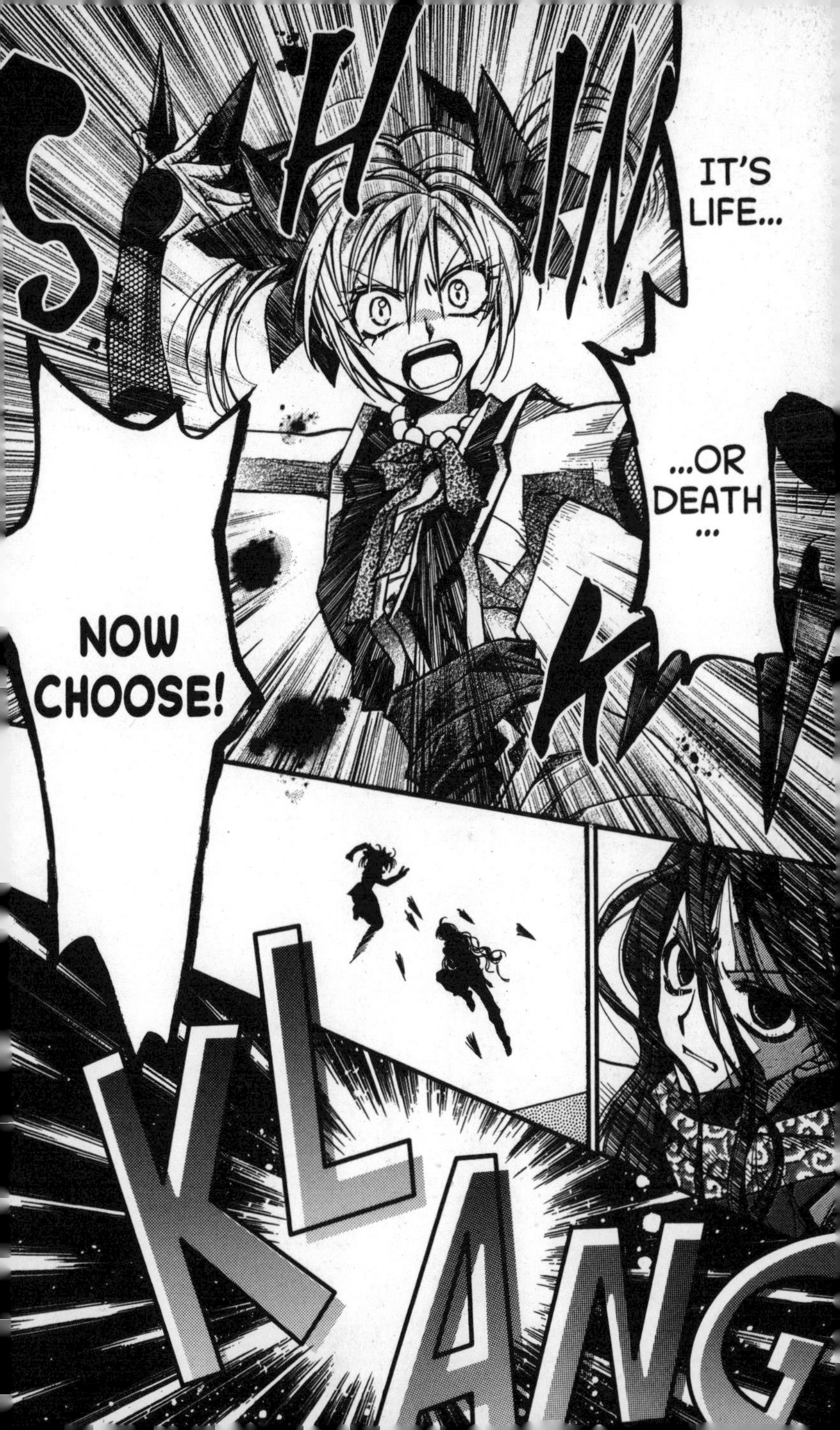
IT'S LIFE...
...OR DEATH...
NOW CHOOSE!
KLANG

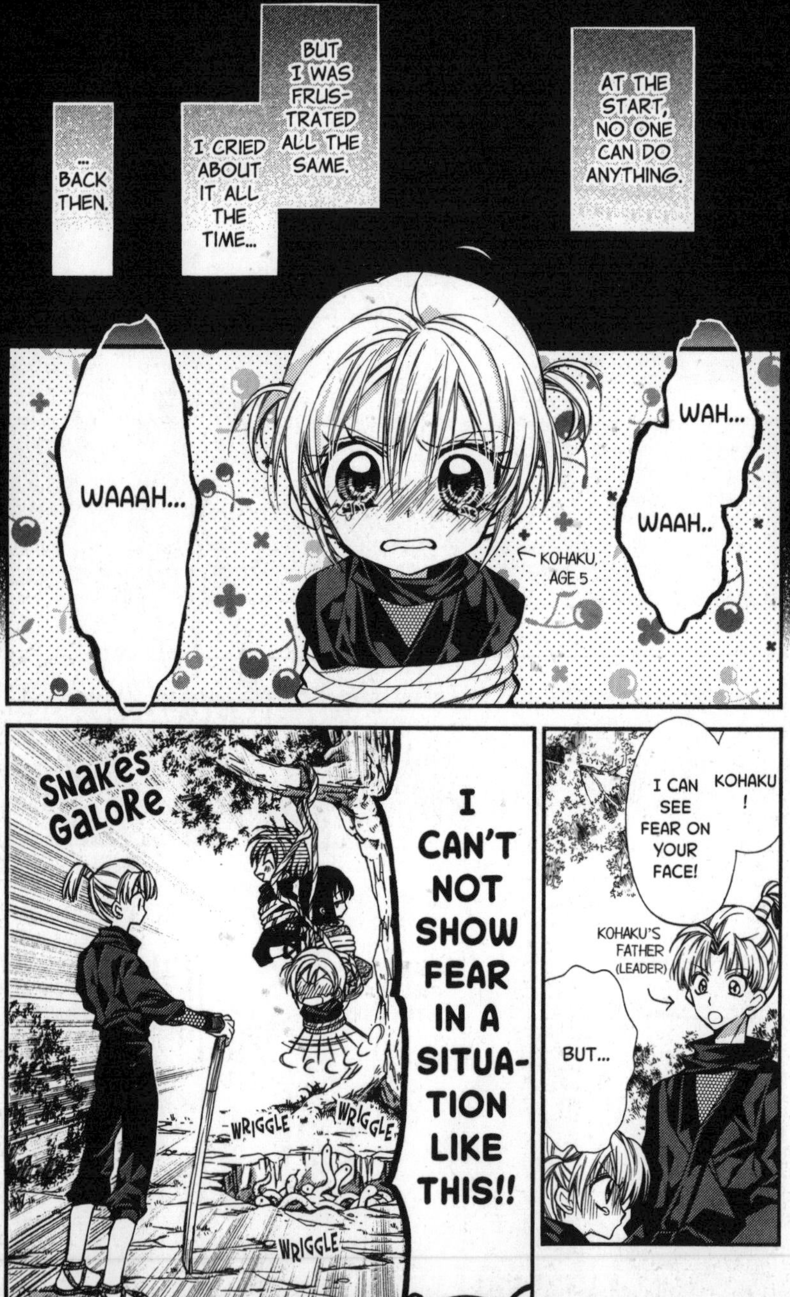
AT THE START, NO ONE CAN DO ANYTHING.
BUT I WAS FRUS-TRATED ALL THE SAME.
I CRIED ABOUT IT ALL THE TIME...
... BACK THEN.
WAH...
WAAH..
← KOHAKU, AGE 5
WAAAH...
KOHAKU!
I CAN SEE FEAR ON YOUR FACE!
KOHAKU'S FATHER (LEADER)
BUT...
I CAN'T NOT SHOW FEAR IN A SITUA-TION LIKE THIS!!
Snakes Galore
WRIGGLE
WRIGGLE
WRIGGLE

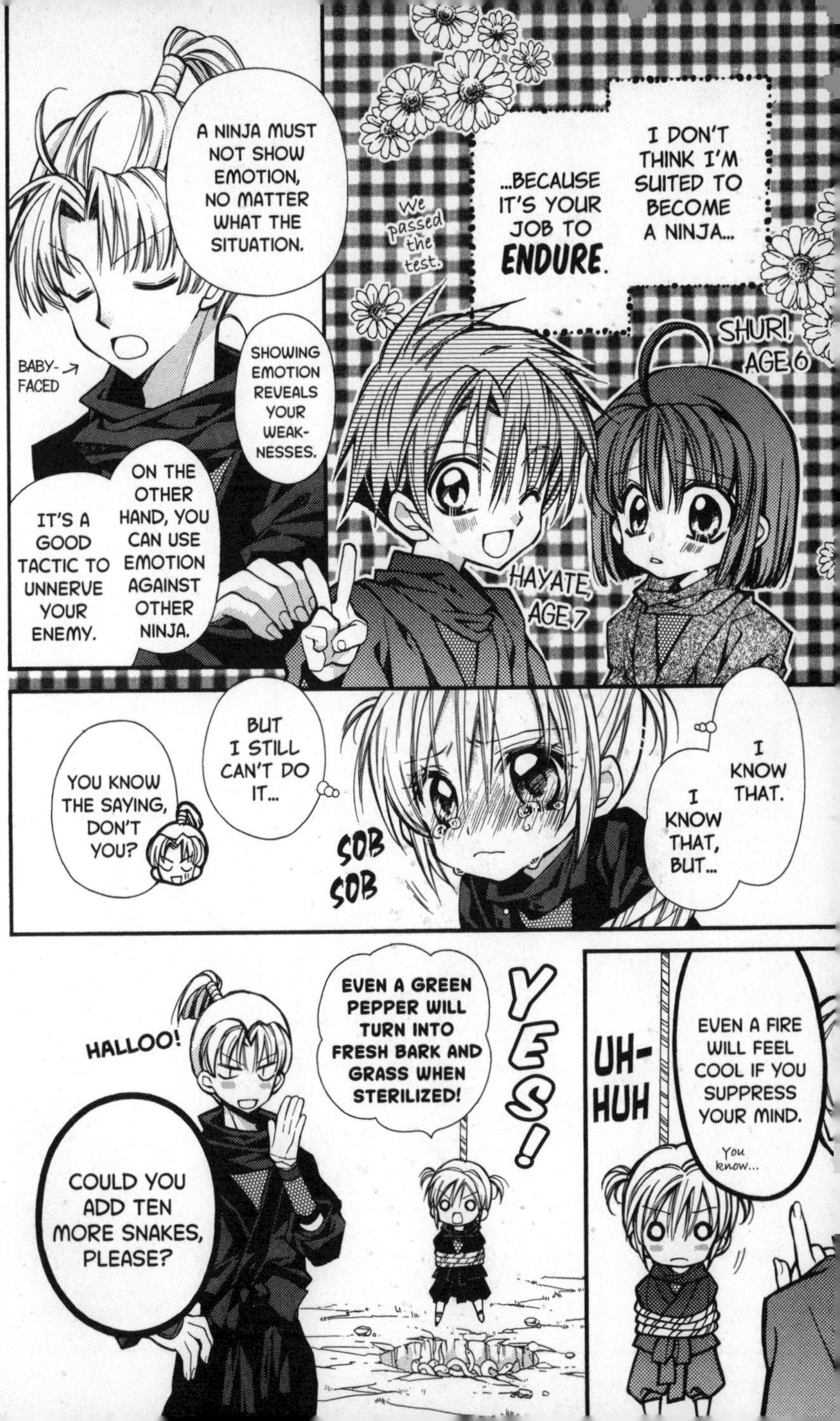
I DON'T THINK I'M SUITED TO BECOME A NINJA...
...BECAUSE IT'S YOUR JOB TO ENDURE.
We passed the test.
SHURI, AGE 6
HAYATE, AGE 7
A NINJA MUST NOT SHOW EMOTION, NO MATTER WHAT THE SITUATION.
SHOWING EMOTION REVEALS YOUR WEAKNESSES.
BABY-FACED
ON THE OTHER HAND, YOU CAN USE EMOTION AGAINST OTHER NINJA.
IT'S A GOOD TACTIC TO UNNERVE YOUR ENEMY.
I KNOW THAT.
I KNOW THAT, BUT...
SOB SOB
BUT I STILL CAN'T DO IT...
YOU KNOW THE SAYING, DON'T YOU?
EVEN A FIRE WILL FEEL COOL IF YOU SUPPRESS YOUR MIND.
You know...
UH-HUH
YES!
EVEN A GREEN PEPPER WILL TURN INTO FRESH BARK AND GRASS WHEN STERILIZED!
HALLOO!
COULD YOU ADD TEN MORE SNAKES, PLEASE?

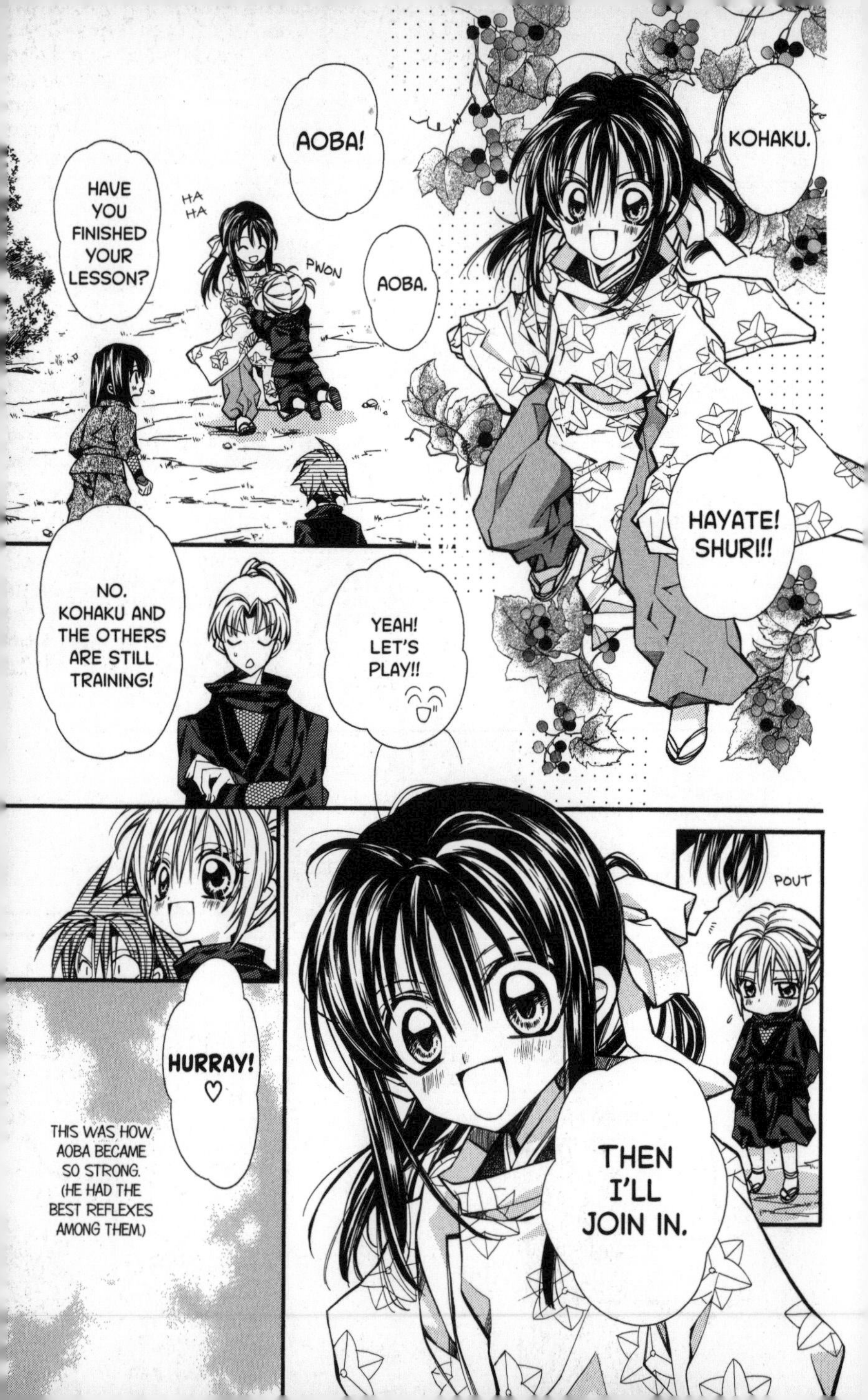
KOHAKU.
HAYATE! SHURI!!
AOBA!
AOBA.
PWON
HA HA
HAVE YOU FINISHED YOUR LESSON?
YEAH! LET'S PLAY!!
NO. KOHAKU AND THE OTHERS ARE STILL TRAINING!
POUT
THEN I'LL JOIN IN.
HURRAY! ♡
THIS WAS HOW AOBA BECAME SO STRONG. (HE HAD THE BEST REFLEXES AMONG THEM.)

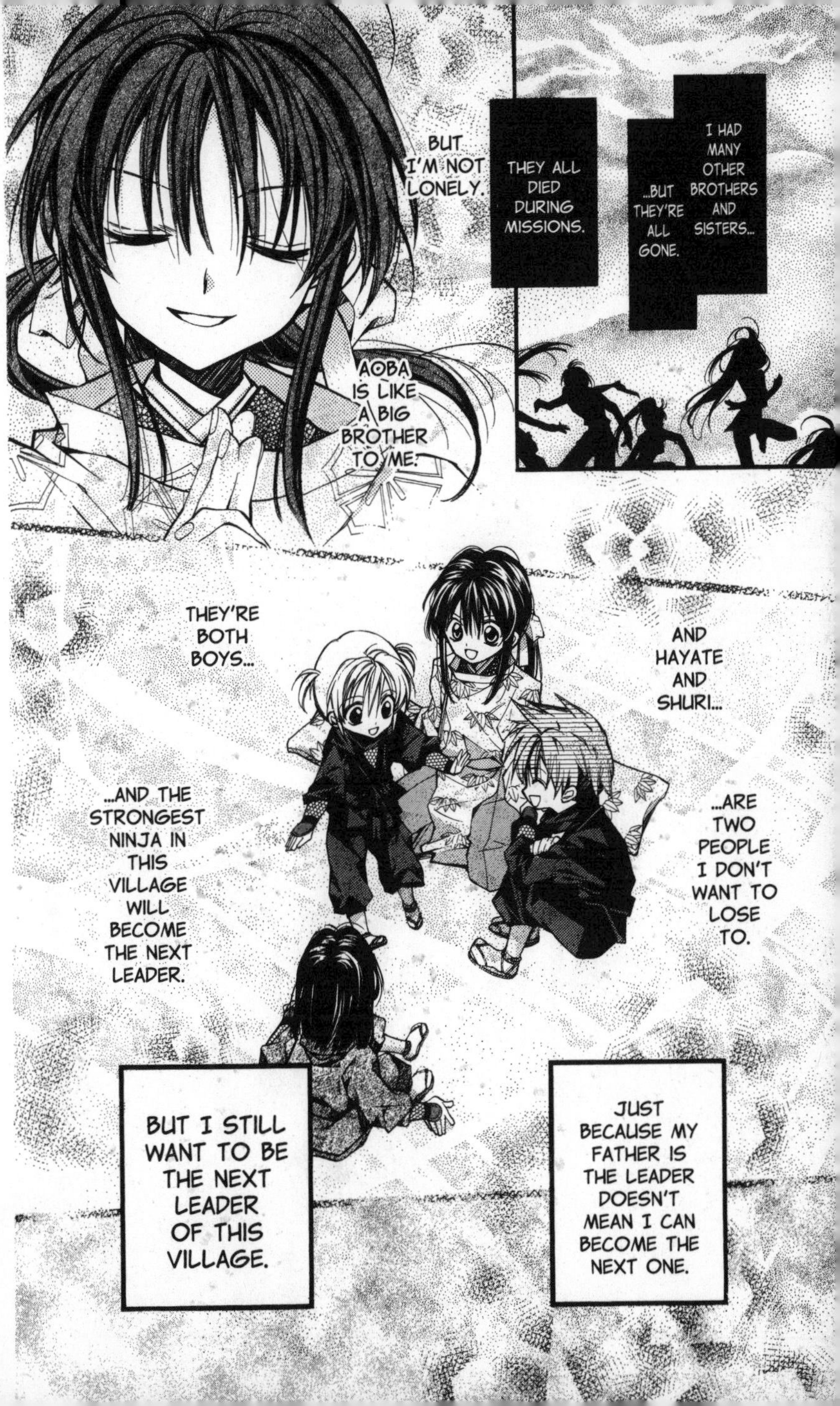
I HAD MANY OTHER BROTHERS AND SISTERS...
...BUT THEY'RE ALL GONE.
THEY ALL DIED DURING MISSIONS.
BUT I'M NOT LONELY.
AOBA IS LIKE A BIG BROTHER TO ME.
AND HAYATE AND SHURI...
...ARE TWO PEOPLE I DON'T WANT TO LOSE TO.
THEY'RE BOTH BOYS...
...AND THE STRONGEST NINJA IN THIS VILLAGE WILL BECOME THE NEXT LEADER.
JUST BECAUSE MY FATHER IS THE LEADER DOESN'T MEAN I CAN BECOME THE NEXT ONE.
BUT I STILL WANT TO BE THE NEXT LEADER OF THIS VILLAGE.

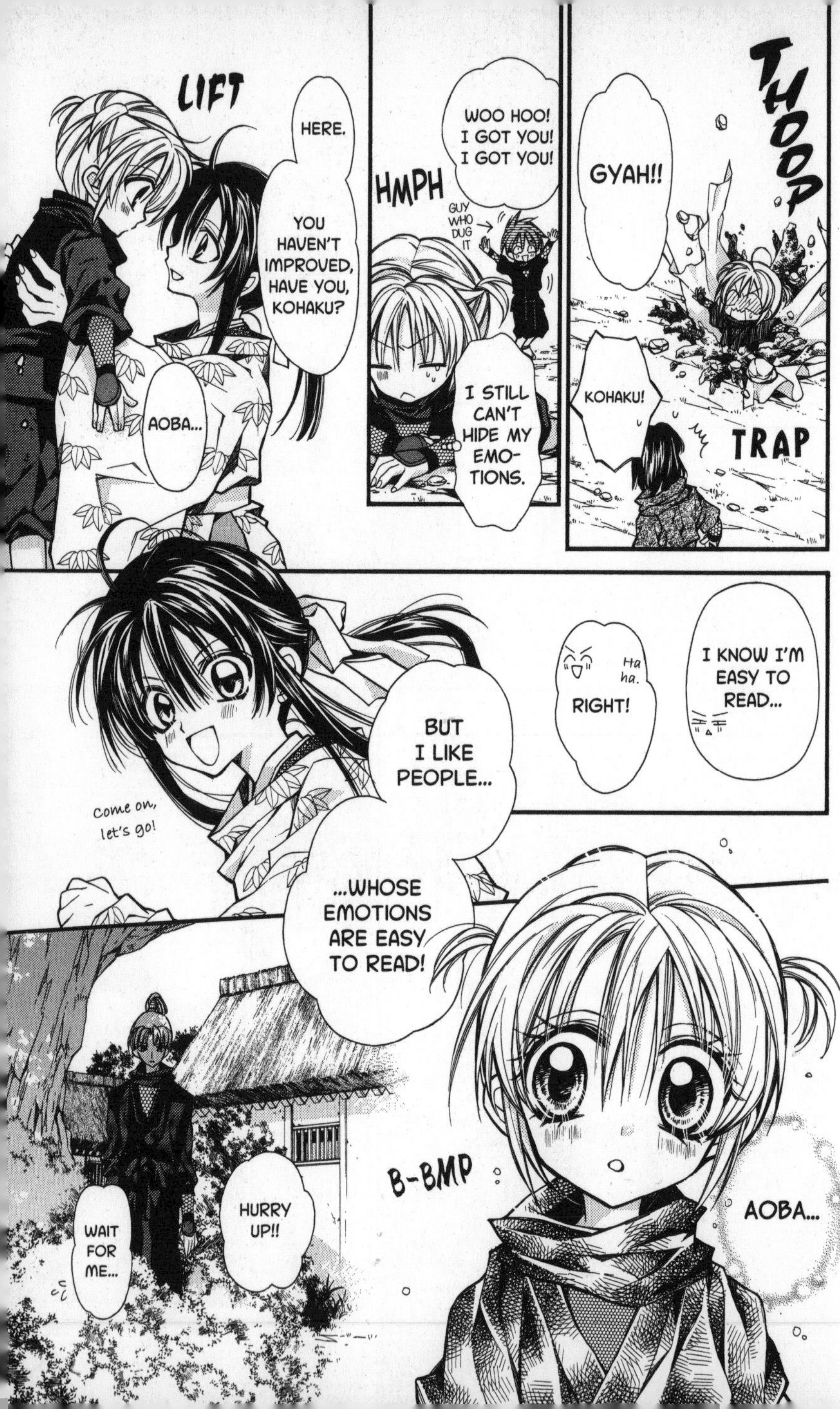
THOOOP
GYAH!!
TRAP
KOHAKU!
WOO HOO! I GOT YOU! I GOT YOU!
HMPH
GUY WHO DUG IT
I STILL CAN'T HIDE MY EMO-TIONS.
LIFT
HERE.
YOU HAVEN'T IMPROVED, HAVE YOU, KOHAKU?
AOBA...
I KNOW I'M EASY TO READ...
RIGHT!
Ha ha.
BUT I LIKE PEOPLE...
Come on, let's go!
...WHOSE EMOTIONS ARE EASY TO READ!
AOBA...
B-BMP
HURRY UP!!
WAIT FOR ME...

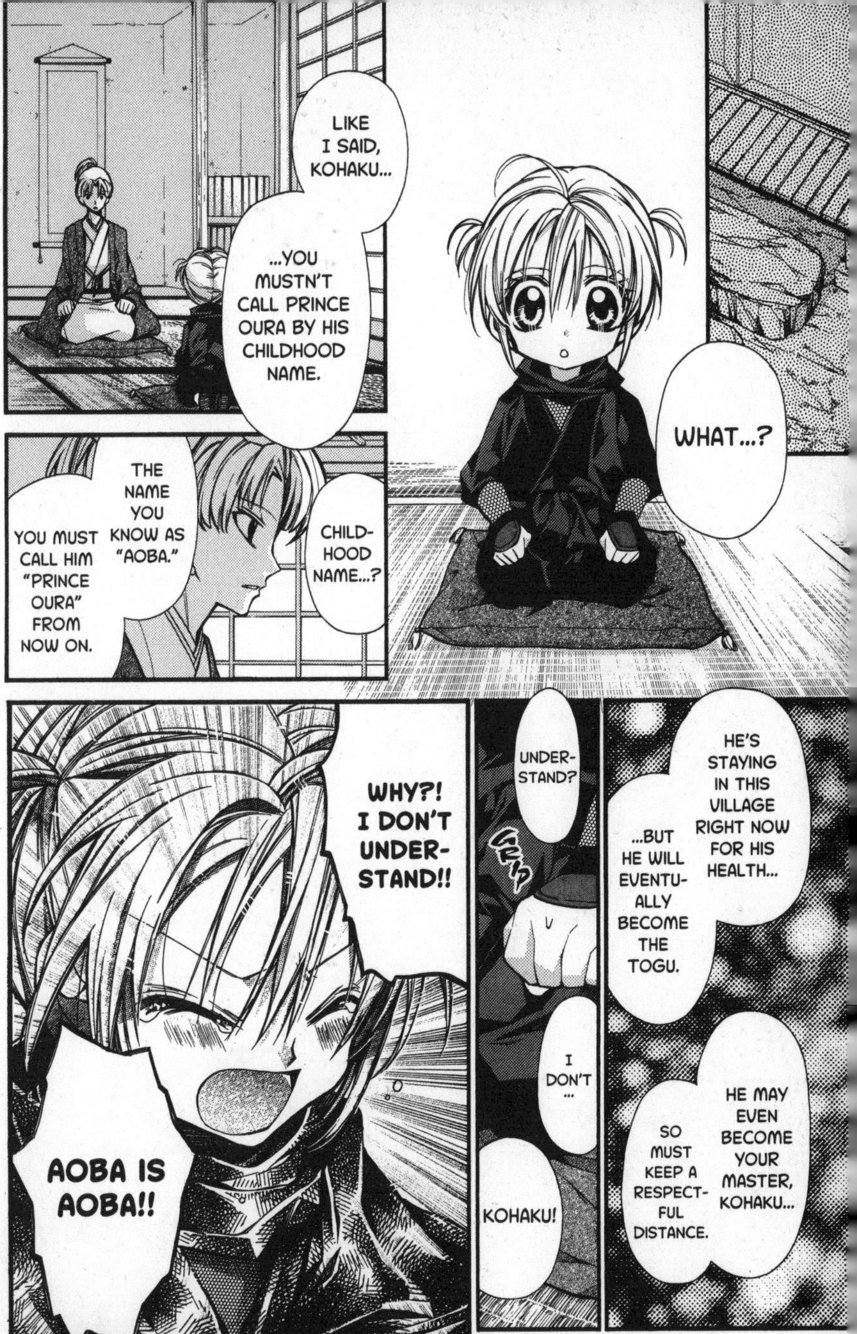
WHAT...?
LIKE I SAID, KOHAKU...
...YOU MUSTN'T CALL PRINCE OURA BY HIS CHILDHOOD NAME.
CHILD-HOOD NAME...?
THE NAME YOU KNOW AS "AOBA."
YOU MUST CALL HIM "PRINCE OURA" FROM NOW ON.
HE'S STAYING IN THIS VILLAGE RIGHT NOW FOR HIS HEALTH...
...BUT HE WILL EVENTU-ALLY BECOME THE TOGU.
HE MAY EVEN BECOME YOUR MASTER, KOHAKU...
SO MUST KEEP A RESPECT-FUL DISTANCE.
UNDER-STAND?
GRIP
I DON'T ...
KOHAKU!
WHY?! I DON'T UNDER-STAND!!
AOBA IS AOBA!!

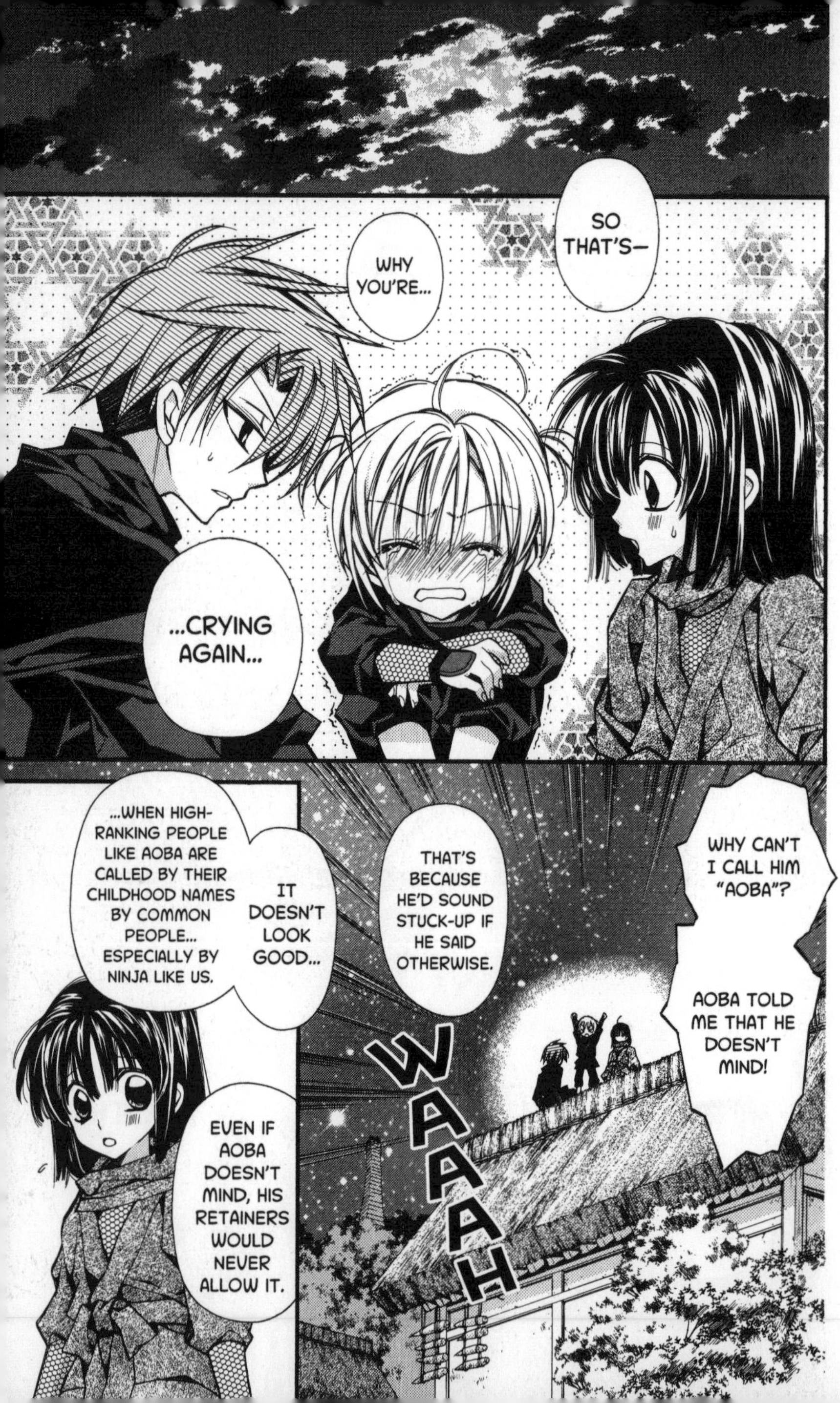
SO THAT'S—
WHY YOU'RE...
...CRYING AGAIN...
WHY CAN'T I CALL HIM "AOBA"?
AOBA TOLD ME THAT HE DOESN'T MIND!
THAT'S BECAUSE HE'D SOUND STUCK-UP IF HE SAID OTHERWISE.
WAAAAH
IT DOESN'T LOOK GOOD...
...WHEN HIGH-RANKING PEOPLE LIKE AOBA ARE CALLED BY THEIR CHILDHOOD NAMES BY COMMON PEOPLE... ESPECIALLY BY NINJA LIKE US.
EVEN IF AOBA DOESN'T MIND, HIS RETAINERS WOULD NEVER ALLOW IT.

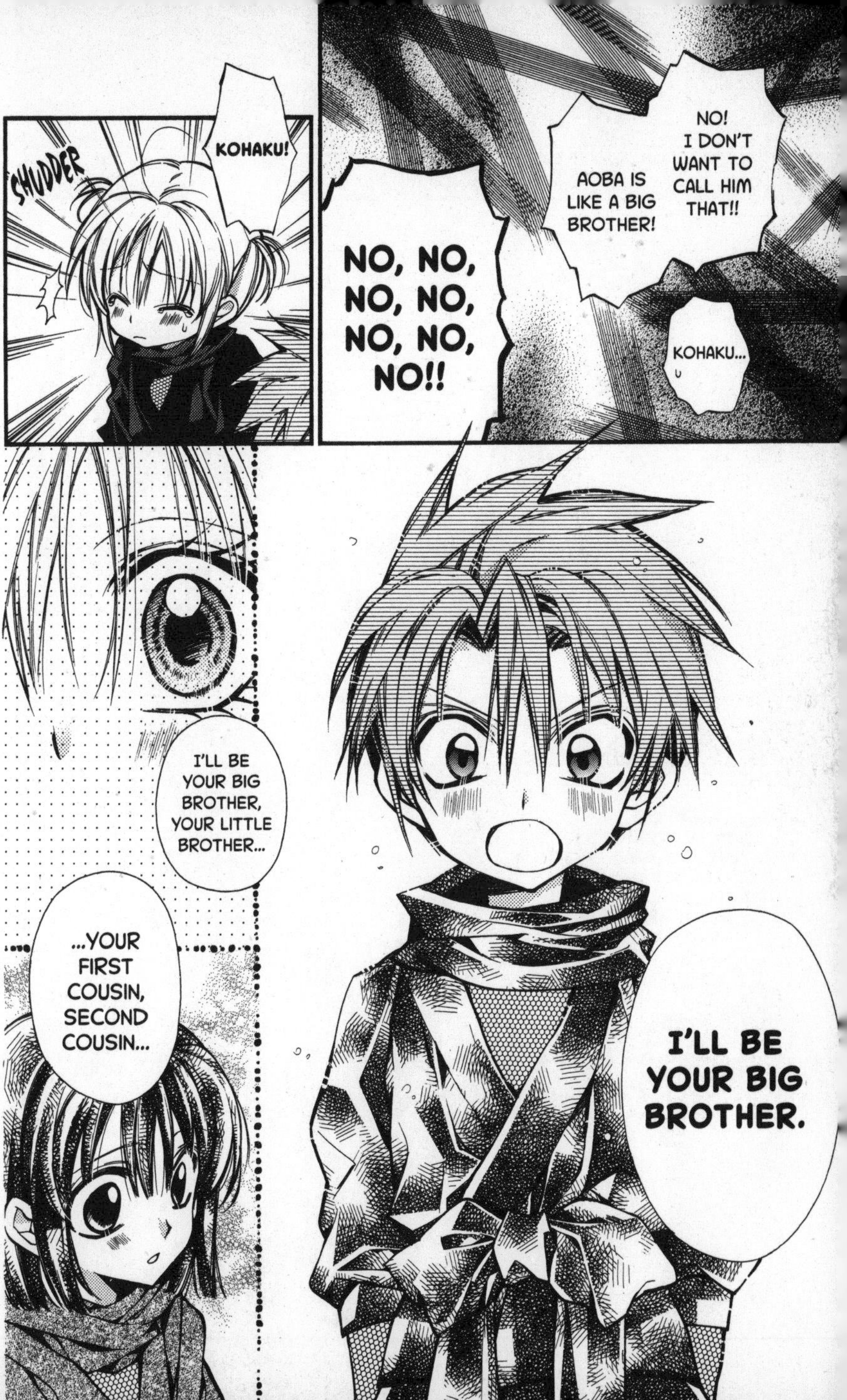
NO! I DON'T WANT TO CALL HIM THAT!!
AOBA IS LIKE A BIG BROTHER!
NO, NO, NO, NO, NO, NO, NO!!
KOHAKU...
KOHAKU!
SHUDDER
I'LL BE YOUR BIG BROTHER.
I'LL BE YOUR BIG BROTHER, YOUR LITTLE BROTHER...
...YOUR FIRST COUSIN, SECOND COUSIN...

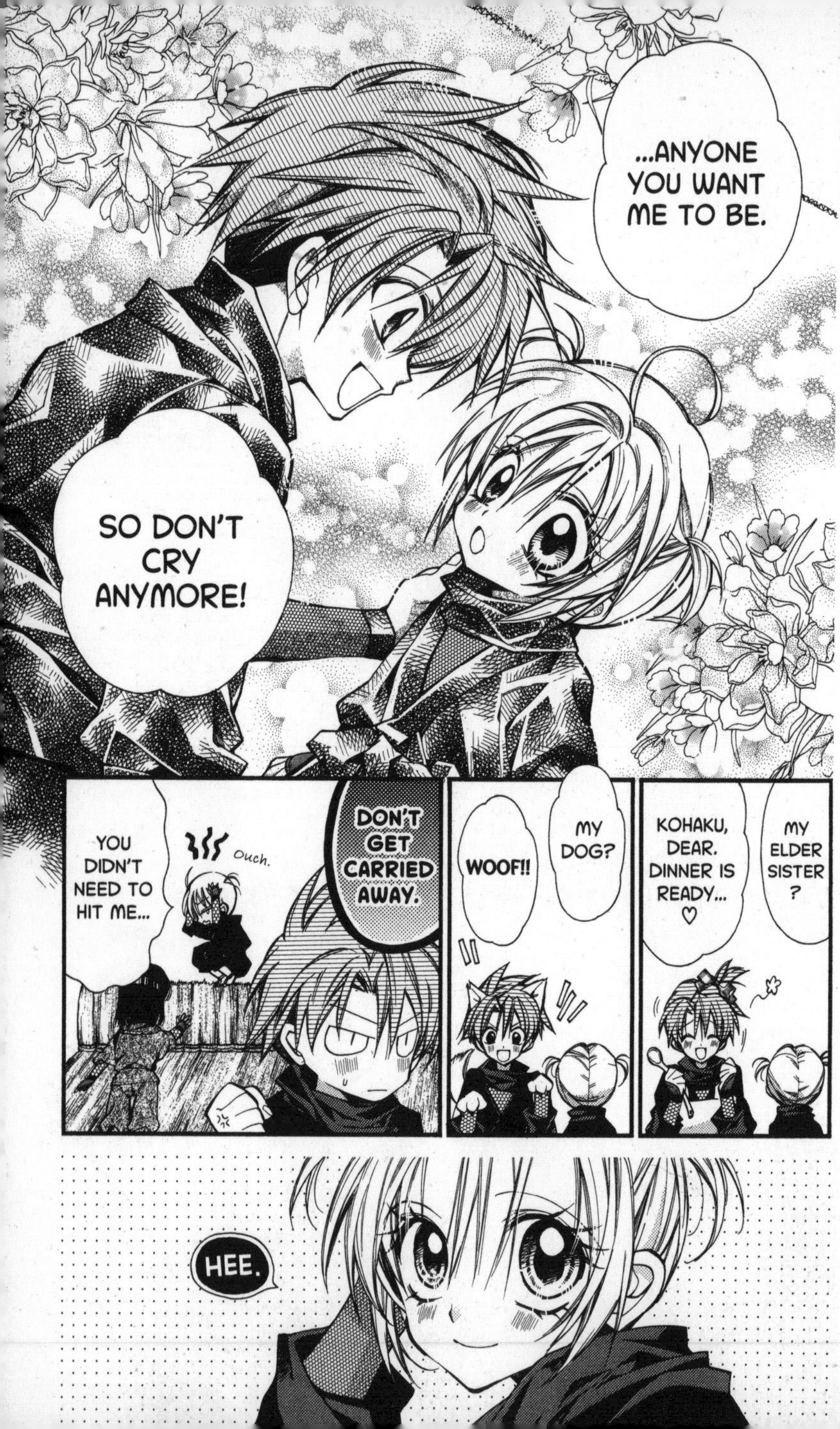
...ANYONE YOU WANT ME TO BE.
SO DON'T CRY ANYMORE!
MY ELDER SISTER?
KOHAKU, DEAR. DINNER IS READY... ♡
MY DOG?
WOOF!!
DON'T GET CARRIED AWAY.
YOU DIDN'T NEED TO HIT ME...
Ouch.
HEE.

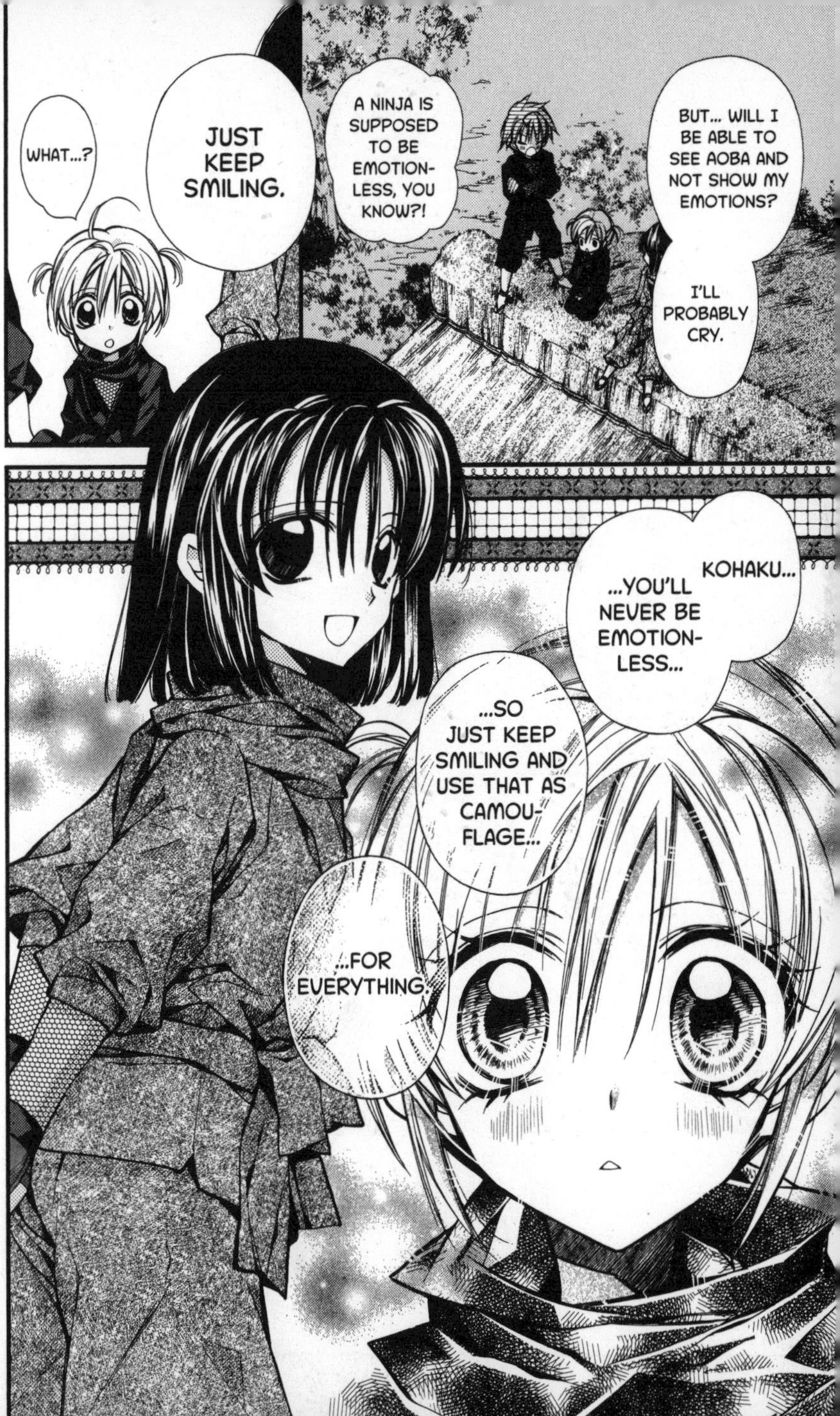
BUT... WILL I BE ABLE TO SEE AOBA AND NOT SHOW MY EMOTIONS?
I'LL PROBABLY CRY.
A NINJA IS SUPPOSED TO BE EMOTIONLESS, YOU KNOW?!
JUST KEEP SMILING.
WHAT...?
KOHAKU...
...YOU'LL NEVER BE EMOTIONLESS...
...SO JUST KEEP SMILING AND USE THAT AS CAMOUFLAGE...
...FOR EVERYTHING.

CCAC

Cocoa Club

I was told "Sure, you can write about it," so I'm going to write about it.

I've made many friends recently, and the people I especially get along with are Mitsuki Saiga-san, Mari Orito-chan, Chicchi, Chiaki Kyan-chan, and Nozomi Sasaki-chan. Together we hold a monthly sleepover called the "Cocoa Club (CCAC)." ♪

It is basically a "girl's get-together" and we chat all night or play Monster Hunter (a PSP game) and whatnot.

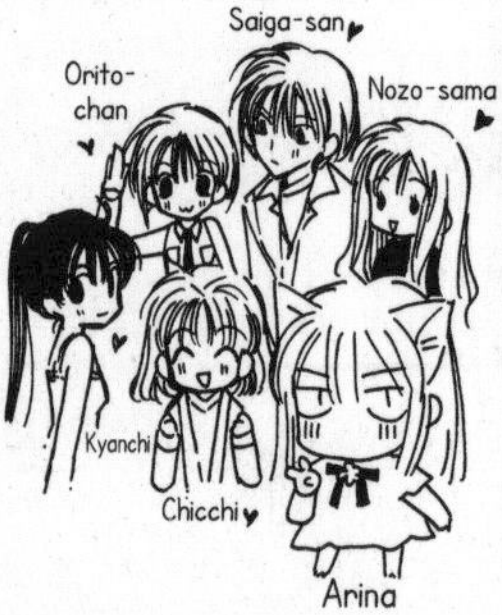
Saiga-san
Orito-chan
Nozo-sama
Kyanchi
Chicchi
Arina

I only got to know them about half a year ago, but we're already best friends. (Well, that's what I think, anyway.) ////

I have such good chemistry with them that I start to feel lonely and unstable when I don't see them once every couple of days.

Most of my other friends were manga artists, so I really enjoy spending time with them.

I write about CCAC on my blog every now and then, so please take a look at it if you'd like. ♪

"Arina Diary"

http://rikukai.arina.lolipop.jp/

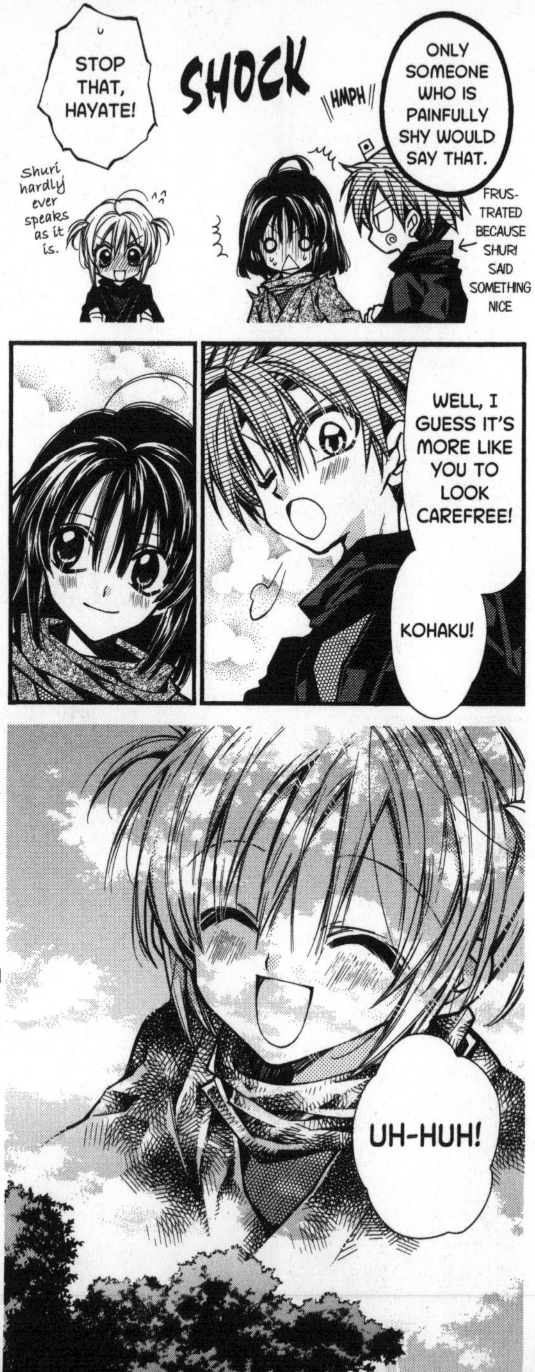
ONLY SOMEONE WHO IS PAINFULLY SHY WOULD SAY THAT.
FRUSTRATED BECAUSE SHURI SAID SOMETHING NICE
HMPH
SHOCK
STOP THAT, HAYATE!
Shuri hardly ever speaks as it is.
WELL, I GUESS IT'S MORE LIKE YOU TO LOOK CAREFREE!
KOHAKU!
UH-HUH!

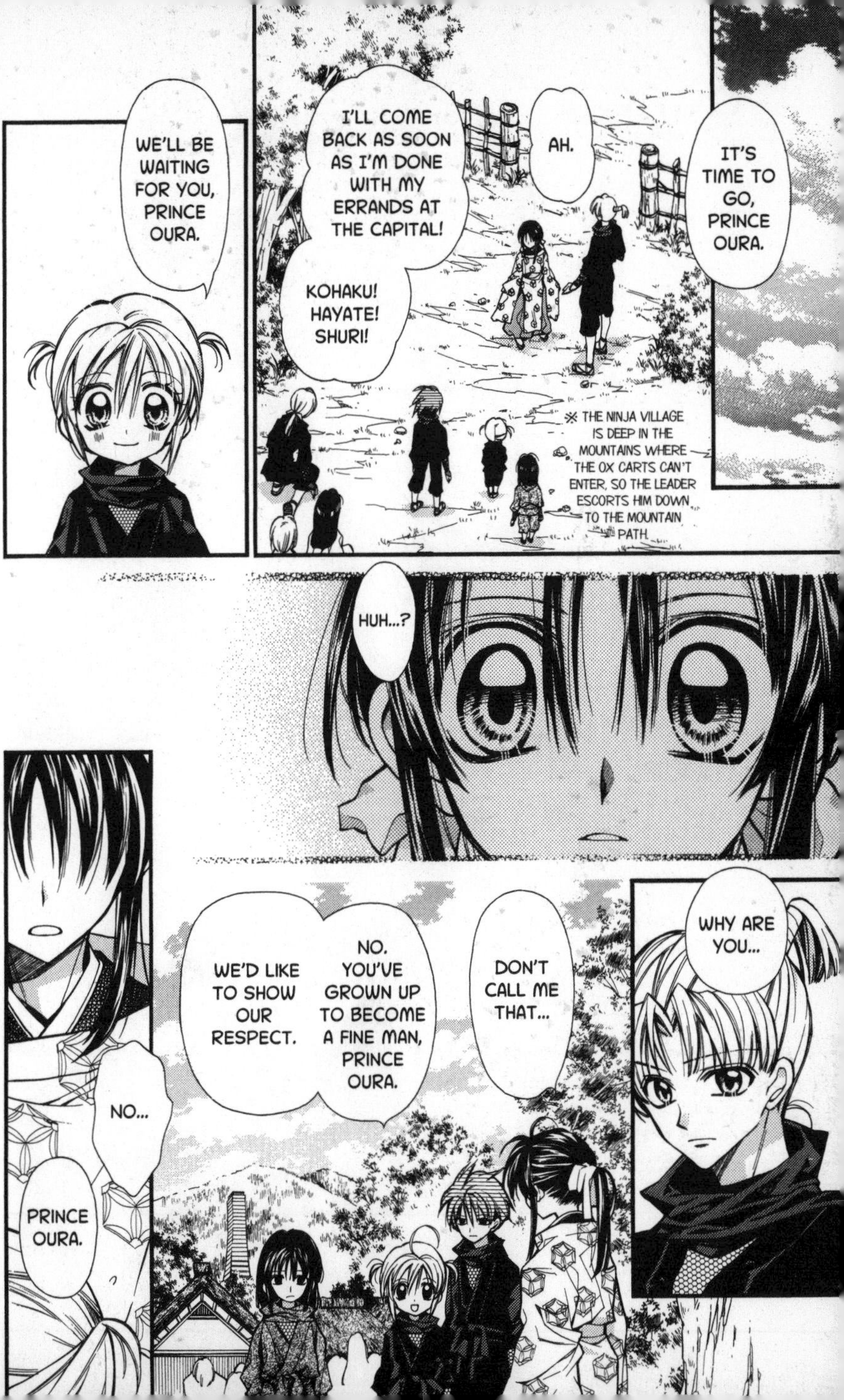
IT'S TIME TO GO, PRINCE OURA.
AH.
I'LL COME BACK AS SOON AS I'M DONE WITH MY ERRANDS AT THE CAPITAL!
KOHAKU! HAYATE! SHURI!
※ THE NINJA VILLAGE IS DEEP IN THE MOUNTAINS WHERE THE OX CARTS CAN'T ENTER, SO THE LEADER ESCORTS HIM DOWN TO THE MOUNTAIN PATH.
WE'LL BE WAITING FOR YOU, PRINCE OURA.
HUH...?
WHY ARE YOU...
DON'T CALL ME THAT...
NO. YOU'VE GROWN UP TO BECOME A FINE MAN, PRINCE OURA.
WE'D LIKE TO SHOW OUR RESPECT.
NO...
PRINCE OURA.

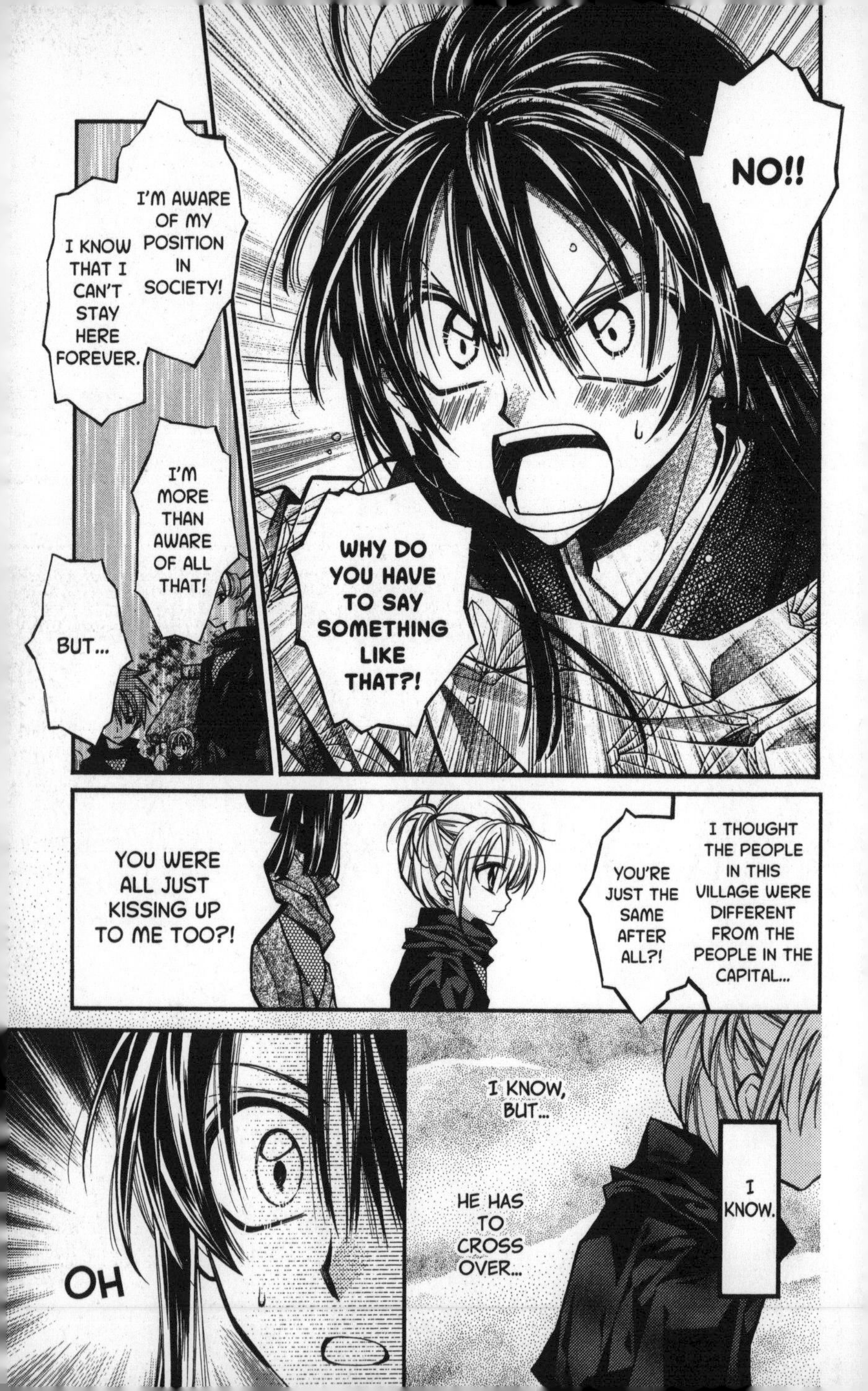
NO!!
WHY DO YOU HAVE TO SAY SOMETHING LIKE THAT?!
I'M AWARE OF MY POSITION IN SOCIETY!
I KNOW THAT I CAN'T STAY HERE FOREVER.
I'M MORE THAN AWARE OF ALL THAT!
BUT...
I THOUGHT THE PEOPLE IN THIS VILLAGE WERE DIFFERENT FROM THE PEOPLE IN THE CAPITAL...
YOU'RE JUST THE SAME AFTER ALL?!
YOU WERE ALL JUST KISSING UP TO ME TOO?!
I KNOW.
I KNOW, BUT...
HE HAS TO CROSS OVER...
OH

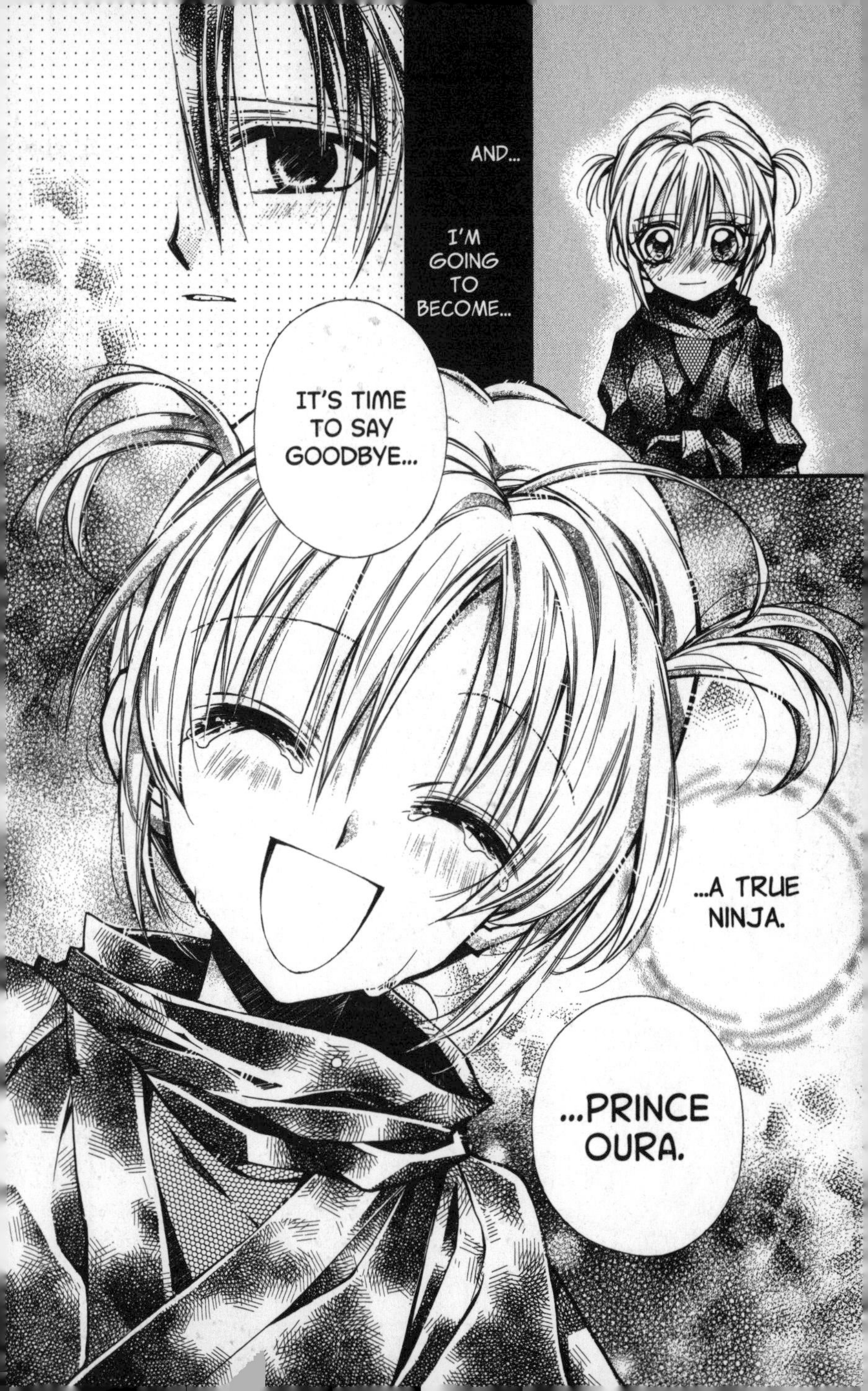
AND...
I'M GOING TO BECOME...
...A TRUE NINJA.
IT'S TIME TO SAY GOODBYE...
...PRINCE OURA.

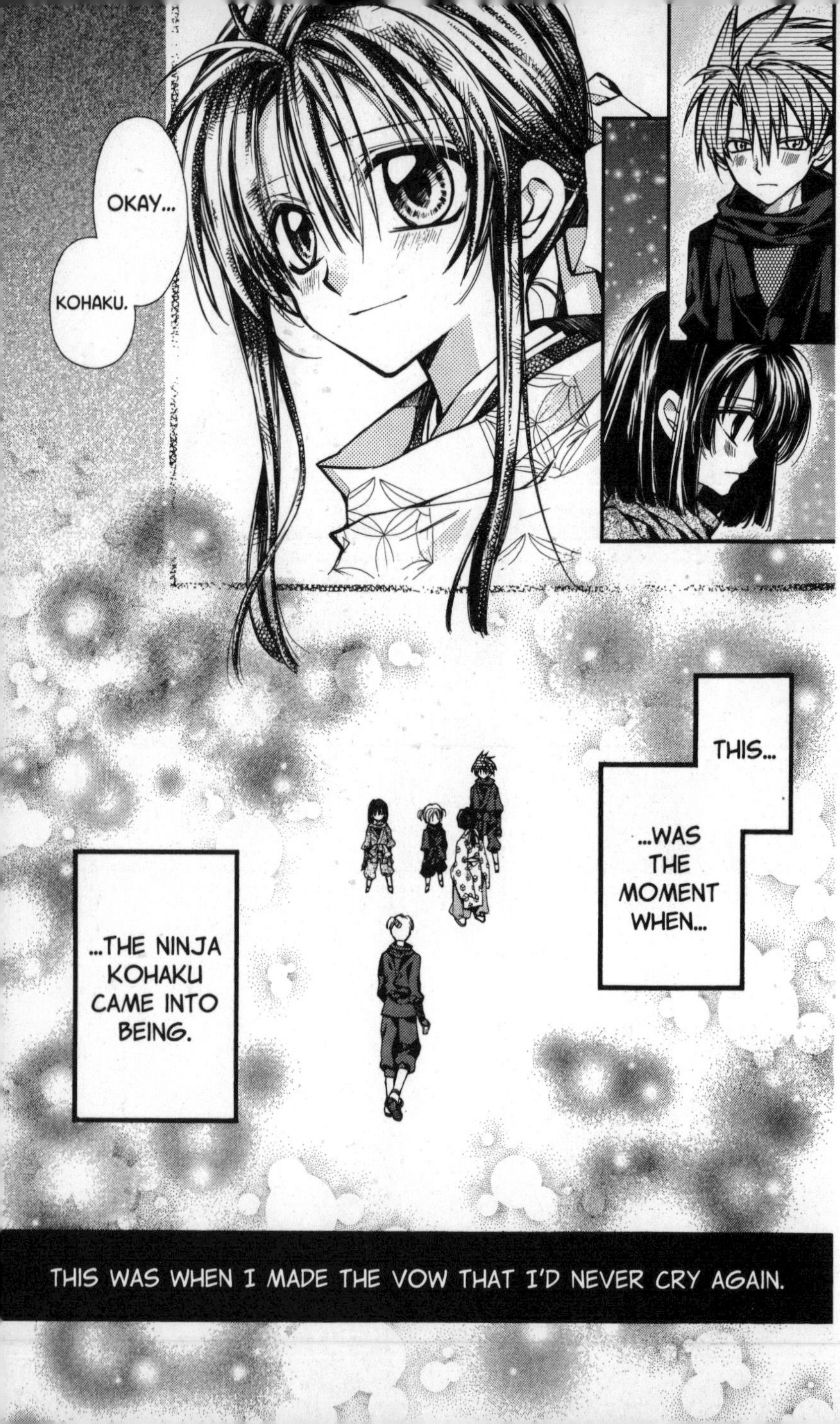
OKAY...
KOHAKU.
THIS...
...WAS THE MOMENT WHEN...
...THE NINJA KOHAKU CAME INTO BEING.
THIS WAS WHEN I MADE THE VOW THAT I'D NEVER CRY AGAIN.

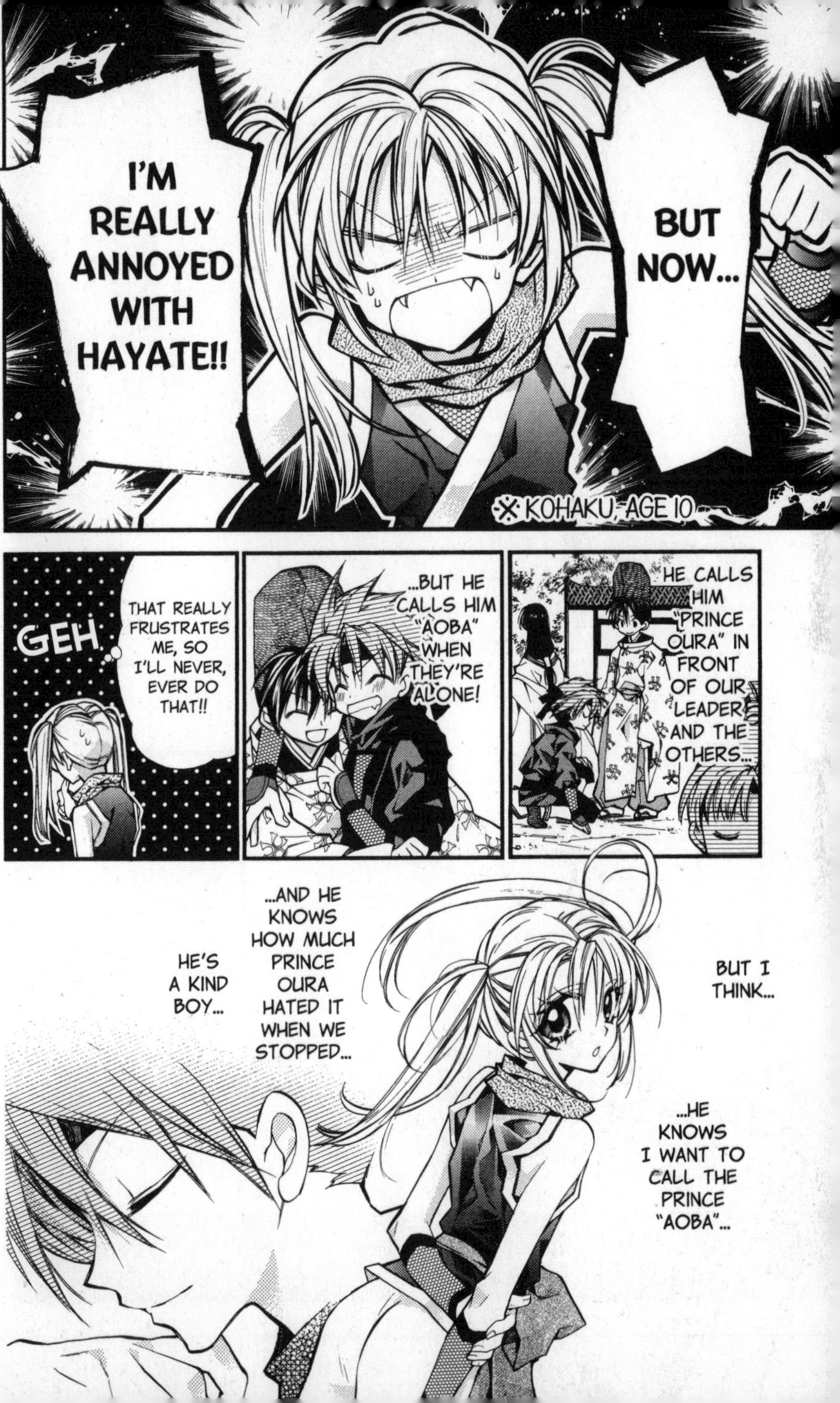
BUT NOW...
I'M REALLY ANNOYED WITH HAYATE!!
※KOHAKU, AGE 10
HE CALLS HIM "PRINCE OURA" IN FRONT OF OUR LEADER AND THE OTHERS...
...BUT HE CALLS HIM "AOBA" WHEN THEY'RE ALONE!
GEH
THAT REALLY FRUSTRATES ME, SO I'LL NEVER, EVER DO THAT!!
BUT I THINK...
...HE KNOWS I WANT TO CALL THE PRINCE "AOBA"...
...AND HE KNOWS HOW MUCH PRINCE OURA HATED IT WHEN WE STOPPED...
HE'S A KIND BOY...

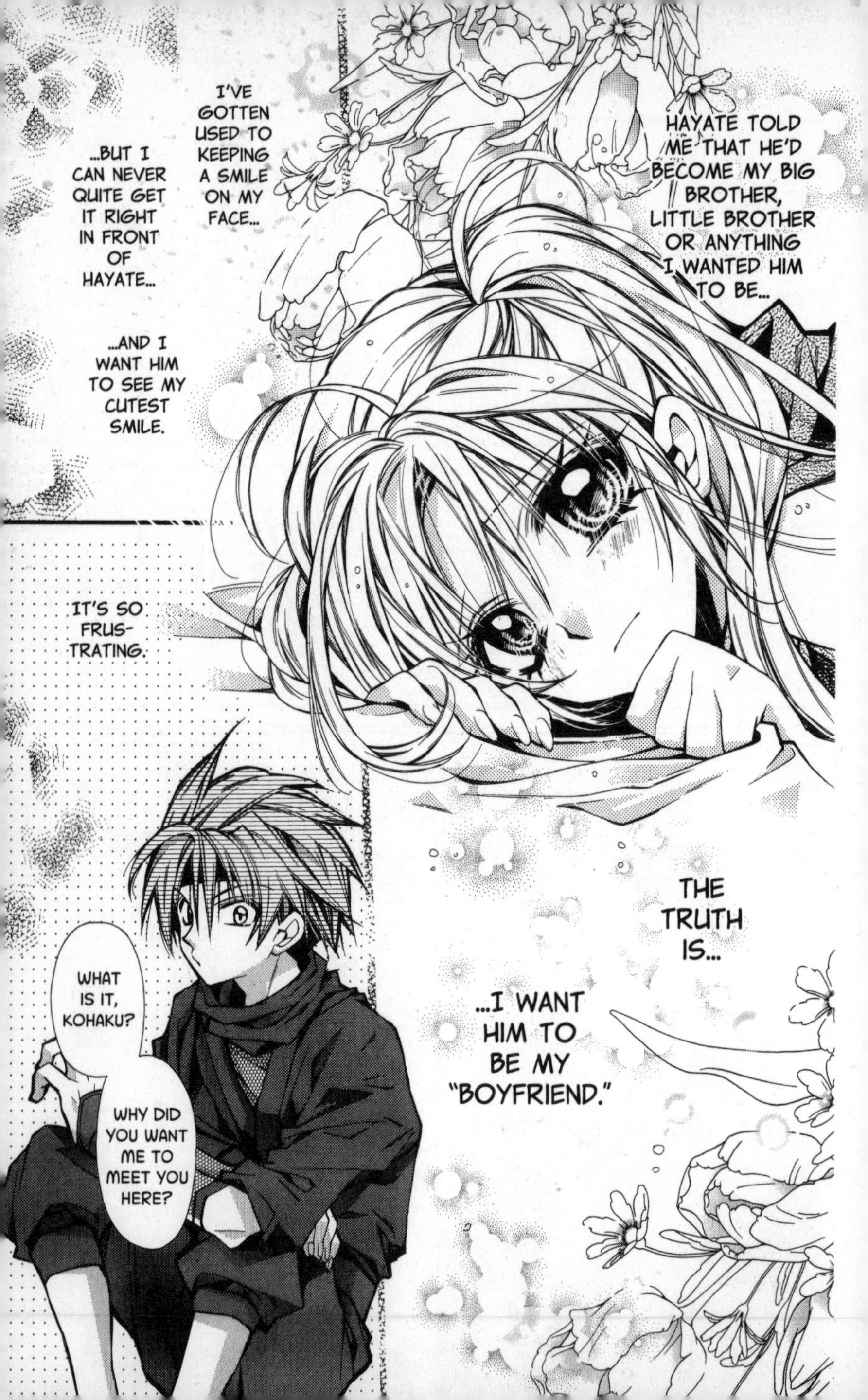
HAYATE TOLD ME THAT HE'D BECOME MY BIG BROTHER, LITTLE BROTHER OR ANYTHING I WANTED HIM TO BE...
I'VE GOTTEN USED TO KEEPING A SMILE ON MY FACE...
...BUT I CAN NEVER QUITE GET IT RIGHT IN FRONT OF HAYATE...
...AND I WANT HIM TO SEE MY CUTEST SMILE.
IT'S SO FRUS-TRATING.
THE TRUTH IS...
...I WANT HIM TO BE MY "BOYFRIEND."
WHAT IS IT, KOHAKU?
WHY DID YOU WANT ME TO MEET YOU HERE?

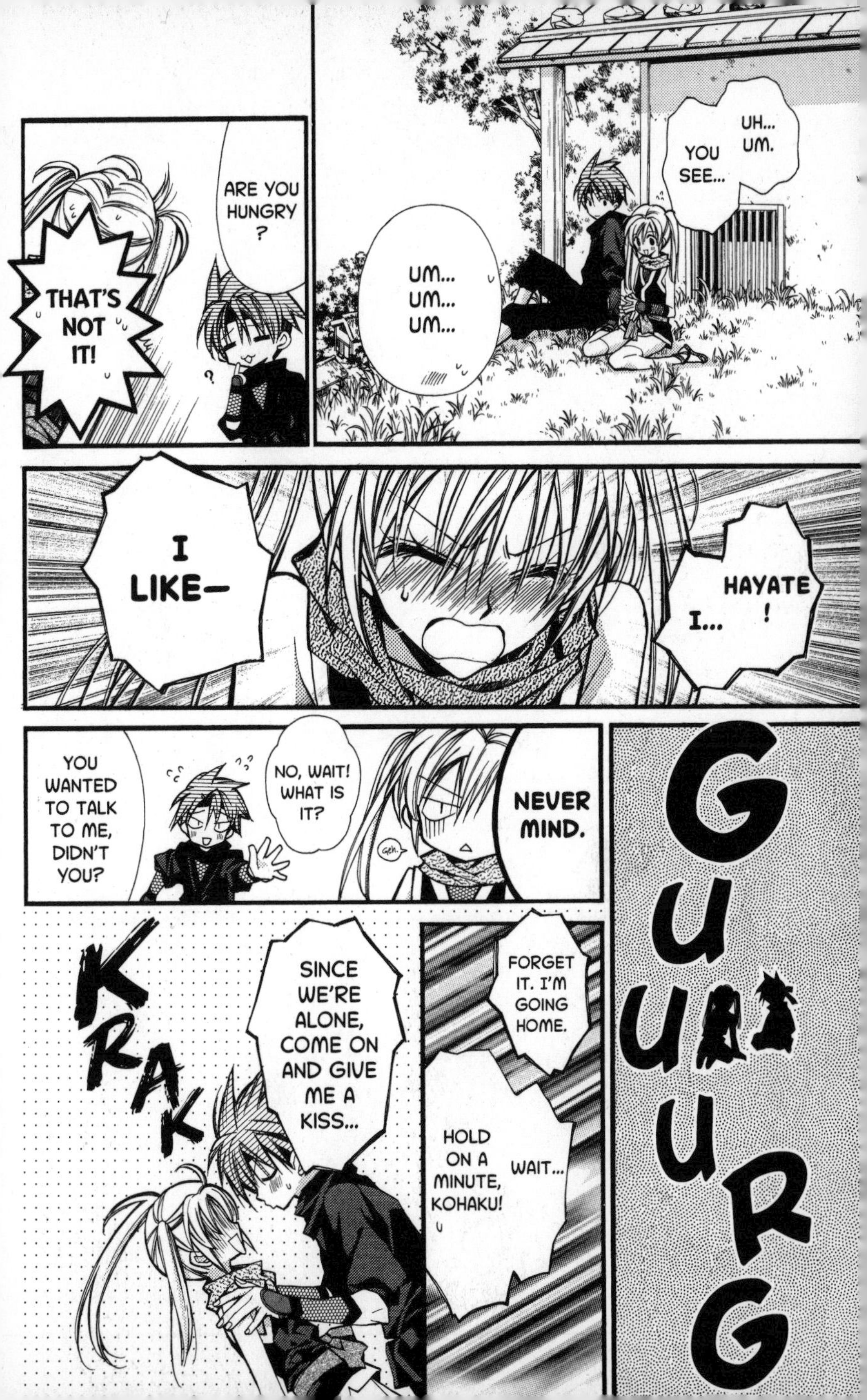
UH... UM.
YOU SEE...
UM... UM... UM...
ARE YOU HUNGRY ?
THAT'S NOT IT!
HAYATE !
I...
I LIKE—
GUUURG
NEVER MIND.
Geh.
NO, WAIT! WHAT IS IT?
YOU WANTED TO TALK TO ME, DIDN'T YOU?
FORGET IT. I'M GOING HOME.
WAIT...
HOLD ON A MINUTE, KOHAKU!
SINCE WE'RE ALONE, COME ON AND GIVE ME A KISS...
KRAK

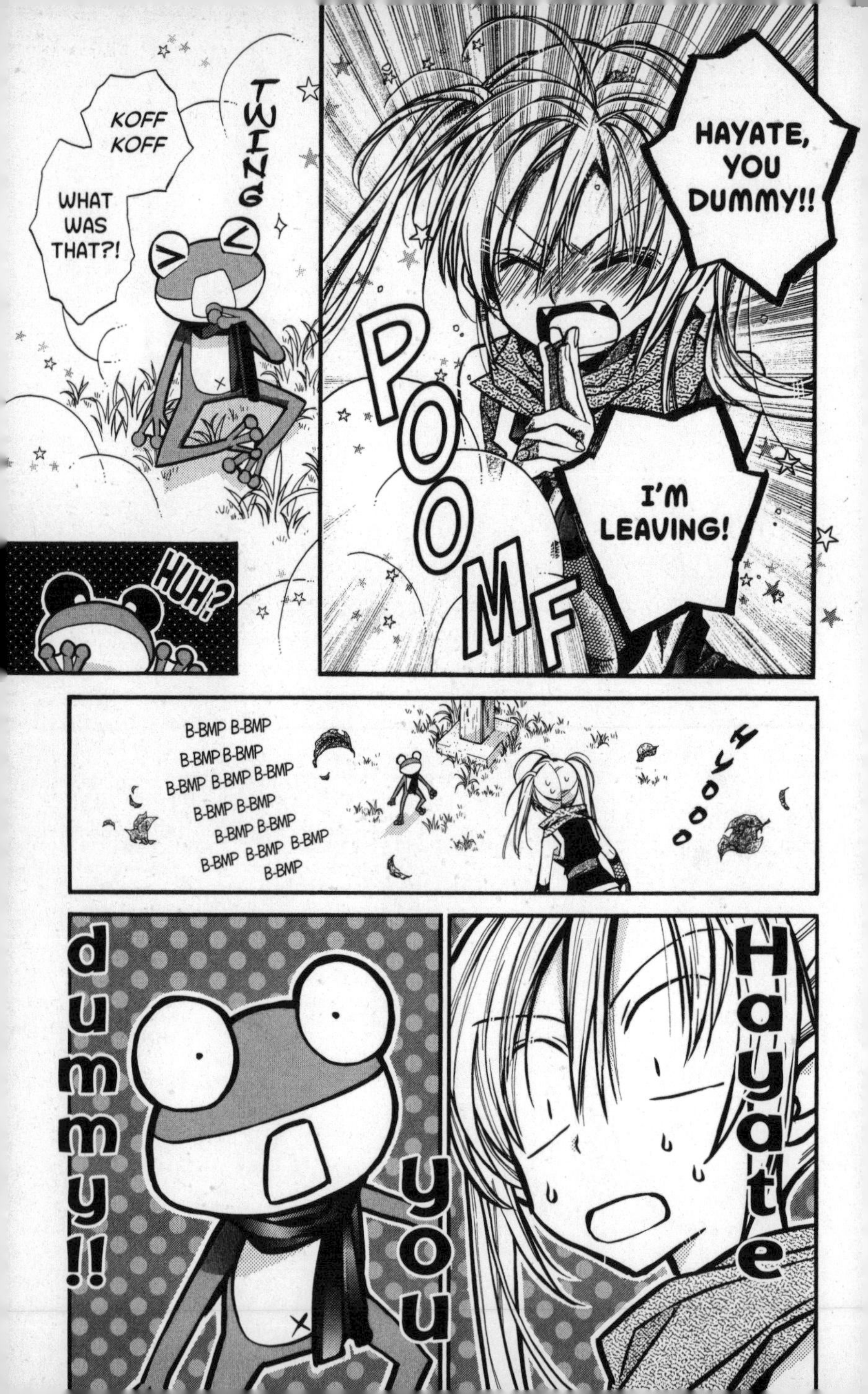
HAYATE, YOU DUMMY!!
I'M LEAVING!
POOMF
TWING
KOFF KOFF
WHAT WAS THAT?!
HUH?
HOOOO
B-BMP B-BMP
B-BMP B-BMP
B-BMP B-BMP B-BMP
B-BMP B-BMP
B-BMP B-BMP
B-BMP B-BMP B-BMP
B-BMP
Hayate
you
dummy!!

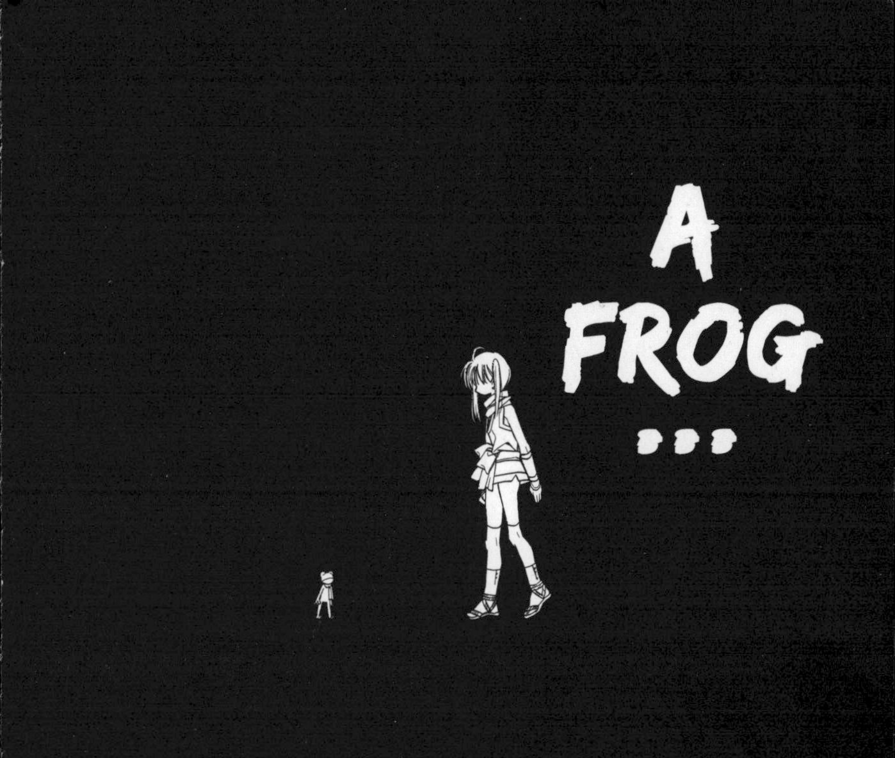
A FROG...

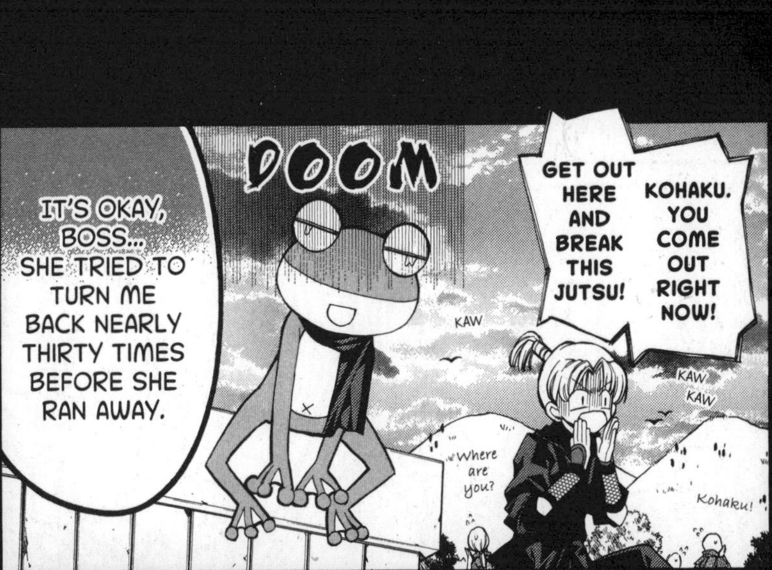
KOHAKU. YOU COME OUT RIGHT NOW!
GET OUT HERE AND BREAK THIS JUTSU!
KAW KAW
Kohaku!
Where are you?
KAW
DOOM
IT'S OKAY, BOSS... SHE TRIED TO TURN ME BACK NEARLY THIRTY TIMES BEFORE SHE RAN AWAY.

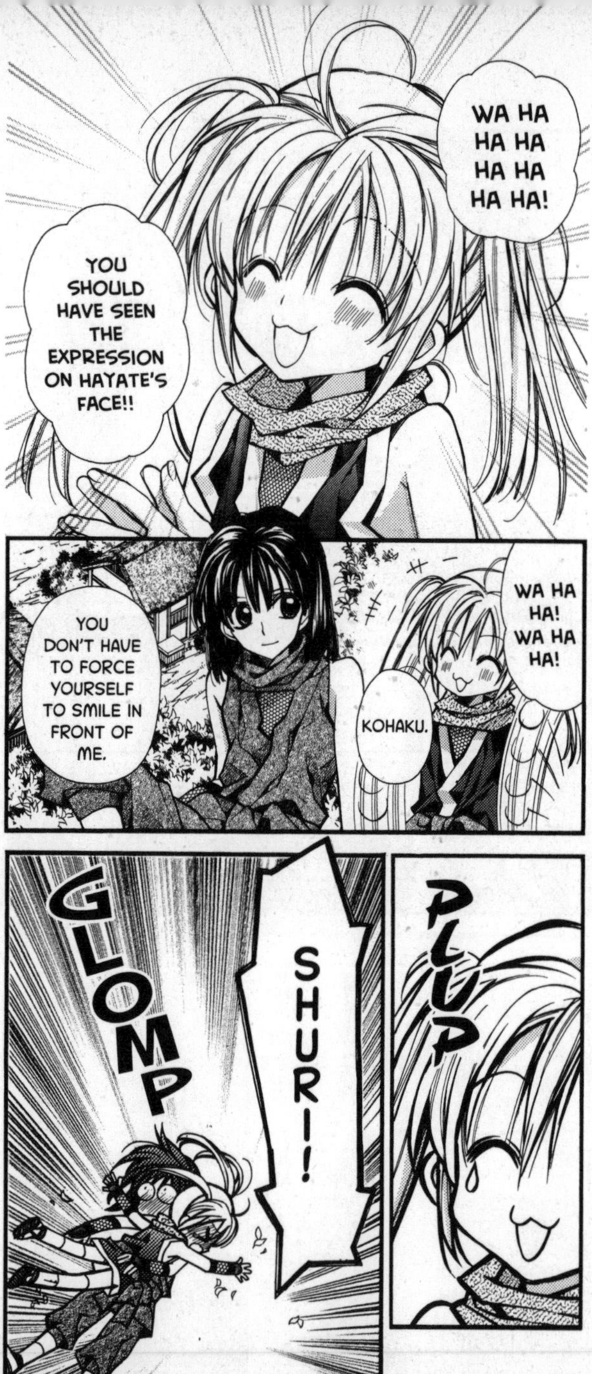
WA HA HA HA HA HA HA HA!
YOU SHOULD HAVE SEEN THE EXPRESSION ON HAYATE'S FACE!!
WA HA HA! WA HA HA!
KOHAKU.
YOU DON'T HAVE TO FORCE YOURSELF TO SMILE IN FRONT OF ME.
PLUP
SHURI!
GLOMP

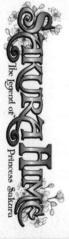

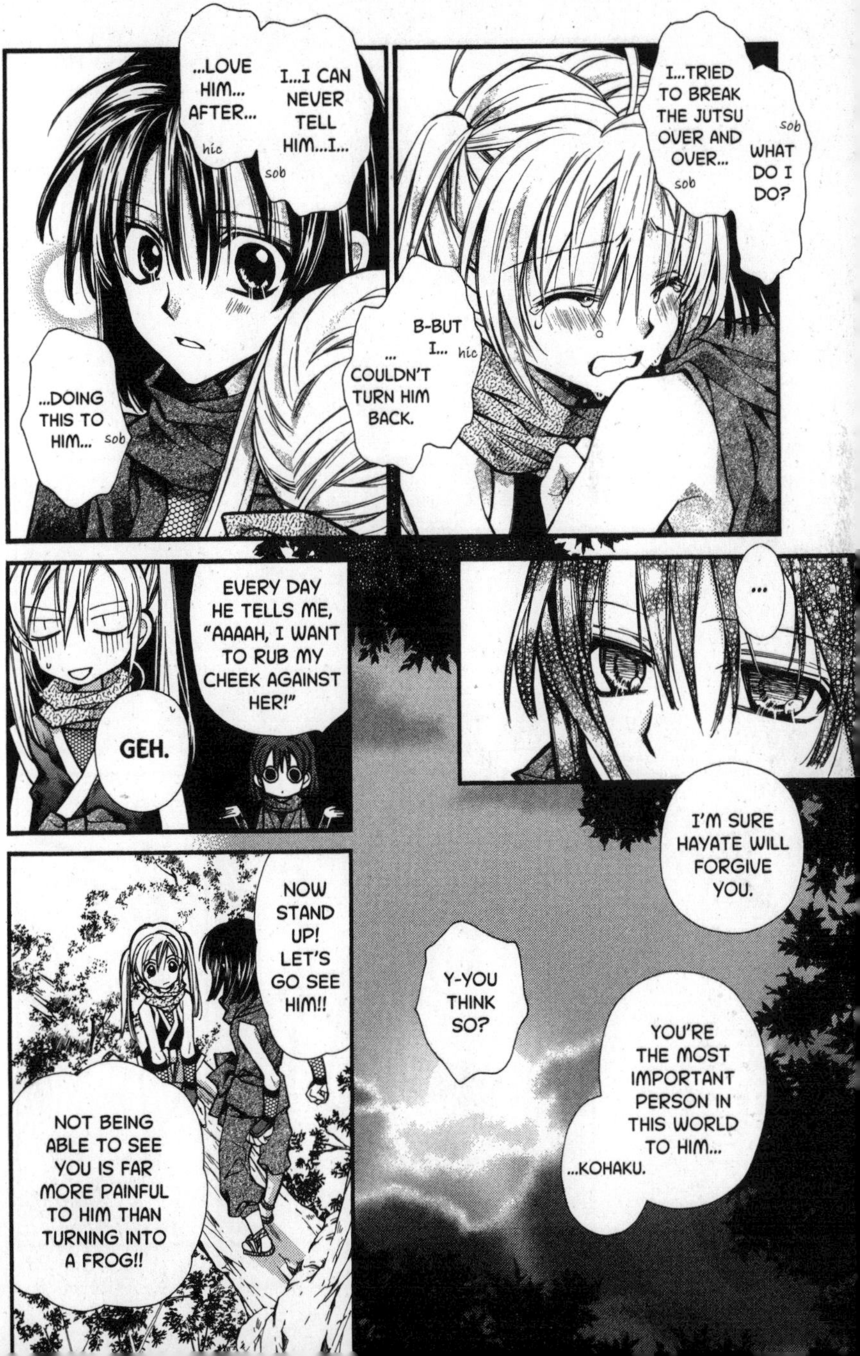
I...TRIED TO BREAK THE JUTSU OVER AND OVER...
sob
sob
WHAT DO I DO?
B-BUT I... ...COULDN'T TURN HIM BACK.
hic
I...I CAN NEVER TELL HIM...I...
sob
...LOVE HIM... AFTER...
hic
...DOING THIS TO HIM...
sob
...
EVERY DAY HE TELLS ME, "AAAAH, I WANT TO RUB MY CHEEK AGAINST HER!"
GEH.
I'M SURE HAYATE WILL FORGIVE YOU.
Y-YOU THINK SO?
YOU'RE THE MOST IMPORTANT PERSON IN THIS WORLD TO HIM... ...KOHAKU.
NOT BEING ABLE TO SEE YOU IS FAR MORE PAINFUL TO HIM THAN TURNING INTO A FROG!!
NOW STAND UP! LET'S GO SEE HIM!!

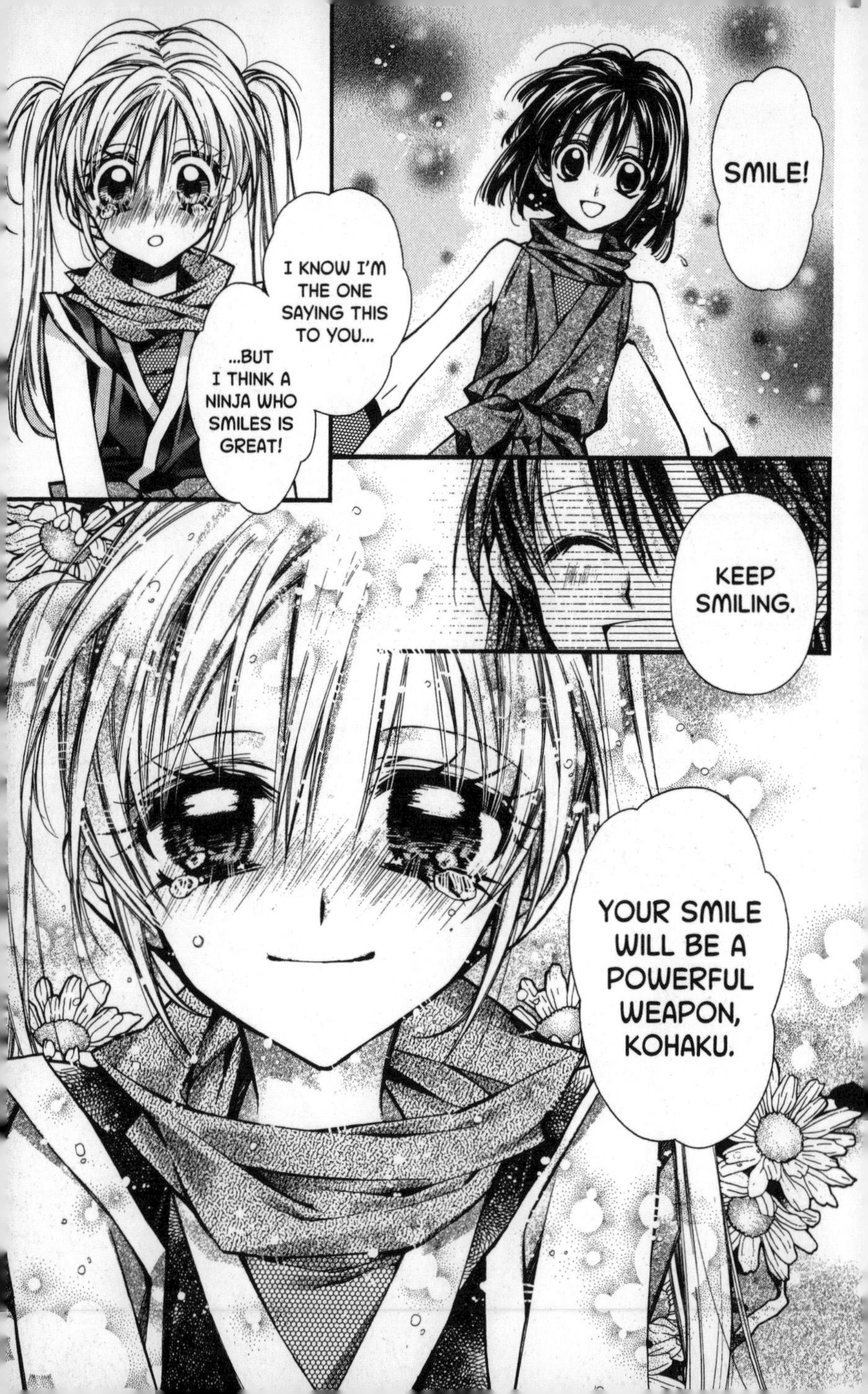
SMILE!
I KNOW I'M THE ONE SAYING THIS TO YOU...
...BUT I THINK A NINJA WHO SMILES IS GREAT!
KEEP SMILING.
YOUR SMILE WILL BE A POWERFUL WEAPON, KOHAKU.

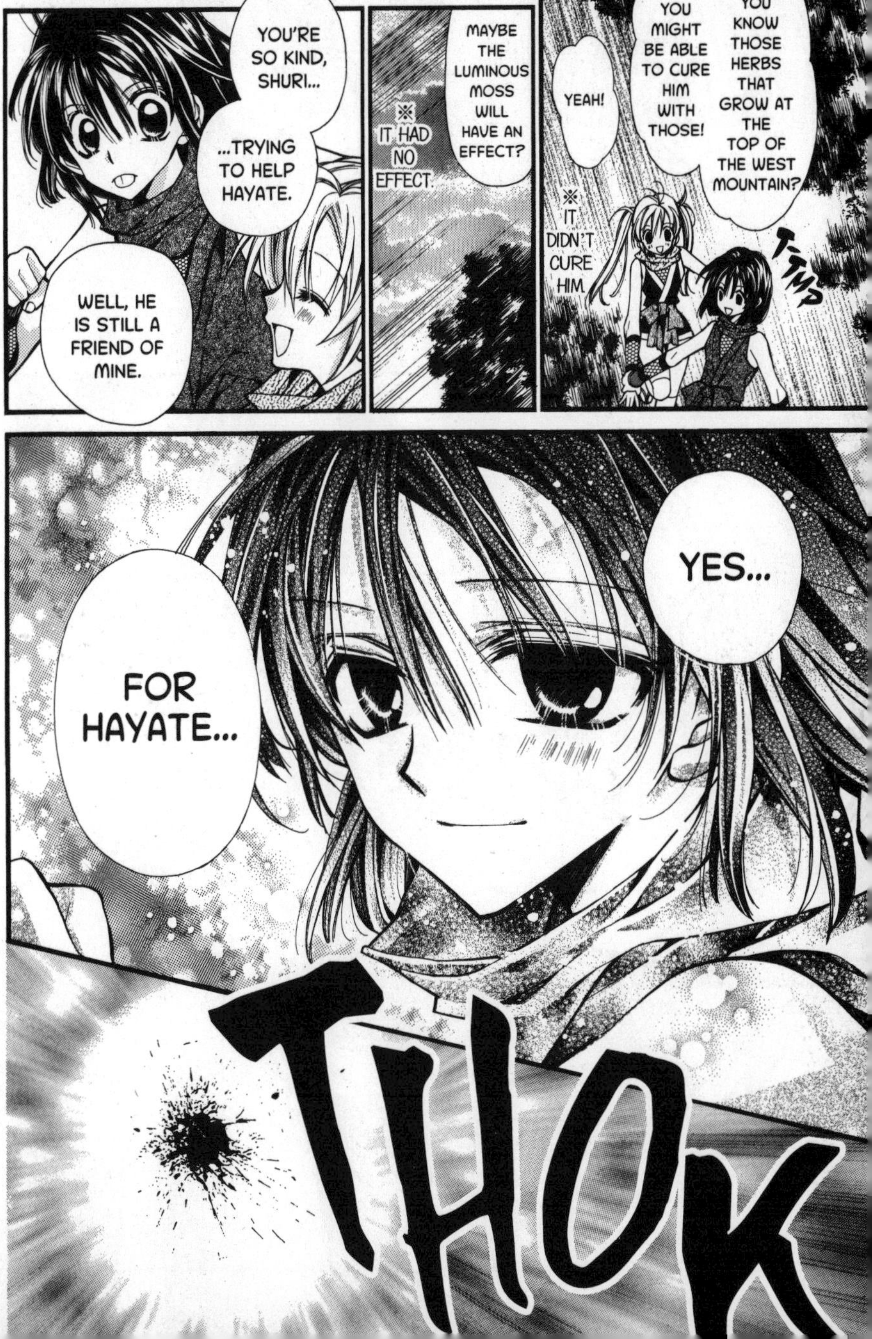
YOU KNOW THOSE HERBS THAT GROW AT THE TOP OF THE WEST MOUNTAIN?
YOU MIGHT BE ABLE TO CURE HIM WITH THOSE!
YEAH!
※ IT DIDN'T CURE HIM
T-TMP
MAYBE THE LUMINOUS MOSS WILL HAVE AN EFFECT?
※ IT HAD NO EFFECT.
YOU'RE SO KIND, SHURI...
...TRYING TO HELP HAYATE.
WELL, HE IS STILL A FRIEND OF MINE.
YES...
FOR HAYATE...
THOK

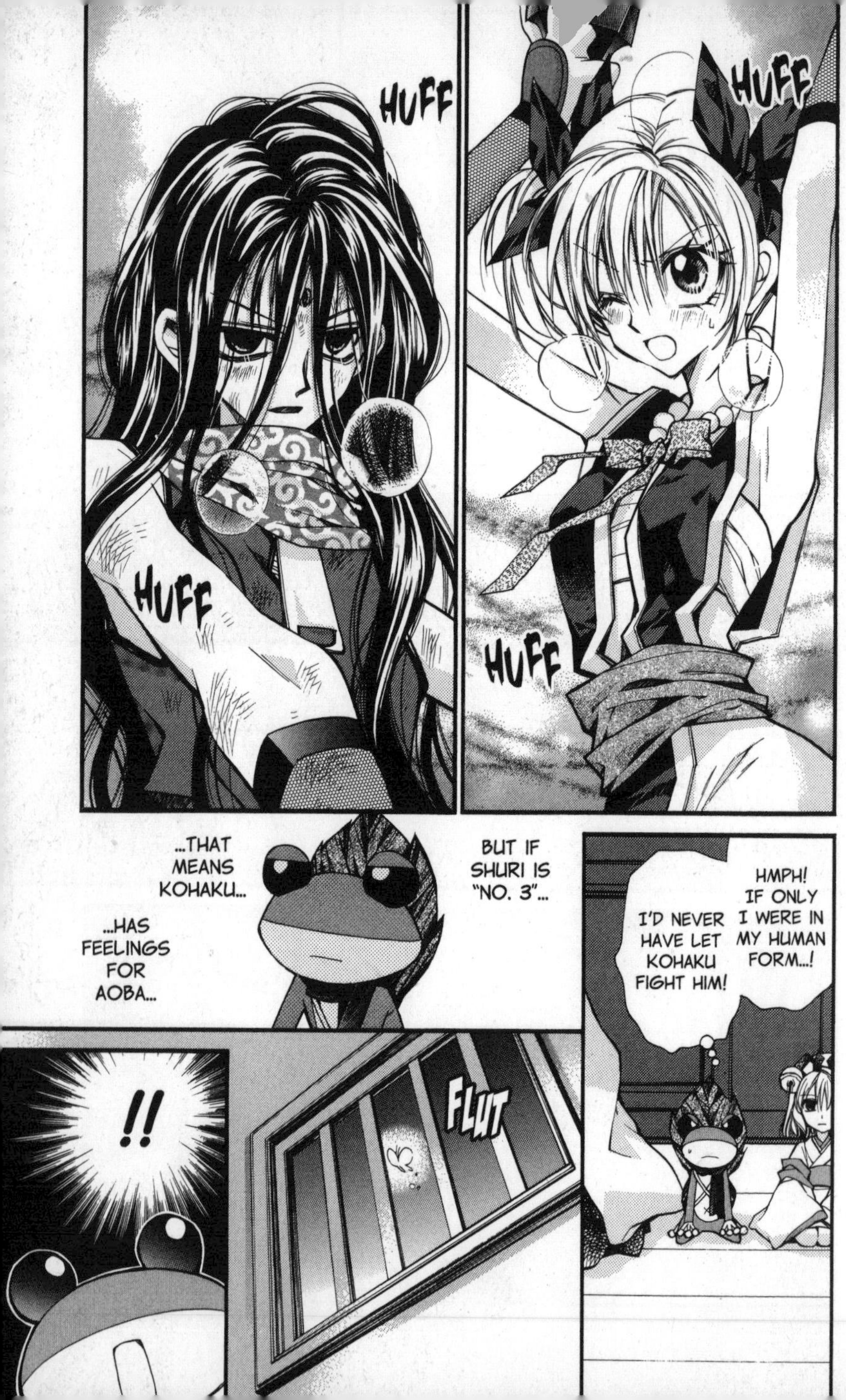
HUFF
HUFF
HUFF
HUFF
HMPH! IF ONLY I WERE IN MY HUMAN FORM...!
I'D NEVER HAVE LET KOHAKU FIGHT HIM!
BUT IF SHURI IS "NO. 3"...
...THAT MEANS KOHAKU...
...HAS FEELINGS FOR AOBA...
FLUT
!!

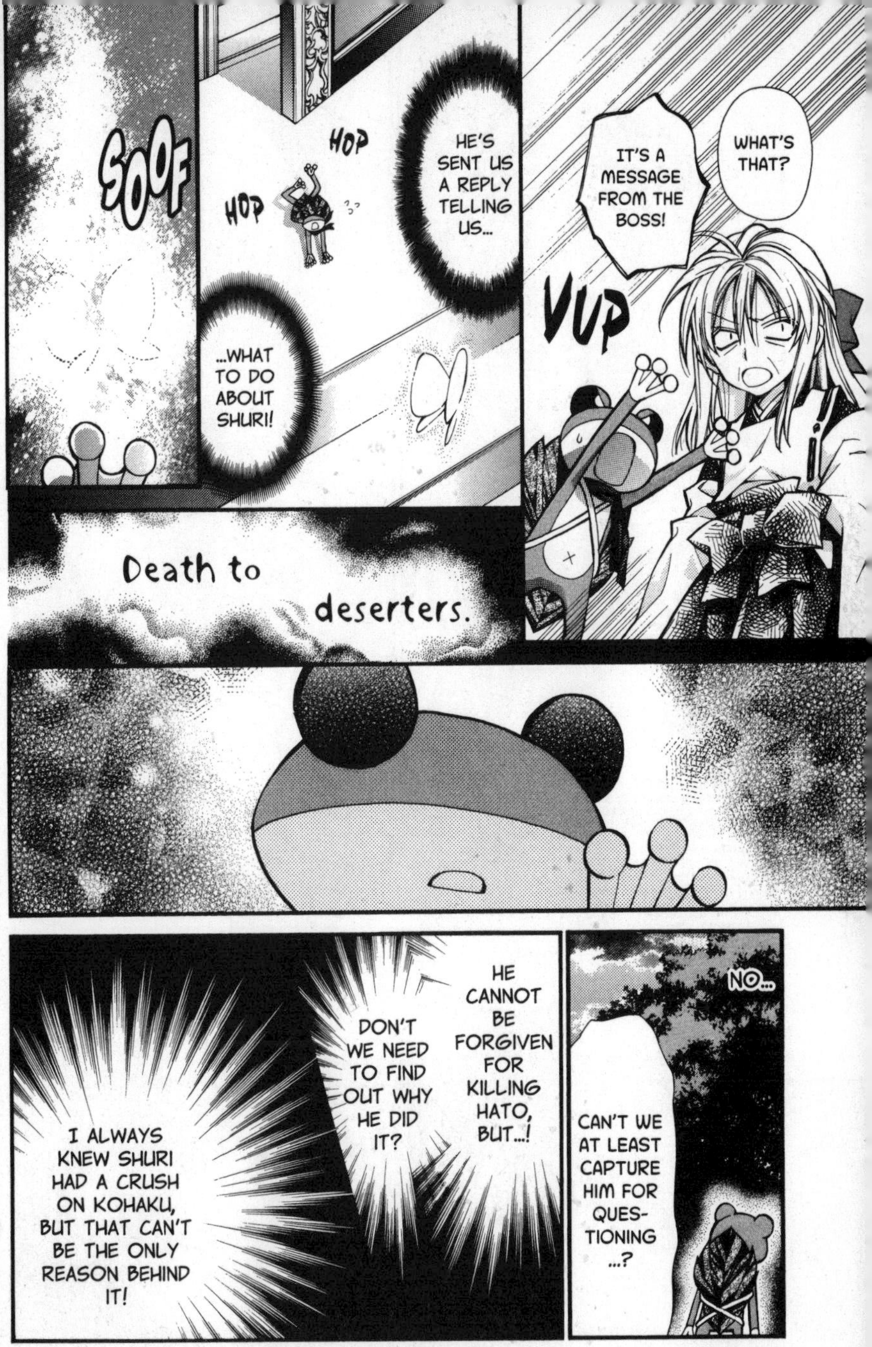
WHAT'S THAT?
IT'S A MESSAGE FROM THE BOSS!
VUP
HE'S SENT US A REPLY TELLING US...
HOP
HOP
...WHAT TO DO ABOUT SHURI!
SOOF
Death to deserters.
NO...
CAN'T WE AT LEAST CAPTURE HIM FOR QUES-TIONING ...?
HE CANNOT BE FORGIVEN FOR KILLING HATO, BUT...!
DON'T WE NEED TO FIND OUT WHY HE DID IT?
I ALWAYS KNEW SHURI HAD A CRUSH ON KOHAKU, BUT THAT CAN'T BE THE ONLY REASON BEHIND IT!

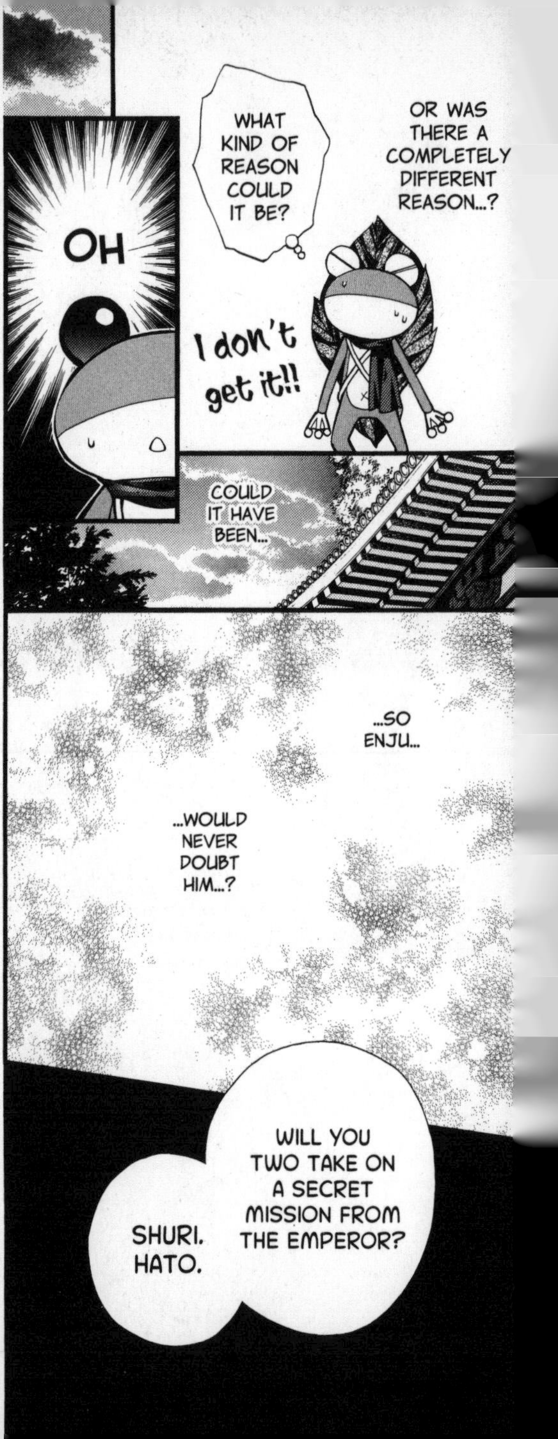
OR WAS THERE A COMPLETELY DIFFERENT REASON...?
WHAT KIND OF REASON COULD IT BE?
I don't get it!!
OH
COULD IT HAVE BEEN...
...SO ENJU...
...WOULD NEVER DOUBT HIM...?
WILL YOU TWO TAKE ON A SECRET MISSION FROM THE EMPEROR?
SHURI. HATO.

I visited Capcom.

I visited Capcom—famous for their games like *Monster Hunter*—for an interview!

I went down to talk to them and play *Poka Poka Felyne Village* for a color article in *Ribon*...

The Felynes were so cute.

I've always liked them because they're cute, but they are even more adorable when they're made into chibis with comical movements. It's a game all cat lovers must get their hands on. (It's a PSP game, by the way. ♪)

All the monsters from the original *Monster Hunter* appear in chibi form and Felyne Elder's younger sister, Felyne Imoto, appears in it too.

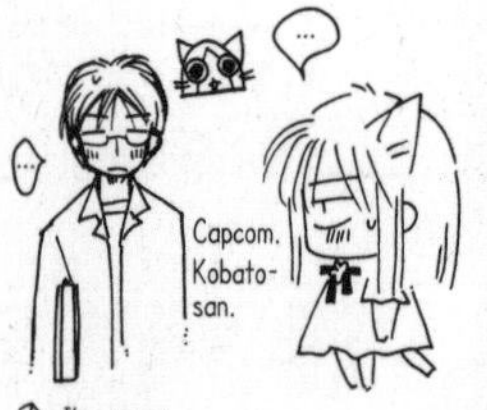
...
...
Capcom. Kobato-san.

I'm sorry.
I wasn't able to draw him well.
He's much more handsome than this.

I had met Kobato-san before at drinking parties and at Monster Hunter meet-ups (my friend's) a couple of times, but I never thought I'd see him for work, so I was kind of embarrassed. (laugh)

I really like game creators. They seem to really love video games. Obviously I've already pre-ordered *Felyne Village*. ♥

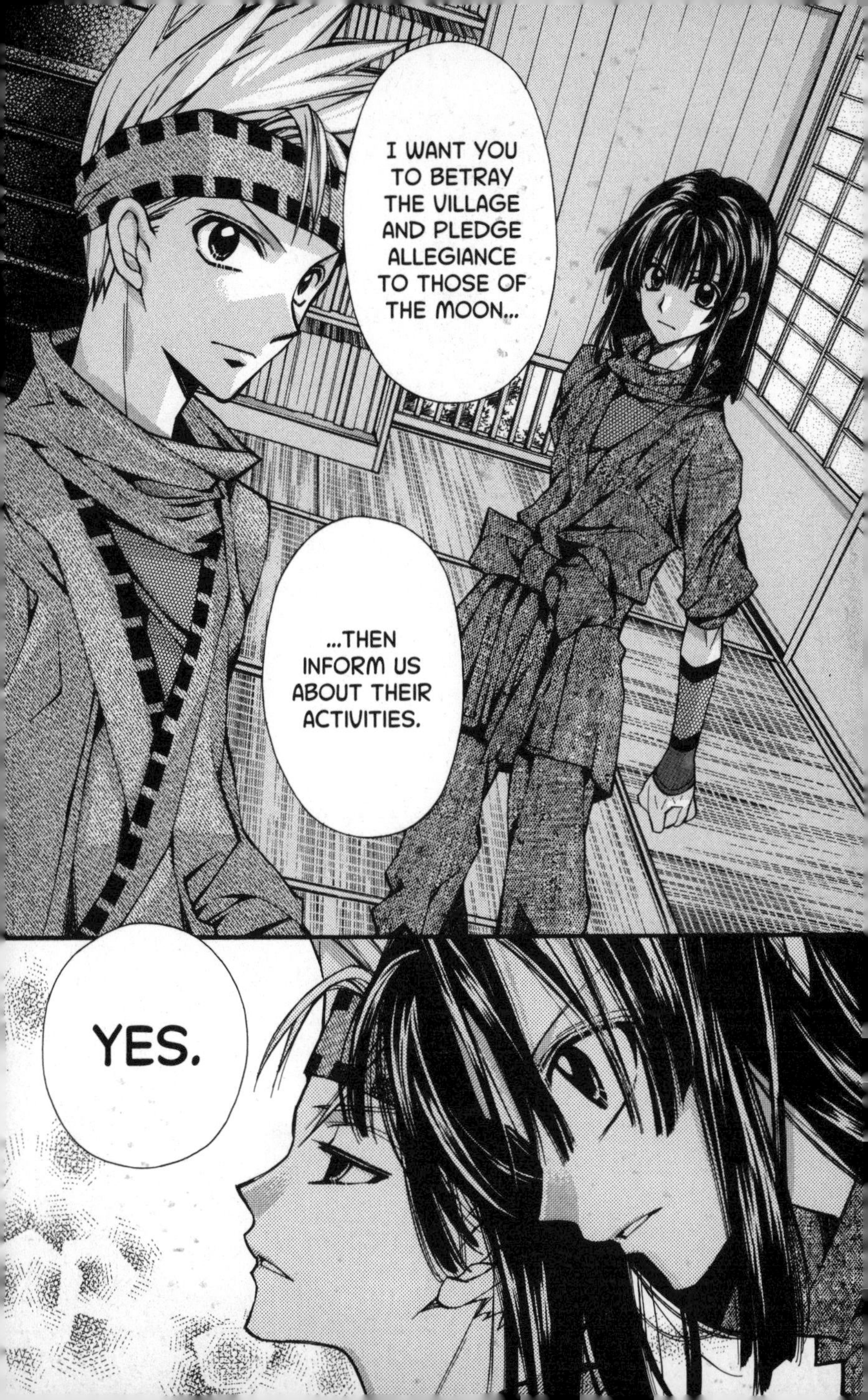
I WANT YOU TO BETRAY THE VILLAGE AND PLEDGE ALLEGIANCE TO THOSE OF THE MOON...
...THEN INFORM US ABOUT THEIR ACTIVITIES.
YES.

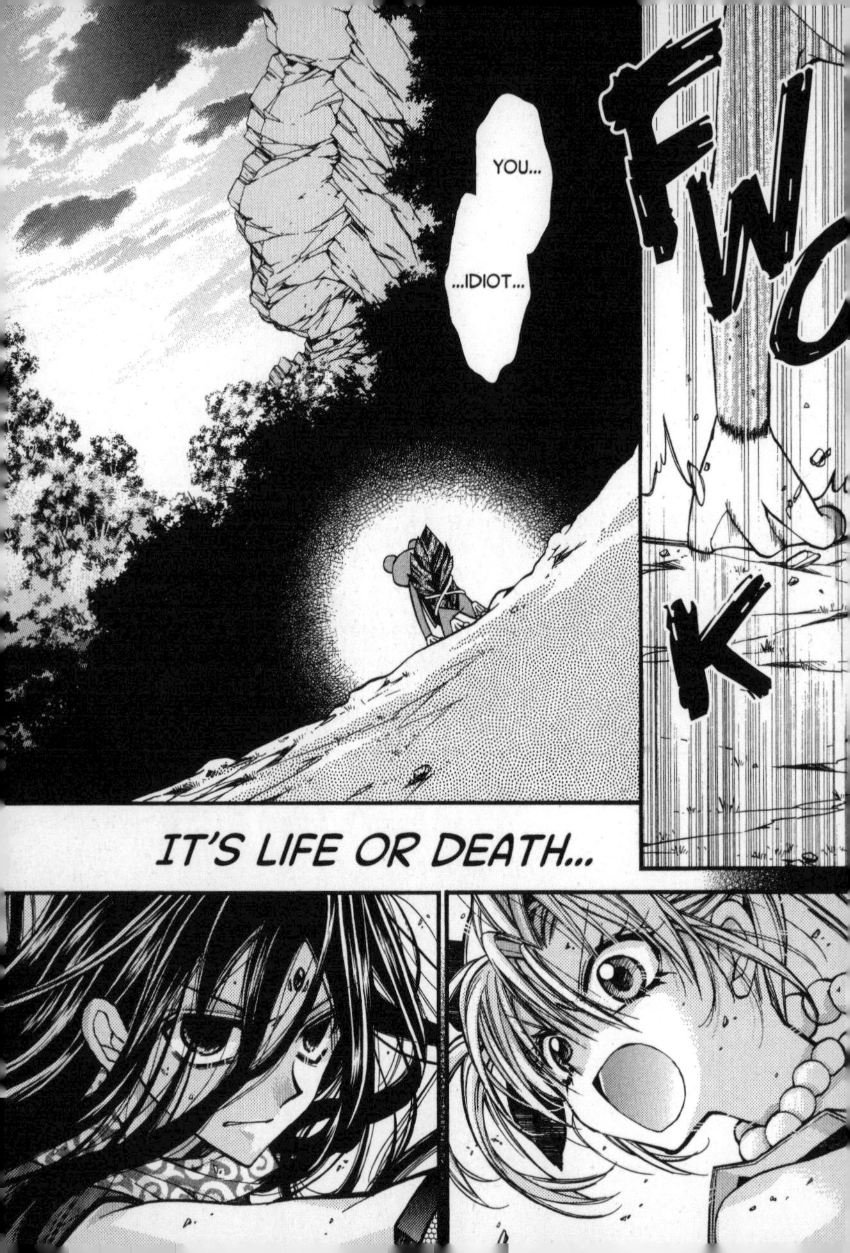
FWOK
YOU...
...IDIOT...
IT'S LIFE OR DEATH...

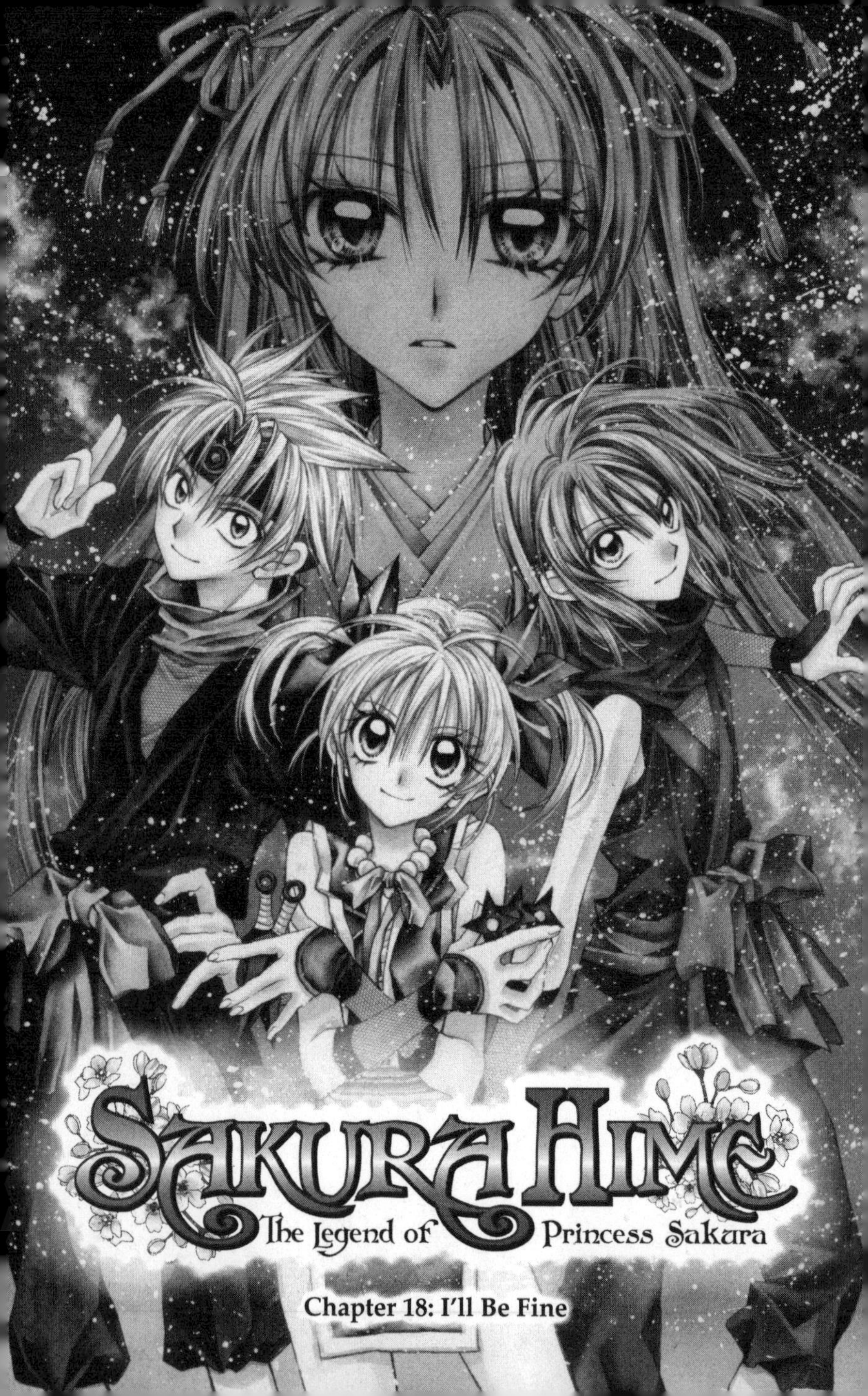
SAKURA HIME
The Legend of Princess Sakura
Chapter 18: I'll Be Fine

YOUR MISSION...

SHURI, YOU IDIOT!

...WAS TO JOIN THE MEMBERS OF THE MOON TO SPY ON ENJU!

Chapter 18: I'll Be Fine

※ I'm giving away the story.

Lead-in A ninja is a shadow.
The only time the shadows shine is when
ninja risk their lives for their master!

The title page illustration was a request from my editor back when I was working on this, and I was asked for something with "three ninja and Sakura." I like it a lot.

Hato seems to have had some fans when he appeared in the magazine. My former editor liked him a lot too and would often say to me, "I'm sure Hayate held a very strong adoration for Hato!" every time we had a meeting. (ᴺ▽ᴺ)ᵛ

The story may be a little somber, but I wanted to include the transition of Shuri gradually pining away. That's why I drew it.

In my opinion, Shuri is the true ninja. Kohaku is still too soft. But as a character in this manga, I want Kohaku to remain the kind person that she is right now, so I have mixed feelings about it. ⚞✑⚟

I want Hayate to prove himself worthy as a guy, but he seems to take the lion's share even when he hasn't done much.

By the way, Rurijo's finger (the leaf) that was on Hayate's back is now inside his ninja kimono.

Also, the lead-ins these days have all been written by my editor.

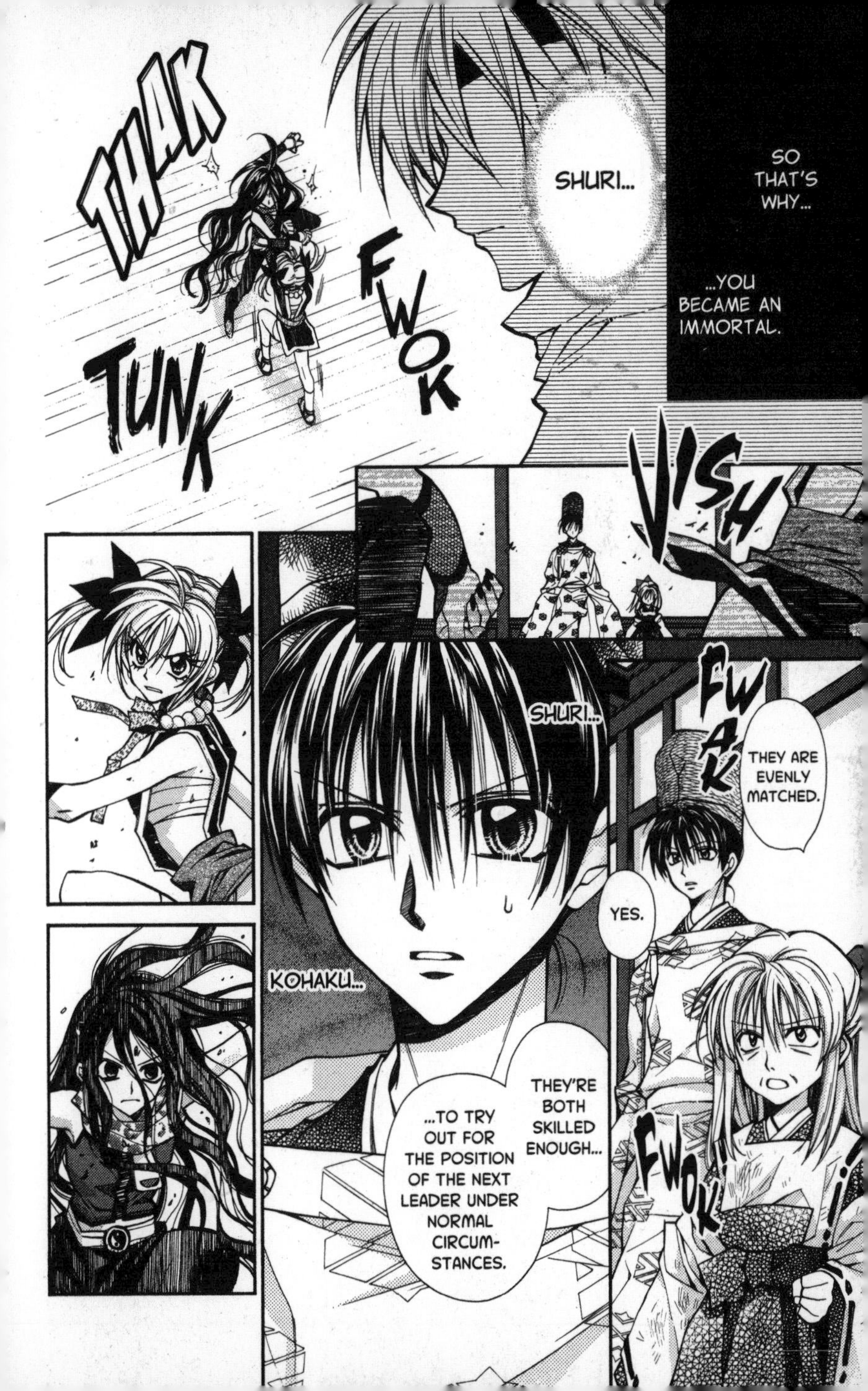
SO THAT'S WHY...
...YOU BECAME AN IMMORTAL.
SHURI...
FWOK
THAK
TUNK
VISH
FWAK
THEY ARE EVENLY MATCHED.
YES.
SHURI...
THEY'RE BOTH SKILLED ENOUGH...
...TO TRY OUT FOR THE POSITION OF THE NEXT LEADER UNDER NORMAL CIRCUM-STANCES.
KOHAKU...
FWOK

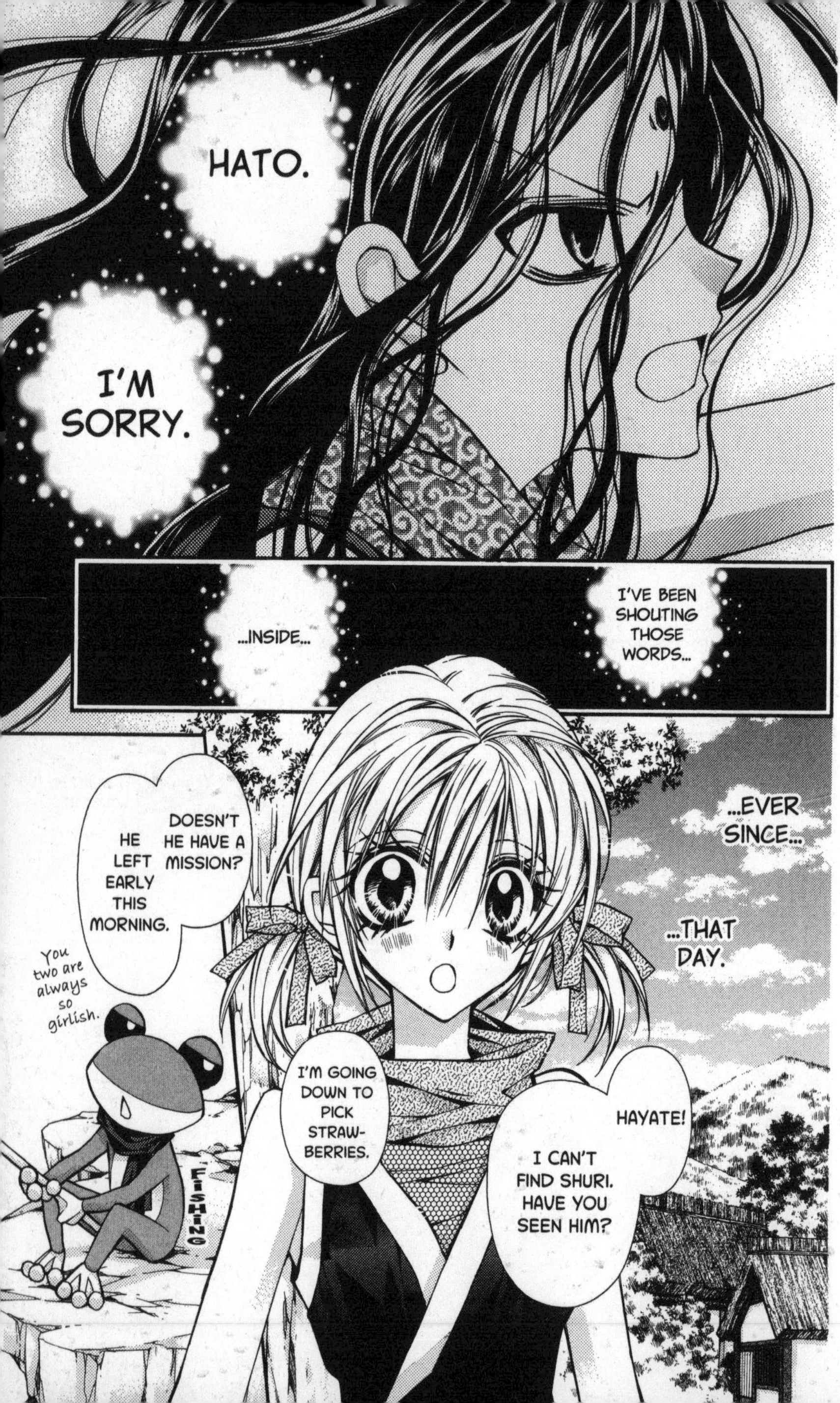
HATO.
I'M SORRY.
I'VE BEEN SHOUTING THOSE WORDS...
...INSIDE...
...EVER SINCE...
...THAT DAY.
HAYATE!
I CAN'T FIND SHURI. HAVE YOU SEEN HIM?
I'M GOING DOWN TO PICK STRAW-BERRIES.
DOESN'T HE HAVE A MISSION?
HE LEFT EARLY THIS MORNING.
You two are always so girlish.
FISHING

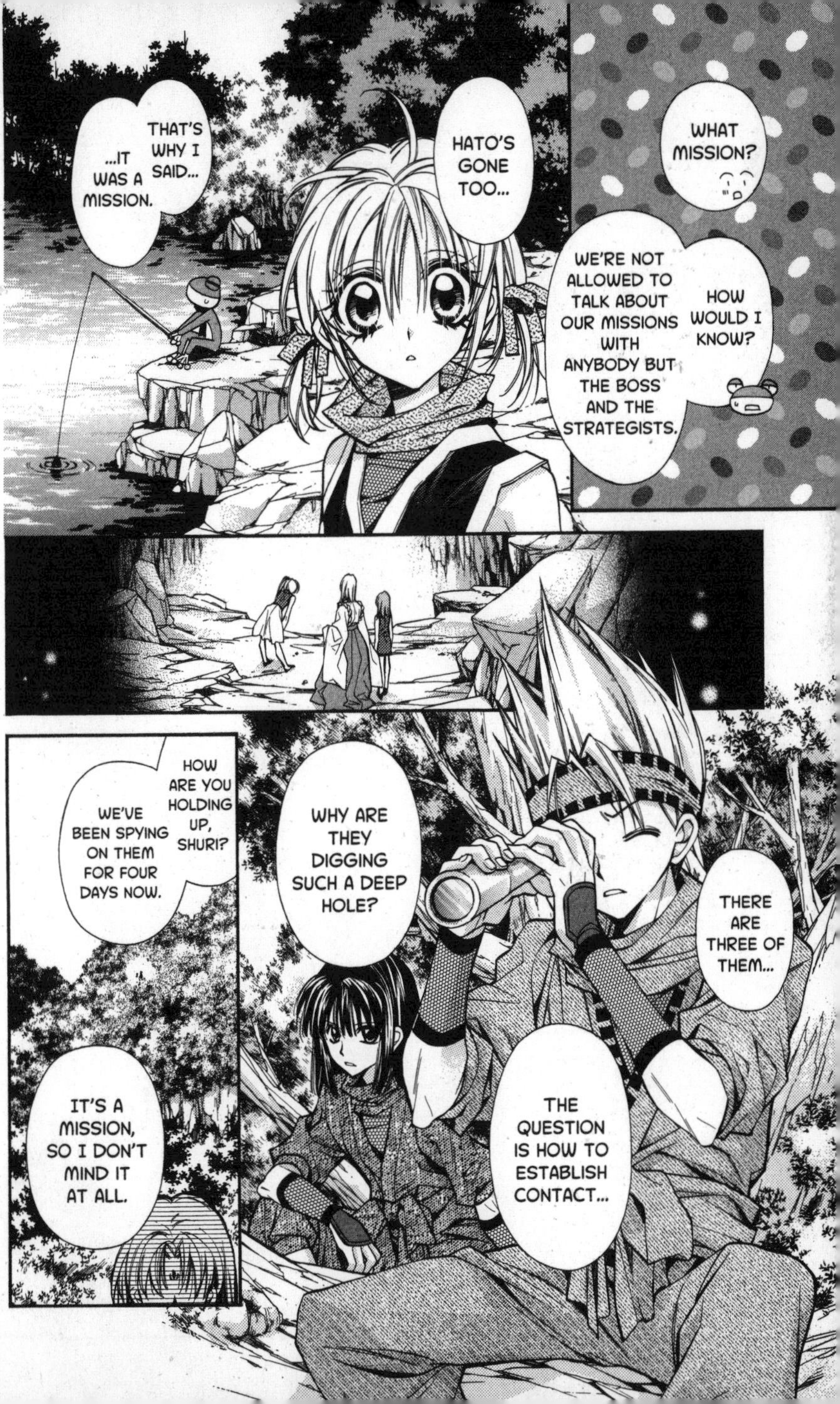
HATO'S GONE TOO...
THAT'S WHY I SAID...
...IT WAS A MISSION.
WHAT MISSION?
HOW WOULD I KNOW?
WE'RE NOT ALLOWED TO TALK ABOUT OUR MISSIONS WITH ANYBODY BUT THE BOSS AND THE STRATEGISTS.
THERE ARE THREE OF THEM...
WHY ARE THEY DIGGING SUCH A DEEP HOLE?
THE QUESTION IS HOW TO ESTABLISH CONTACT...
WE'VE BEEN SPYING ON THEM FOR FOUR DAYS NOW.
HOW ARE YOU HOLDING UP, SHURI?
IT'S A MISSION, SO I DON'T MIND IT AT ALL.

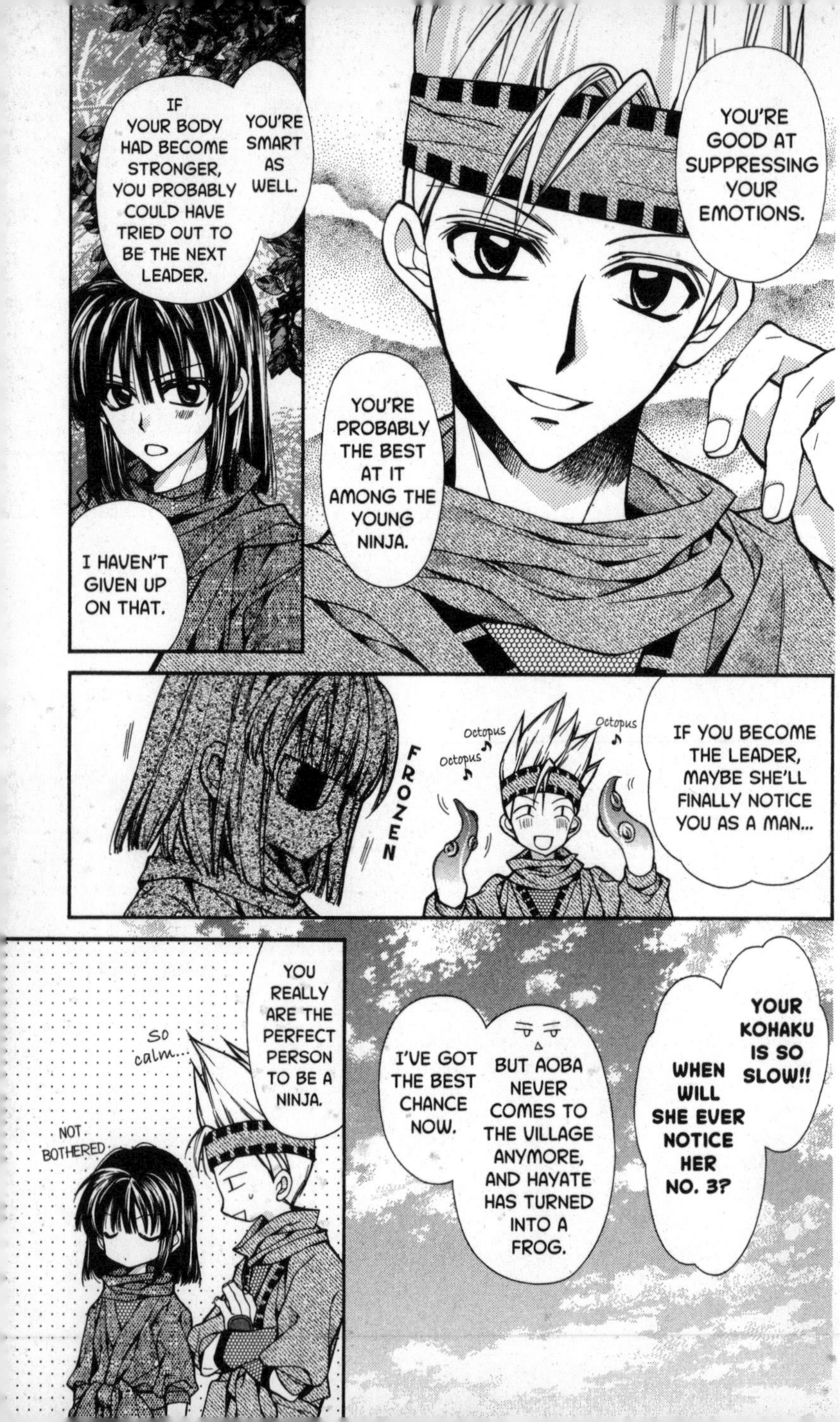

YOU'RE GOOD AT SUPPRESSING YOUR EMOTIONS.
YOU'RE SMART AS WELL.
IF YOUR BODY HAD BECOME STRONGER, YOU PROBABLY COULD HAVE TRIED OUT TO BE THE NEXT LEADER.
YOU'RE PROBABLY THE BEST AT IT AMONG THE YOUNG NINJA.
I HAVEN'T GIVEN UP ON THAT.
IF YOU BECOME THE LEADER, MAYBE SHE'LL FINALLY NOTICE YOU AS A MAN...
Octopus
Octopus
Octopus
FROZEN
YOUR KOHAKU IS SO SLOW!!
WHEN WILL SHE EVER NOTICE HER NO. 3?
BUT AOBA NEVER COMES TO THE VILLAGE ANYMORE, AND HAYATE HAS TURNED INTO A FROG.
I'VE GOT THE BEST CHANCE NOW.
YOU REALLY ARE THE PERFECT PERSON TO BE A NINJA.
So calm...
NOT BOTHERED

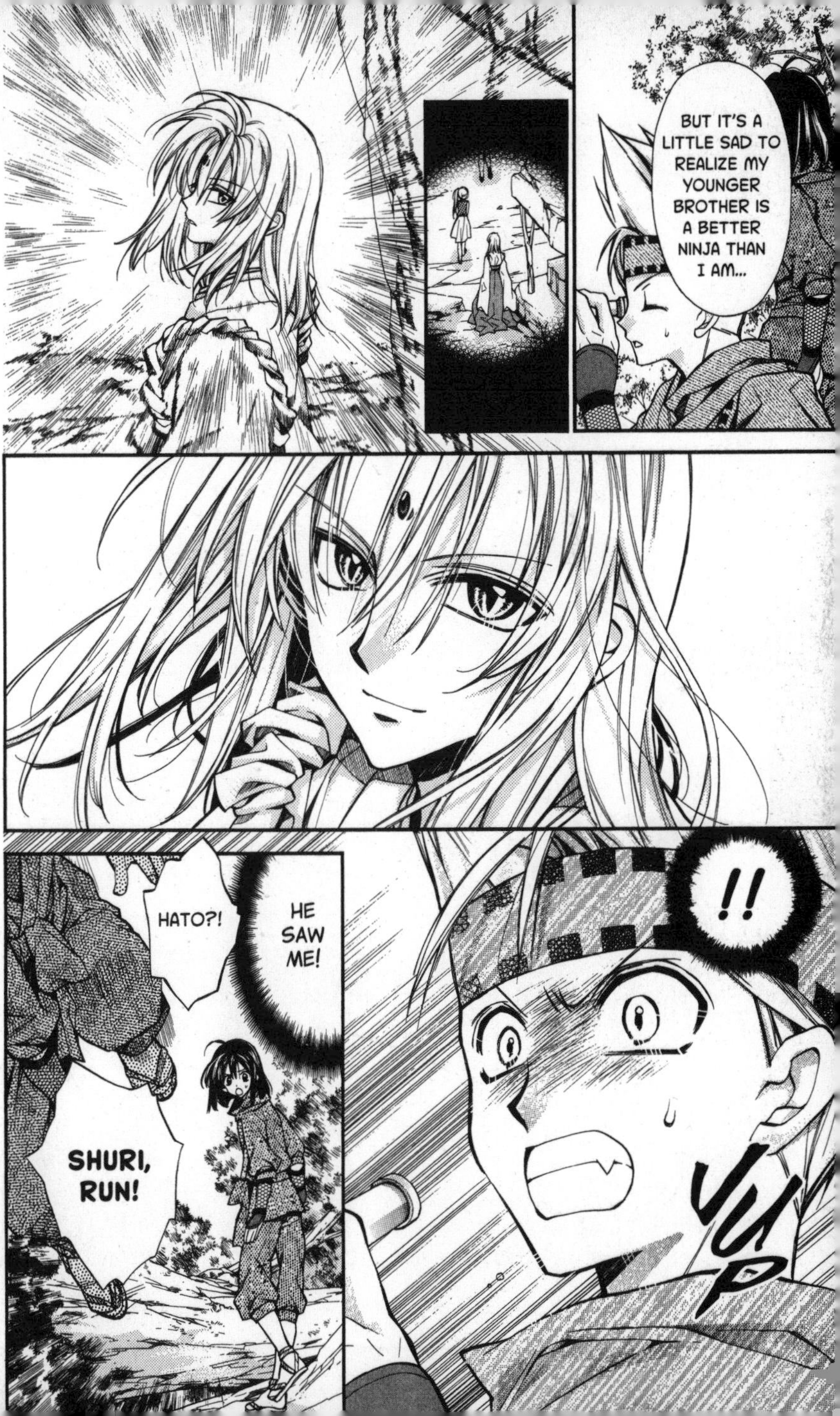
BUT IT'S A LITTLE SAD TO REALIZE MY YOUNGER BROTHER IS A BETTER NINJA THAN I AM...
!!
VUUP
HE SAW ME!
HATO?!
SHURI, RUN!

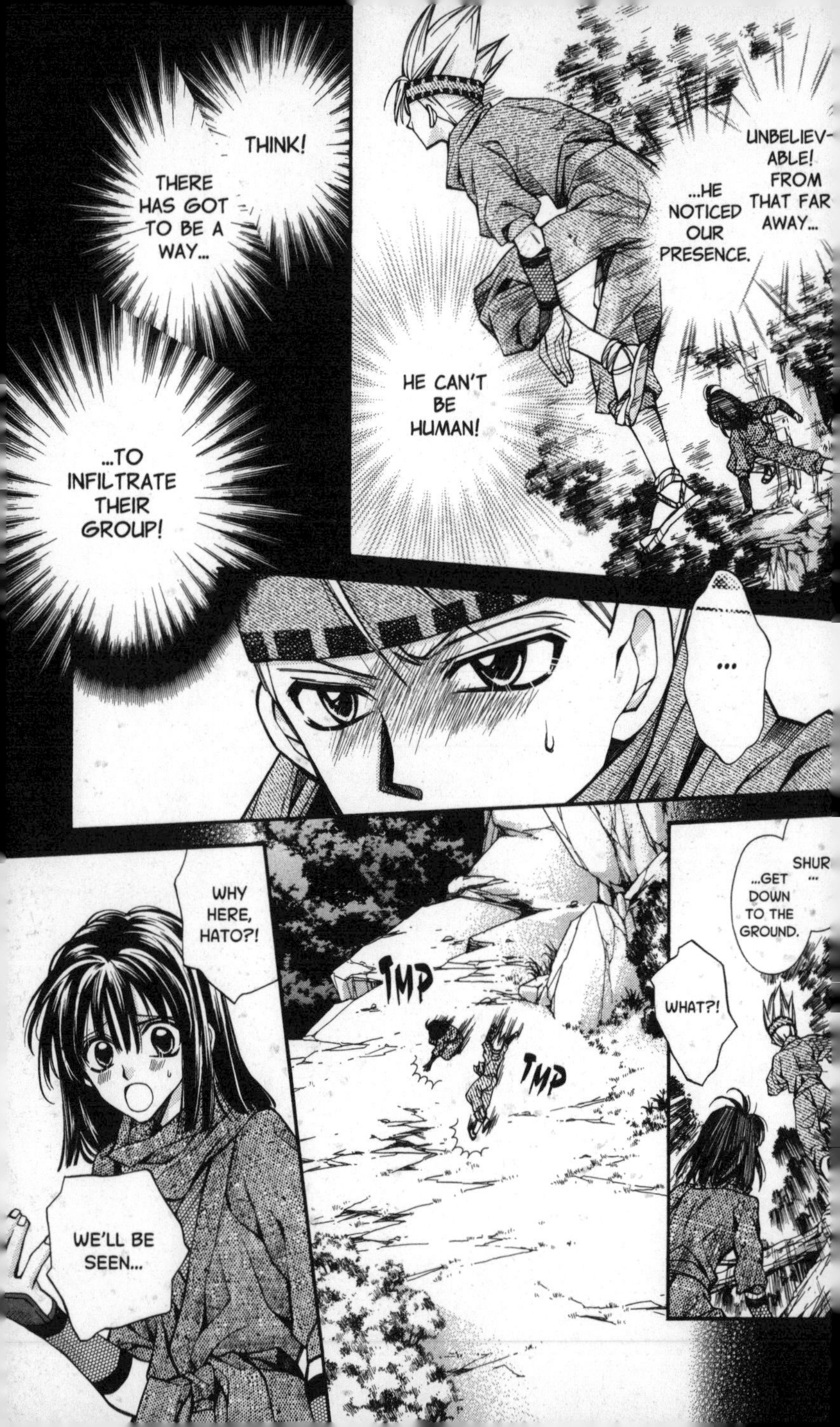
UNBELIEV-ABLE! FROM THAT FAR AWAY...
...HE NOTICED OUR PRESENCE.
HE CAN'T BE HUMAN!
THINK!
THERE HAS GOT TO BE A WAY...
...TO INFILTRATE THEIR GROUP!
...
SHUR...
...GET DOWN TO THE GROUND.
WHAT?!
TMP
TMP
WHY HERE, HATO?!
WE'LL BE SEEN...

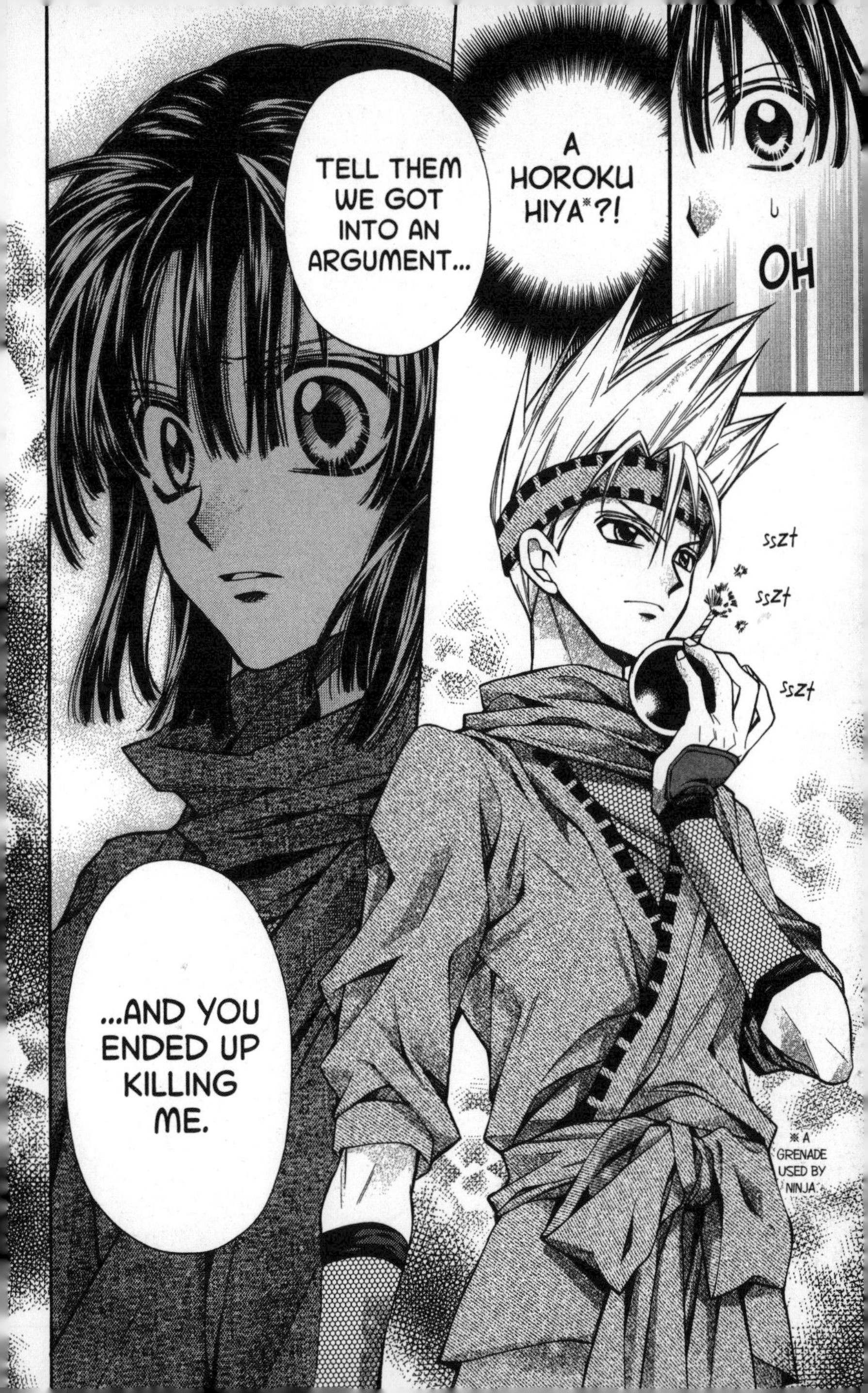
OH
A HOROKU HIYA*?!
TELL THEM WE GOT INTO AN ARGUMENT...
SSZT
SSZT
SSZT
...AND YOU ENDED UP KILLING ME.
* A GRENADE USED BY NINJA.

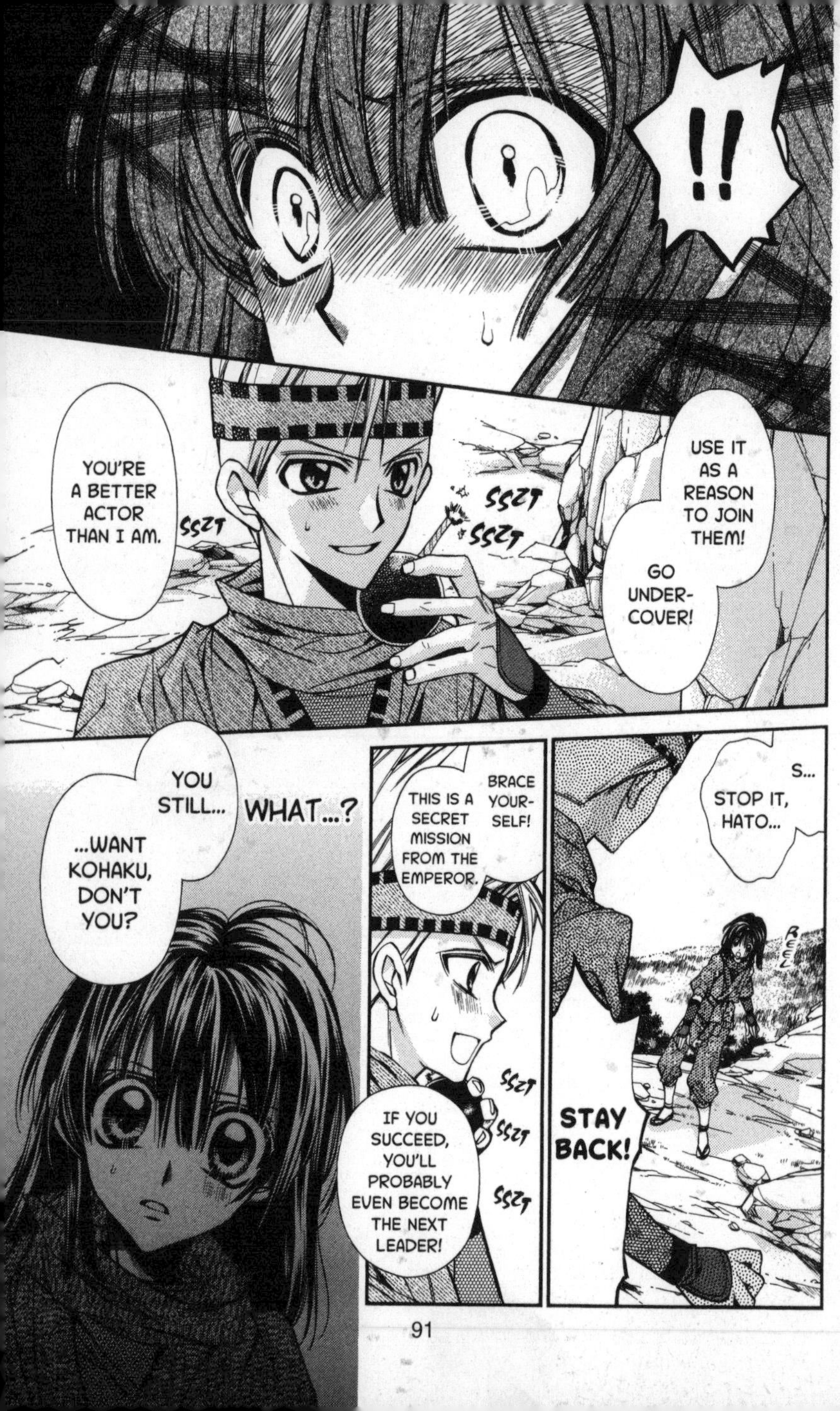
!!
USE IT AS A REASON TO JOIN THEM!
GO UNDER-COVER!
SSZT
SSZT
SSZT
YOU'RE A BETTER ACTOR THAN I AM.
S... STOP IT, HATO...
REEL
STAY BACK!
BRACE YOURSELF!
THIS IS A SECRET MISSION FROM THE EMPEROR.
SSZT
SSZT
SSZT
IF YOU SUCCEED, YOU'LL PROBABLY EVEN BECOME THE NEXT LEADER!
WHAT...?
YOU STILL...
...WANT KOHAKU, DON'T YOU?

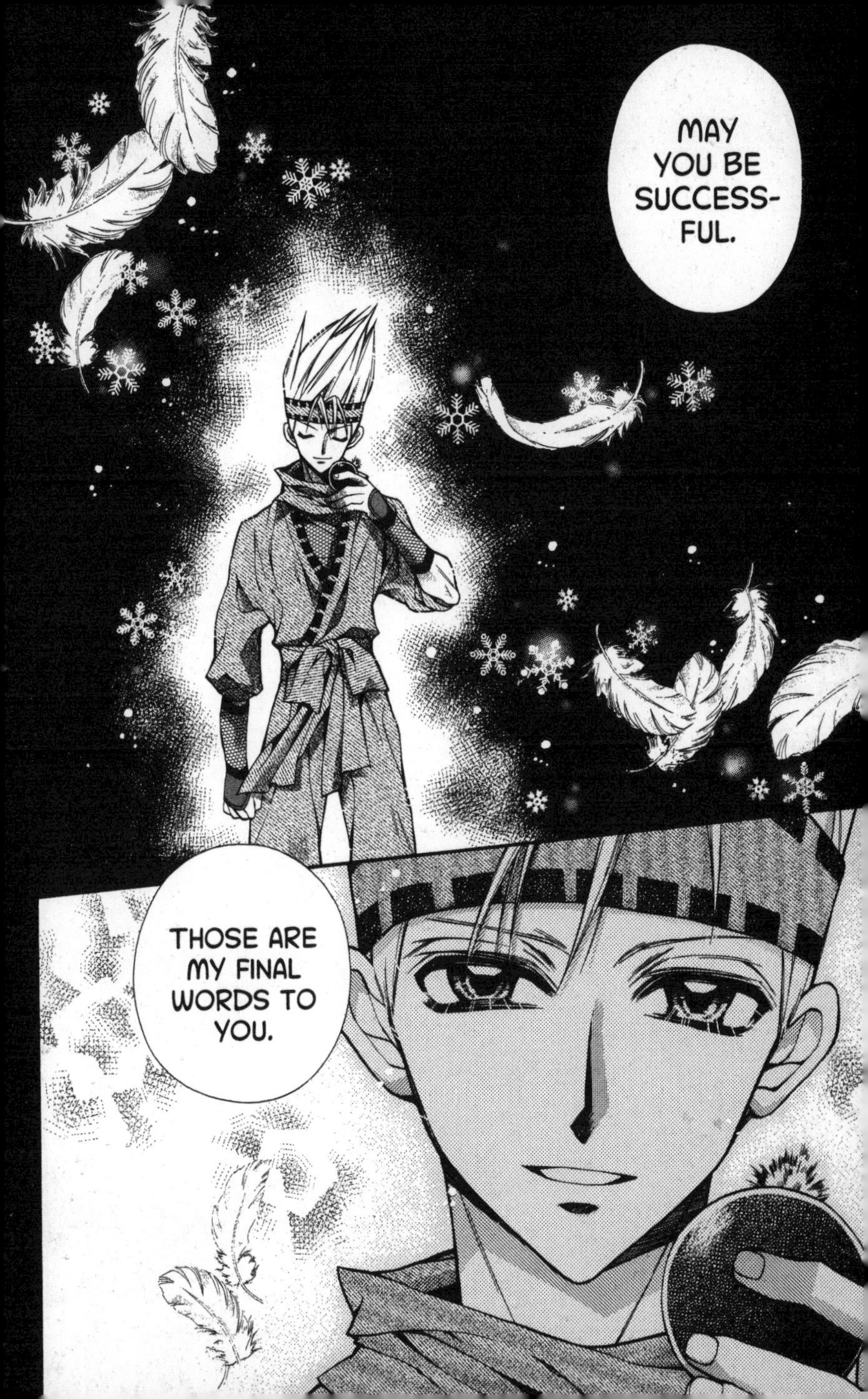
MAY YOU BE SUCCESS-FUL.
THOSE ARE MY FINAL WORDS TO YOU.

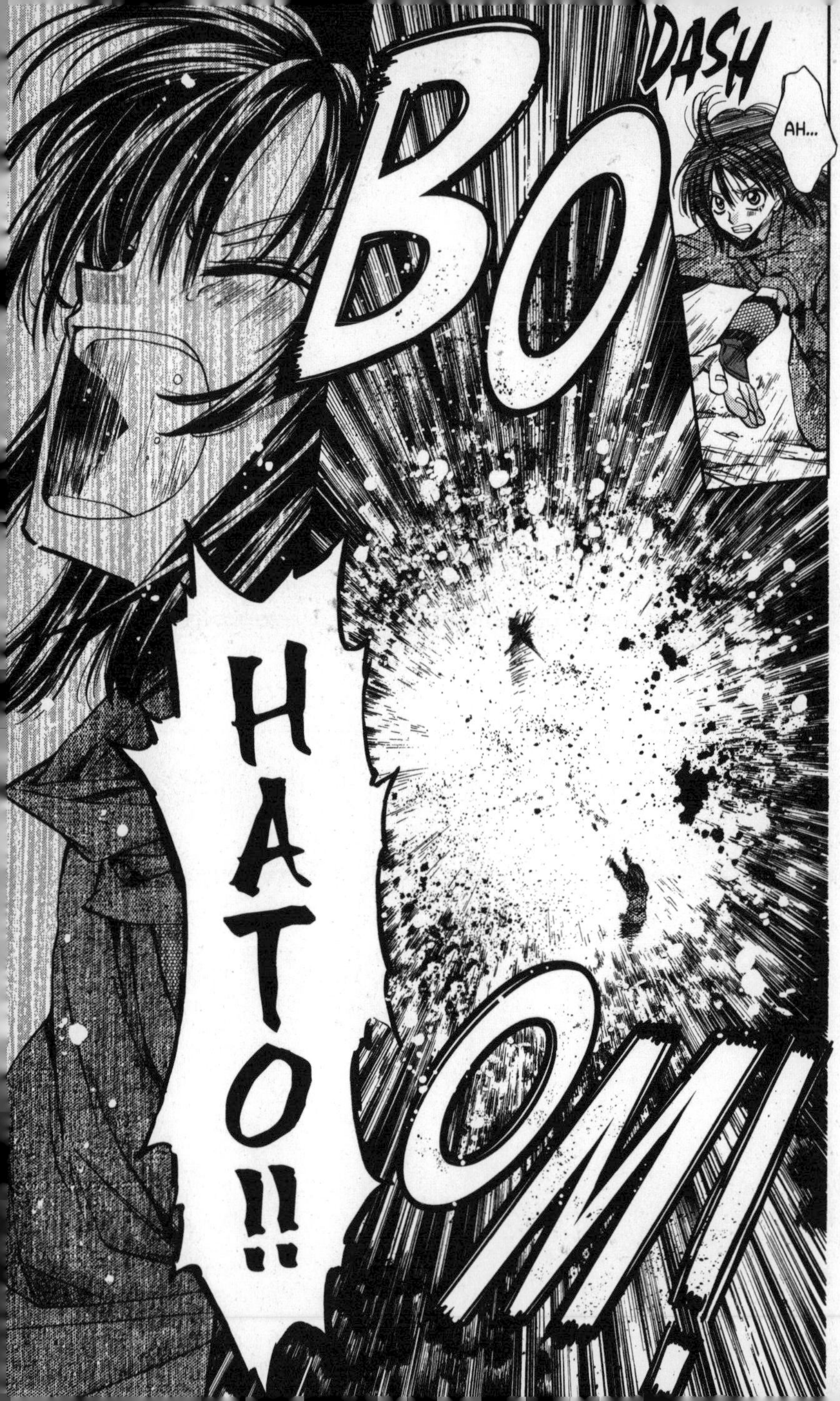
DASH
AH...
BOOM
HATO!!

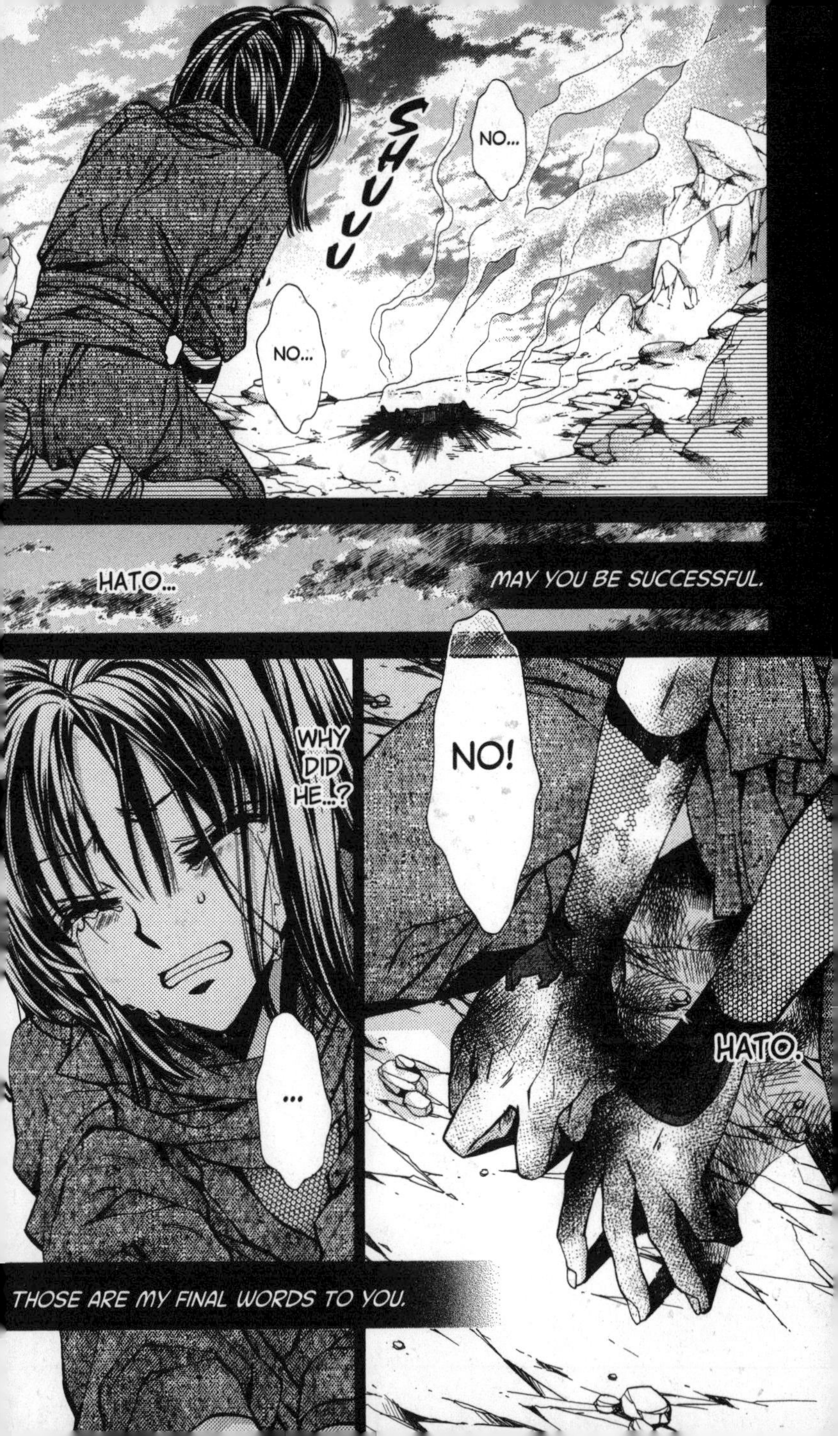
NO...
SHUUUUU
NO...
MAY YOU BE SUCCESSFUL.
HATO...
NO!
HATO.
WHY DID HE...?
...
THOSE ARE MY FINAL WORDS TO YOU.

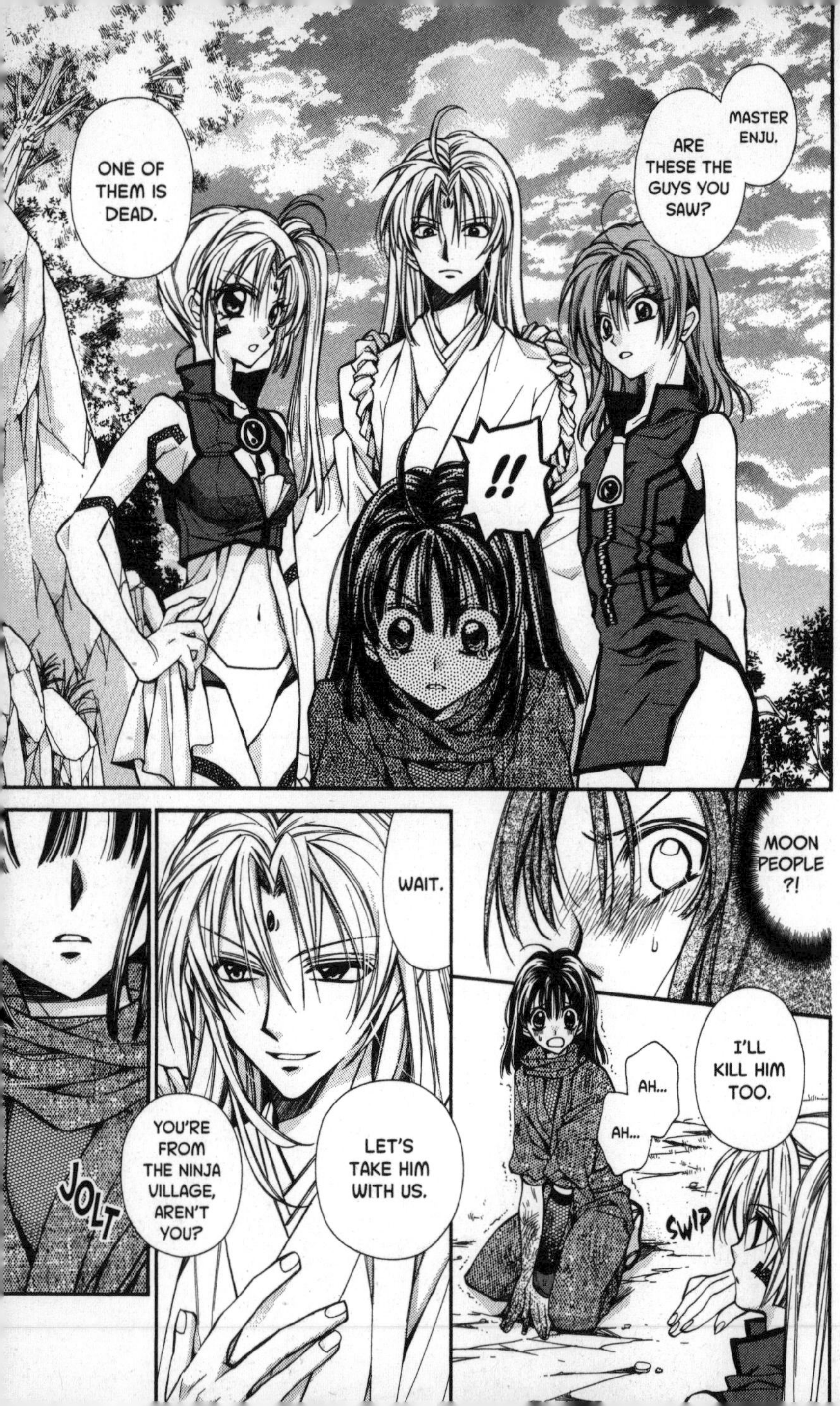

MASTER ENJU.
ARE THESE THE GUYS YOU SAW?
ONE OF THEM IS DEAD.
!!
MOON PEOPLE ?!
I'LL KILL HIM TOO.
AH...
AH...
SWIP
WAIT.
LET'S TAKE HIM WITH US.
YOU'RE FROM THE NINJA VILLAGE, AREN'T YOU?
JOLT

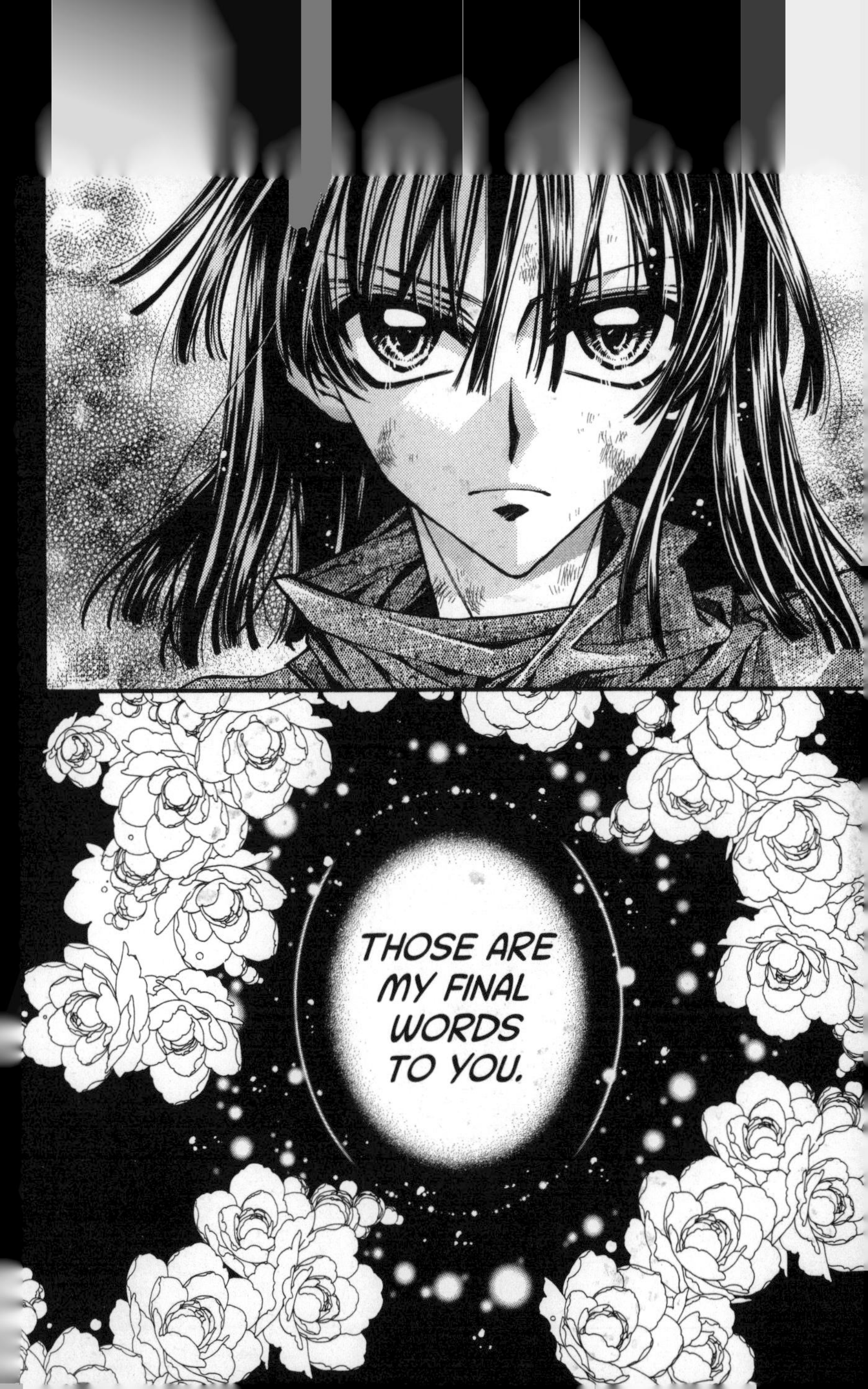
THOSE ARE MY FINAL WORDS TO YOU.

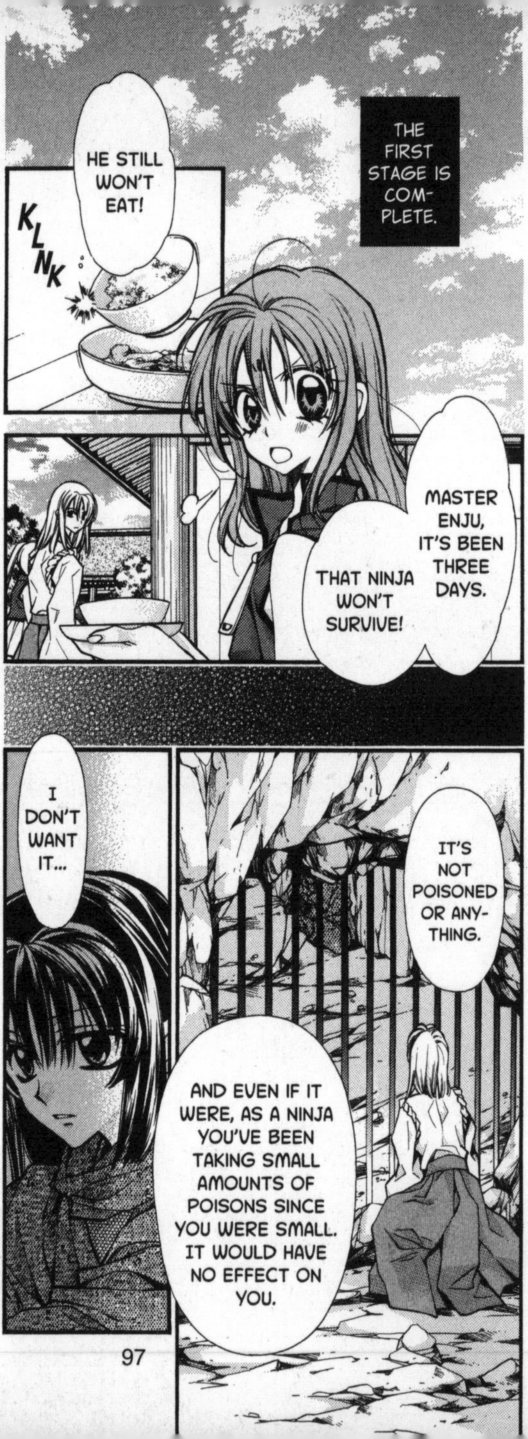
THE FIRST STAGE IS COM-PLETE.
HE STILL WON'T EAT!
KLNK
MASTER ENJU, IT'S BEEN THREE DAYS.
THAT NINJA WON'T SURVIVE!
IT'S NOT POISONED OR ANY-THING.
AND EVEN IF IT WERE, AS A NINJA YOU'VE BEEN TAKING SMALL AMOUNTS OF POISONS SINCE YOU WERE SMALL. IT WOULD HAVE NO EFFECT ON YOU.
I DON'T WANT IT...

Final Comments

I'm sorry I went through this so hurriedly.

Um, this is volume 5, but to everybody's surprise, volume 6 of *Sakura Hime: The Legend of Princess Sakura* will come out on August 12 in Japan. The chapters had piled up, so fortunately the volumes can be released over a short period of time.

I wonder whom I should draw for the cover of the next volume?

✿Special Thanks✿

Nakame, Miichi, Sakakura-san, Konako, Kawanishi-san, Yamada-san, Ikurun, Hina-chan, Nami-san, and Kyomoto-san.

Ammonite Inc.
Shueisha, Ribon Editorial Department
Editor T-san
Editor F-san

Kawatani-san, Kawatani Design

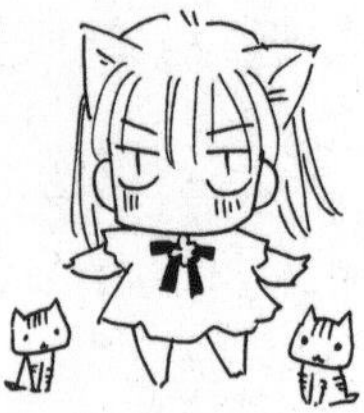

Riku & Kai

See you all in volume 6!!

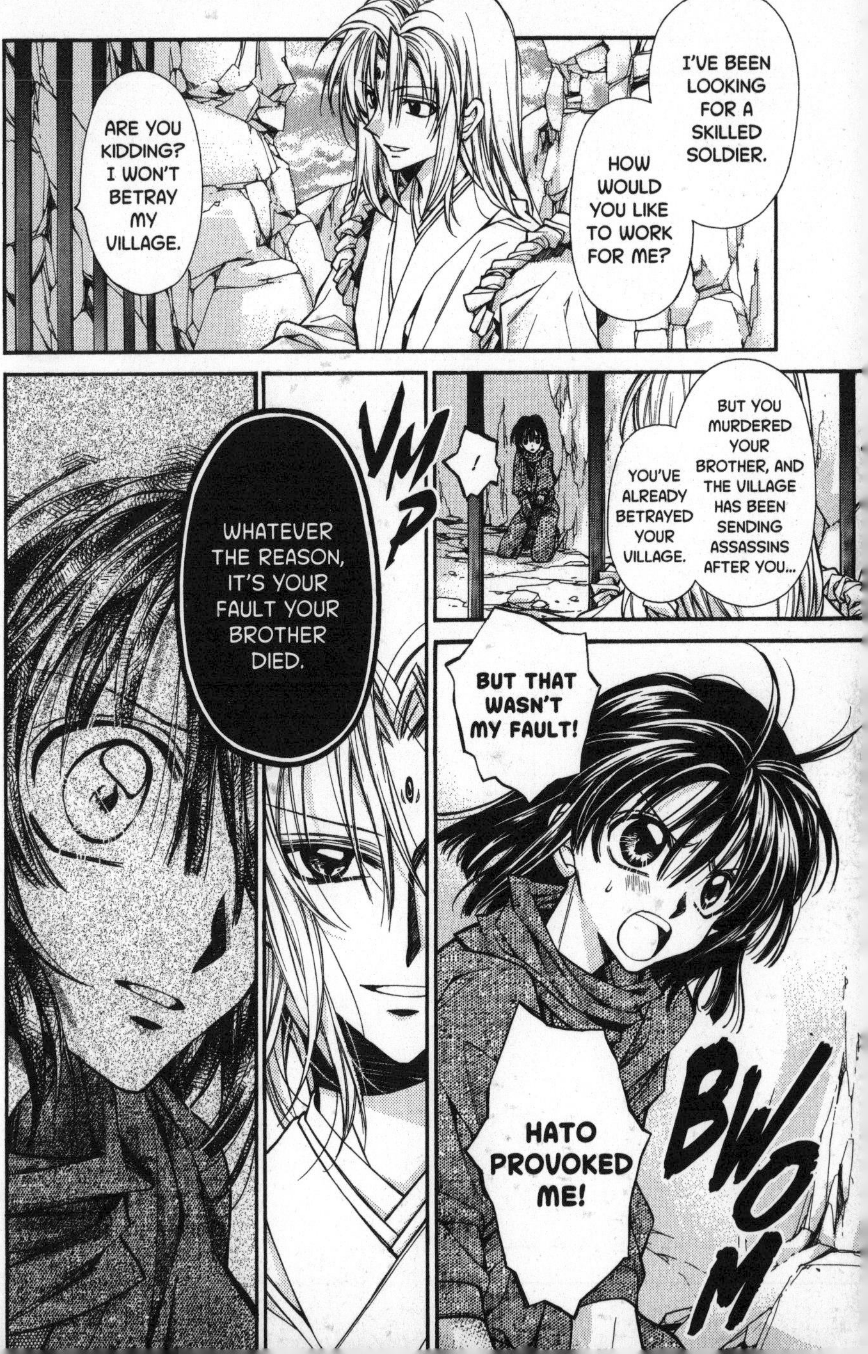
I'VE BEEN LOOKING FOR A SKILLED SOLDIER.
HOW WOULD YOU LIKE TO WORK FOR ME?
ARE YOU KIDDING? I WON'T BETRAY MY VILLAGE.
BUT YOU MURDERED YOUR BROTHER, AND THE VILLAGE HAS BEEN SENDING ASSASSINS AFTER YOU...
YOU'VE ALREADY BETRAYED YOUR VILLAGE.
!
BUT THAT WASN'T MY FAULT!
BWOM
HATO PROVOKED ME!
VMP
WHATEVER THE REASON, IT'S YOUR FAULT YOUR BROTHER DIED.

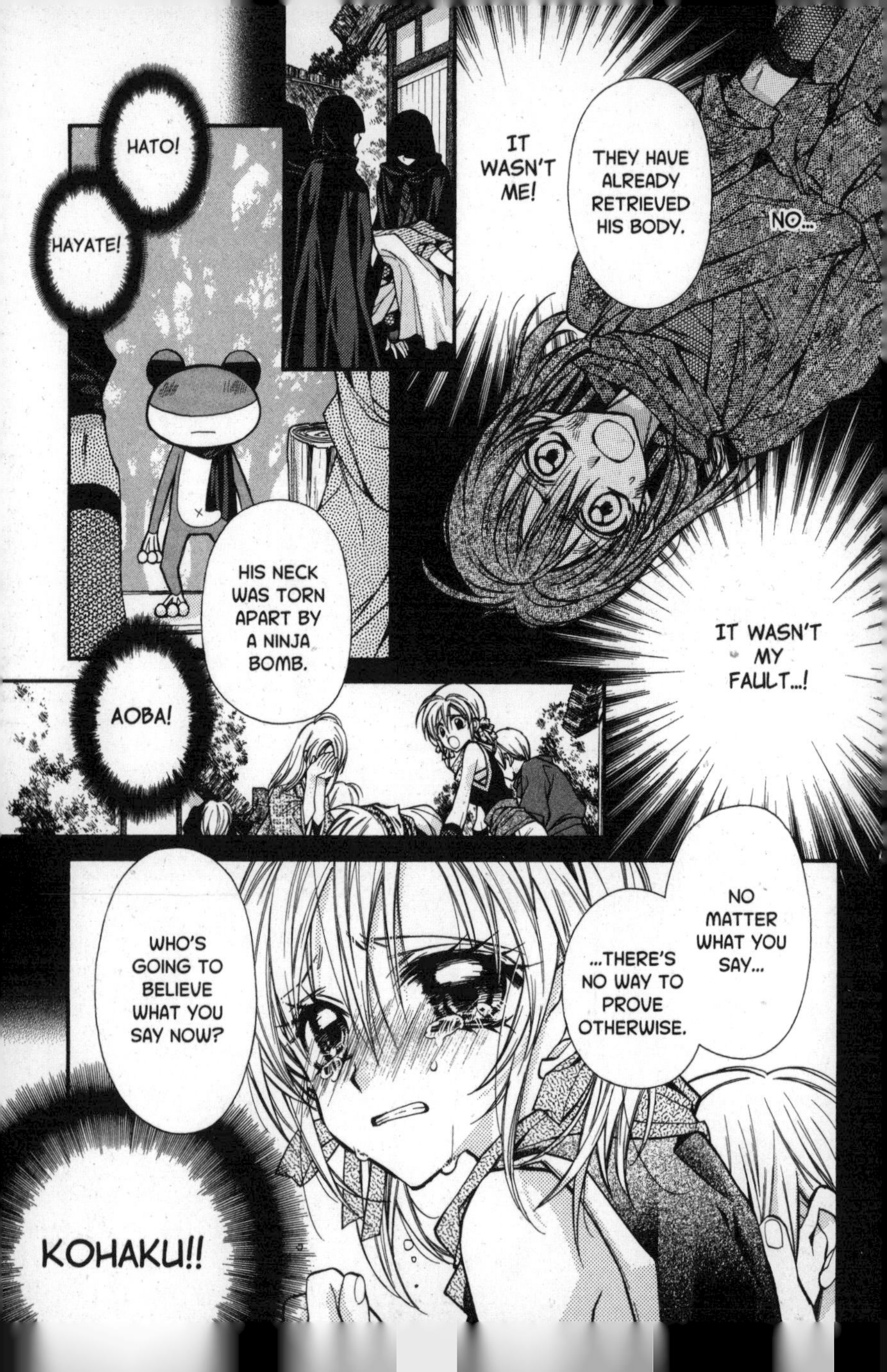
THEY HAVE ALREADY RETRIEVED HIS BODY.
IT WASN'T ME!
NO...
IT WASN'T MY FAULT...!
HIS NECK WAS TORN APART BY A NINJA BOMB.
HATO!
HAYATE!
AOBA!
NO MATTER WHAT YOU SAY...
...THERE'S NO WAY TO PROVE OTHERWISE.
WHO'S GOING TO BELIEVE WHAT YOU SAY NOW?
KOHAKU!!

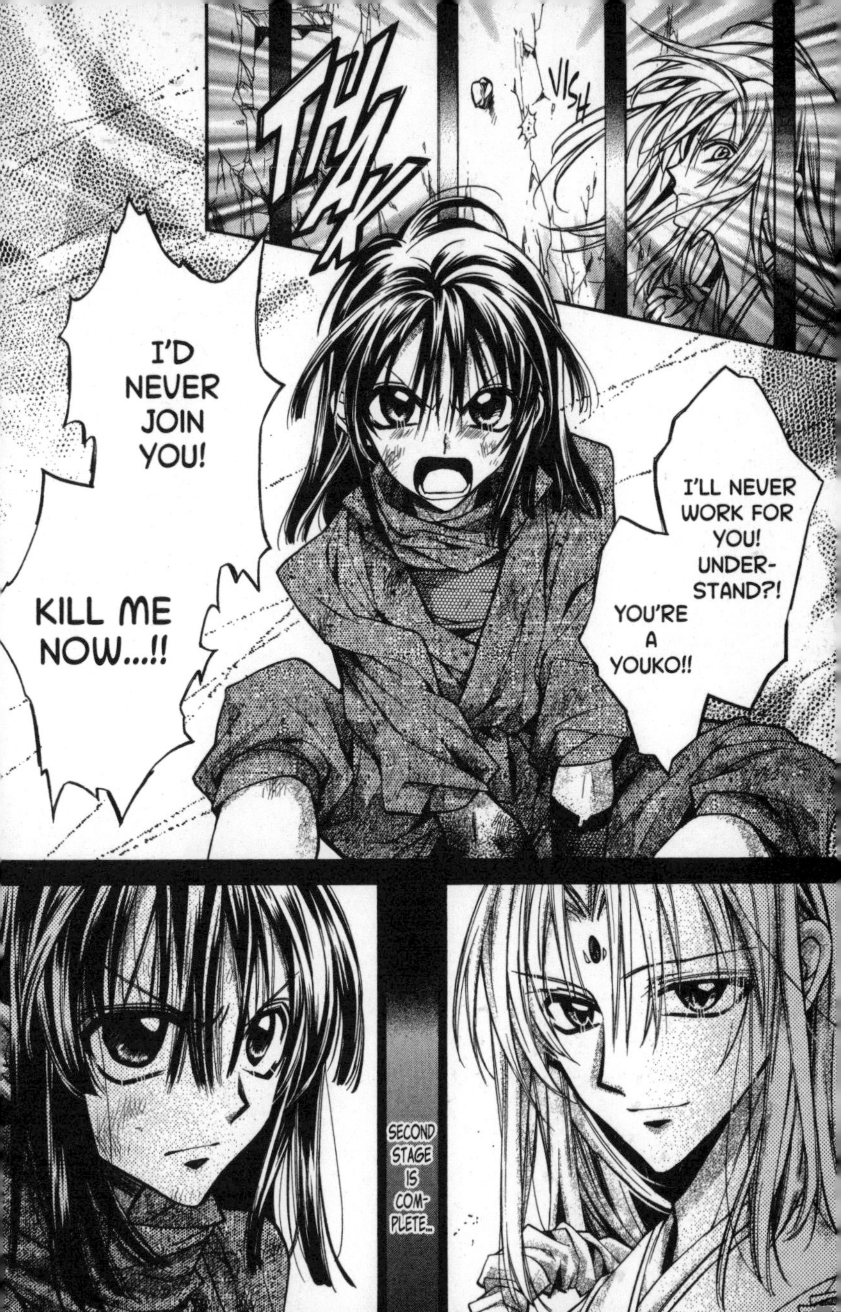
VISH
THK
I'LL NEVER WORK FOR YOU! UNDER-STAND?!
YOU'RE A YOUKO!!
I'D NEVER JOIN YOU!
KILL ME NOW...!!
SECOND STAGE IS COM-PLETE...

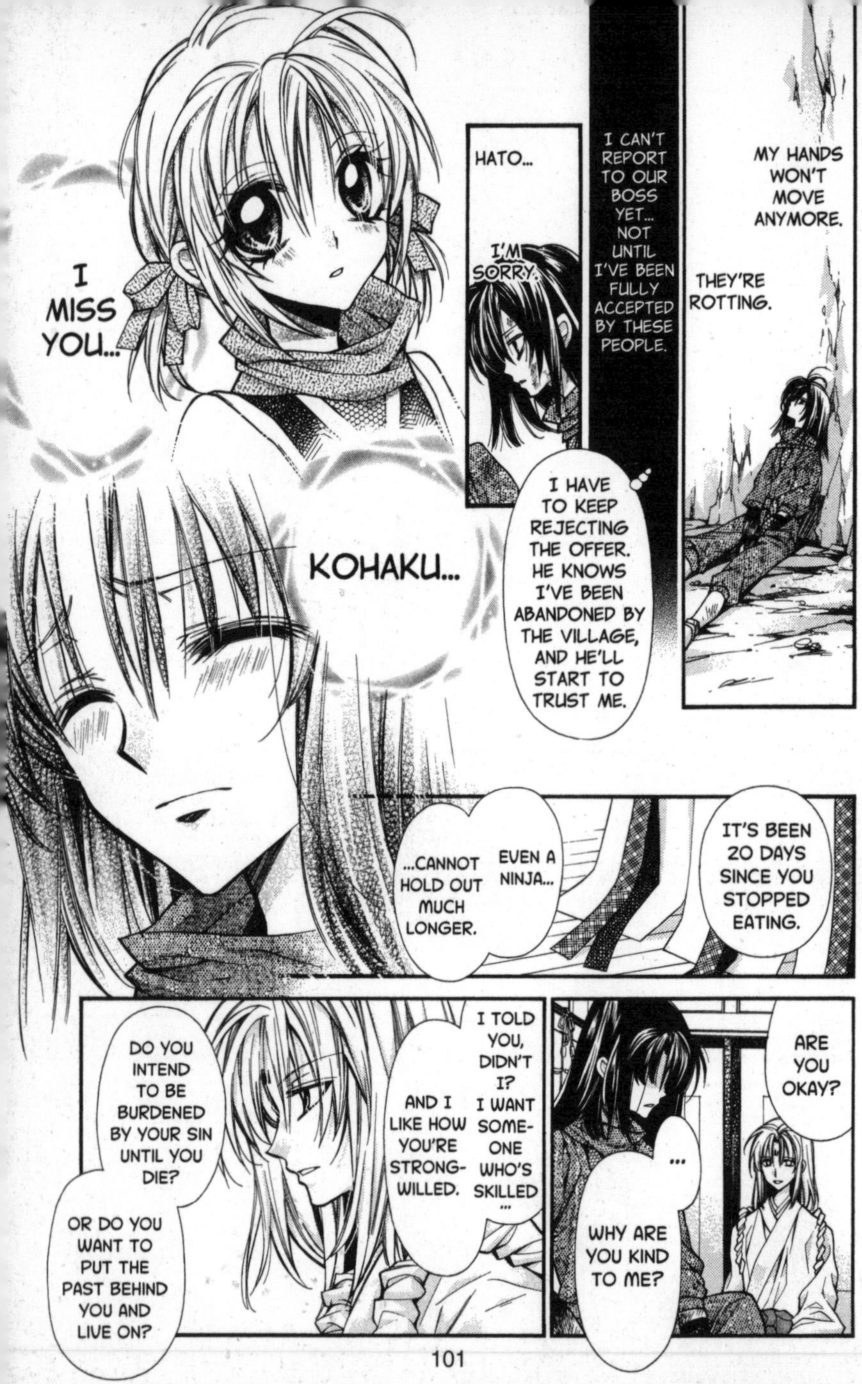
MY HANDS WON'T MOVE ANYMORE.
THEY'RE ROTTING.
I CAN'T REPORT TO OUR BOSS YET... NOT UNTIL I'VE BEEN FULLY ACCEPTED BY THESE PEOPLE.
HATO...
I'M SORRY.
I MISS YOU...
I HAVE TO KEEP REJECTING THE OFFER. HE KNOWS I'VE BEEN ABANDONED BY THE VILLAGE, AND HE'LL START TO TRUST ME.
KOHAKU...
IT'S BEEN 20 DAYS SINCE YOU STOPPED EATING.
EVEN A NINJA...
...CANNOT HOLD OUT MUCH LONGER.
ARE YOU OKAY?
...
WHY ARE YOU KIND TO ME?
I TOLD YOU, DIDN'T I? I WANT SOME-ONE WHO'S SKILLED...
AND I LIKE HOW YOU'RE STRONG-WILLED.
DO YOU INTEND TO BE BURDENED BY YOUR SIN UNTIL YOU DIE?
OR DO YOU WANT TO PUT THE PAST BEHIND YOU AND LIVE ON?

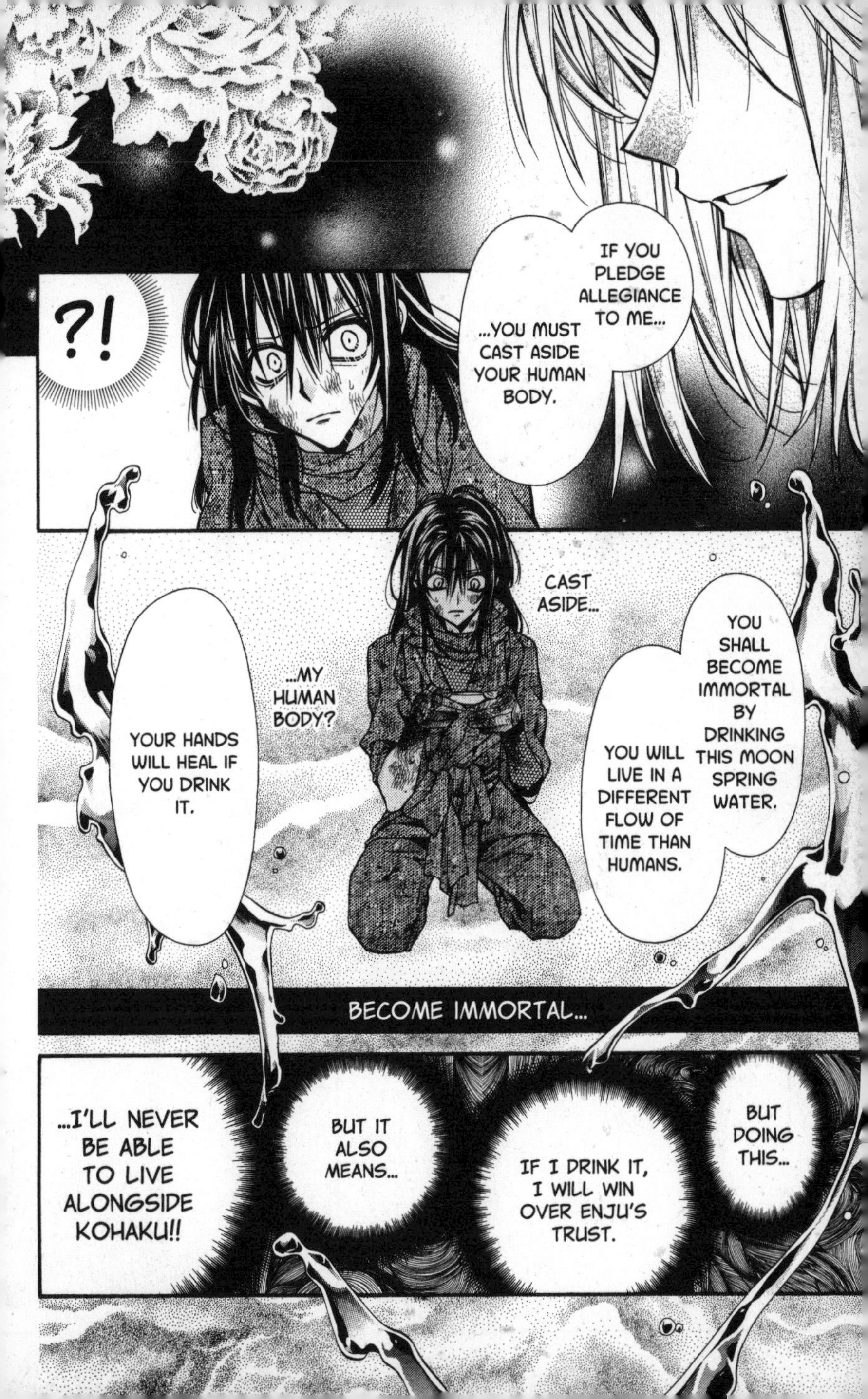
IF YOU PLEDGE ALLEGIANCE TO ME...
...YOU MUST CAST ASIDE YOUR HUMAN BODY.
?!
YOU SHALL BECOME IMMORTAL BY DRINKING THIS MOON SPRING WATER.
YOU WILL LIVE IN A DIFFERENT FLOW OF TIME THAN HUMANS.
CAST ASIDE...
...MY HUMAN BODY?
YOUR HANDS WILL HEAL IF YOU DRINK IT.
BECOME IMMORTAL...
BUT DOING THIS...
IF I DRINK IT, I WILL WIN OVER ENJU'S TRUST.
BUT IT ALSO MEANS...
...I'LL NEVER BE ABLE TO LIVE ALONGSIDE KOHAKU!!

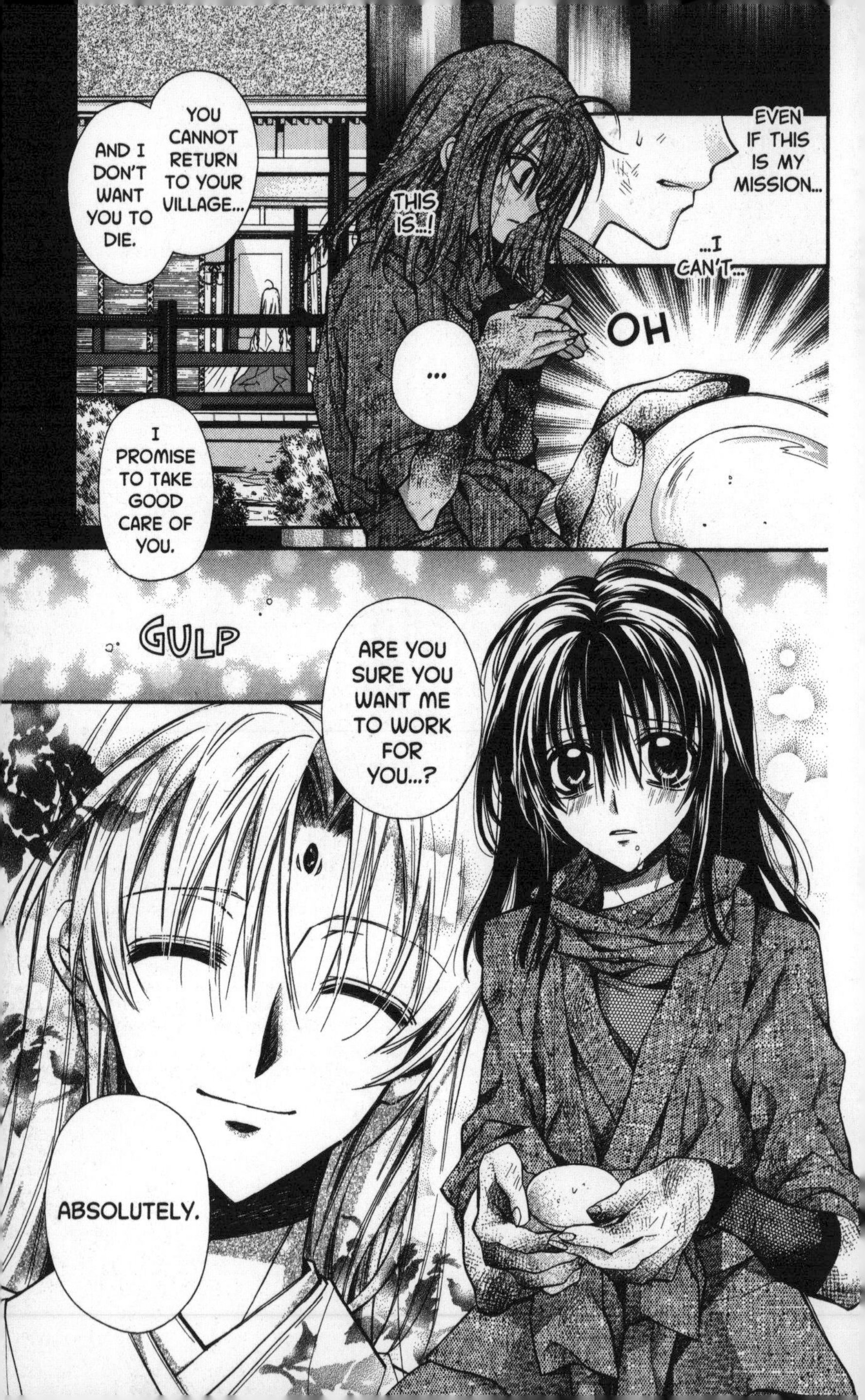
EVEN IF THIS IS MY MISSION...
YOU CANNOT RETURN TO YOUR VILLAGE...
AND I DON'T WANT YOU TO DIE.
THIS IS...!
...I CAN'T...
OH
...
I PROMISE TO TAKE GOOD CARE OF YOU.
GULP
ARE YOU SURE YOU WANT ME TO WORK FOR YOU...?
ABSOLUTELY.

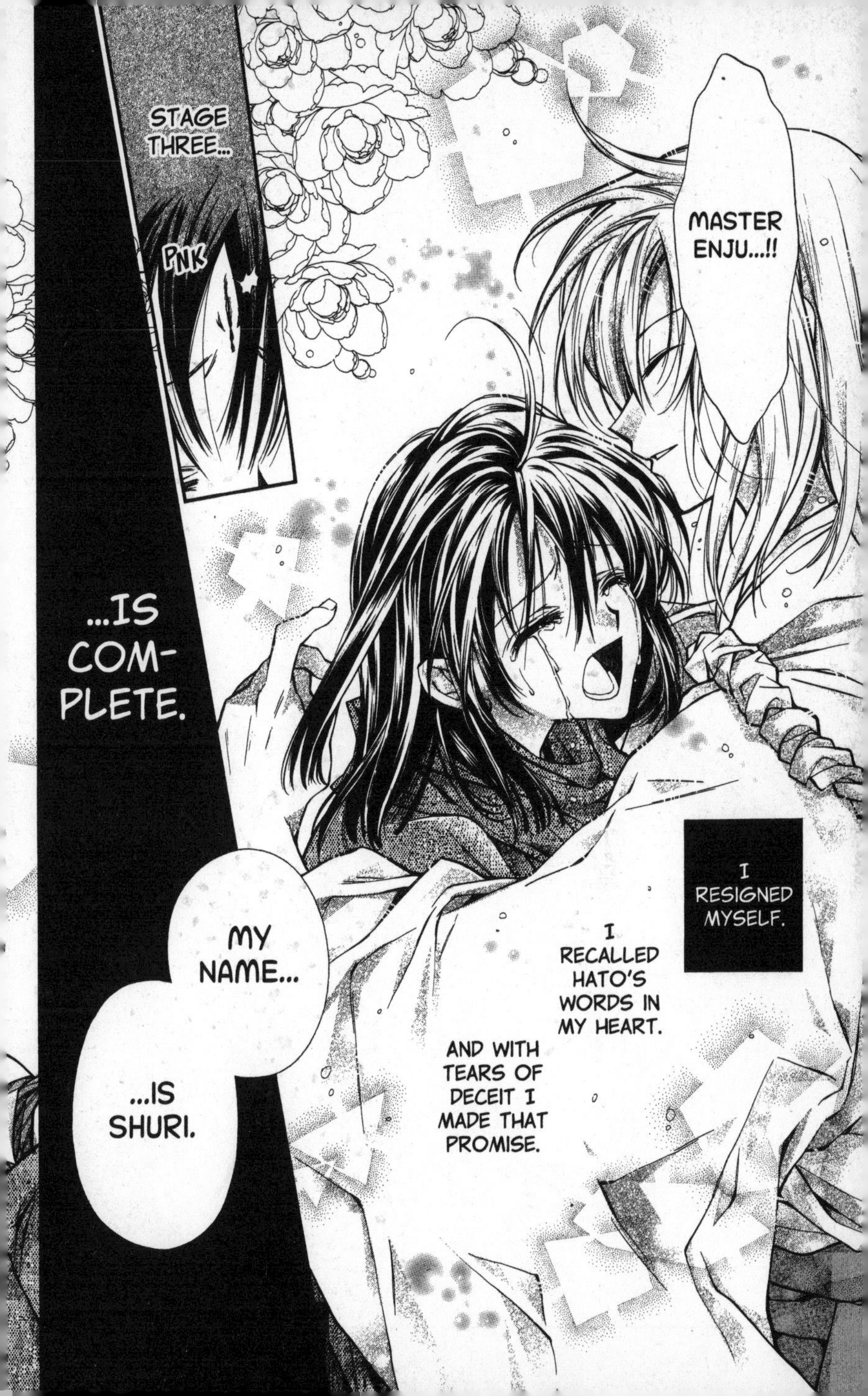
MASTER ENJU...!!
STAGE THREE...
PNK
...IS COM-PLETE.
I RESIGNED MYSELF.
I RECALLED HATO'S WORDS IN MY HEART.
AND WITH TEARS OF DECEIT I MADE THAT PROMISE.
MY NAME...
...IS SHURI.

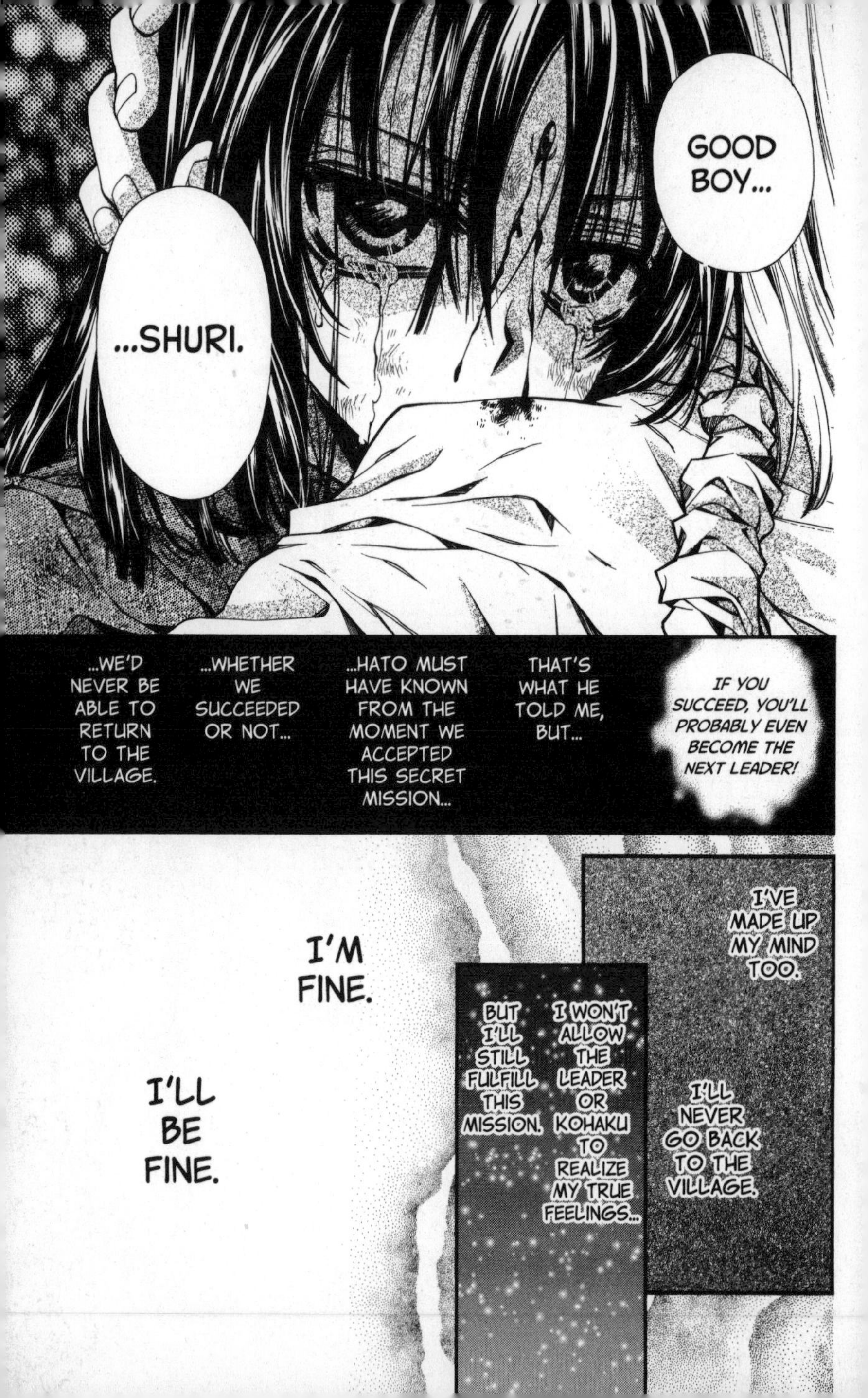
GOOD BOY...
...SHURI.
IF YOU SUCCEED, YOU'LL PROBABLY EVEN BECOME THE NEXT LEADER!
THAT'S WHAT HE TOLD ME, BUT...
...HATO MUST HAVE KNOWN FROM THE MOMENT WE ACCEPTED THIS SECRET MISSION...
...WHETHER WE SUCCEEDED OR NOT...
...WE'D NEVER BE ABLE TO RETURN TO THE VILLAGE.
I'VE MADE UP MY MIND TOO.
I'LL NEVER GO BACK TO THE VILLAGE.
I WON'T ALLOW THE LEADER OR KOHAKU TO REALIZE MY TRUE FEELINGS...
BUT I'LL STILL FULFILL THIS MISSION.
I'M FINE.
I'LL BE FINE.

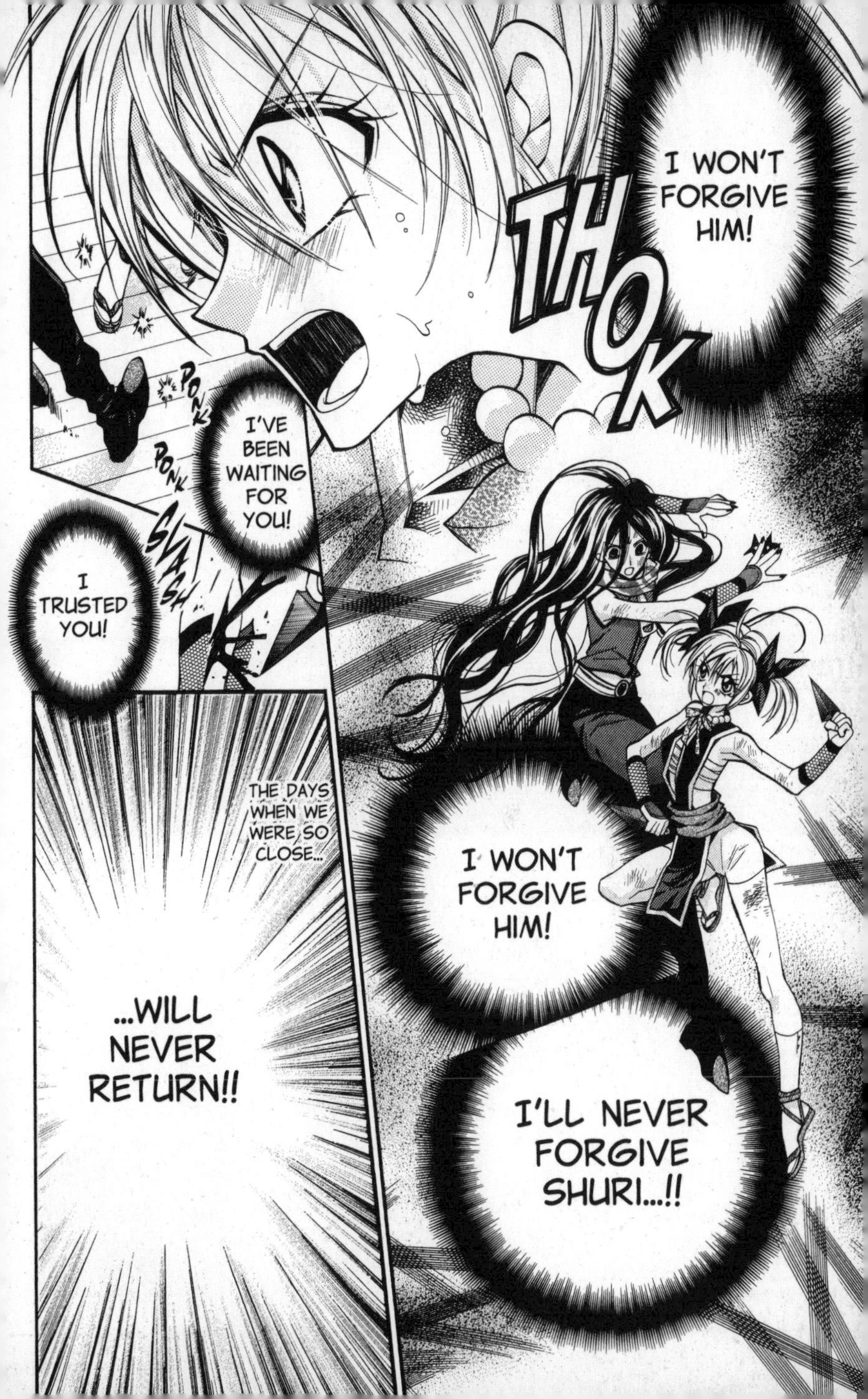

I WON'T FORGIVE HIM!
THOK
I'VE BEEN WAITING FOR YOU!
PONK
PONK
SLASH
I TRUSTED YOU!
I WON'T FORGIVE HIM!
I'LL NEVER FORGIVE SHURI...!!
THE DAYS WHEN WE WERE SO CLOSE...
...WILL NEVER RETURN!!

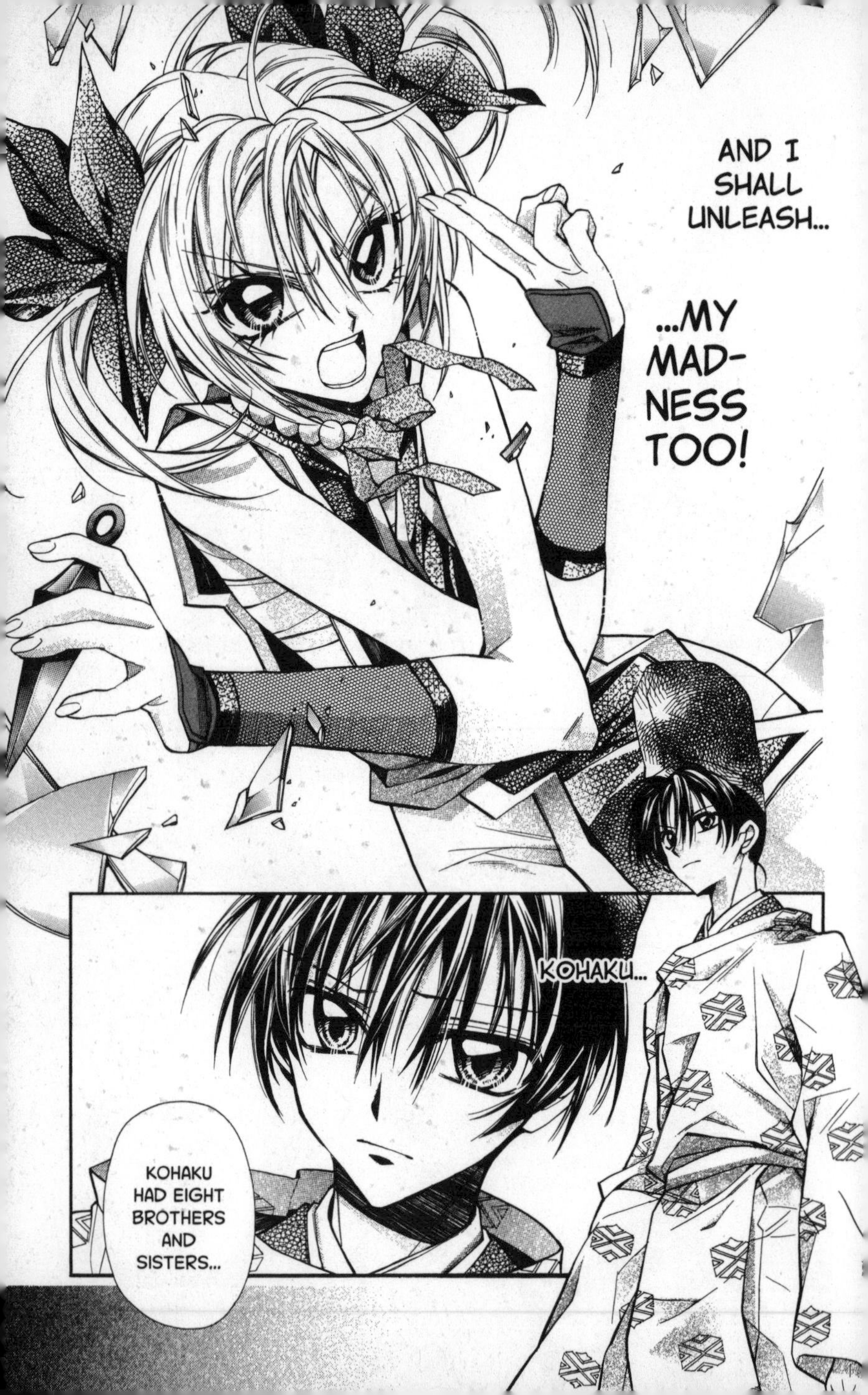
AND I SHALL UNLEASH...
...MY MAD-NESS TOO!
KOHAKU...
KOHAKU HAD EIGHT BROTHERS AND SISTERS...

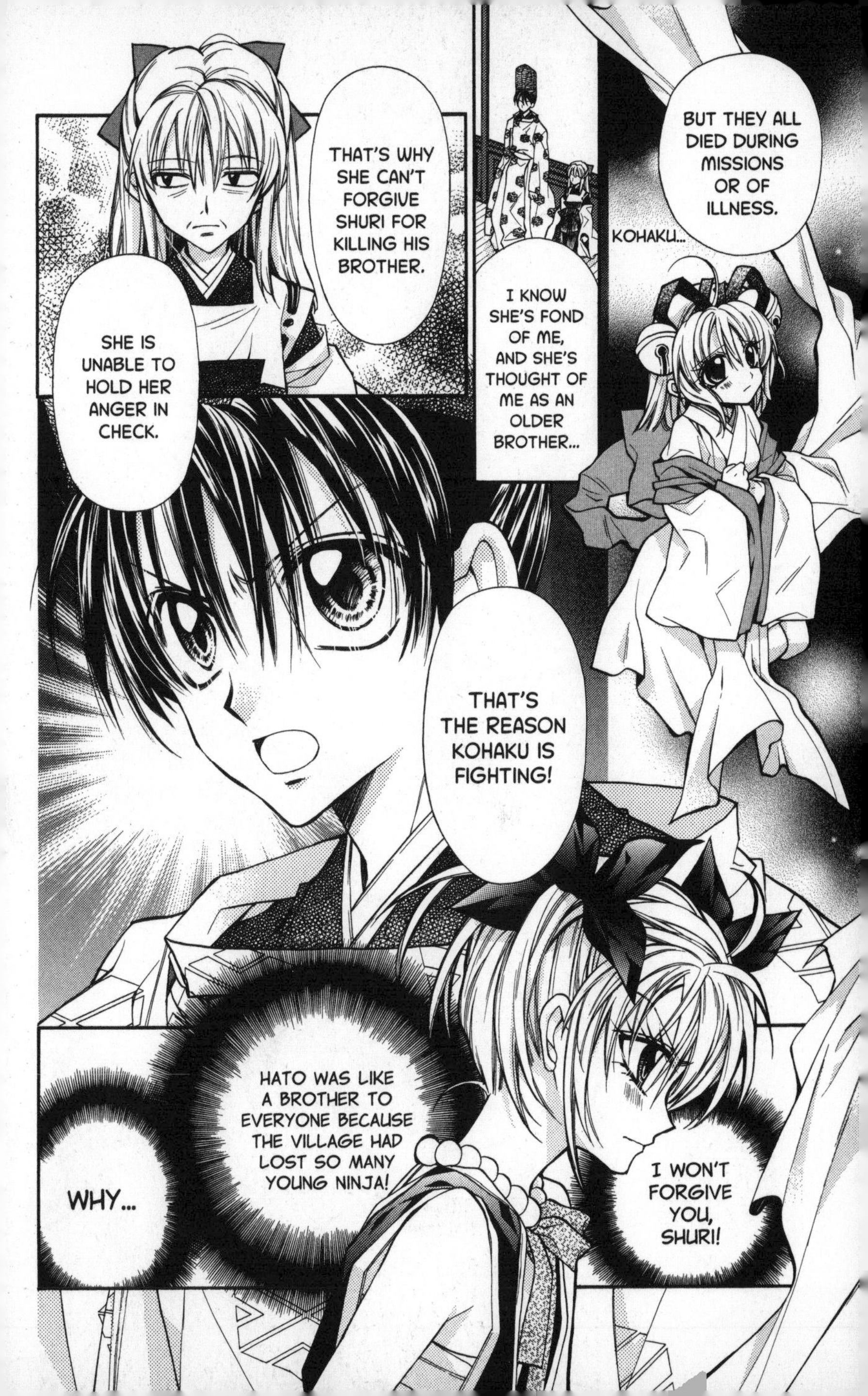
BUT THEY ALL DIED DURING MISSIONS OR OF ILLNESS.
KOHAKU...
I KNOW SHE'S FOND OF ME, AND SHE'S THOUGHT OF ME AS AN OLDER BROTHER...
THAT'S WHY SHE CAN'T FORGIVE SHURI FOR KILLING HIS BROTHER.
SHE IS UNABLE TO HOLD HER ANGER IN CHECK.
THAT'S THE REASON KOHAKU IS FIGHTING!
HATO WAS LIKE A BROTHER TO EVERYONE BECAUSE THE VILLAGE HAD LOST SO MANY YOUNG NINJA!
I WON'T FORGIVE YOU, SHURI!
WHY...

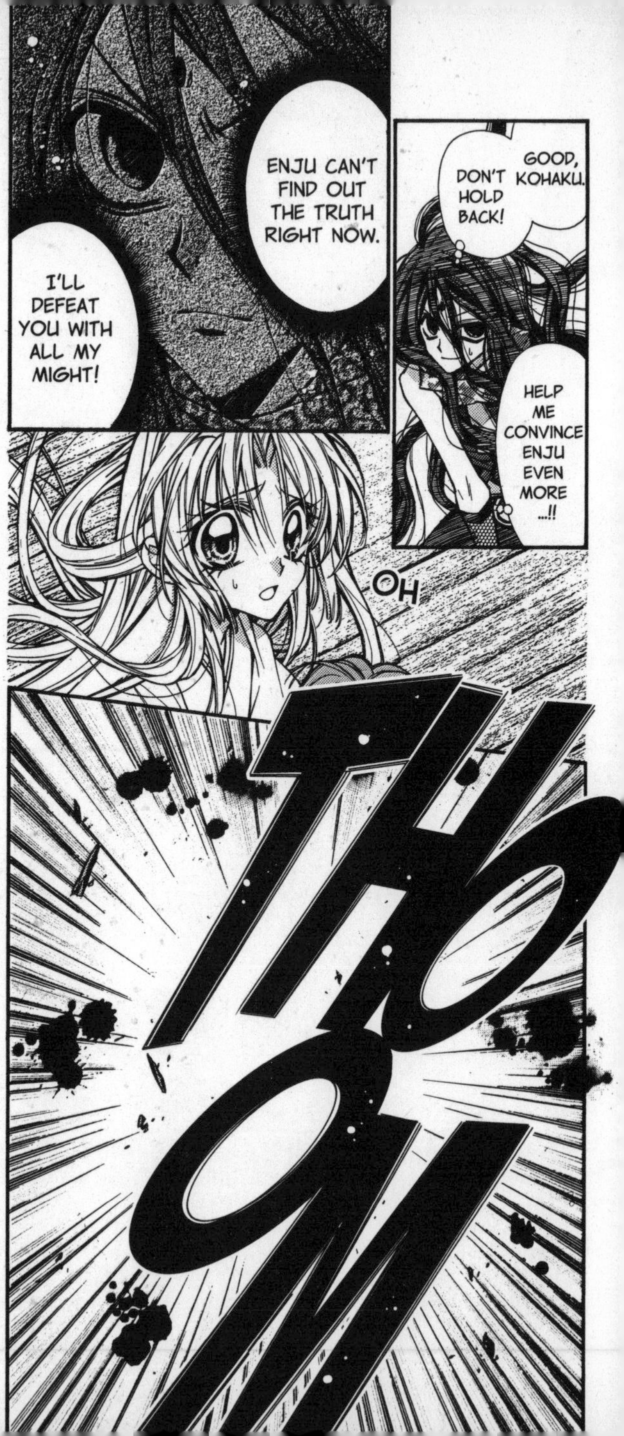
GOOD, KOHAKU. DON'T HOLD BACK!
HELP ME CONVINCE ENJU EVEN MORE ...!!
ENJU CAN'T FIND OUT THE TRUTH RIGHT NOW.
I'LL DEFEAT YOU WITH ALL MY MIGHT!
OH
THOOM

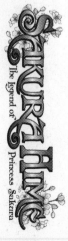

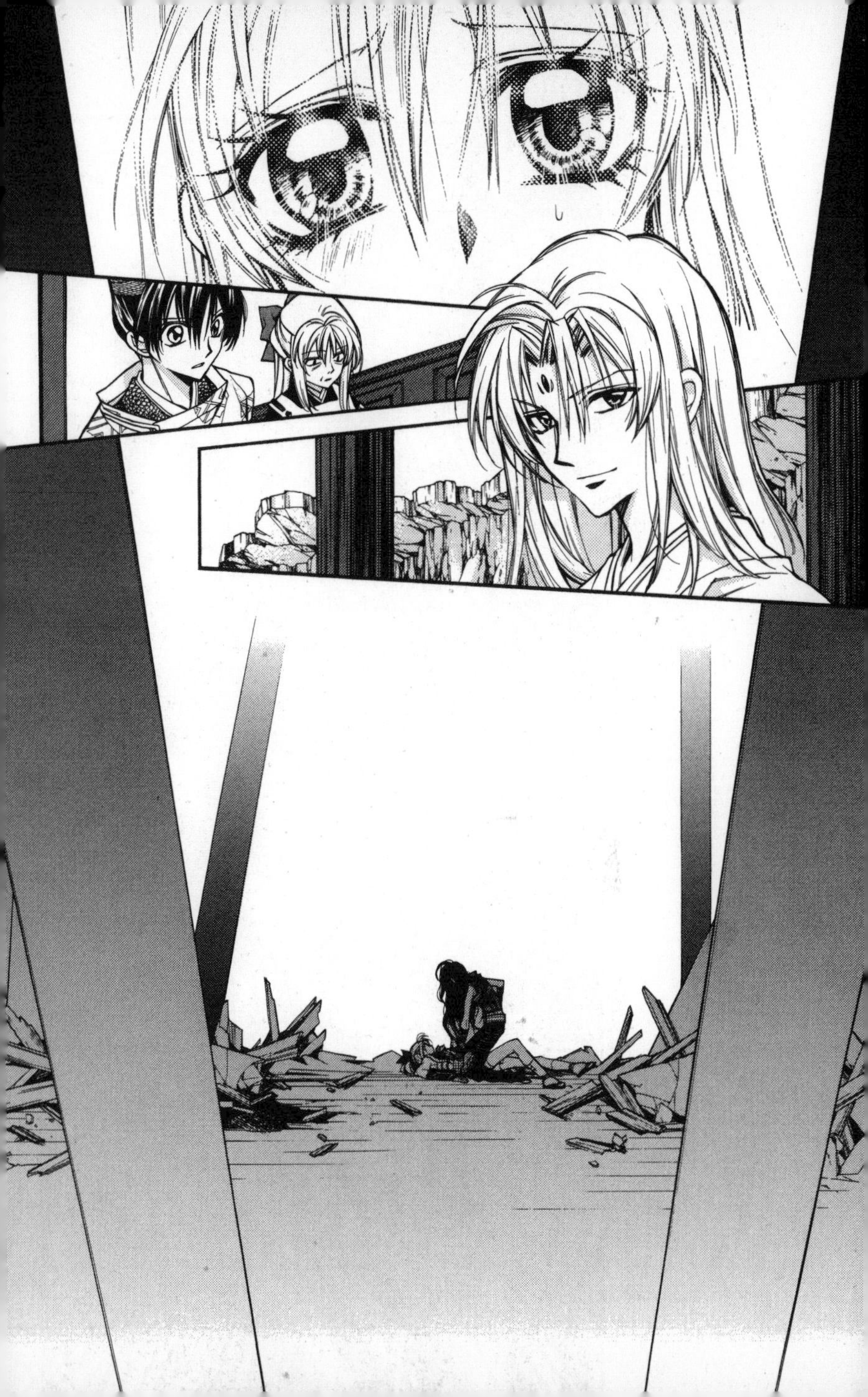

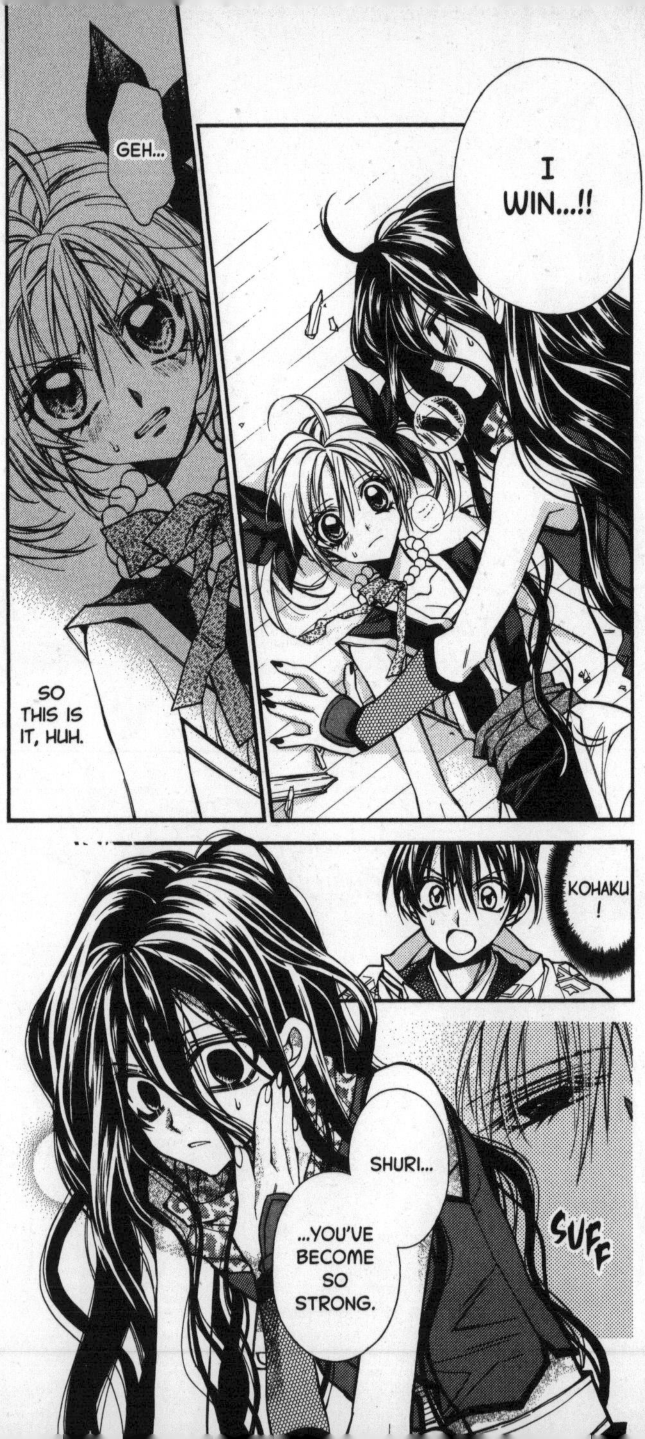
I WIN...!!
GEH...
SO THIS IS IT, HUH.
KOHAKU!
SHURI...
...YOU'VE BECOME SO STRONG.
SUFF

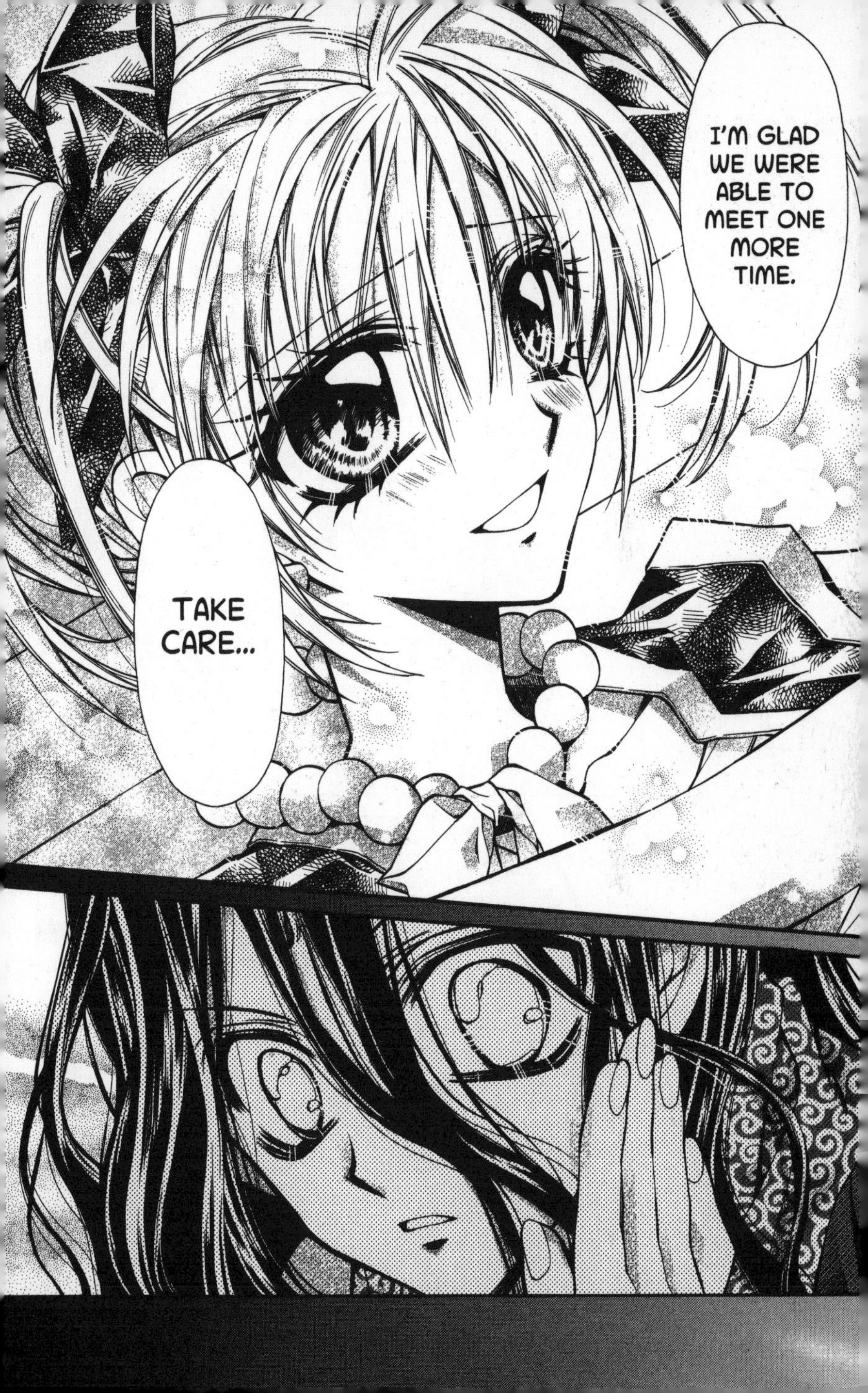
I'M GLAD WE WERE ABLE TO MEET ONE MORE TIME.
TAKE CARE...

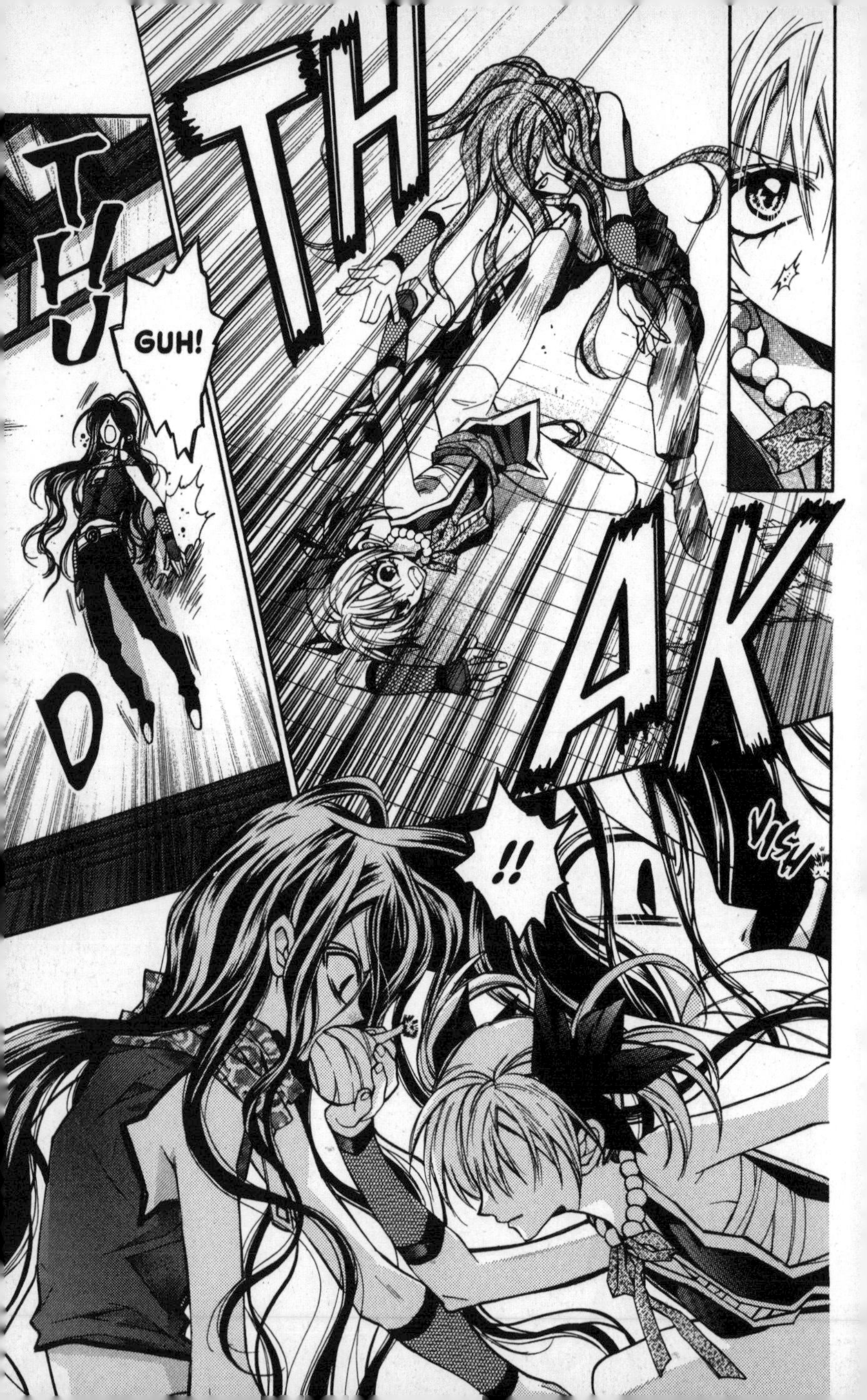
TH
AK
THU
GUH!
D
!!
VISH

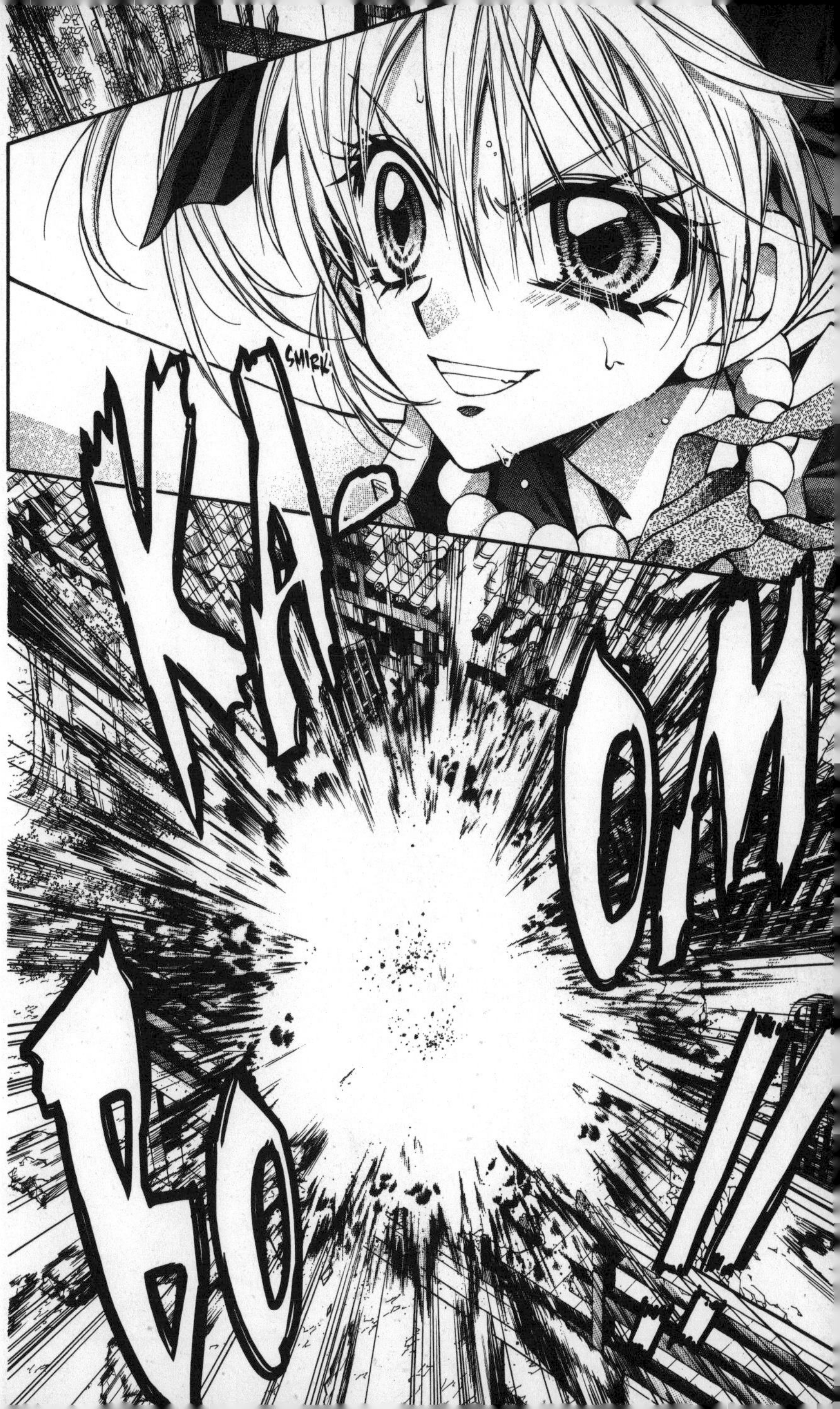
SMIRK
KABOOM!!

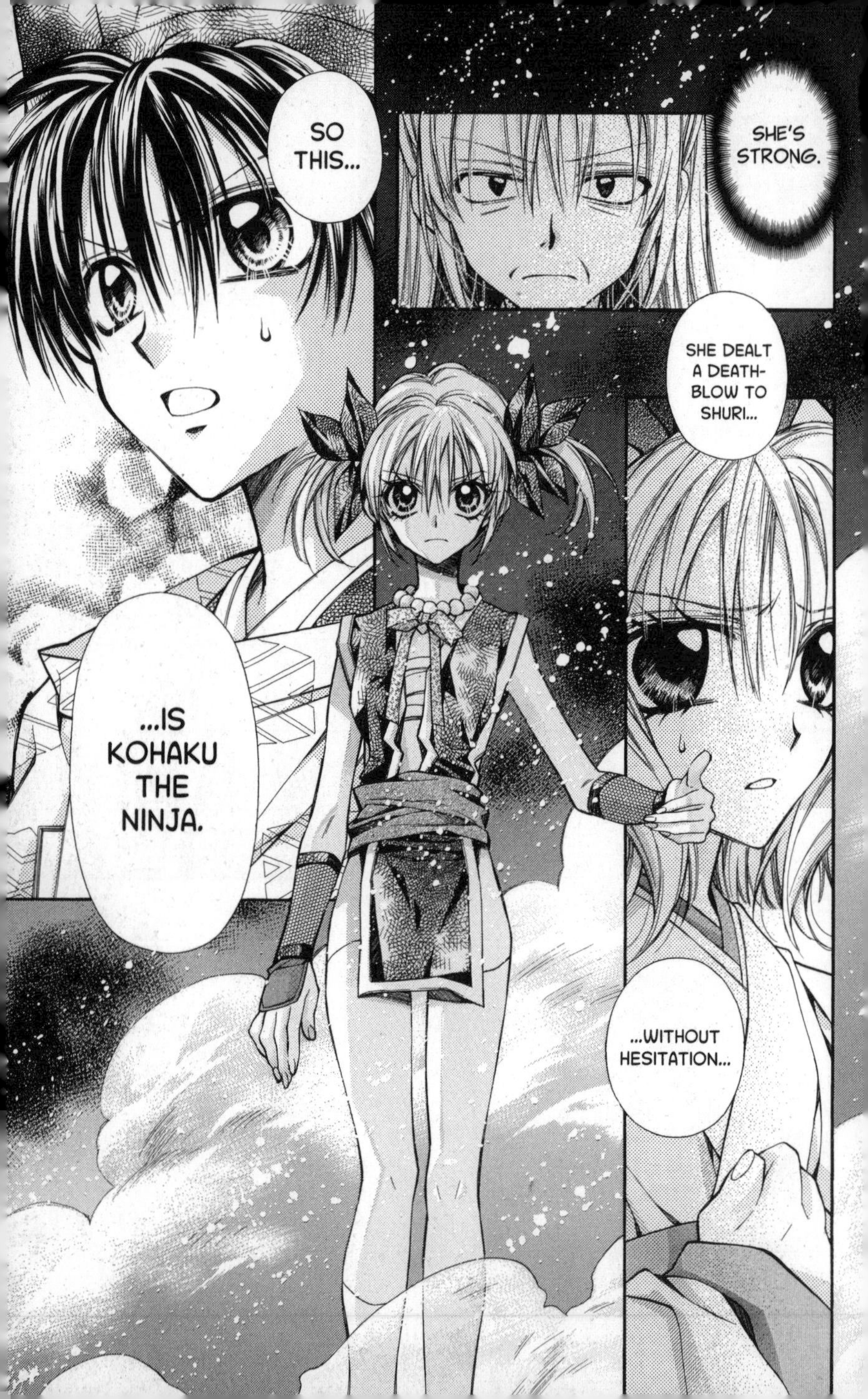
SHE'S STRONG.
SHE DEALT A DEATH-BLOW TO SHURI...
...WITHOUT HESITATION...
SO THIS...
...IS KOHAKU THE NINJA.

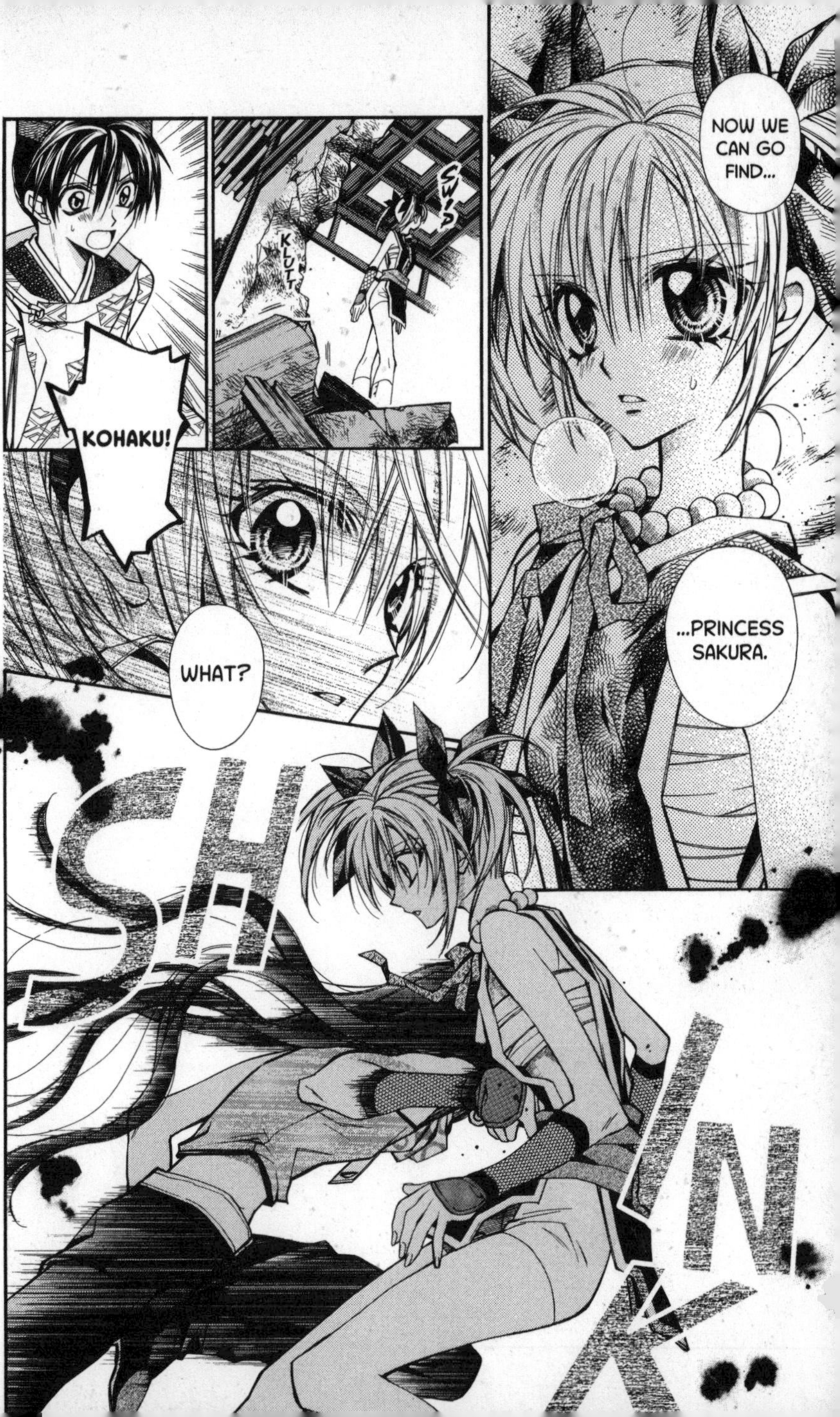
NOW WE CAN GO FIND...
...PRINCESS SAKURA.
SWIP
KLUTT
KOHAKU!
WHAT?
SHINK

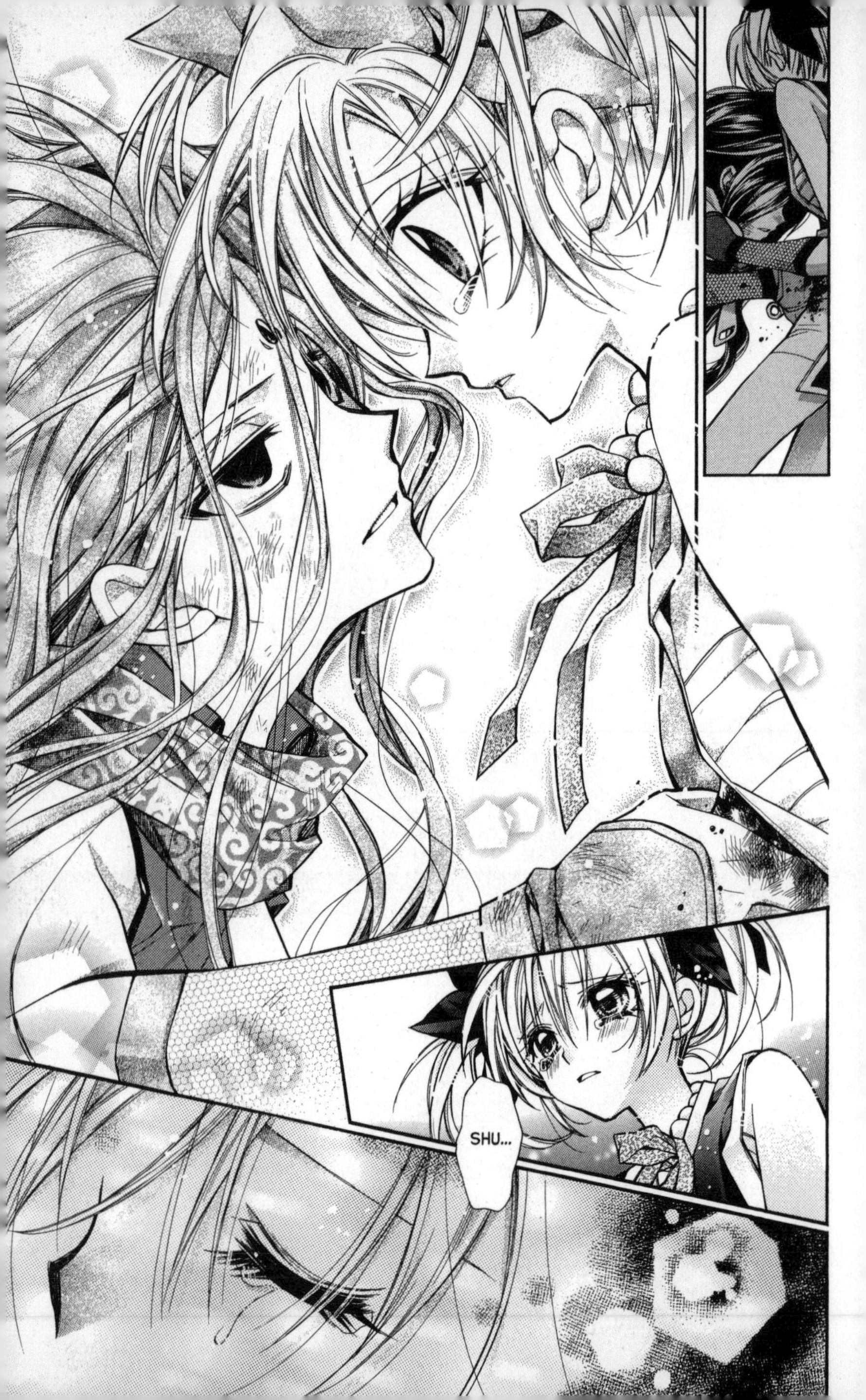
SHU...

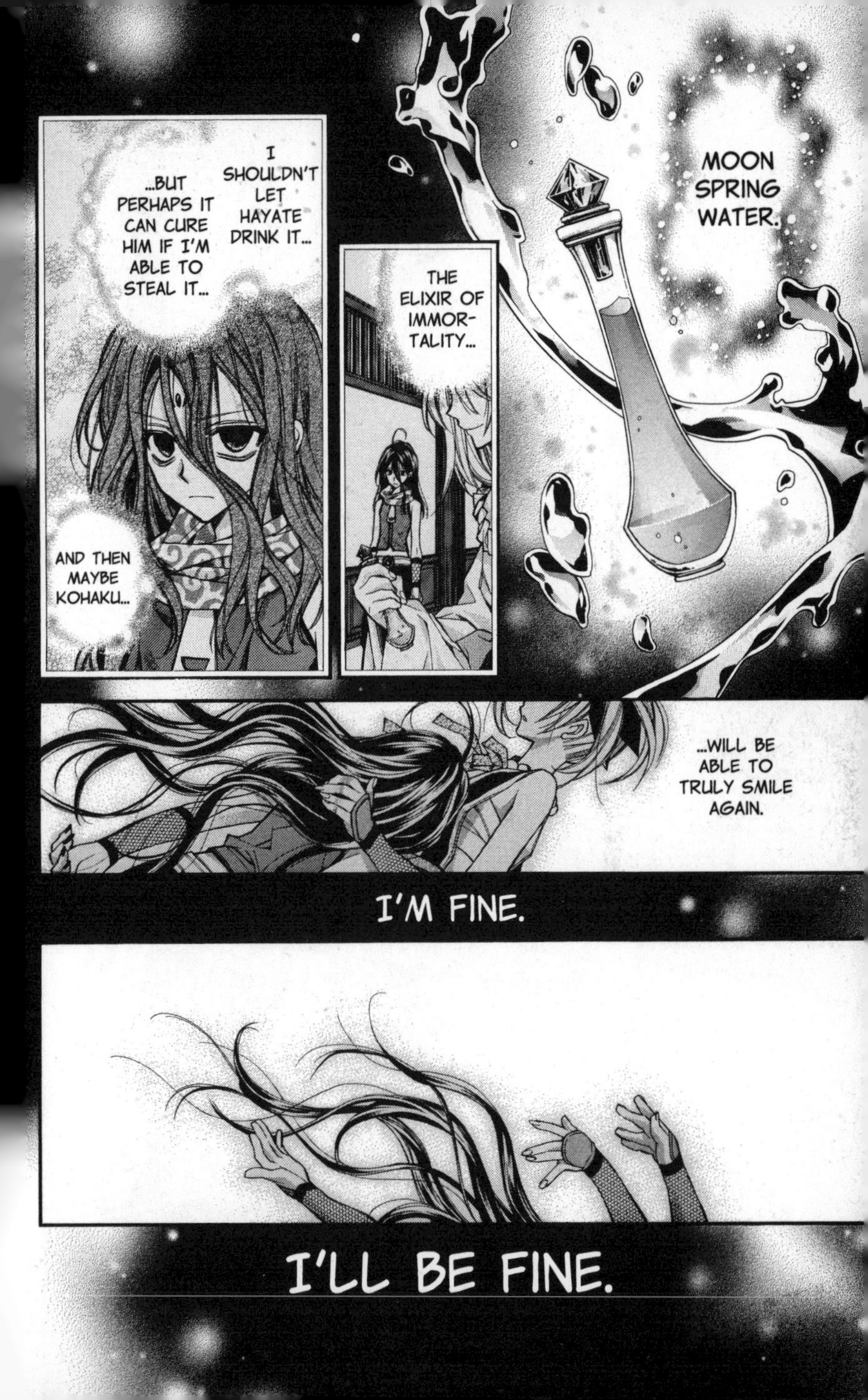
MOON SPRING WATER.
THE ELIXIR OF IMMORTALITY...
I SHOULDN'T LET HAYATE DRINK IT...
...BUT PERHAPS IT CAN CURE HIM IF I'M ABLE TO STEAL IT...
AND THEN MAYBE KOHAKU...
...WILL BE ABLE TO TRULY SMILE AGAIN.
I'M FINE.
I'LL BE FINE.

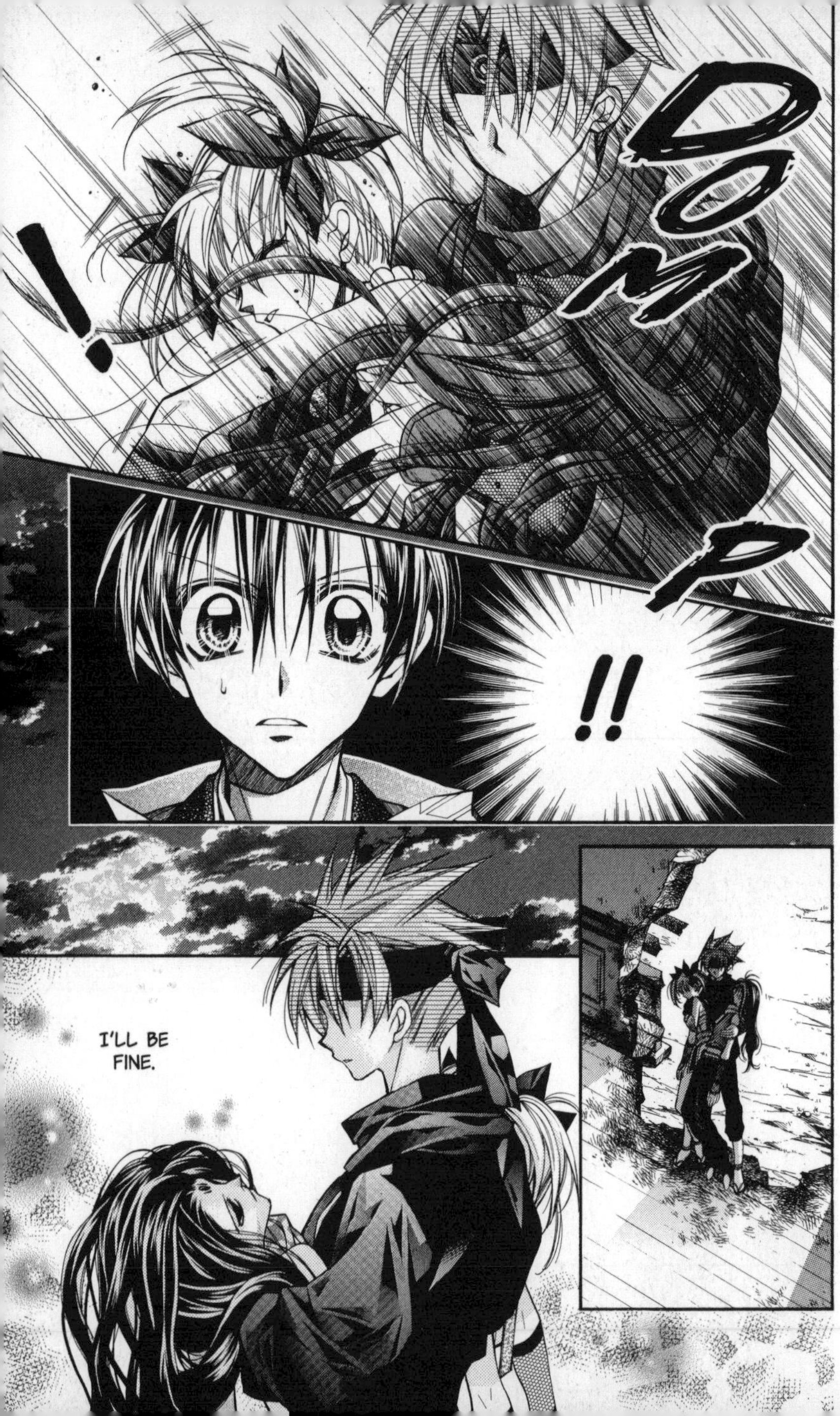
DOMP
!
!!
I'LL BE FINE.

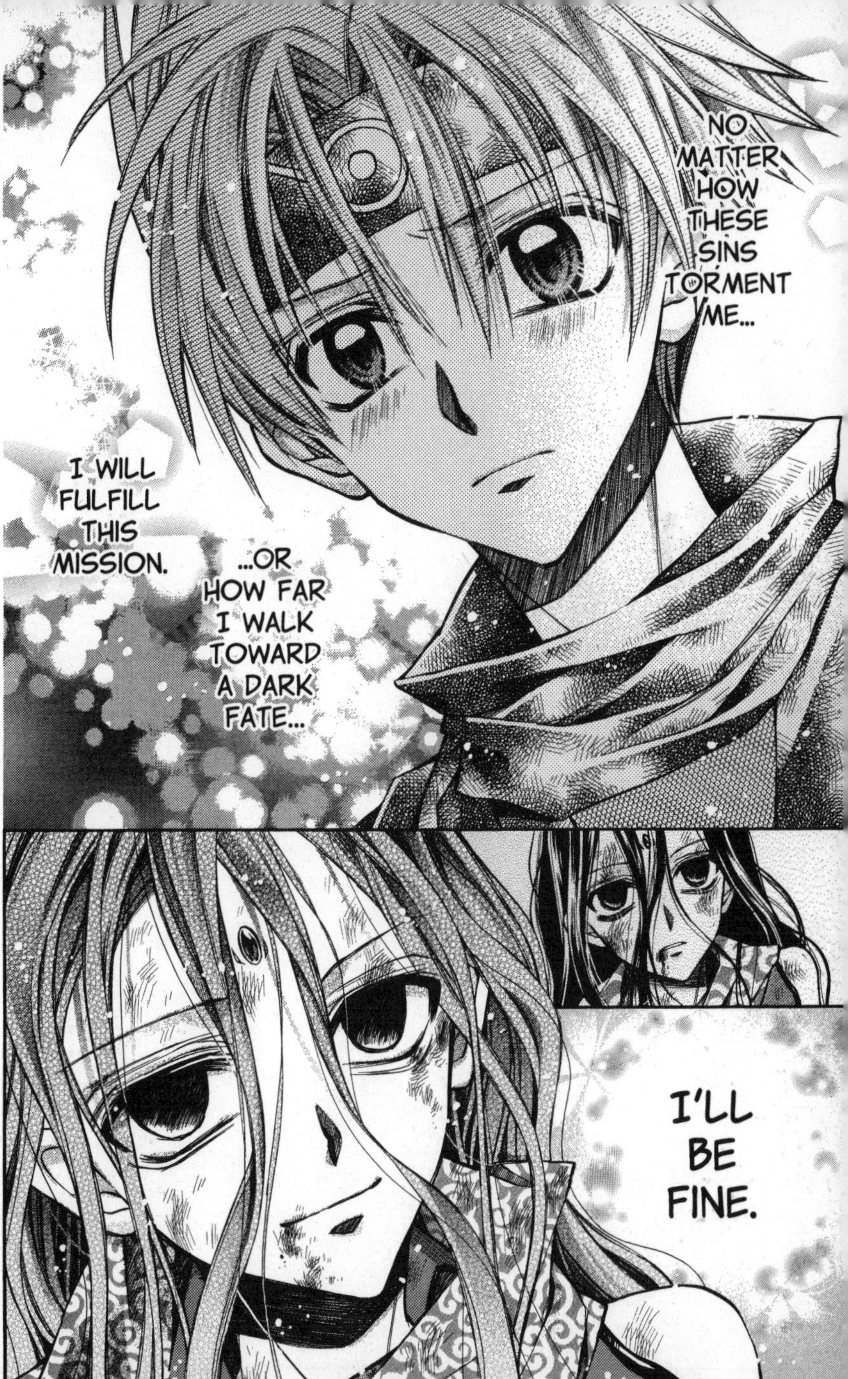
NO MATTER HOW THESE SINS TORMENT ME...
...OR HOW FAR I WALK TOWARD A DARK FATE...
I WILL FULFILL THIS MISSION.
I'LL BE FINE.

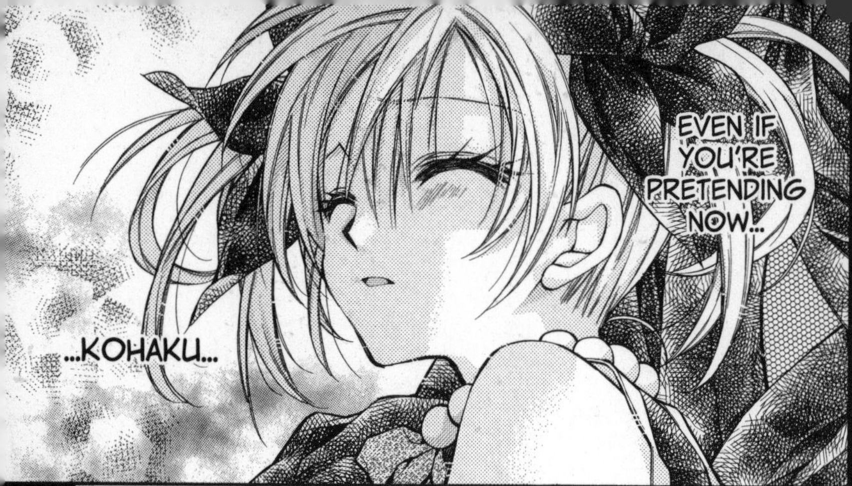
EVEN IF YOU'RE PRETENDING NOW...
...KOHAKU...

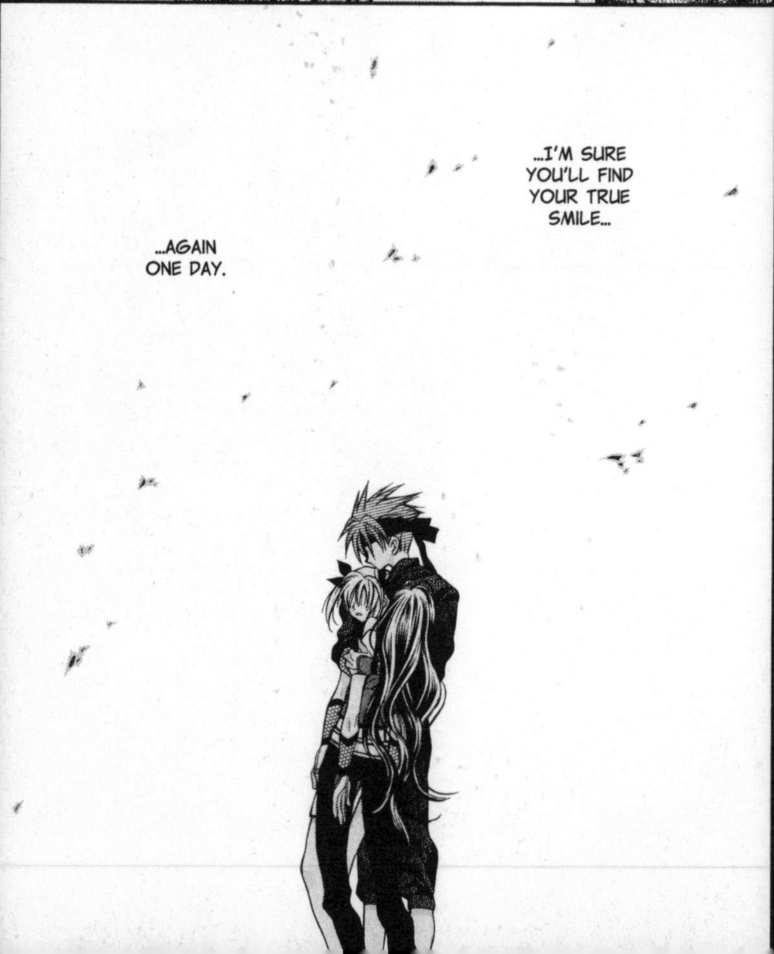
...I'M SURE YOU'LL FIND YOUR TRUE SMILE...
...AGAIN ONE DAY.

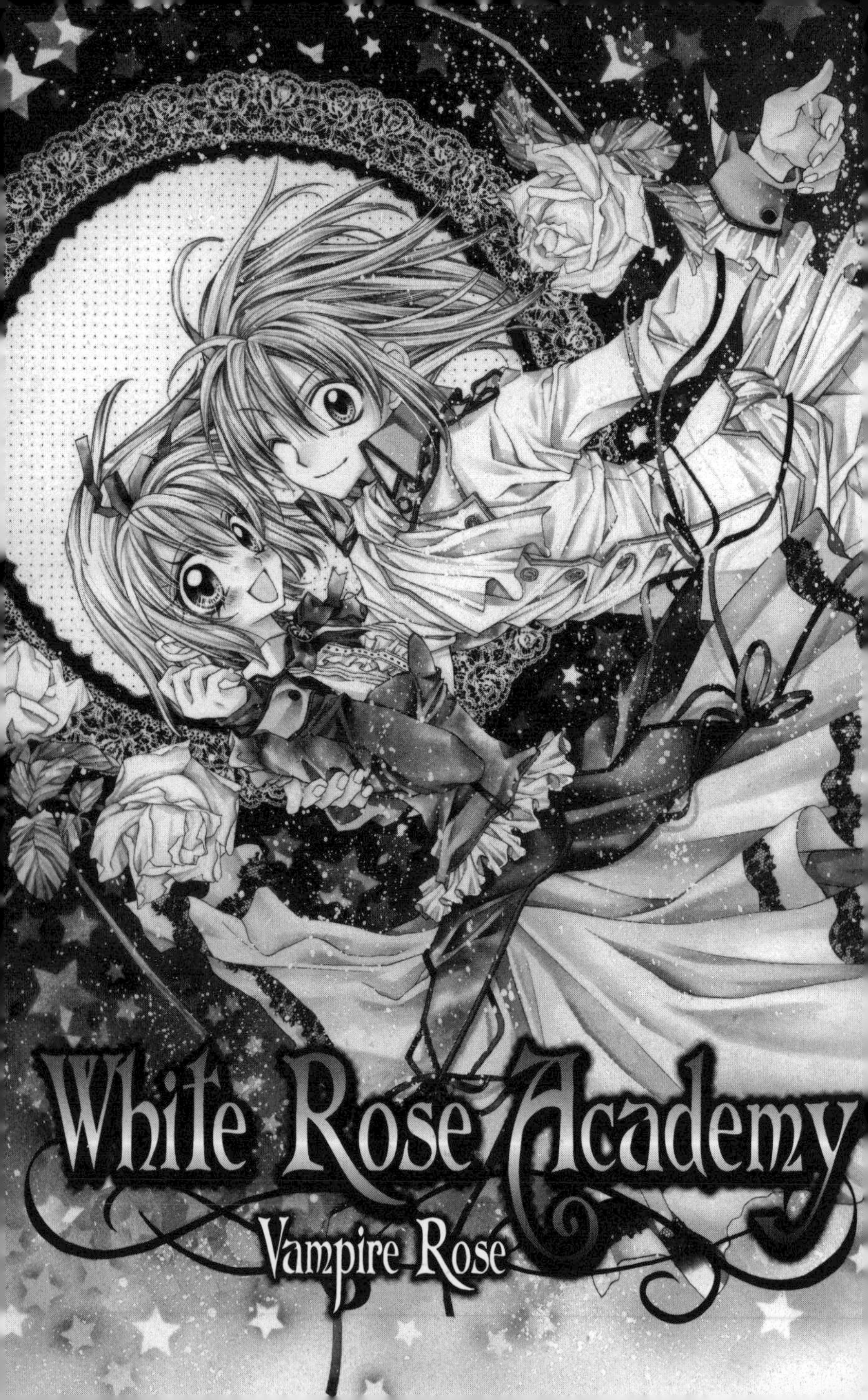
White Rose Academy
Vampire Rose

One-Shot ☆ "White Rose Academy: Vampire Rose"

☀ I'm giving away the story.

This is a 50-page story. I started drawing manga when I was 15 years old. (I made my debut when I was 18 years old.) Back then I was lucky enough to be given a series before I really had the proper skills to draw manga, so I'm still bad at coming up with one-shots. And this was 50 pages too. It was very difficult.

I wanted to include a magic spell and make the story slightly supernatural. When I was small, I found a book on magic (I forget the title, sorry) at the library, and the book had a magic spell in it. I didn't really believe it would work (but maybe...). But I was a little interested... So that's why I wanted to write about it. (By the way, the spell in that book was "Sakana saka saka sakanashan," and it was very different from the spell that appears in this. I liked that spell. ♥

To be honest, I have a thing for the occult. I have tons of books about Out-of-Place Artifacts (OOParts) and Unidentified Marine Animals (UMA). UFOs are interesting too.

I have the urge to draw something western when I'm working on *Sakura-Hime: The Legend of Princess Sakura.* (I want to use lots of lace and things! You know...)

My favorite character is Hikaru. ♪

A castle's rose is reflected
upon the door.

A singing ring
and a silver bird.

Fade away, fade away,
labyrinth.

Who are you?

IT'S A MAGIC SPELL...

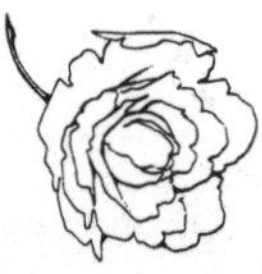

...I'VE KNOWN SINCE I WAS SMALL.

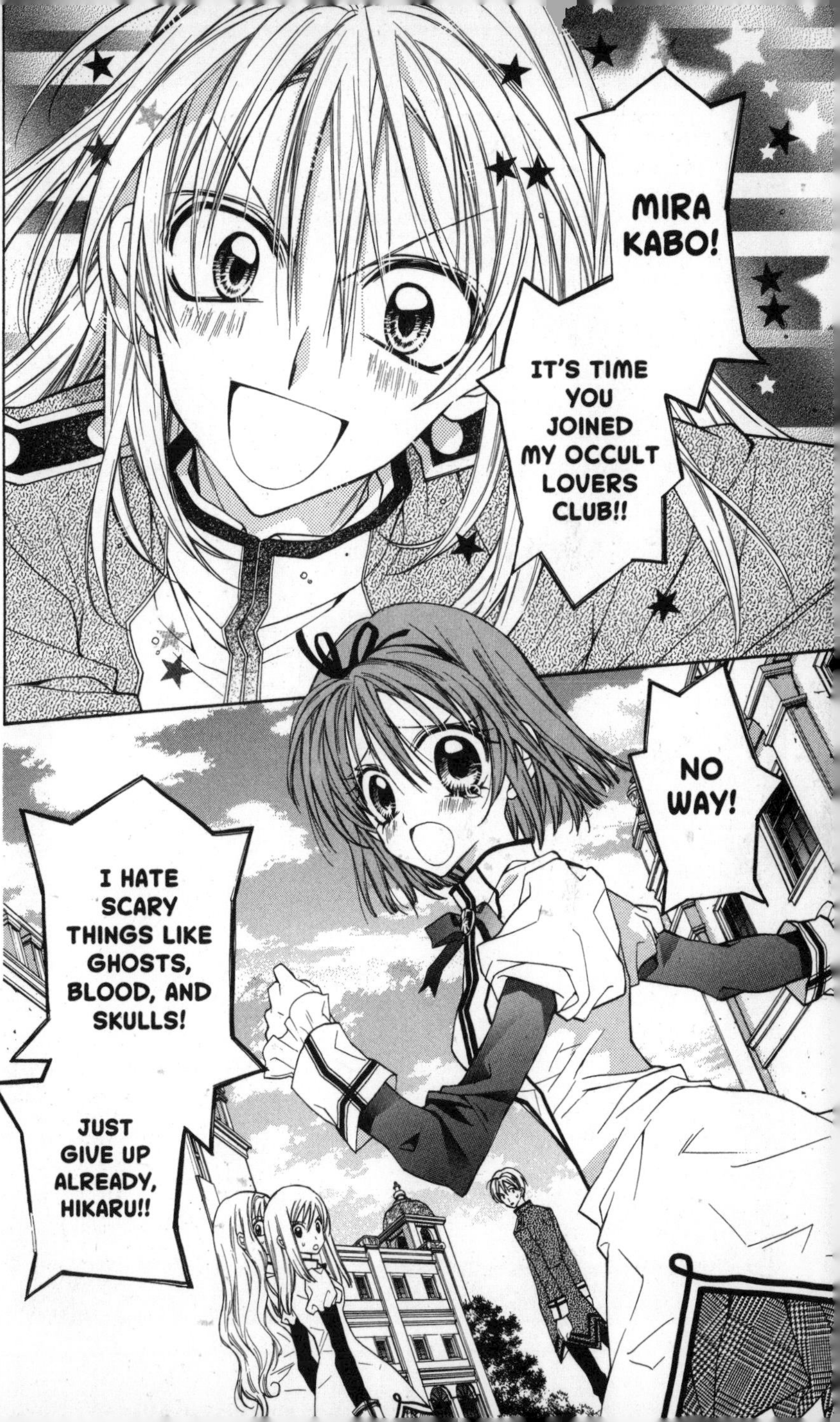
MIRA KABO!
IT'S TIME YOU JOINED MY OCCULT LOVERS CLUB!!
NO WAY!
I HATE SCARY THINGS LIKE GHOSTS, BLOOD, AND SKULLS!
JUST GIVE UP ALREADY, HIKARU!!

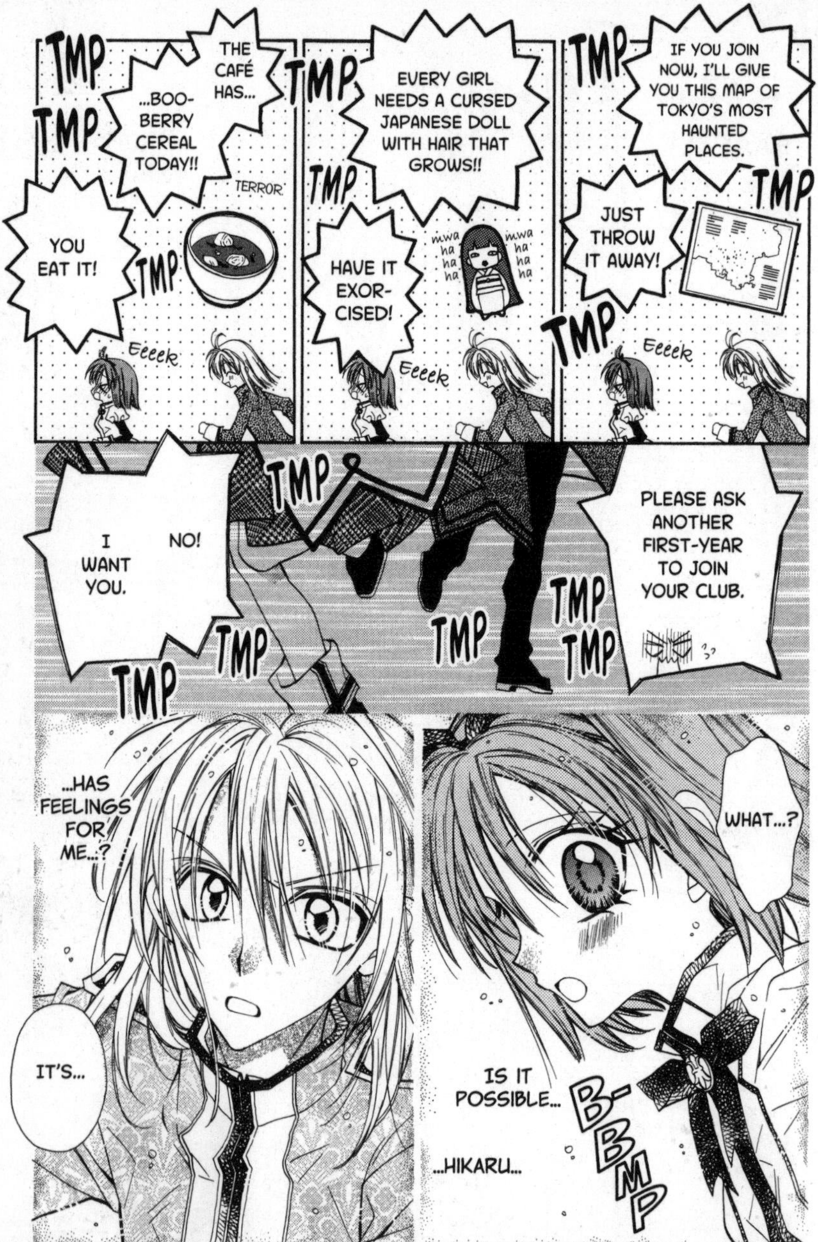
TMP
IF YOU JOIN NOW, I'LL GIVE YOU THIS MAP OF TOKYO'S MOST HAUNTED PLACES.
TMP
JUST THROW IT AWAY!
TMP
Eeeek
TMP
EVERY GIRL NEEDS A CURSED JAPANESE DOLL WITH HAIR THAT GROWS!!
TMP
mwa ha ha ha
mwa ha ha ha
HAVE IT EXORCISED!
Eeeek
THE CAFÉ HAS...
...BOO-BERRY CEREAL TODAY!!
TMP
TMP
TERROR
YOU EAT IT!
TMP
Eeeek
PLEASE ASK ANOTHER FIRST-YEAR TO JOIN YOUR CLUB.
TMP
TMP
TMP
TMP
NO!
I WANT YOU.
TMP
TMP
WHAT...?
IS IT POSSIBLE...
...HIKARU...
B-BMP
...HAS FEELINGS FOR ME...?
IT'S...

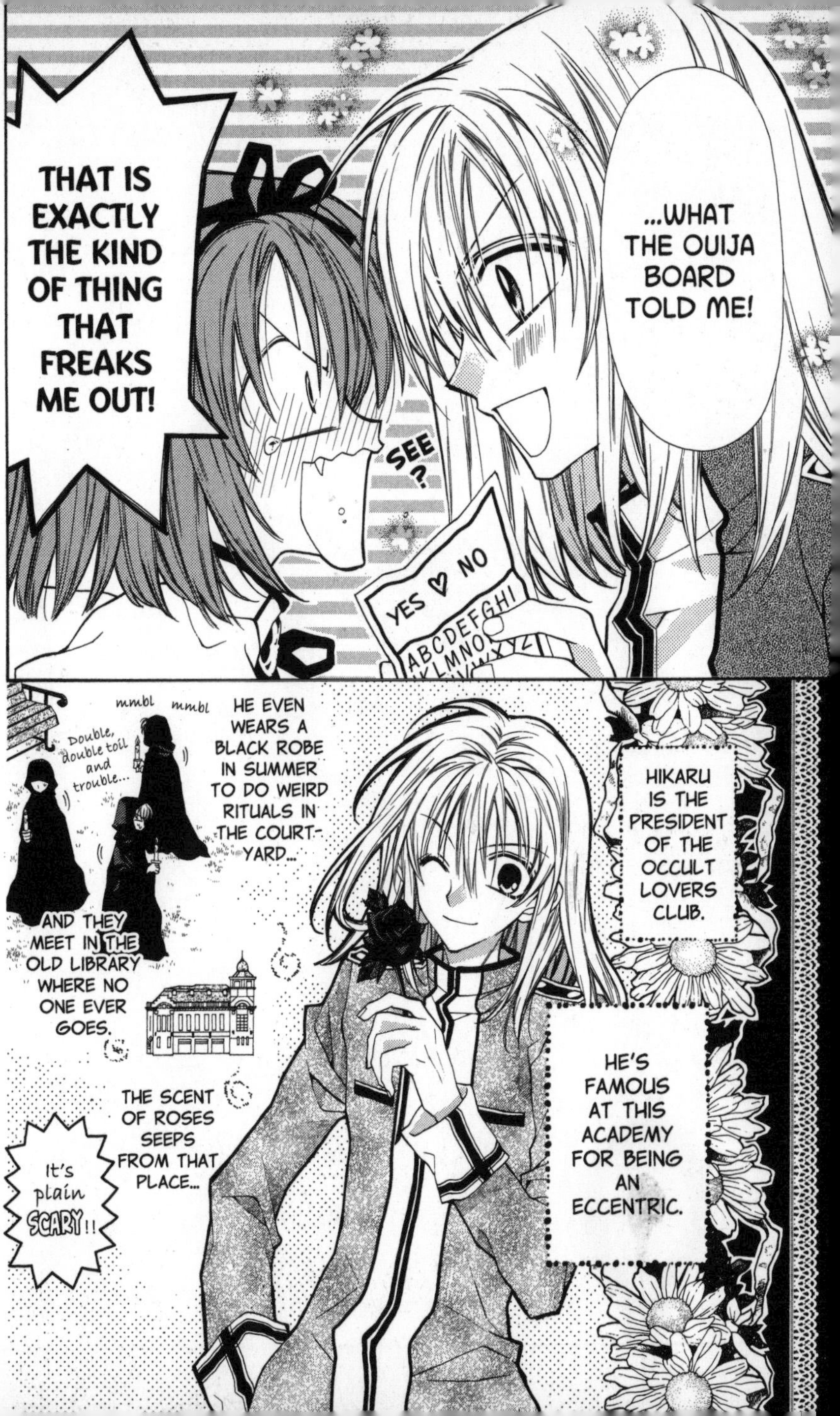

...WHAT THE OUIJA BOARD TOLD ME!
SEE?
YES ♡ NO
THAT IS EXACTLY THE KIND OF THING THAT FREAKS ME OUT!
HIKARU IS THE PRESIDENT OF THE OCCULT LOVERS CLUB.
HE'S FAMOUS AT THIS ACADEMY FOR BEING AN ECCENTRIC.
HE EVEN WEARS A BLACK ROBE IN SUMMER TO DO WEIRD RITUALS IN THE COURT-YARD...
mmbl mmbl
Double, double toil and trouble...
AND THEY MEET IN THE OLD LIBRARY WHERE NO ONE EVER GOES.
THE SCENT OF ROSES SEEPS FROM THAT PLACE...
It's plain SCARY!!

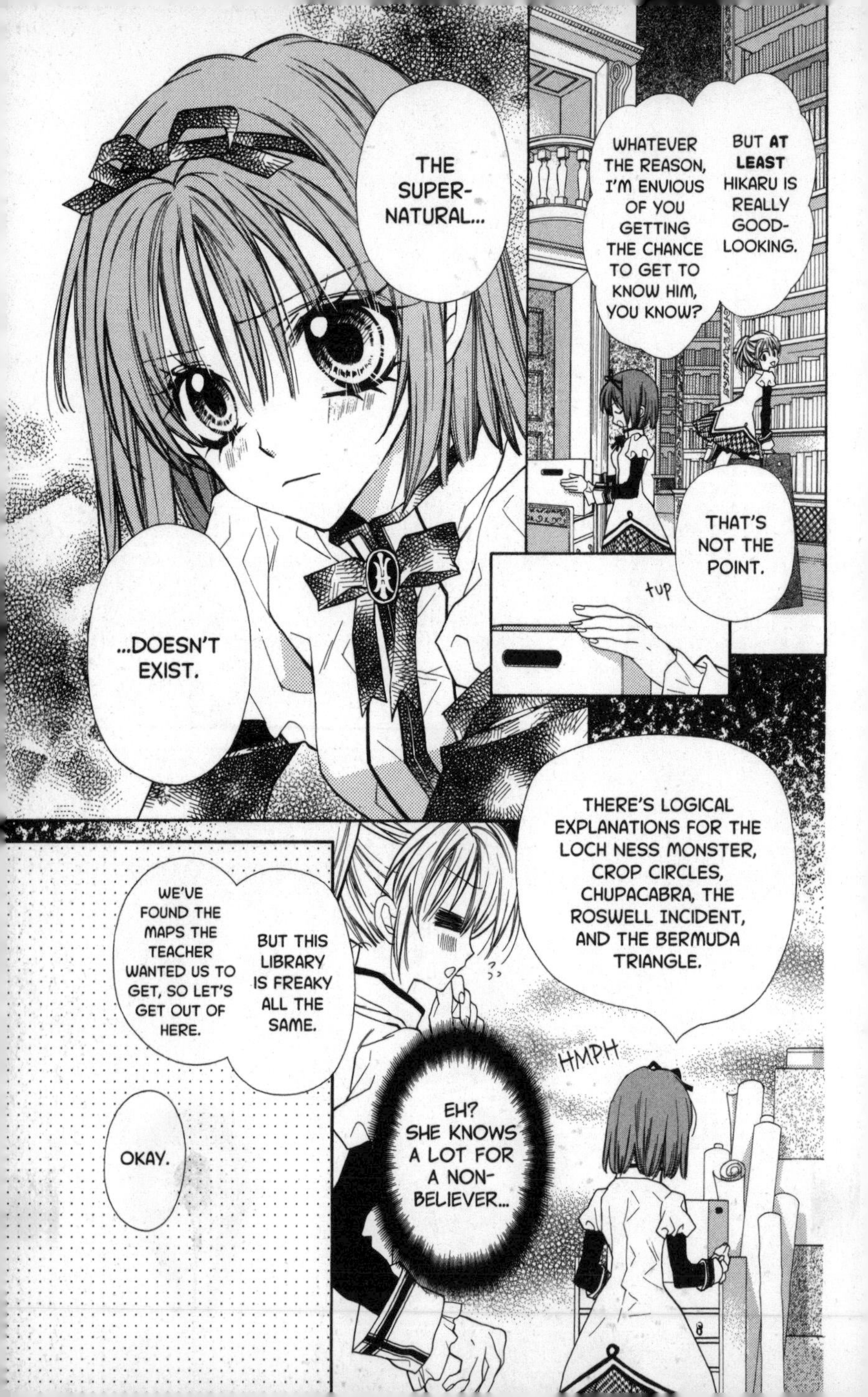
BUT AT LEAST HIKARU IS REALLY GOOD-LOOKING.
WHATEVER THE REASON, I'M ENVIOUS OF YOU GETTING THE CHANCE TO GET TO KNOW HIM, YOU KNOW?
THAT'S NOT THE POINT.
tup
THE SUPER-NATURAL...
...DOESN'T EXIST.
THERE'S LOGICAL EXPLANATIONS FOR THE LOCH NESS MONSTER, CROP CIRCLES, CHUPACABRA, THE ROSWELL INCIDENT, AND THE BERMUDA TRIANGLE.
HMPH
EH? SHE KNOWS A LOT FOR A NON-BELIEVER...
BUT THIS LIBRARY IS FREAKY ALL THE SAME.
WE'VE FOUND THE MAPS THE TEACHER WANTED US TO GET, SO LET'S GET OUT OF HERE.
OKAY.

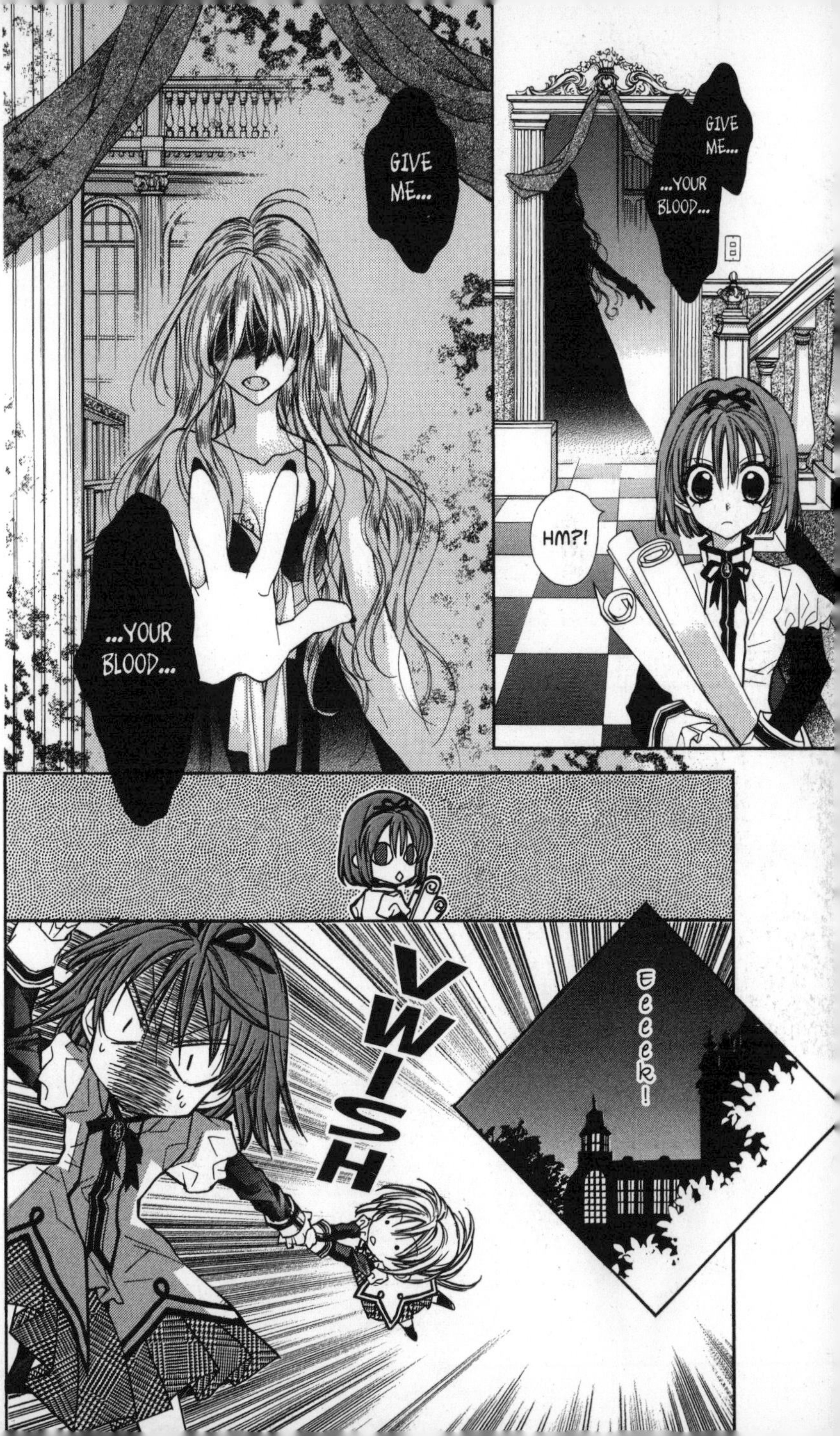
GIVE ME...
...YOUR BLOOD...
HM?!
GIVE ME...
...YOUR BLOOD...
Eeeek!
VWISH

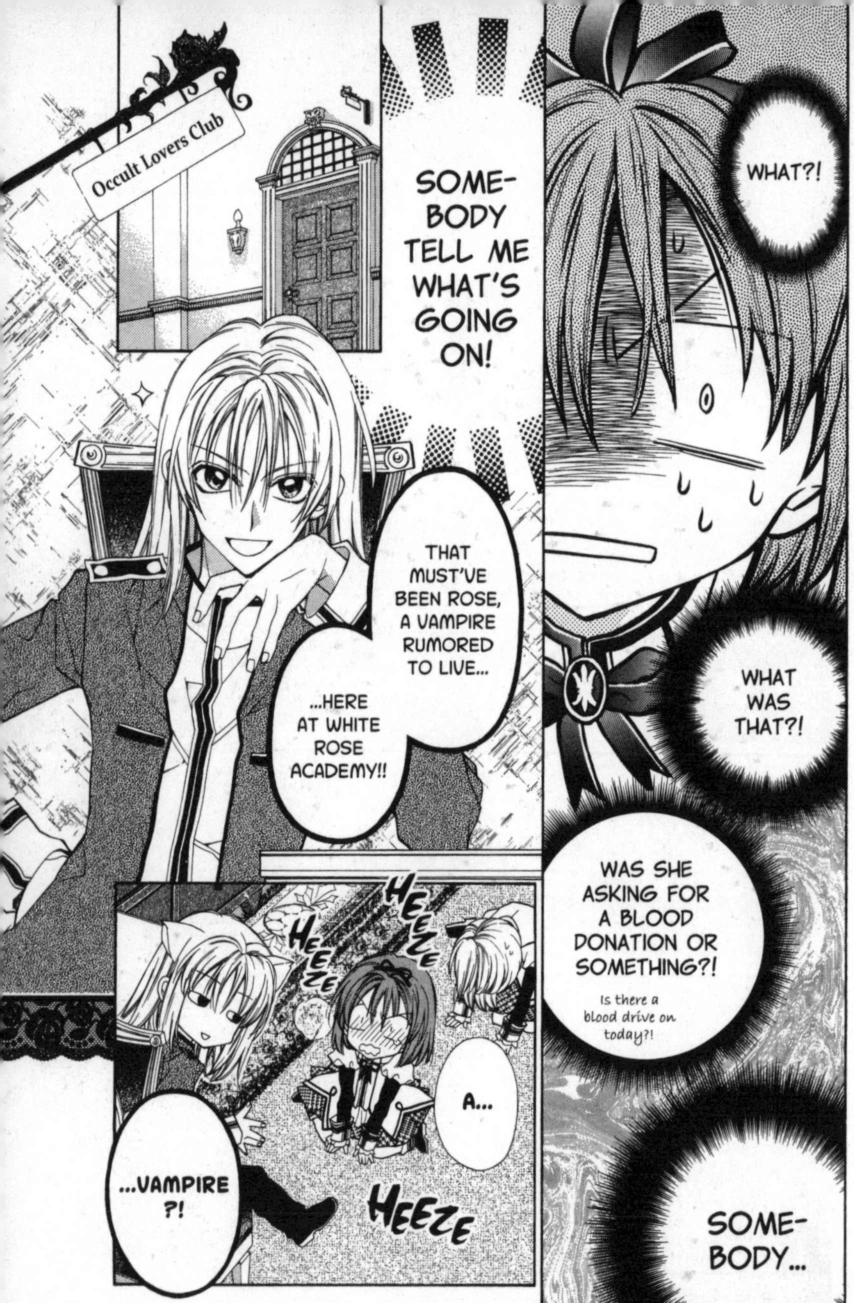
WHAT?!
WHAT WAS THAT?!
WAS SHE ASKING FOR A BLOOD DONATION OR SOMETHING?!
Is there a blood drive on today?!
SOME-BODY...
SOME-BODY TELL ME WHAT'S GOING ON!
Occult Lovers Club
THAT MUST'VE BEEN ROSE, A VAMPIRE RUMORED TO LIVE...
...HERE AT WHITE ROSE ACADEMY!!
HEEZE
HEEZE
A...
...VAMPIRE ?!
HEEZE

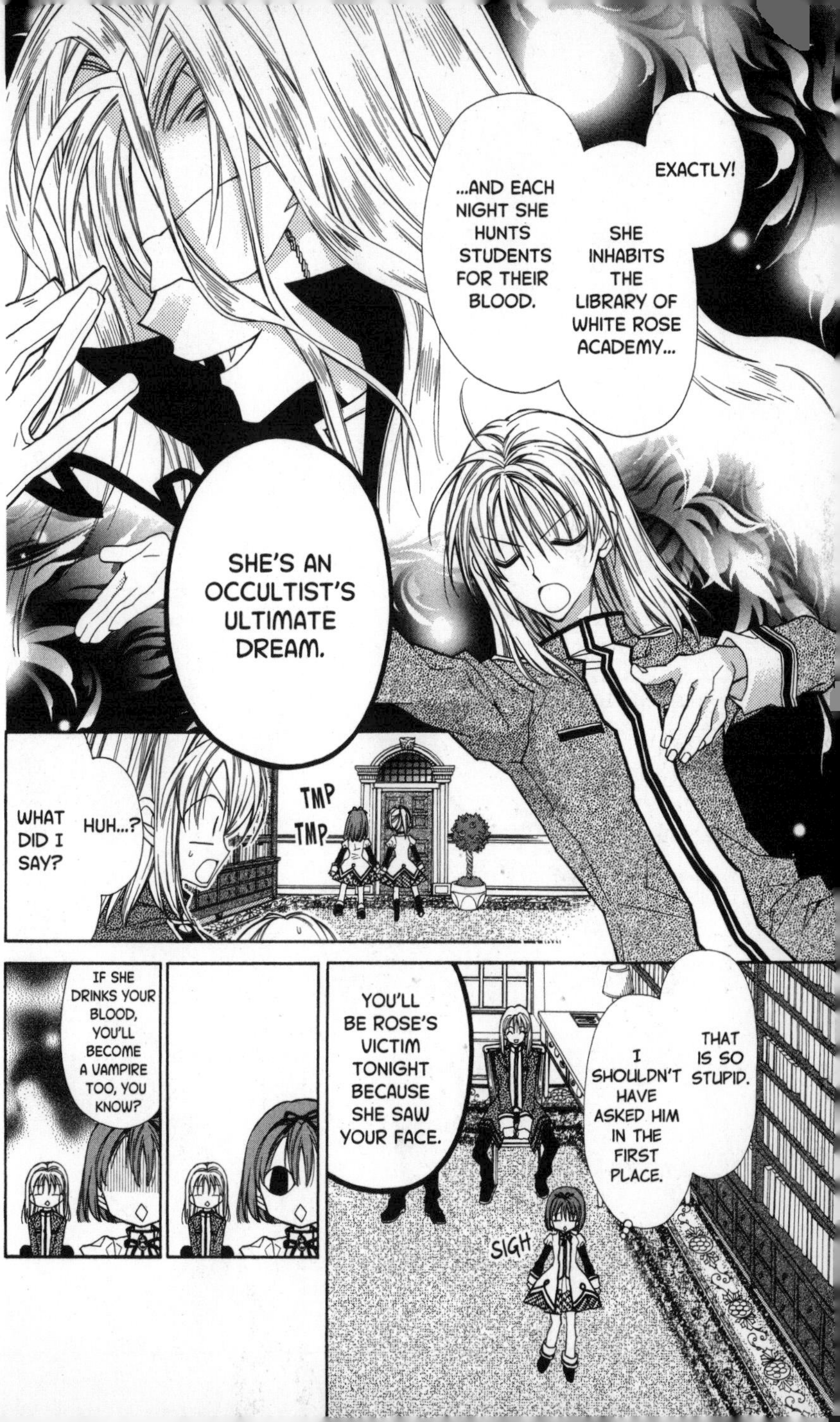
EXACTLY!
SHE INHABITS THE LIBRARY OF WHITE ROSE ACADEMY...
...AND EACH NIGHT SHE HUNTS STUDENTS FOR THEIR BLOOD.
SHE'S AN OCCULTIST'S ULTIMATE DREAM.
TMP
TMP
HUH...?
WHAT DID I SAY?
THAT IS SO STUPID.
I SHOULDN'T HAVE ASKED HIM IN THE FIRST PLACE.
SIGH
YOU'LL BE ROSE'S VICTIM TONIGHT BECAUSE SHE SAW YOUR FACE.
IF SHE DRINKS YOUR BLOOD, YOU'LL BECOME A VAMPIRE TOO, YOU KNOW?

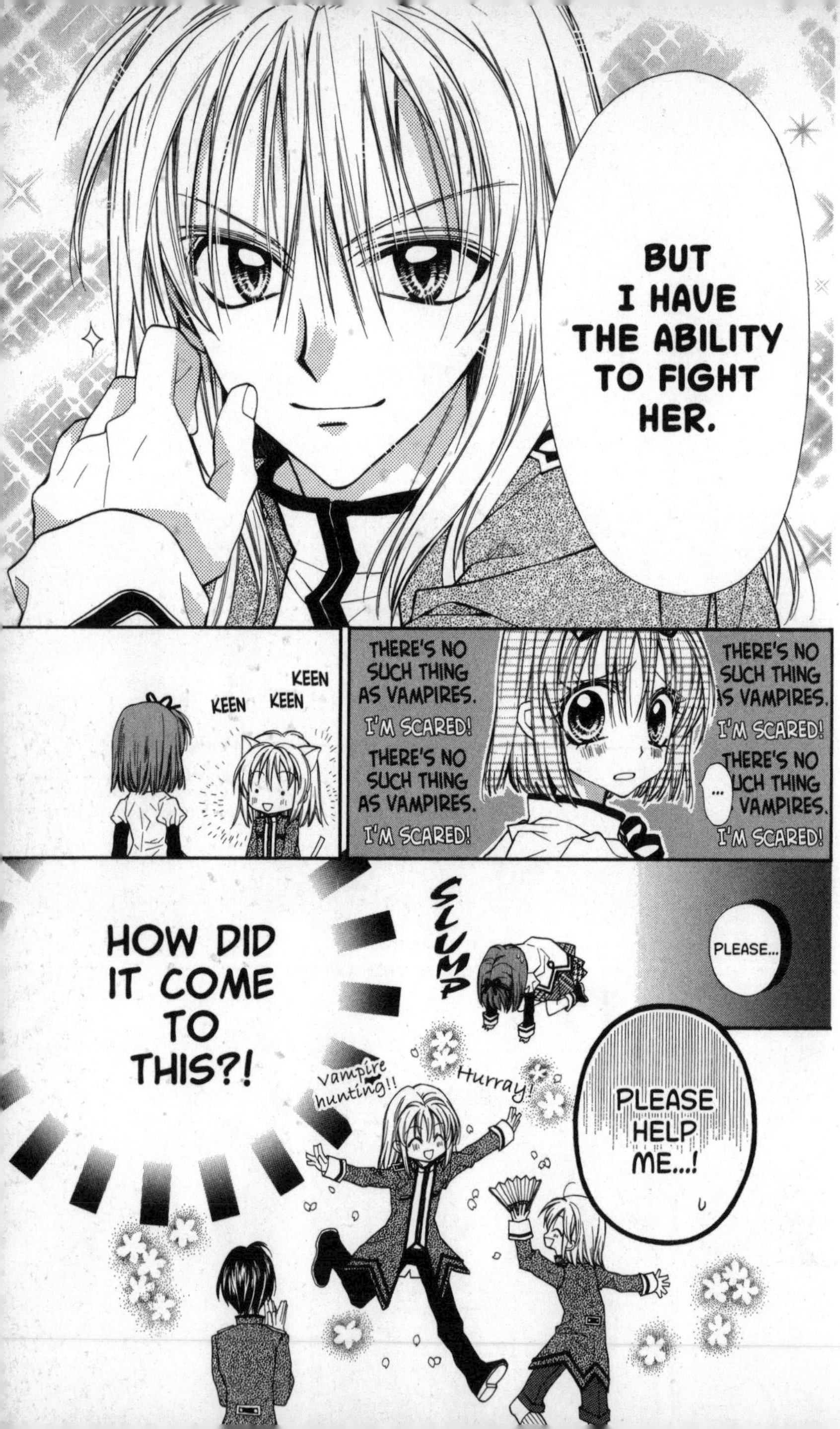
BUT I HAVE THE ABILITY TO FIGHT HER.
THERE'S NO SUCH THING S VAMPIRES.
I'M SCARED!
THERE'S NO UCH THING VAMPIRES.
I'M SCARED!
...
THERE'S NO SUCH THING AS VAMPIRES.
I'M SCARED!
THERE'S NO SUCH THING AS VAMPIRES.
I'M SCARED!
KEEN
KEEN
KEEN
PLEASE...
SLUMP
PLEASE HELP ME...!
Hurray!
vampire hunting!!
HOW DID IT COME TO THIS?!

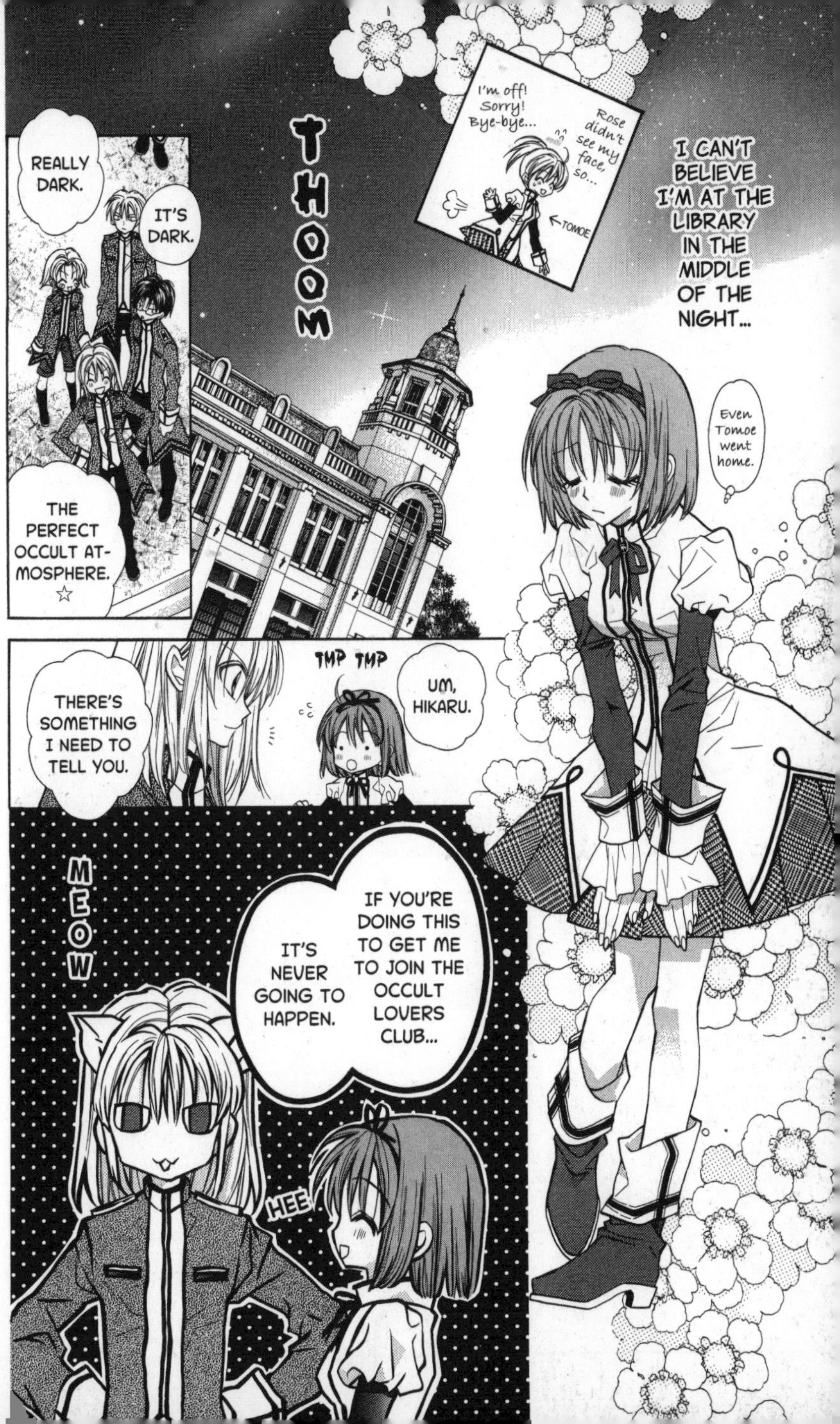
Rose didn't see my face, so...
I'm off! Sorry! Bye-bye...
←TOMOE
I CAN'T BELIEVE I'M AT THE LIBRARY IN THE MIDDLE OF THE NIGHT...
Even Tomoe went home.
THOOM
IT'S DARK.
REALLY DARK.
THE PERFECT OCCULT AT-MOSPHERE. ☆
TMP TMP
UM, HIKARU.
THERE'S SOMETHING I NEED TO TELL YOU.
IF YOU'RE DOING THIS TO GET ME TO JOIN THE OCCULT LOVERS CLUB...
IT'S NEVER GOING TO HAPPEN.
MEOW
HEE

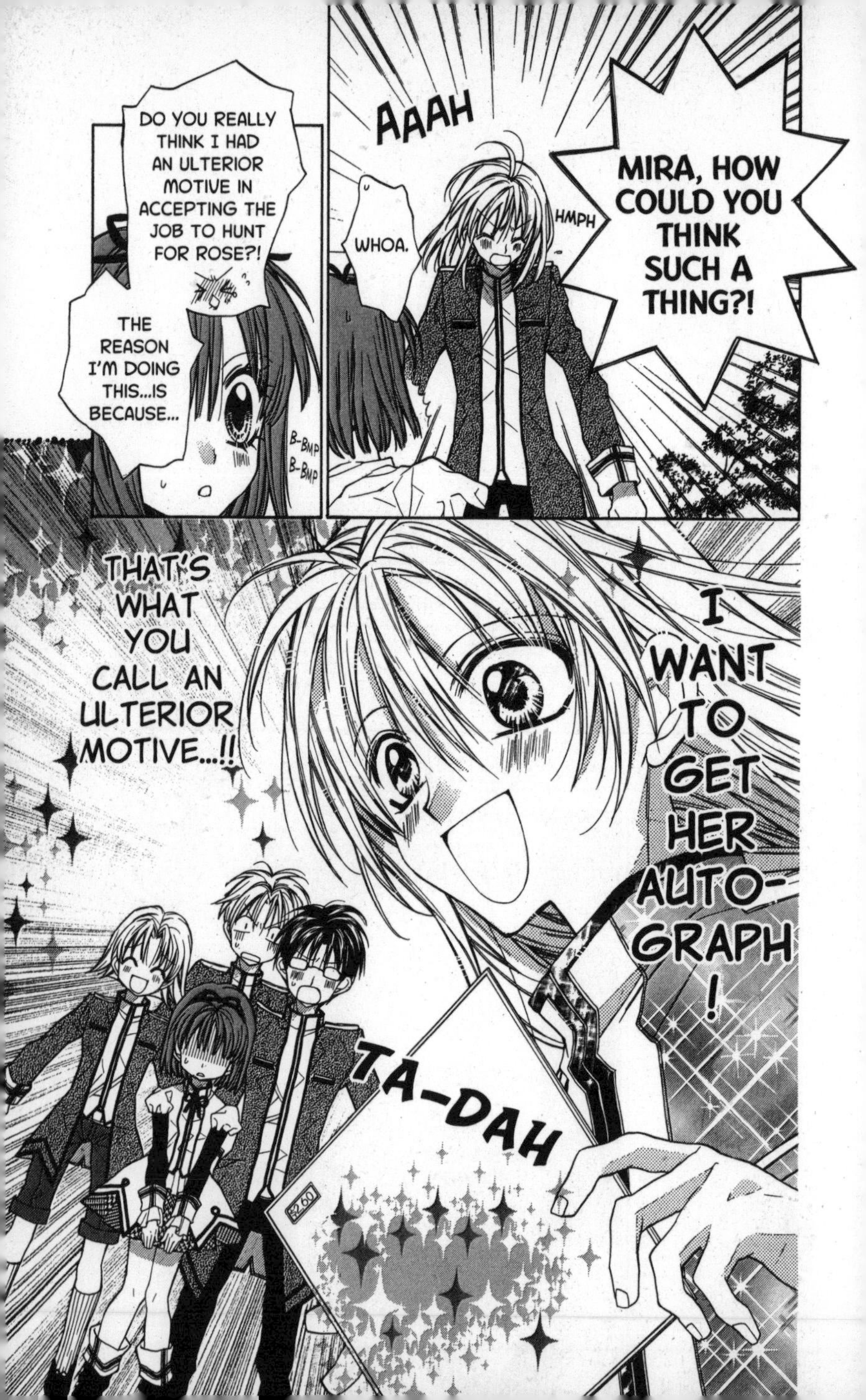
MIRA, HOW COULD YOU THINK SUCH A THING?!
AAAH
HMPH
WHOA.
DO YOU REALLY THINK I HAD AN ULTERIOR MOTIVE IN ACCEPTING THE JOB TO HUNT FOR ROSE?!
THE REASON I'M DOING THIS...IS BECAUSE...
B-BMP B-BMP
I WANT TO GET HER AUTO-GRAPH!
TA-DAH
THAT'S WHAT YOU CALL AN ULTERIOR MOTIVE...!!

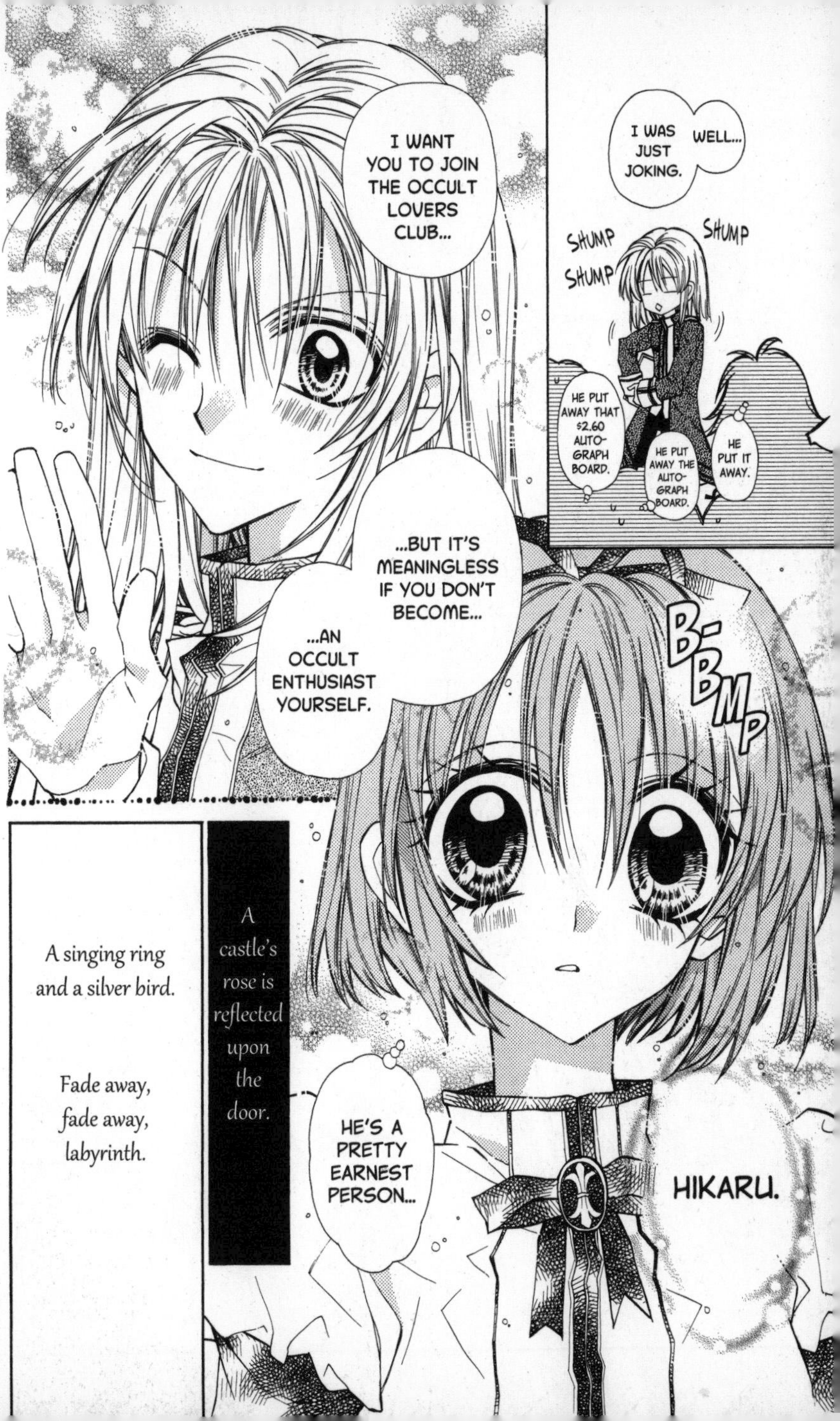
WELL...
I WAS JUST JOKING.
SHUMP
SHUMP
SHUMP
HE PUT IT AWAY.
HE PUT AWAY THE AUTOGRAPH BOARD.
HE PUT AWAY THAT $2.60 AUTOGRAPH BOARD.
I WANT YOU TO JOIN THE OCCULT LOVERS CLUB...
...BUT IT'S MEANINGLESS IF YOU DON'T BECOME...
...AN OCCULT ENTHUSIAST YOURSELF.
B-BMP
HIKARU.
HE'S A PRETTY EARNEST PERSON...
A castle's rose is reflected upon the door.
A singing ring and a silver bird.
Fade away, fade away, labyrinth.

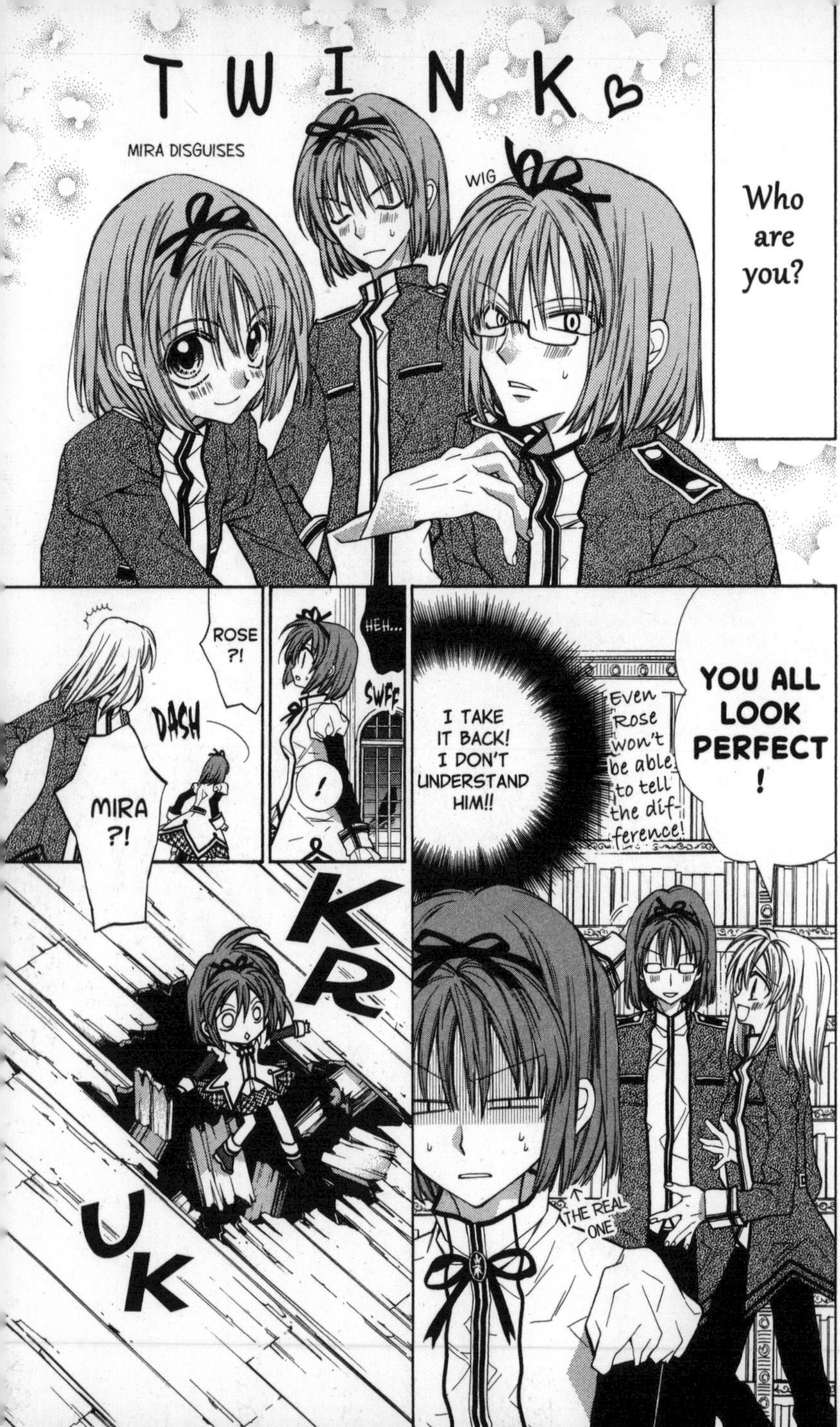
Who are you?
TWINK ♡
WIG
MIRA DISGUISES
YOU ALL LOOK PERFECT!
Even Rose won't be able to tell the difference!
I TAKE IT BACK! I DON'T UNDERSTAND HIM!!
THE REAL ONE
HEH...
SWFF
!
ROSE ?!
DASH
MIRA ?!
KR
UK

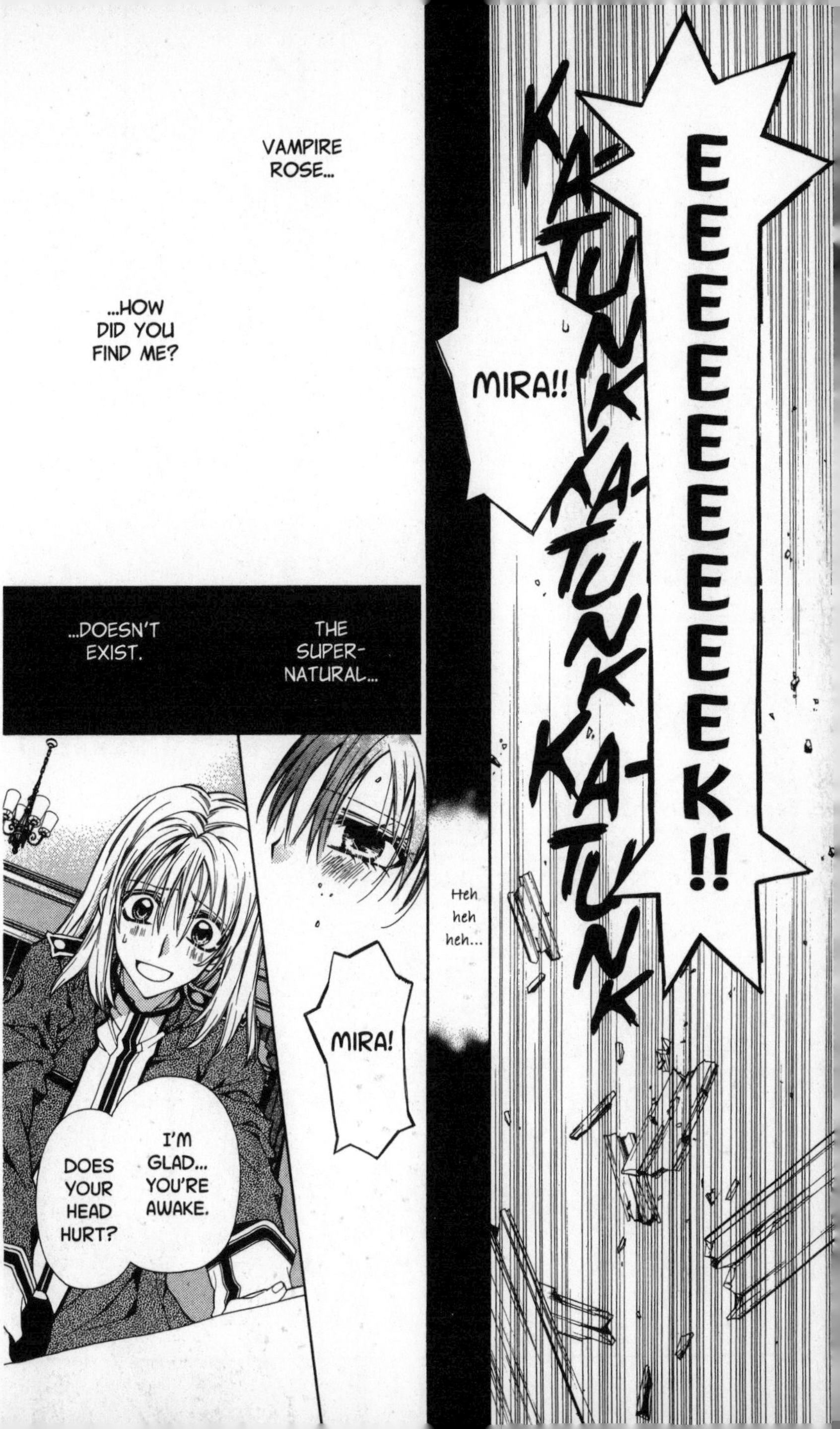
EEEEEEEEEEEK!!
KA-TUNK KA-TUNK KA-TUNK
MIRA!!
Heh heh heh...
VAMPIRE ROSE...
...HOW DID YOU FIND ME?
THE SUPER-NATURAL...
...DOESN'T EXIST.
MIRA!
I'M GLAD... YOU'RE AWAKE.
DOES YOUR HEAD HURT?

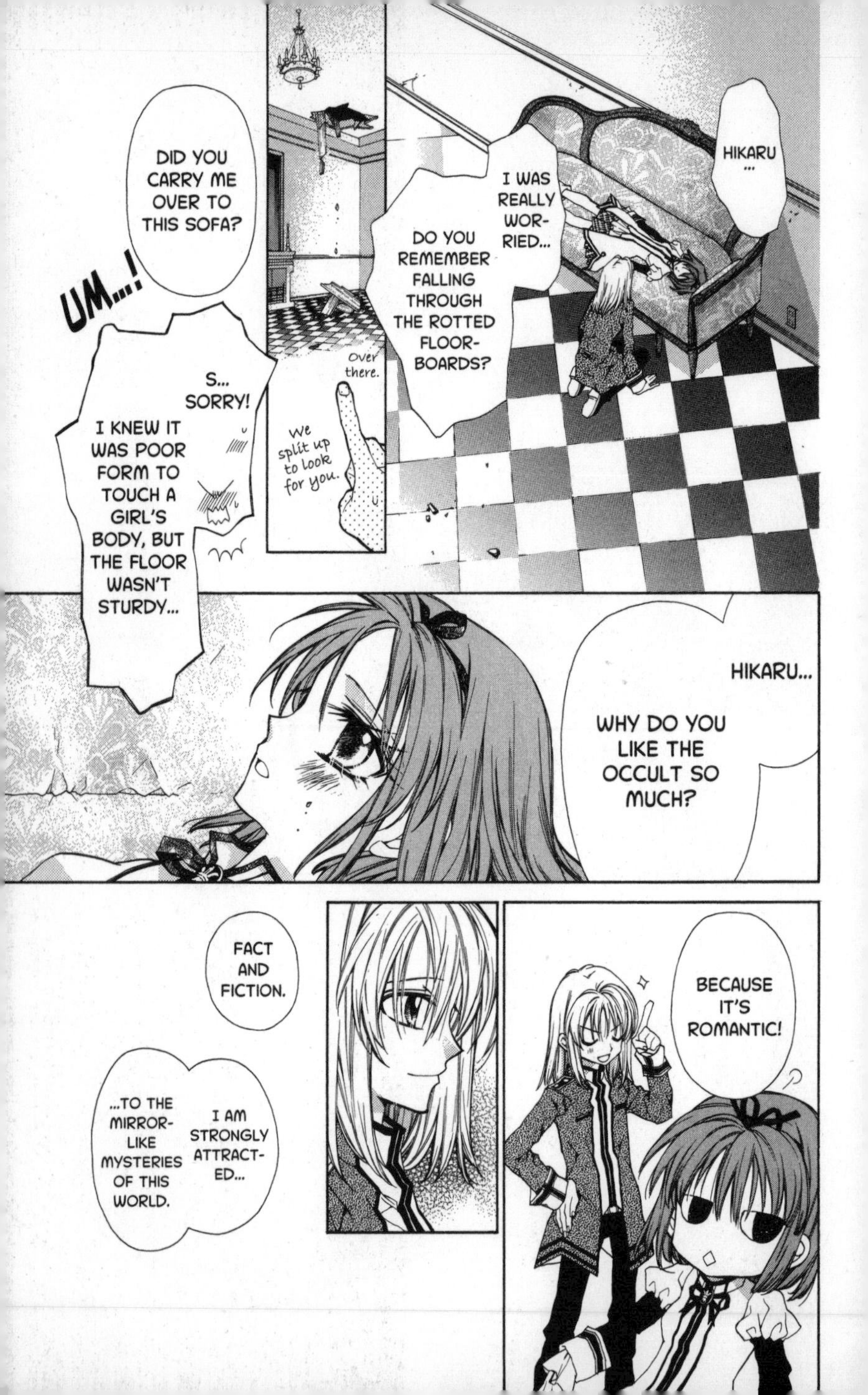
HIKARU ...
I WAS REALLY WOR-RIED...
DO YOU REMEMBER FALLING THROUGH THE ROTTED FLOOR-BOARDS?
DID YOU CARRY ME OVER TO THIS SOFA?
UM...!
S... SORRY! I KNEW IT WAS POOR FORM TO TOUCH A GIRL'S BODY, BUT THE FLOOR WASN'T STURDY...
Over there.
We split up to look for you.
HIKARU... WHY DO YOU LIKE THE OCCULT SO MUCH?
BECAUSE IT'S ROMANTIC!
FACT AND FICTION.
I AM STRONGLY ATTRACT-ED...
...TO THE MIRROR-LIKE MYSTERIES OF THIS WORLD.

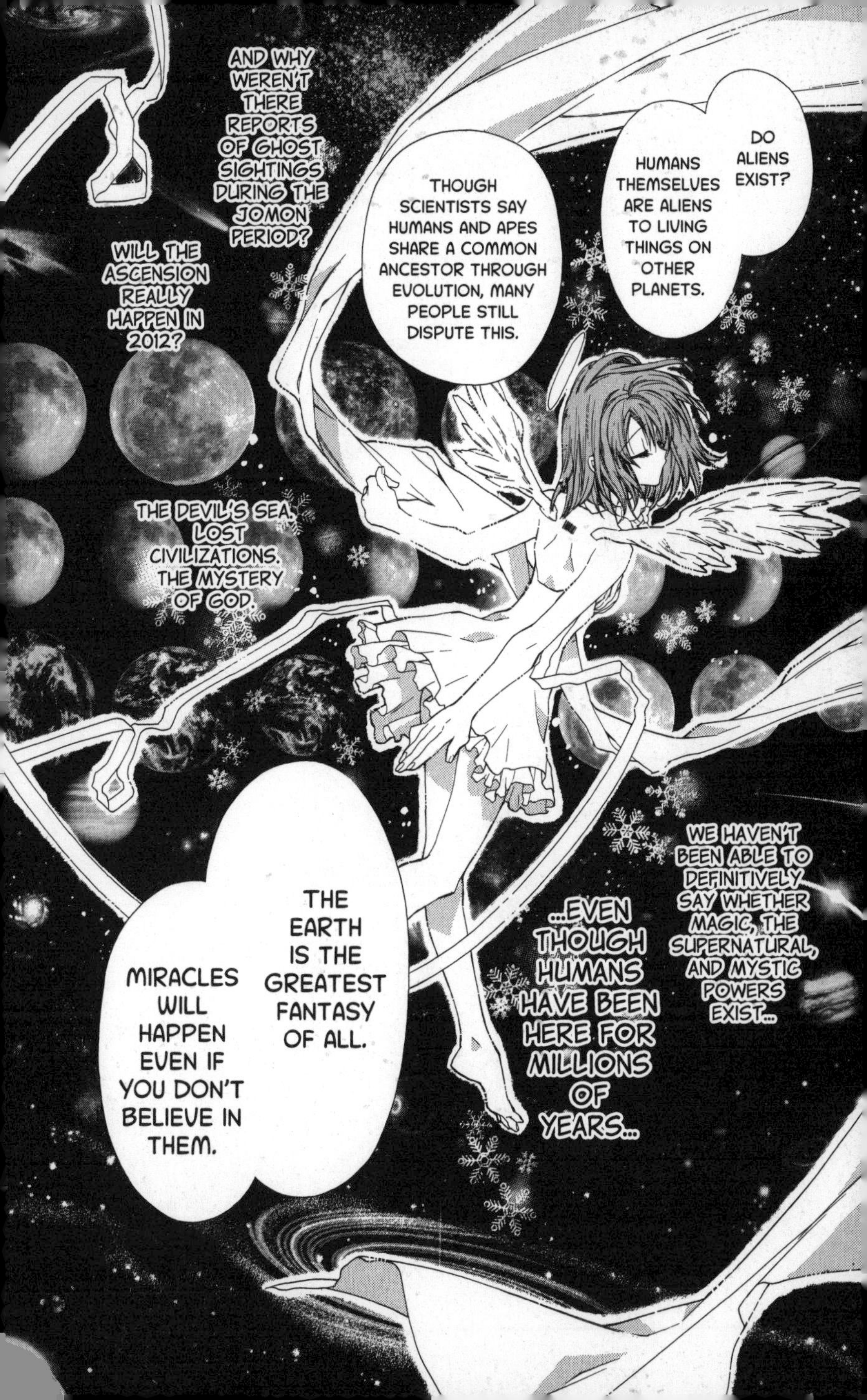
DO ALIENS EXIST?
HUMANS THEMSELVES ARE ALIENS TO LIVING THINGS ON OTHER PLANETS.
THOUGH SCIENTISTS SAY HUMANS AND APES SHARE A COMMON ANCESTOR THROUGH EVOLUTION, MANY PEOPLE STILL DISPUTE THIS.
AND WHY WEREN'T THERE REPORTS OF GHOST SIGHTINGS DURING THE JOMON PERIOD?
WILL THE ASCENSION REALLY HAPPEN IN 2012?
THE DEVIL'S SEA. LOST CIVILIZATIONS. THE MYSTERY OF GOD.
WE HAVEN'T BEEN ABLE TO DEFINITIVELY SAY WHETHER MAGIC, THE SUPERNATURAL, AND MYSTIC POWERS EXIST...
...EVEN THOUGH HUMANS HAVE BEEN HERE FOR MILLIONS OF YEARS...
THE EARTH IS THE GREATEST FANTASY OF ALL.
MIRACLES WILL HAPPEN EVEN IF YOU DON'T BELIEVE IN THEM.

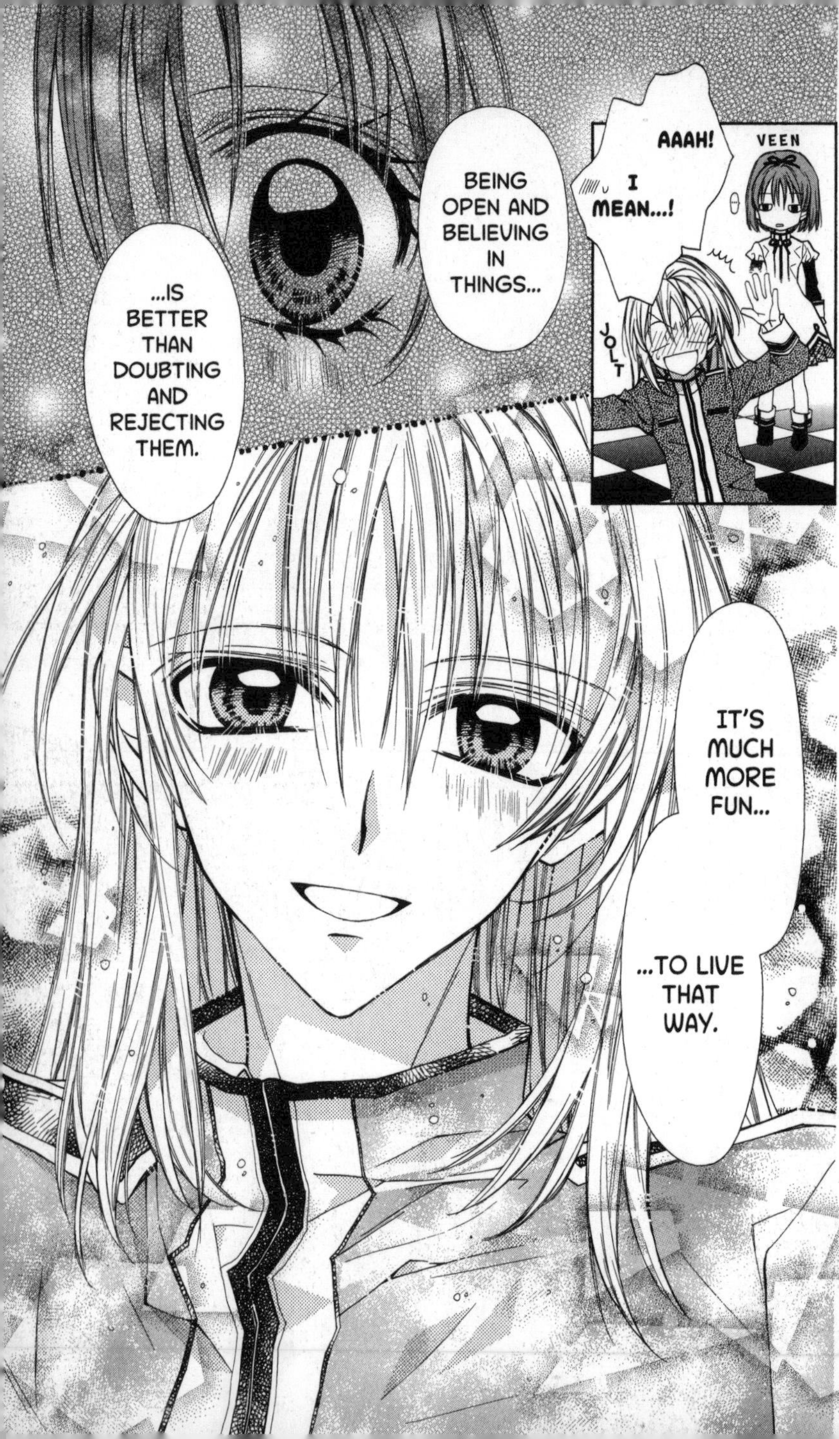

VEEN
AAAH!
I MEAN...!
JOLT
BEING OPEN AND BELIEVING IN THINGS...
...IS BETTER THAN DOUBTING AND REJECTING THEM.
IT'S MUCH MORE FUN...
...TO LIVE THAT WAY.

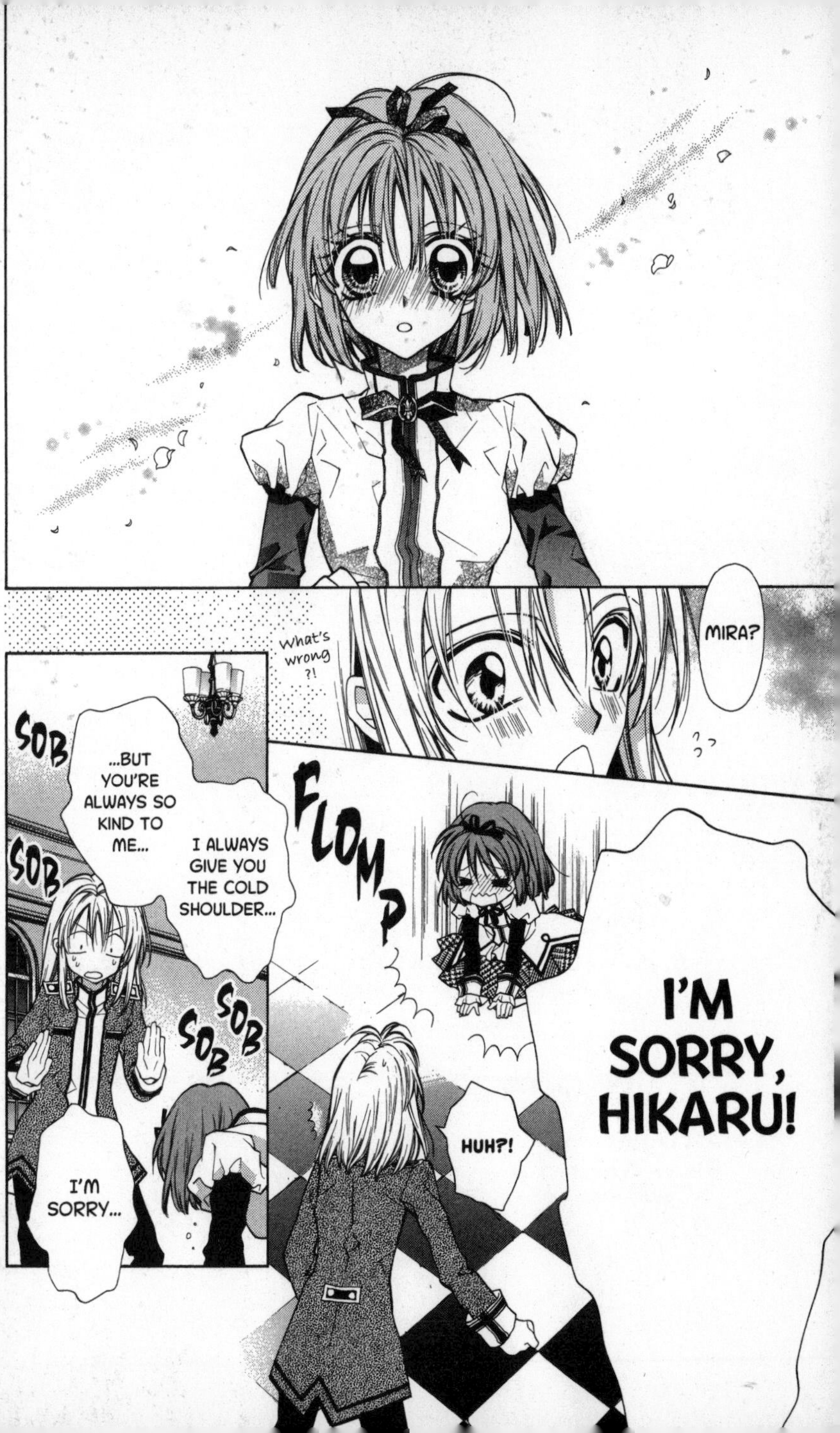
MIRA?
What's wrong ?!
I'M SORRY, HIKARU!
FLOMP
HUH?!
SOB
I ALWAYS GIVE YOU THE COLD SHOULDER...
...BUT YOU'RE ALWAYS SO KIND TO ME...
SOB
SOB
SOB
I'M SORRY...

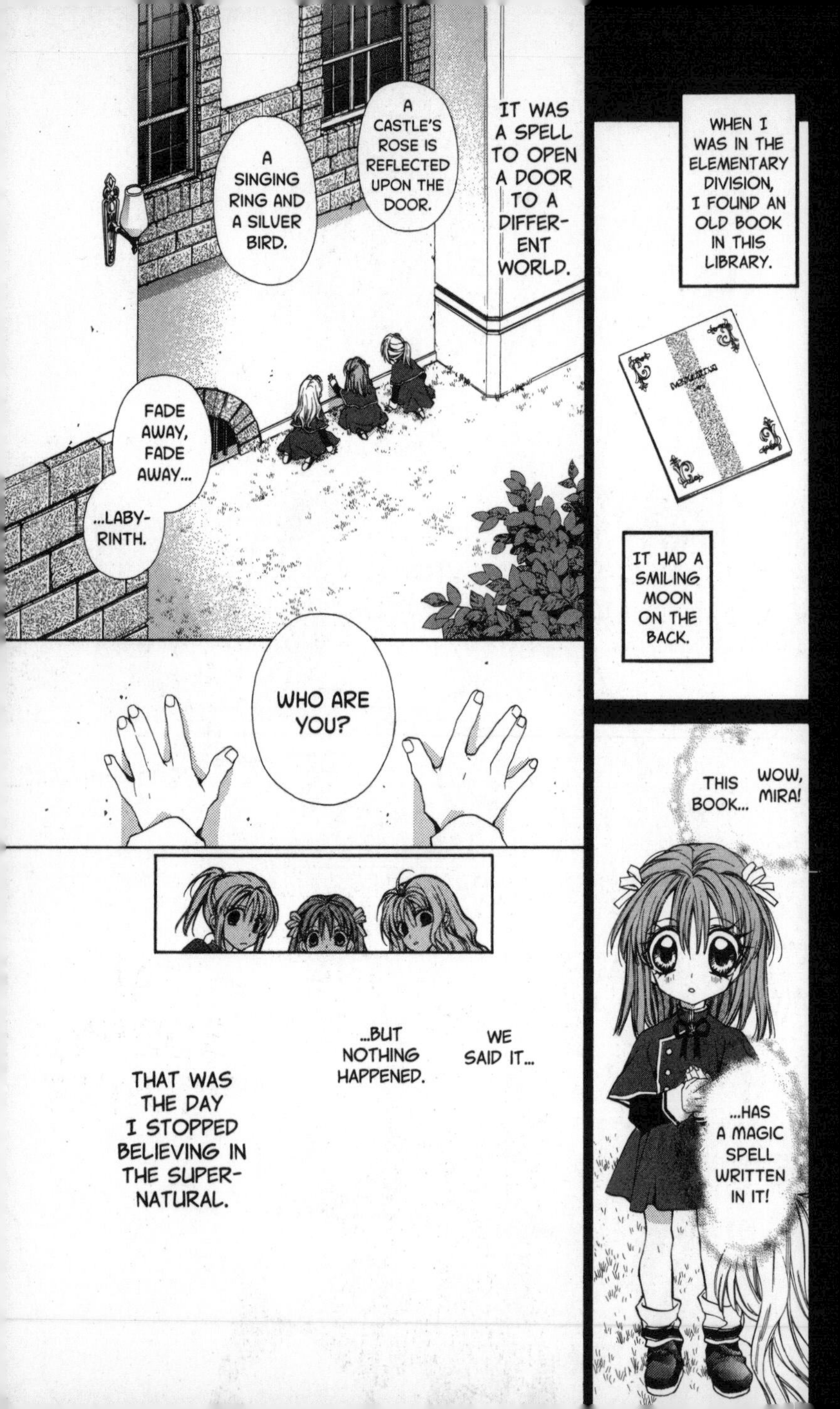
WHEN I WAS IN THE ELEMENTARY DIVISION, I FOUND AN OLD BOOK IN THIS LIBRARY.
IT HAD A SMILING MOON ON THE BACK.
WOW, MIRA!
THIS BOOK...
...HAS A MAGIC SPELL WRITTEN IN IT!
IT WAS A SPELL TO OPEN A DOOR TO A DIFFERENT WORLD.
A CASTLE'S ROSE IS REFLECTED UPON THE DOOR.
A SINGING RING AND A SILVER BIRD.
FADE AWAY, FADE AWAY...
...LABYRINTH.
WHO ARE YOU?
WE SAID IT...
...BUT NOTHING HAPPENED.
THAT WAS THE DAY I STOPPED BELIEVING IN THE SUPERNATURAL.

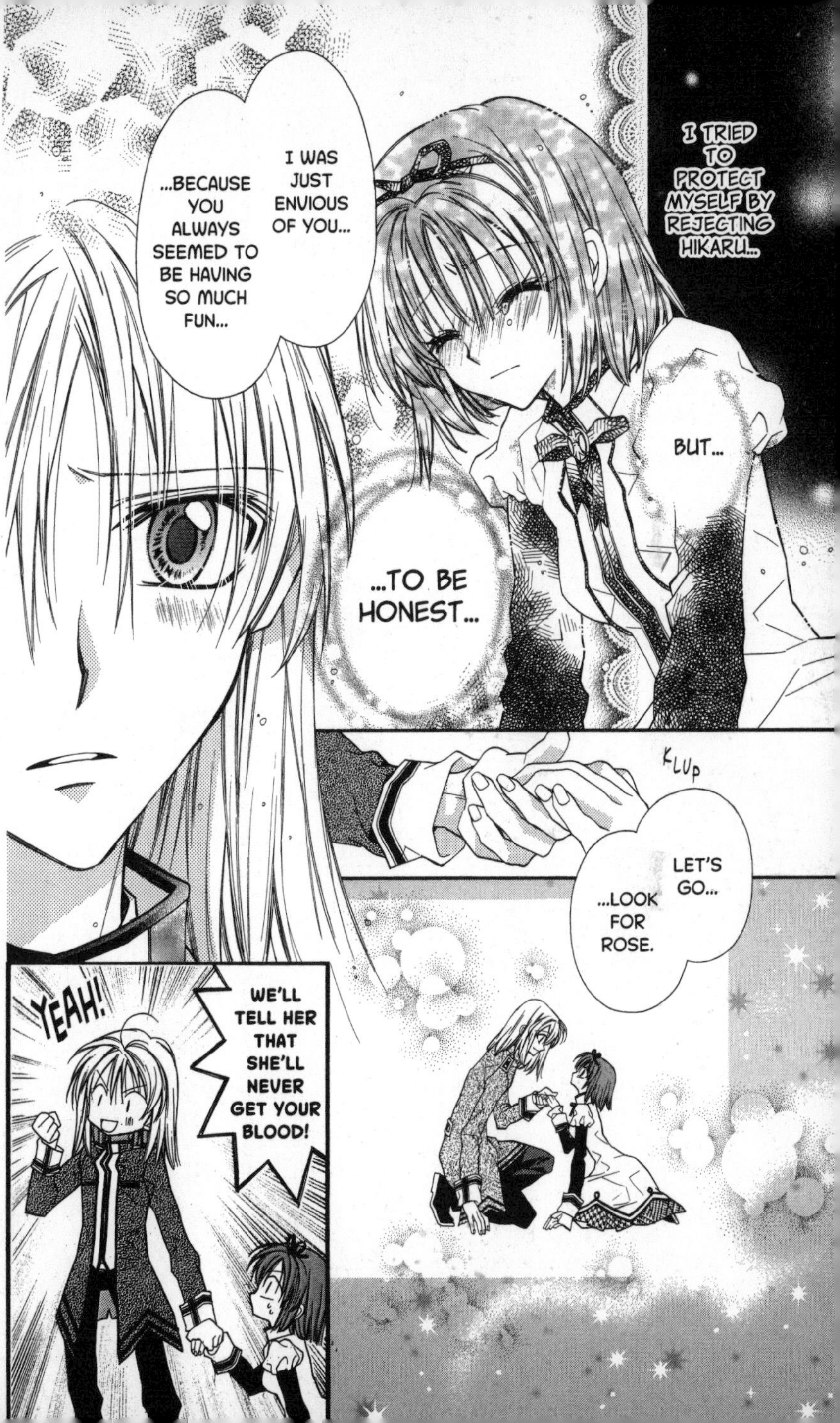
I TRIED TO PROTECT MYSELF BY REJECTING HIKARU...
BUT...
...TO BE HONEST...
I WAS JUST ENVIOUS OF YOU...
...BECAUSE YOU ALWAYS SEEMED TO BE HAVING SO MUCH FUN...
KLUP
LET'S GO...
...LOOK FOR ROSE.
YEAH!
WE'LL TELL HER THAT SHE'LL NEVER GET YOUR BLOOD!

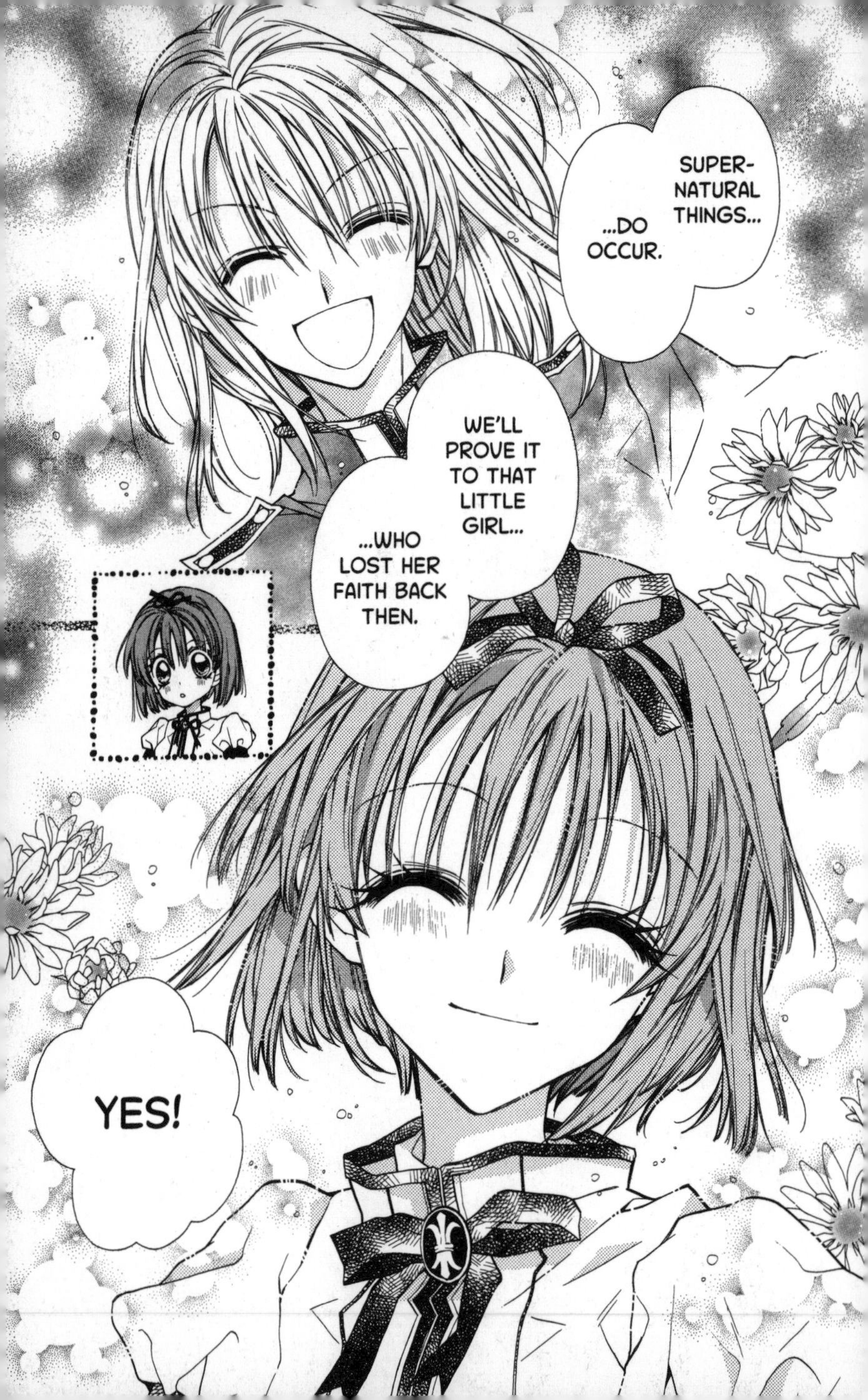
SUPER-NATURAL THINGS...
...DO OCCUR.
WE'LL PROVE IT TO THAT LITTLE GIRL...
...WHO LOST HER FAITH BACK THEN.
YES!

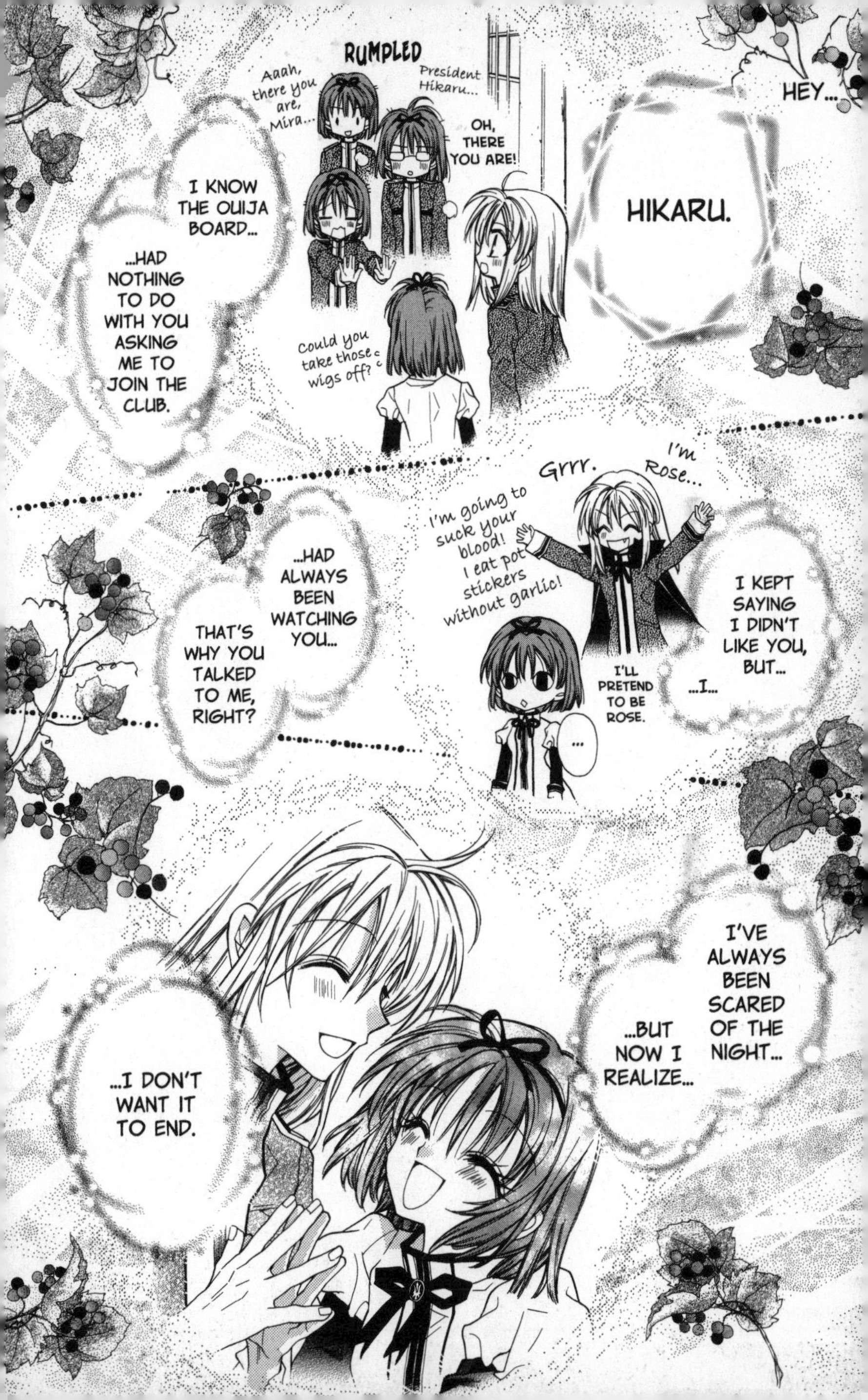
HEY...
HIKARU.
RUMPLED
President Hikaru...
Aaah, there you are, Mira...
OH, THERE YOU ARE!
Could you take those wigs off?
I KNOW THE OUIJA BOARD...
...HAD NOTHING TO DO WITH YOU ASKING ME TO JOIN THE CLUB.
I KEPT SAYING I DIDN'T LIKE YOU, BUT...
...I...
I'm Rose...
Grrr.
I'm going to suck your blood! I eat pot stickers without garlic!
I'LL PRETEND TO BE ROSE.
...
...HAD ALWAYS BEEN WATCHING YOU...
THAT'S WHY YOU TALKED TO ME, RIGHT?
I'VE ALWAYS BEEN SCARED OF THE NIGHT...
...BUT NOW I REALIZE...
...I DON'T WANT IT TO END.

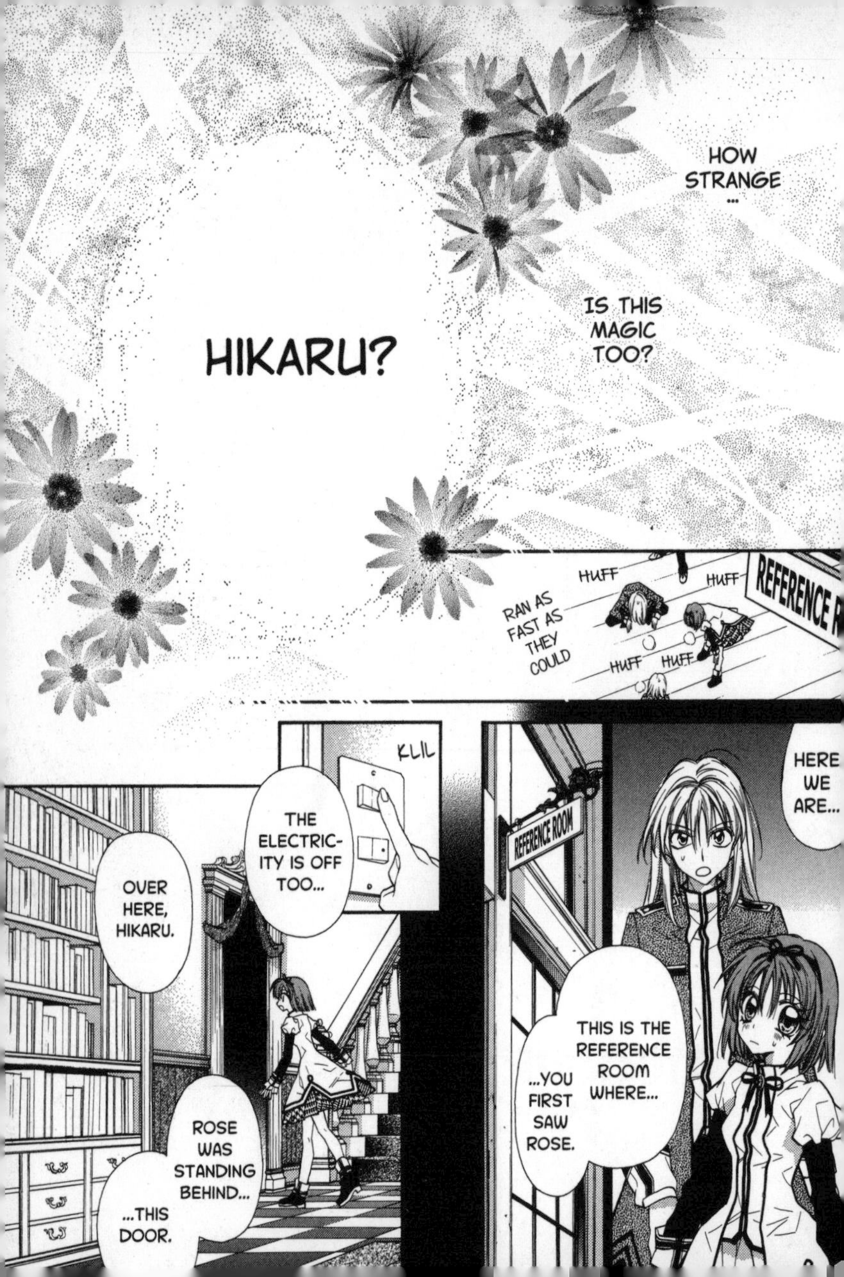
HOW STRANGE...
IS THIS MAGIC TOO?
HIKARU?
HUFF
HUFF
RAN AS FAST AS THEY COULD
HUFF
HUFF
HERE WE ARE...
REFERENCE ROOM
THIS IS THE REFERENCE ROOM WHERE...
...YOU FIRST SAW ROSE.
KLIL
THE ELECTRICITY IS OFF TOO...
OVER HERE, HIKARU.
ROSE WAS STANDING BEHIND...
...THIS DOOR.

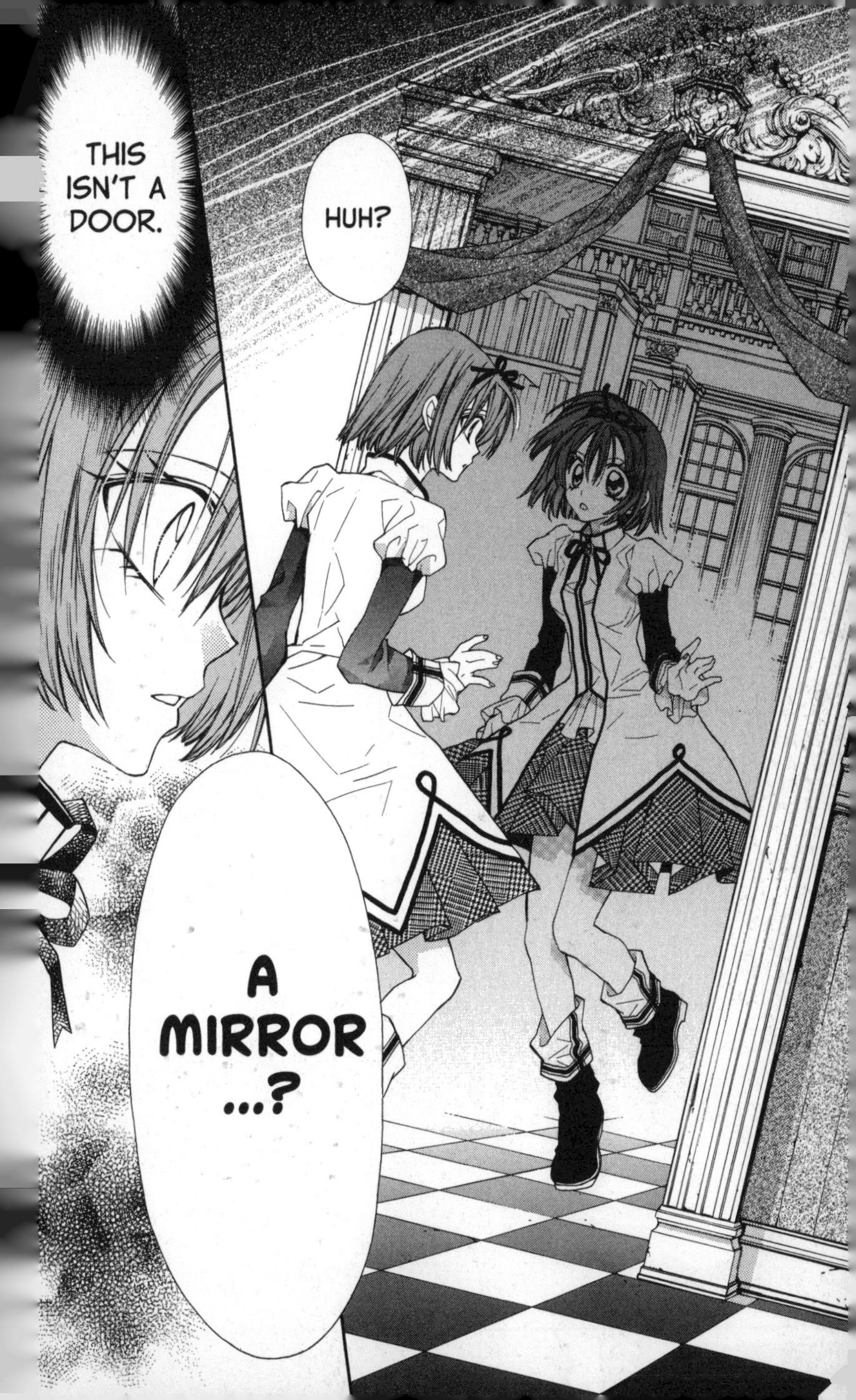
HUH?
THIS ISN'T A DOOR.
A MIRROR ...?

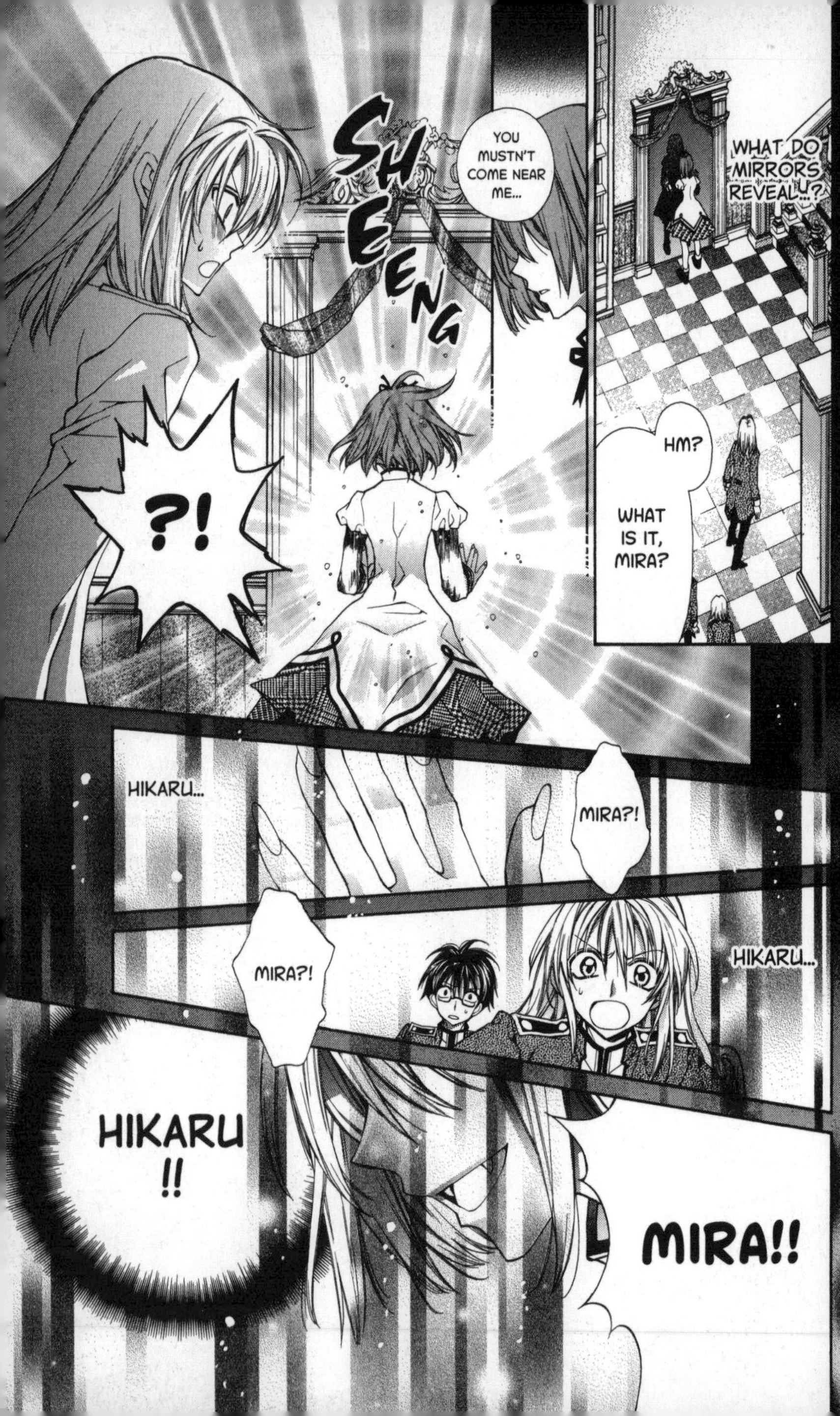
WHAT DO MIRRORS REVEAL...?
HM?
WHAT IS IT, MIRA?
YOU MUSTN'T COME NEAR ME...
SHEEENG
?!
MIRA?!
HIKARU...
HIKARU...
MIRA?!
MIRA!!
HIKARU!!

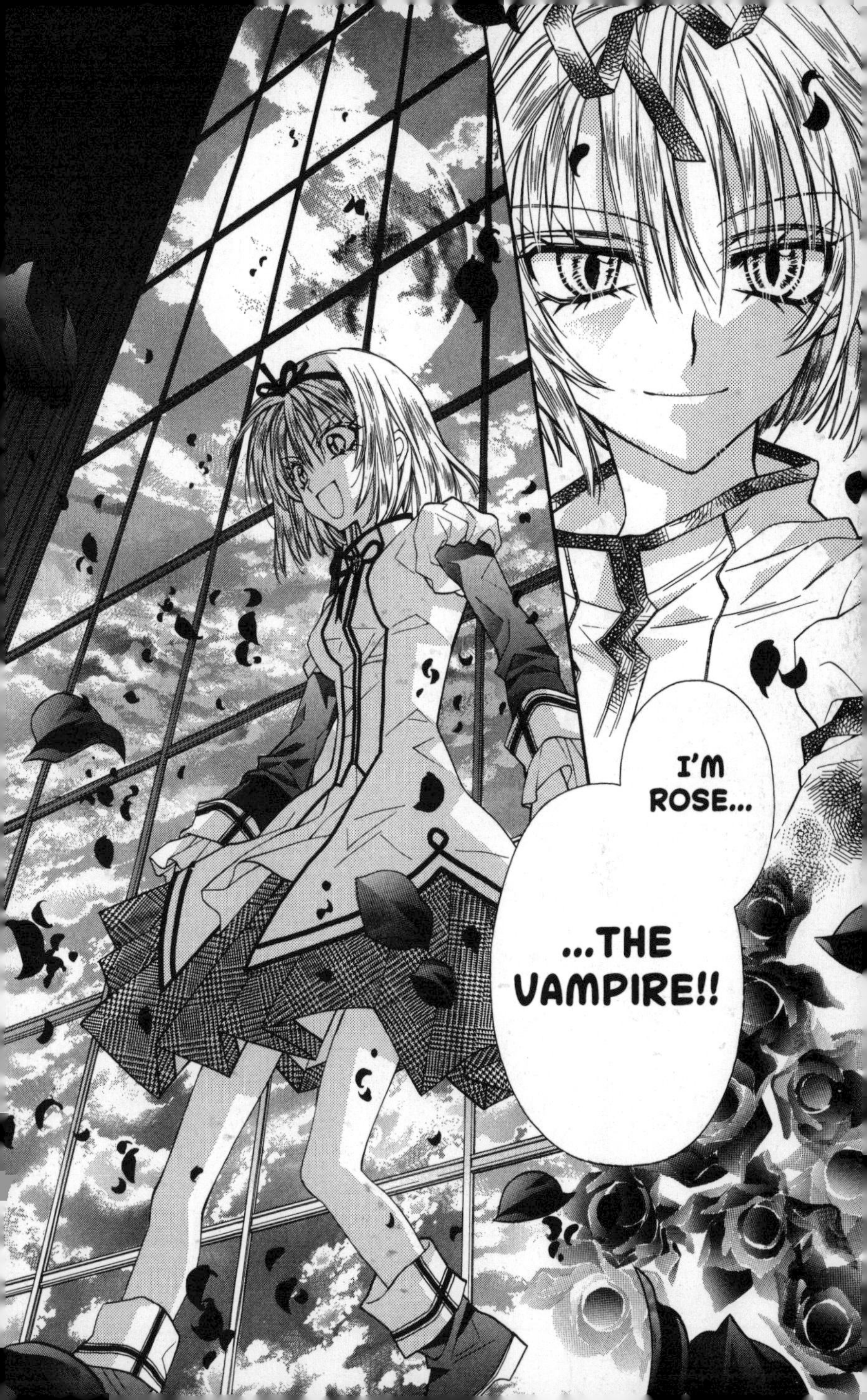
I'M ROSE...
...THE VAMPIRE!!

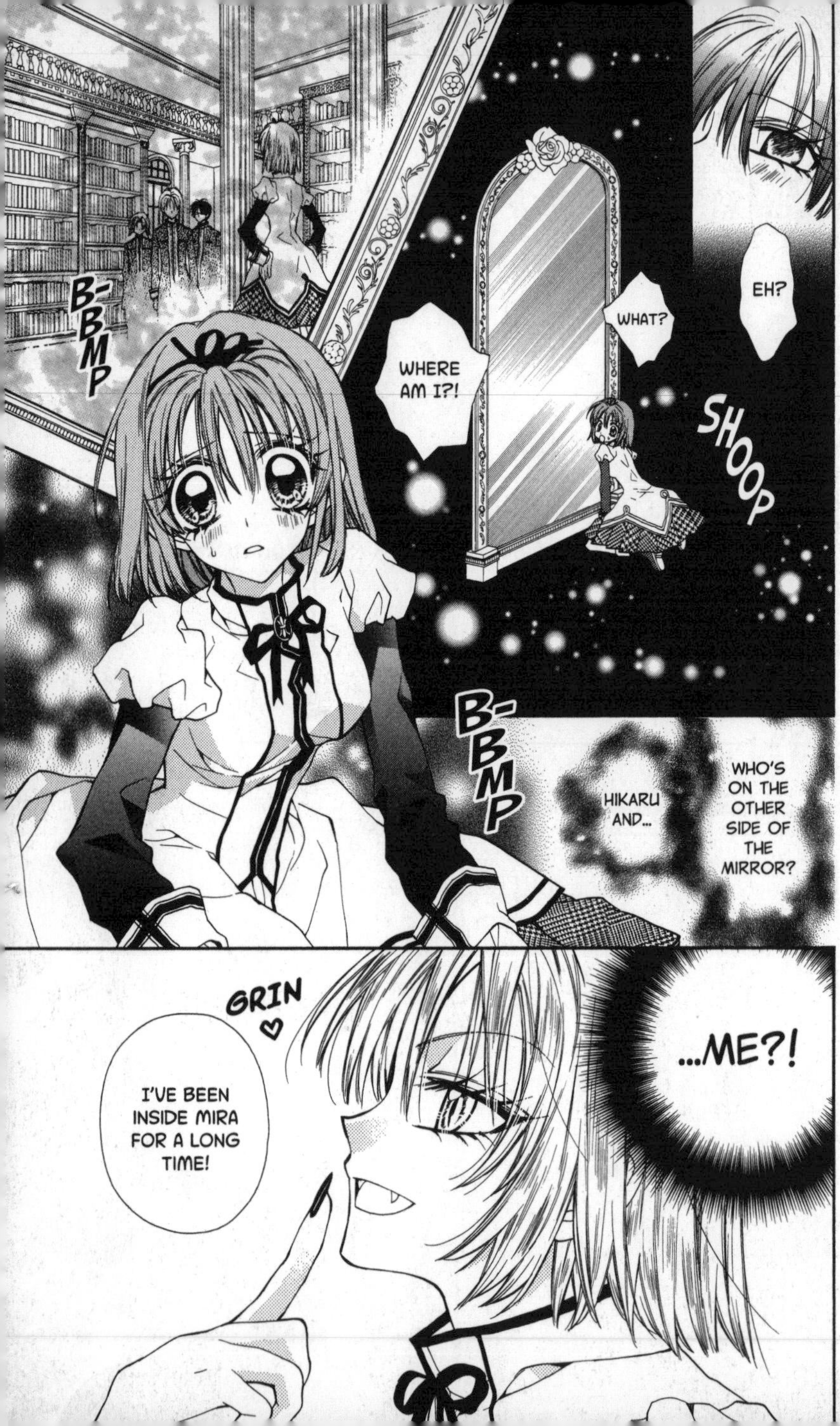
EH?
WHAT?
SHOOP
WHERE AM I?!
B-BMP
WHO'S ON THE OTHER SIDE OF THE MIRROR?
HIKARU AND...
B-BMP
...ME?!
GRIN ♥
I'VE BEEN INSIDE MIRA FOR A LONG TIME!

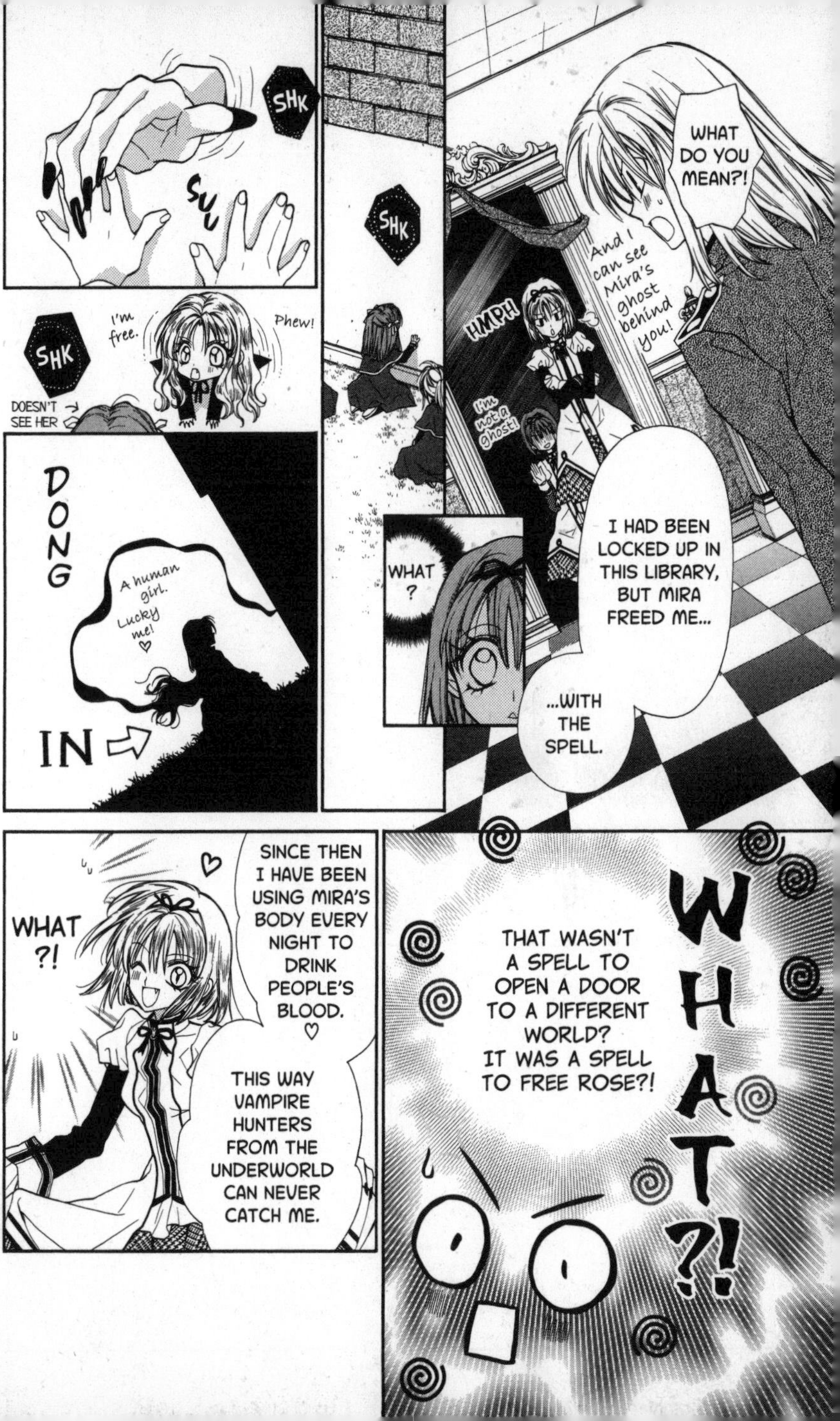
WHAT DO YOU MEAN?!
And I can see Mira's ghost behind you!
HMPH
I'm not a ghost!
I HAD BEEN LOCKED UP IN THIS LIBRARY, BUT MIRA FREED ME...
WHAT ?
...WITH THE SPELL.
SHK
SHK
SHK
SUU
SHK
Phew!
I'm free.
DOESN'T SEE HER
DONG
A human girl. Lucky me! ♡
IN
THAT WASN'T A SPELL TO OPEN A DOOR TO A DIFFERENT WORLD? IT WAS A SPELL TO FREE ROSE?!
WHAT ?!
SINCE THEN I HAVE BEEN USING MIRA'S BODY EVERY NIGHT TO DRINK PEOPLE'S BLOOD. ♡
WHAT ?!
THIS WAY VAMPIRE HUNTERS FROM THE UNDERWORLD CAN NEVER CATCH ME.

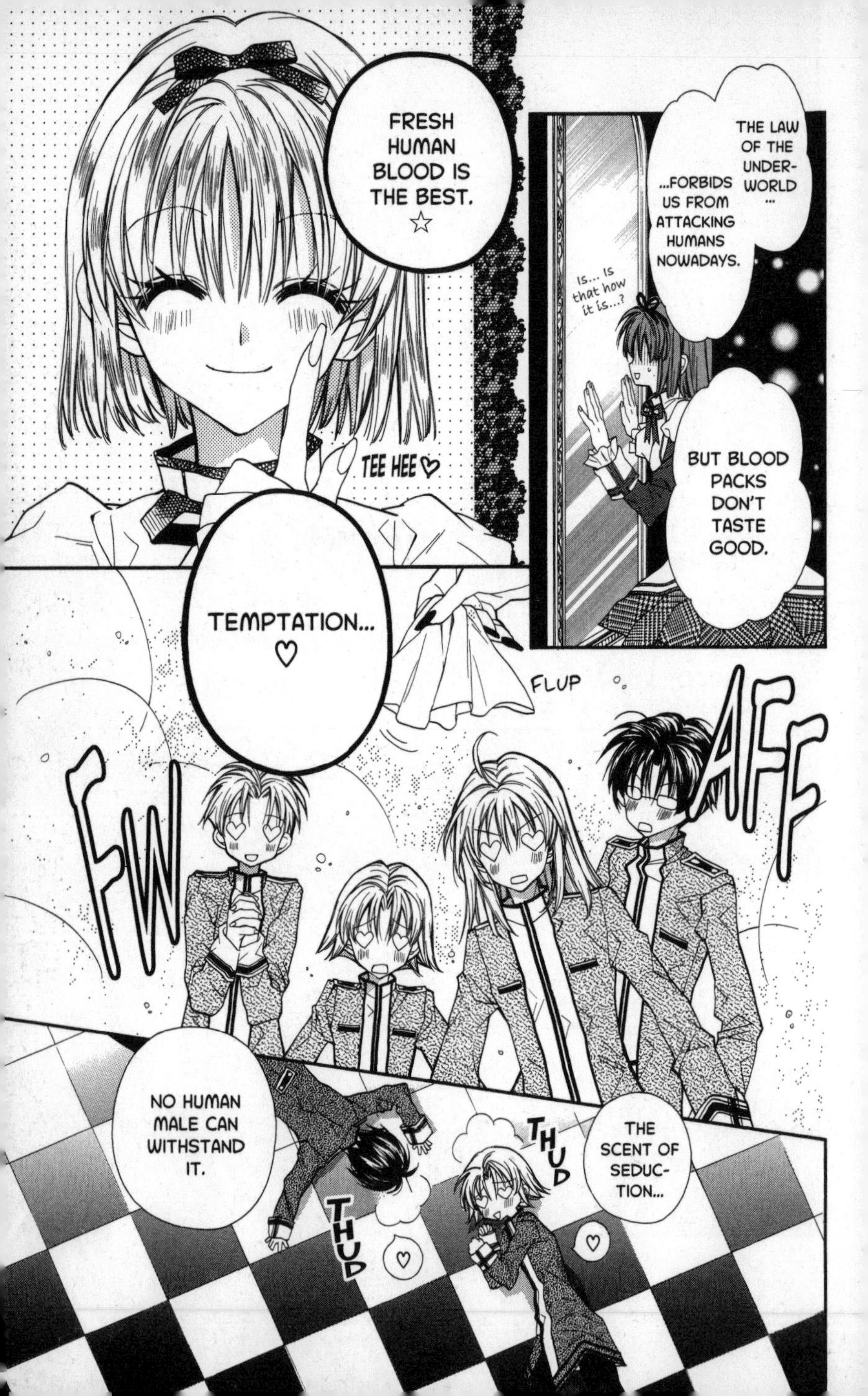
THE LAW OF THE UNDER-WORLD...
...FORBIDS US FROM ATTACKING HUMANS NOWADAYS.
Is... is that how it is...?
BUT BLOOD PACKS DON'T TASTE GOOD.
FRESH HUMAN BLOOD IS THE BEST. ☆
TEE HEE ♡
TEMPTATION... ♡
FLUP
FWAFF
THE SCENT OF SEDUC-TION...
THUD
NO HUMAN MALE CAN WITHSTAND IT.
THUD
♡
♡

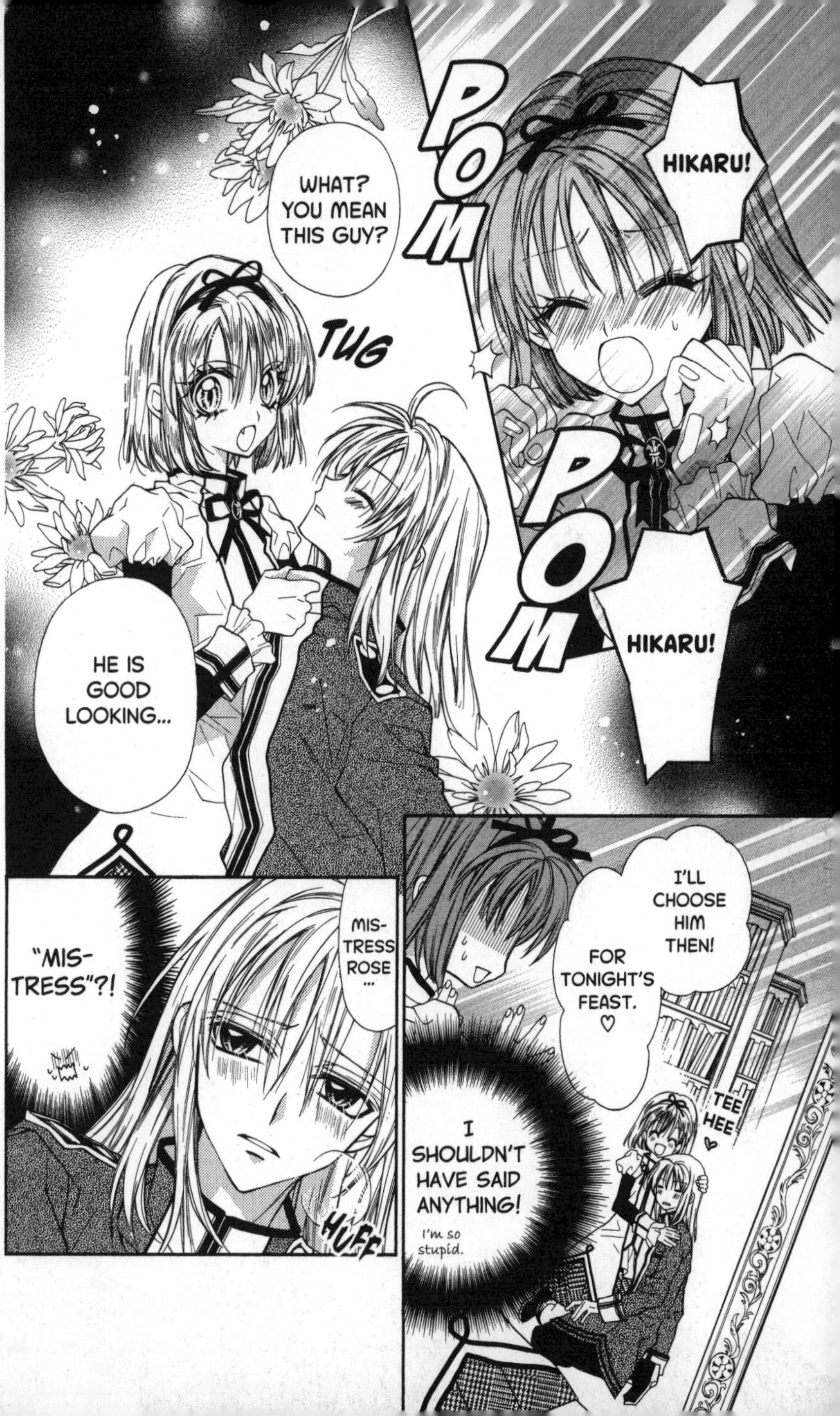
HIKARU!
POM
POM
HIKARU!
WHAT? YOU MEAN THIS GUY?
TUG
HE IS GOOD LOOKING...
I'LL CHOOSE HIM THEN!
FOR TONIGHT'S FEAST. ♡
TEE HEE ♡
I SHOULDN'T HAVE SAID ANYTHING!
I'm so stupid.
MIS-TRESS ROSE...
"MIS-TRESS"?!
HUFF

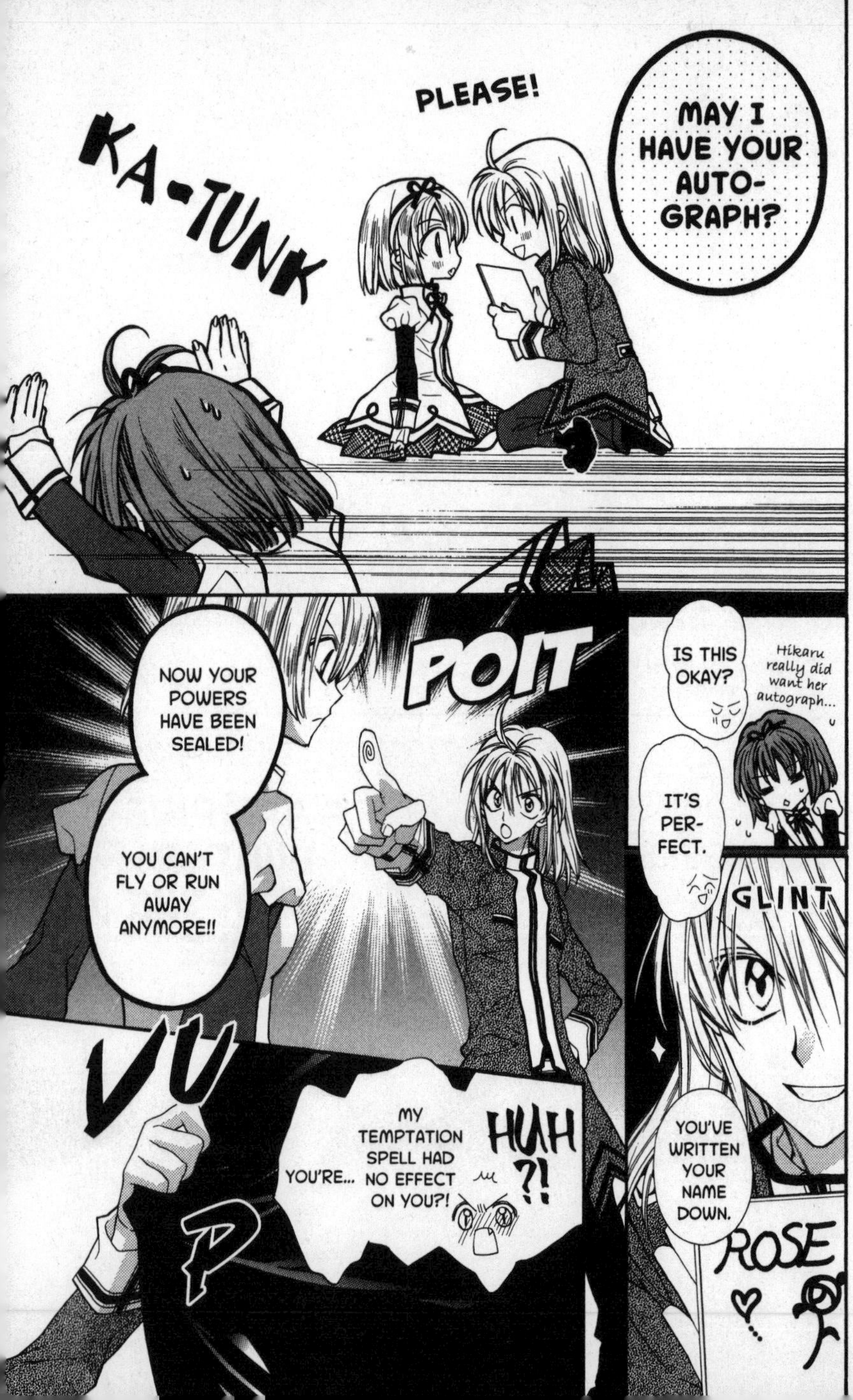
MAY I HAVE YOUR AUTO-GRAPH?
PLEASE!
KA-TUNK
IS THIS OKAY?
Hikaru really did want her autograph...
IT'S PER-FECT.
GLINT
YOU'VE WRITTEN YOUR NAME DOWN.
ROSE
POIT
NOW YOUR POWERS HAVE BEEN SEALED!
YOU CAN'T FLY OR RUN AWAY ANYMORE!!
HUH?!
MY TEMPTATION SPELL HAD NO EFFECT ON YOU?!
YOU'RE...
VU
P

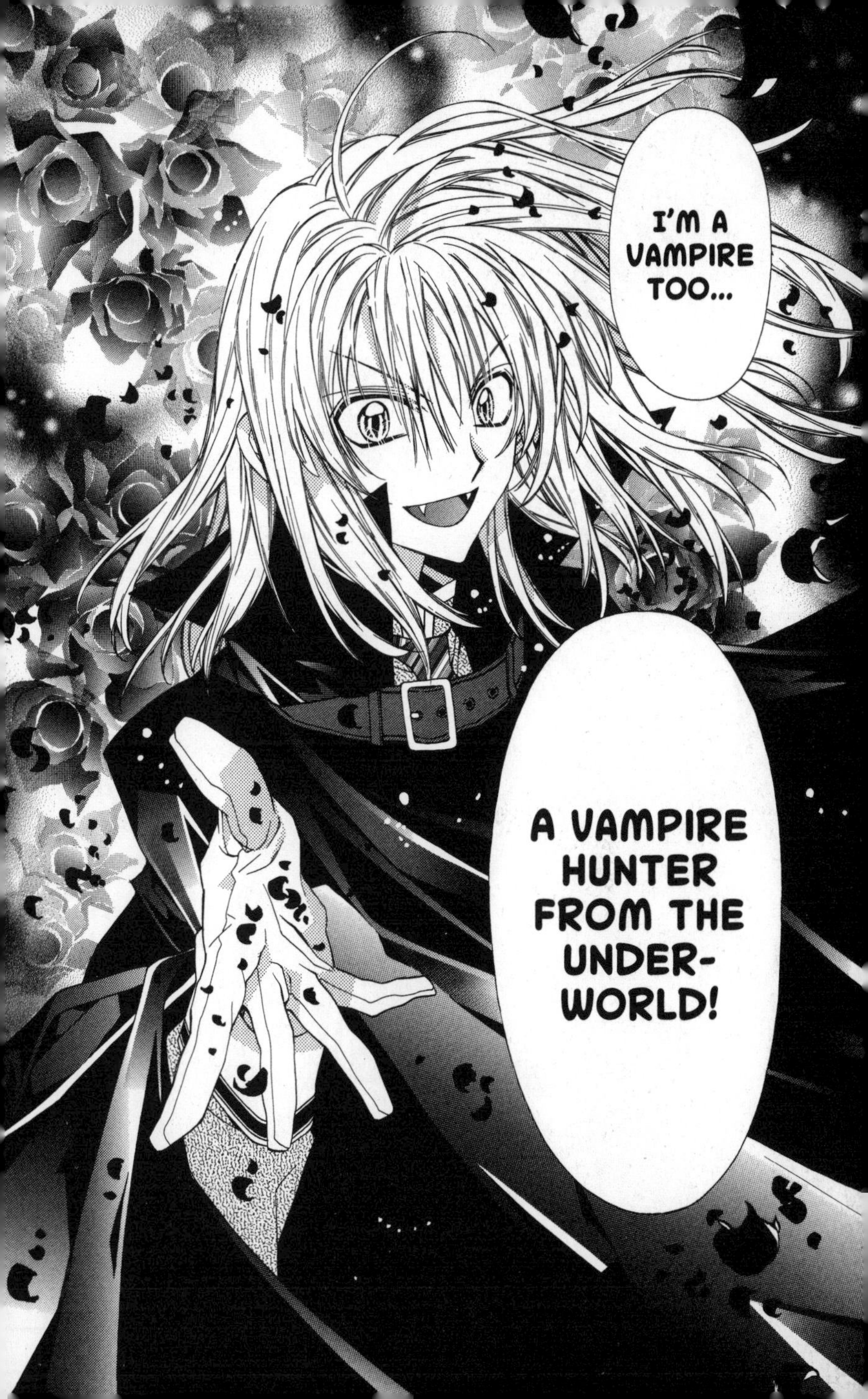
I'M A VAMPIRE TOO...
A VAMPIRE HUNTER FROM THE UNDER-WORLD!

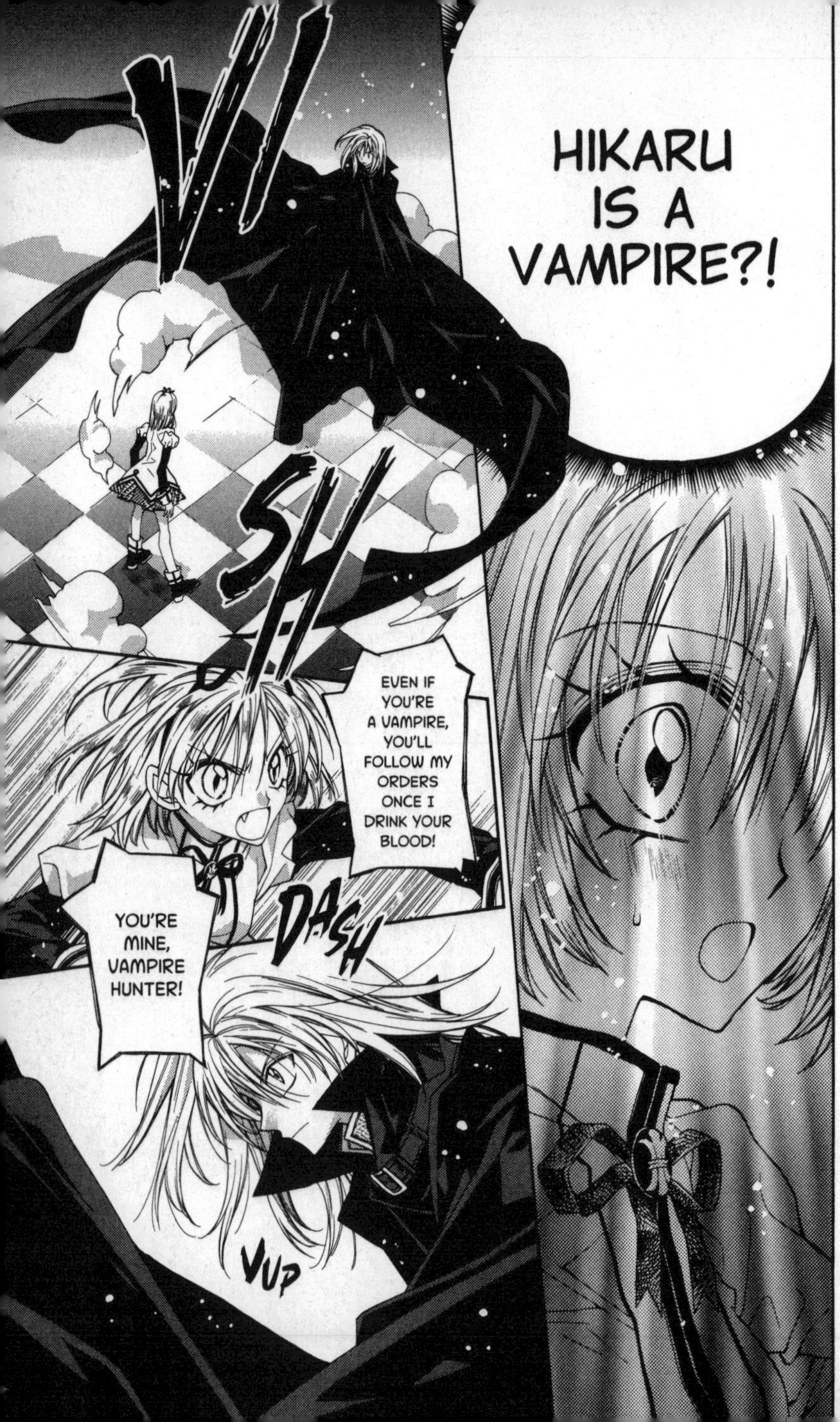
HIKARU IS A VAMPIRE?!
VU
SH
EVEN IF YOU'RE A VAMPIRE, YOU'LL FOLLOW MY ORDERS ONCE I DRINK YOUR BLOOD!
DASH
YOU'RE MINE, VAMPIRE HUNTER!
VUP

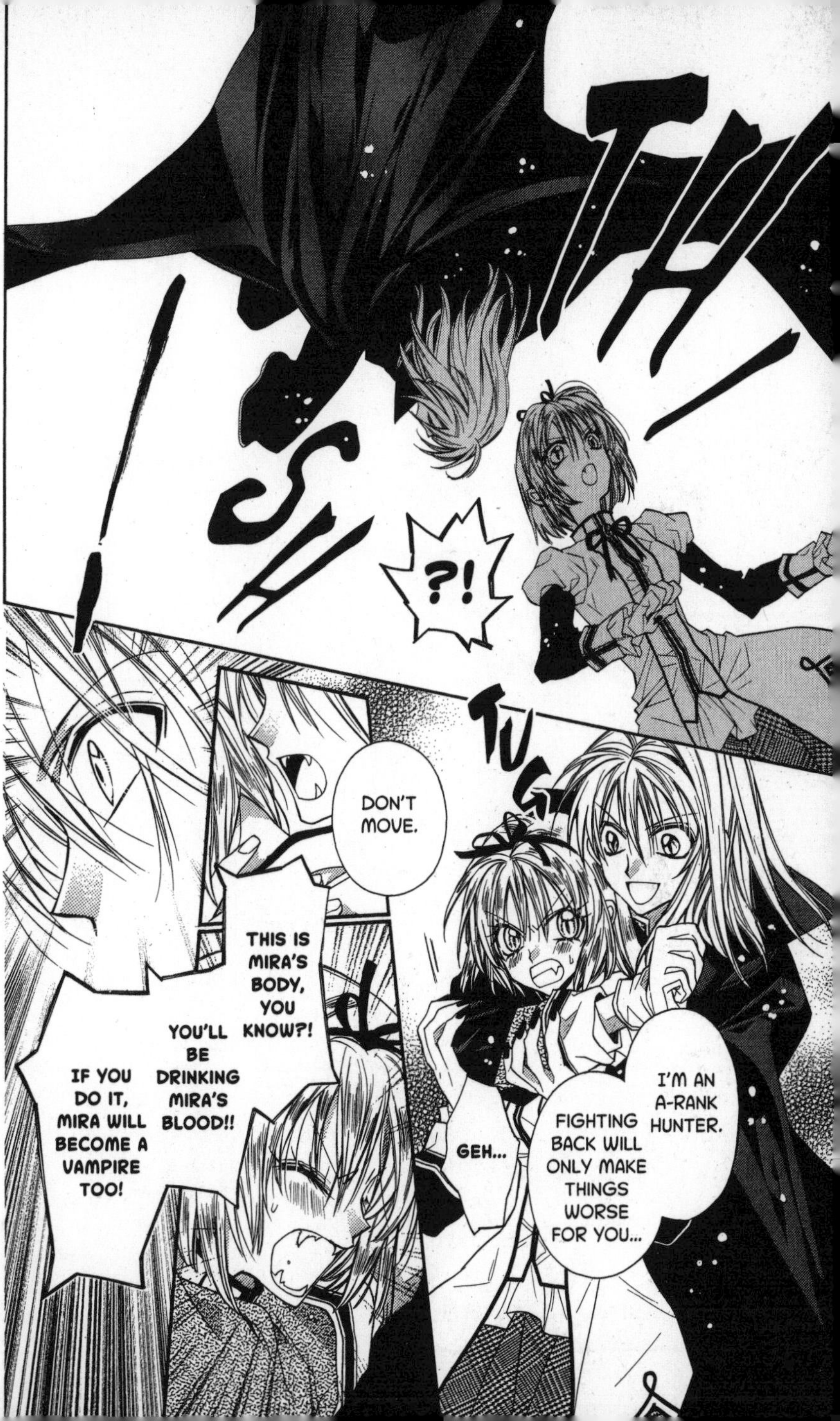
?!
TUG
I'M AN A-RANK HUNTER.
FIGHTING BACK WILL ONLY MAKE THINGS WORSE FOR YOU...
GEH...
DON'T MOVE.
THIS IS MIRA'S BODY, YOU KNOW?!
YOU'LL BE DRINKING MIRA'S BLOOD!!
IF YOU DO IT, MIRA WILL BECOME A VAMPIRE TOO!

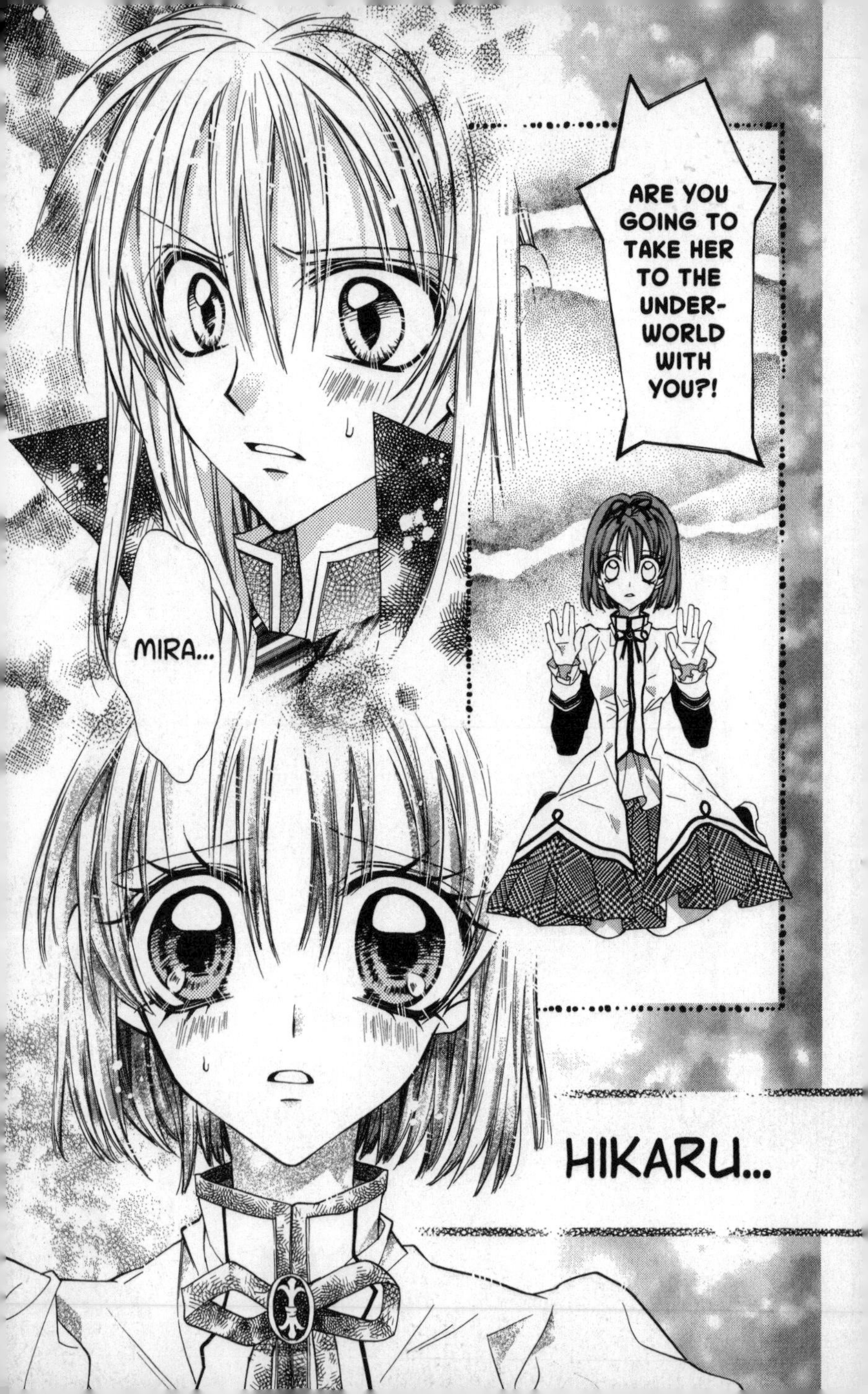
ARE YOU GOING TO TAKE HER TO THE UNDER-WORLD WITH YOU?!
MIRA...
HIKARU...

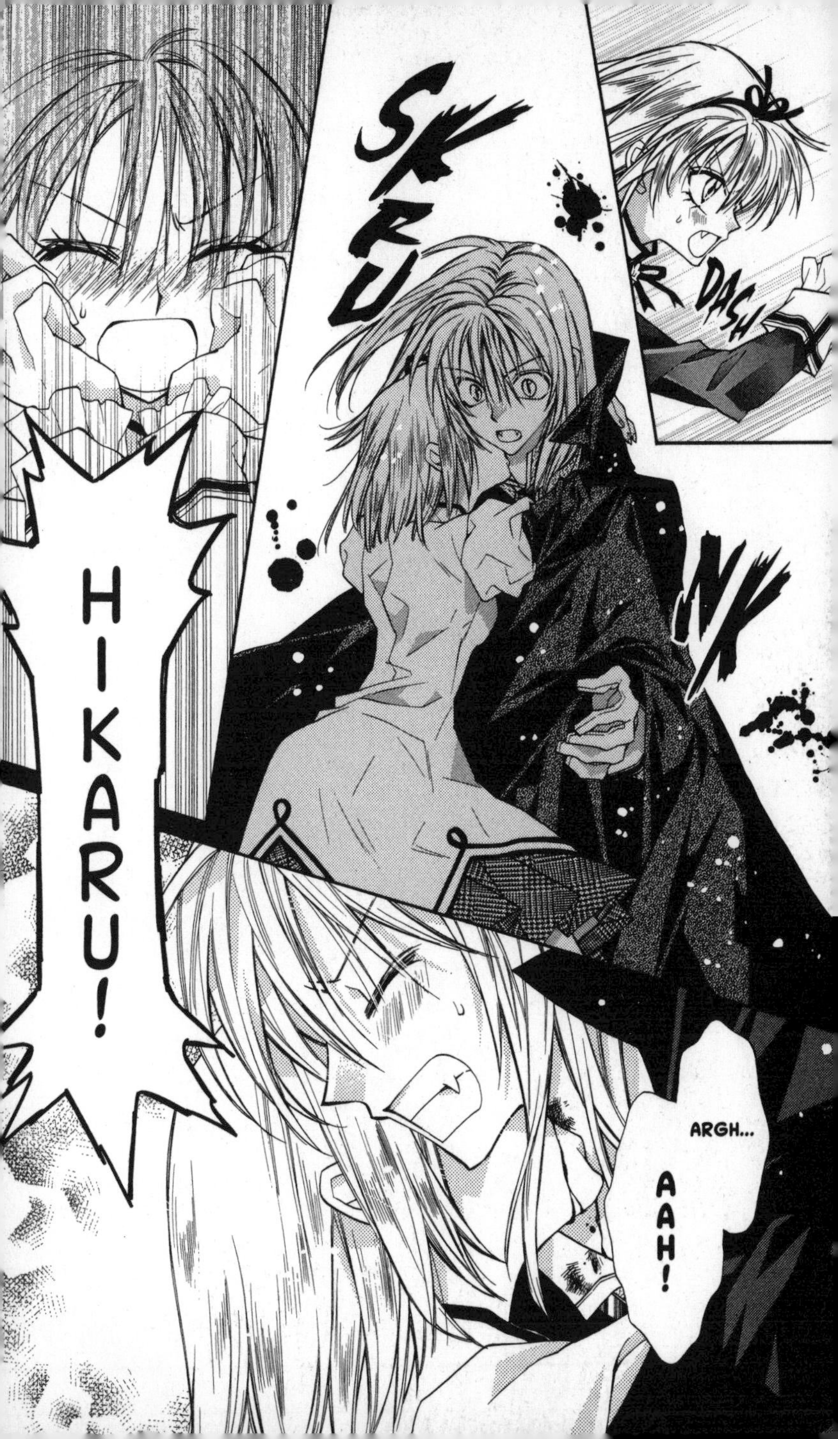
DASH
SKRU
NK
HIKARU!
ARGH...
AAH!

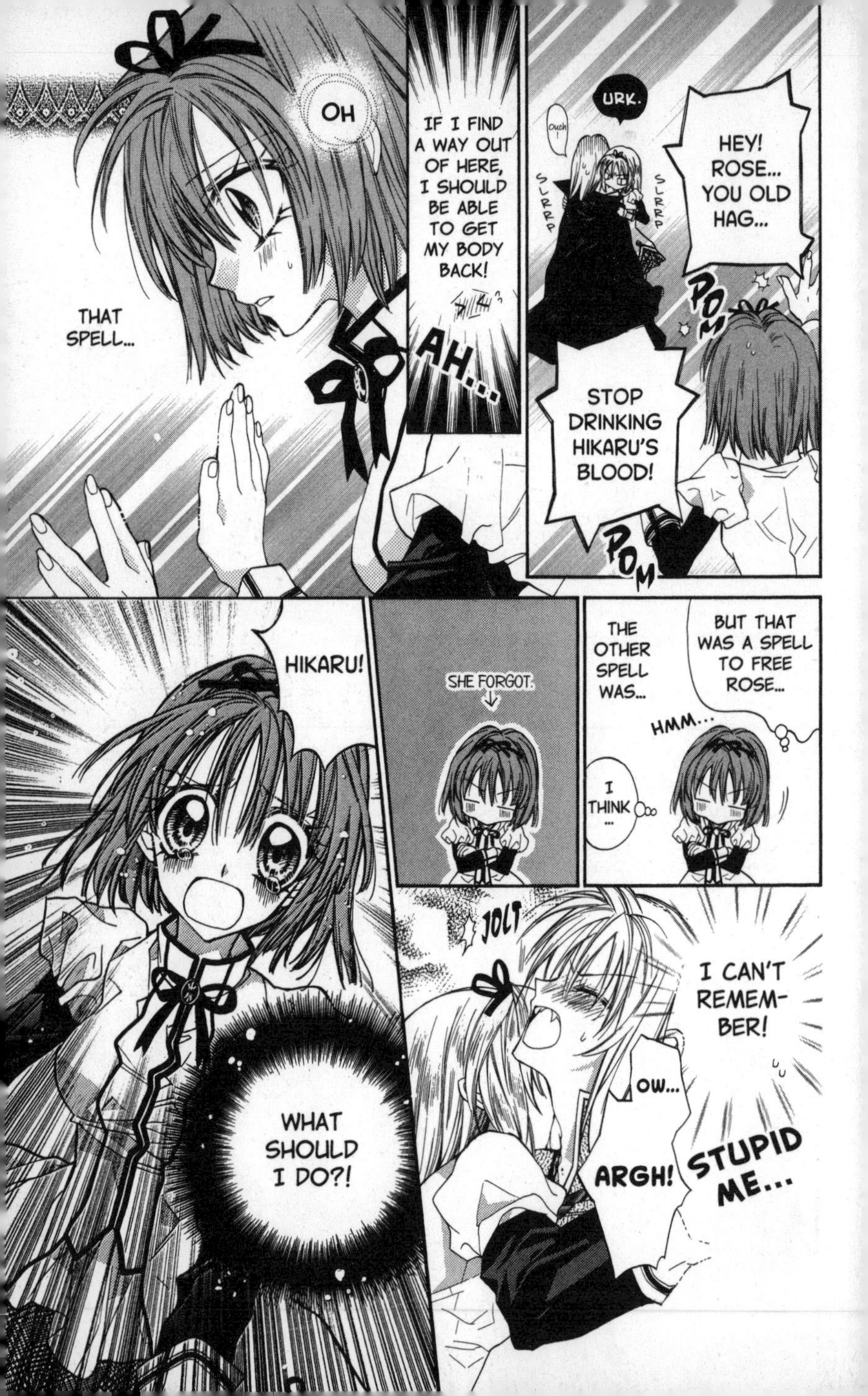

HEY! ROSE... YOU OLD HAG...
URK.
Ouch!
SLRRP
SLRRP
POM
STOP DRINKING HIKARU'S BLOOD!
POM
IF I FIND A WAY OUT OF HERE, I SHOULD BE ABLE TO GET MY BODY BACK!
AH...
OH
THAT SPELL...
BUT THAT WAS A SPELL TO FREE ROSE...
THE OTHER SPELL WAS...
HMM...
I THINK...
SHE FORGOT.
JOLT
I CAN'T REMEMBER!
OW...
STUPID ME...
ARGH!
HIKARU!
WHAT SHOULD I DO?!

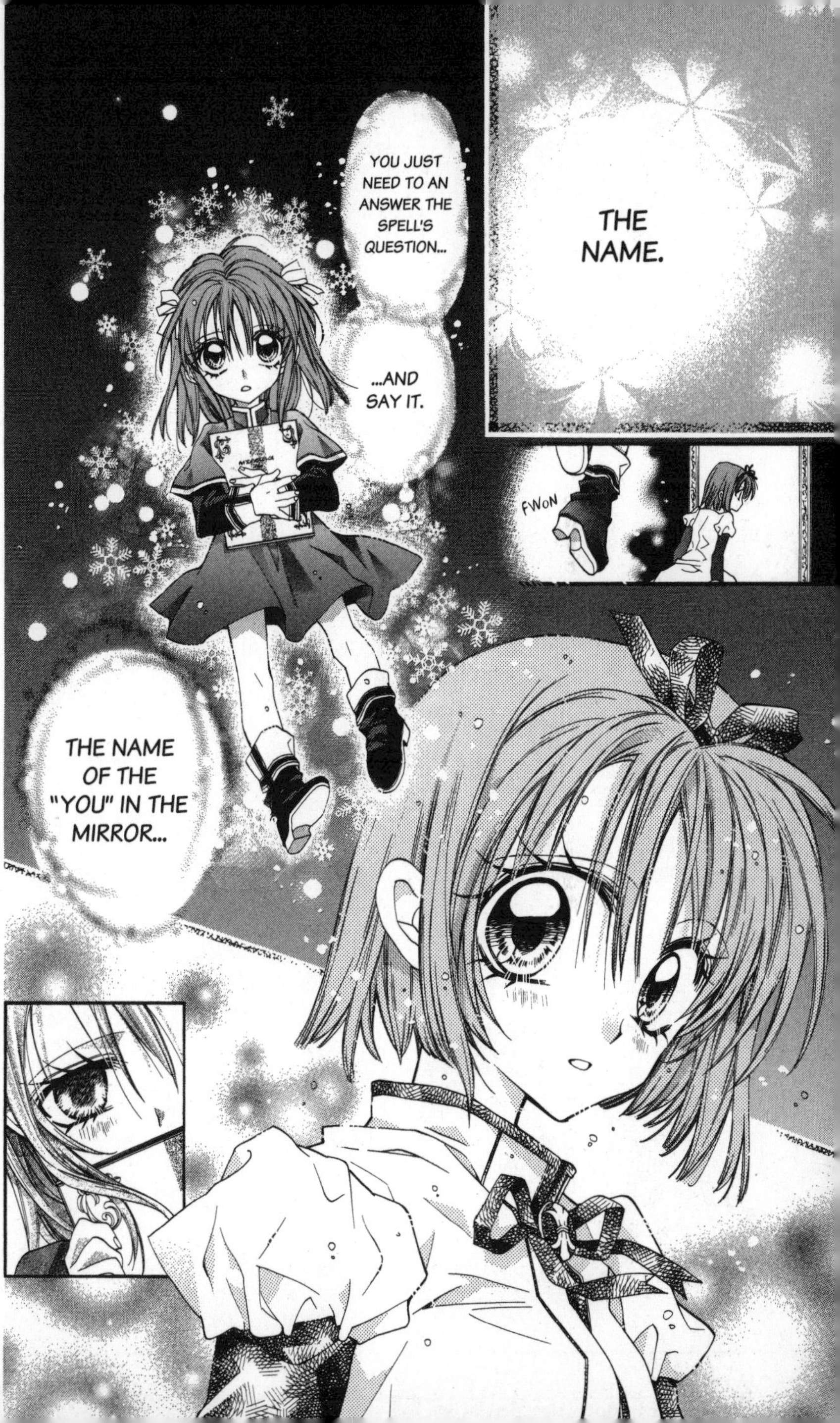
THE NAME.
FWON
YOU JUST NEED TO AN ANSWER THE SPELL'S QUESTION...
...AND SAY IT.
THE NAME OF THE "YOU" IN THE MIRROR...

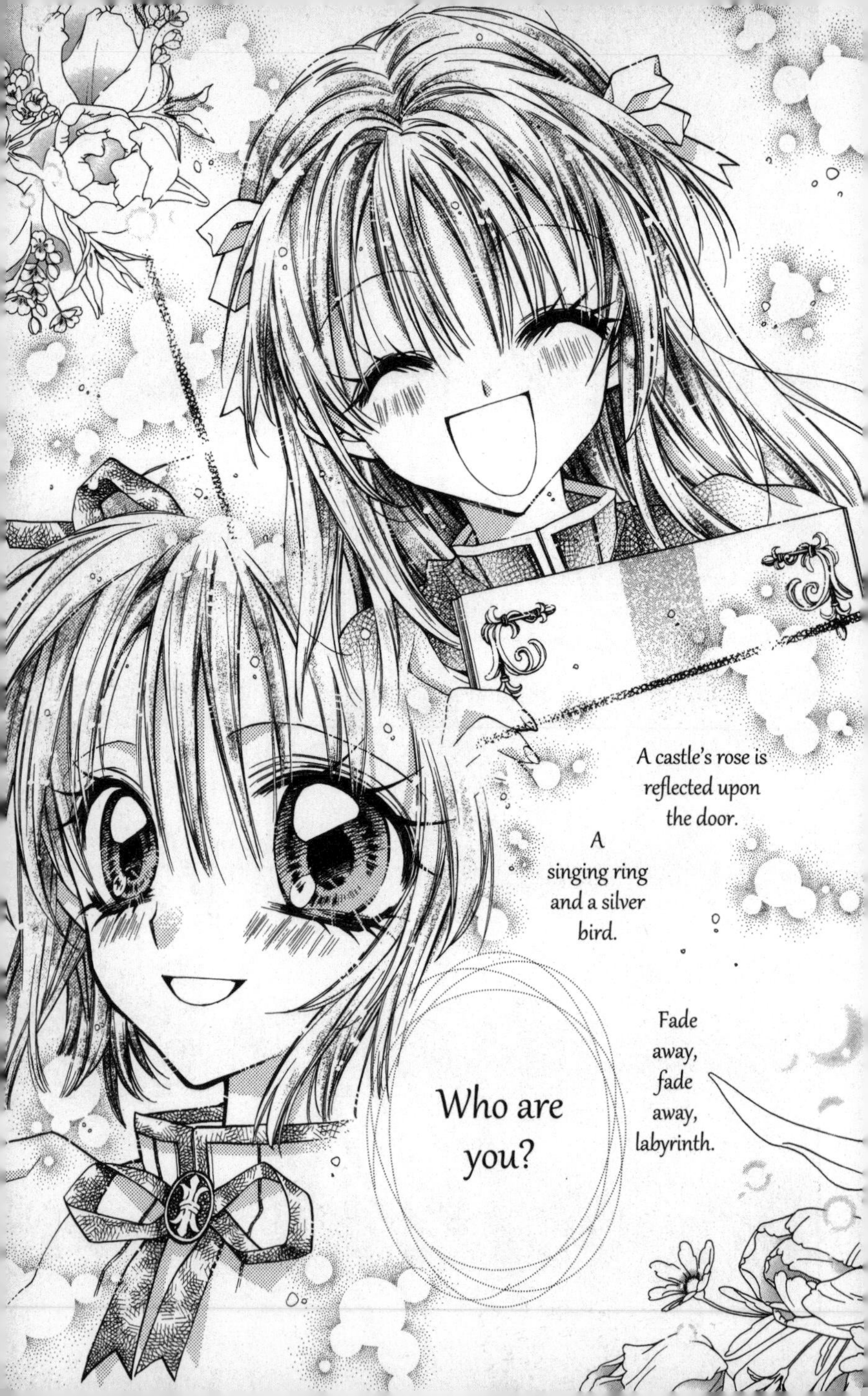
A castle's rose is reflected upon the door.
A singing ring and a silver bird.
Fade away, fade away, labyrinth.
Who are you?

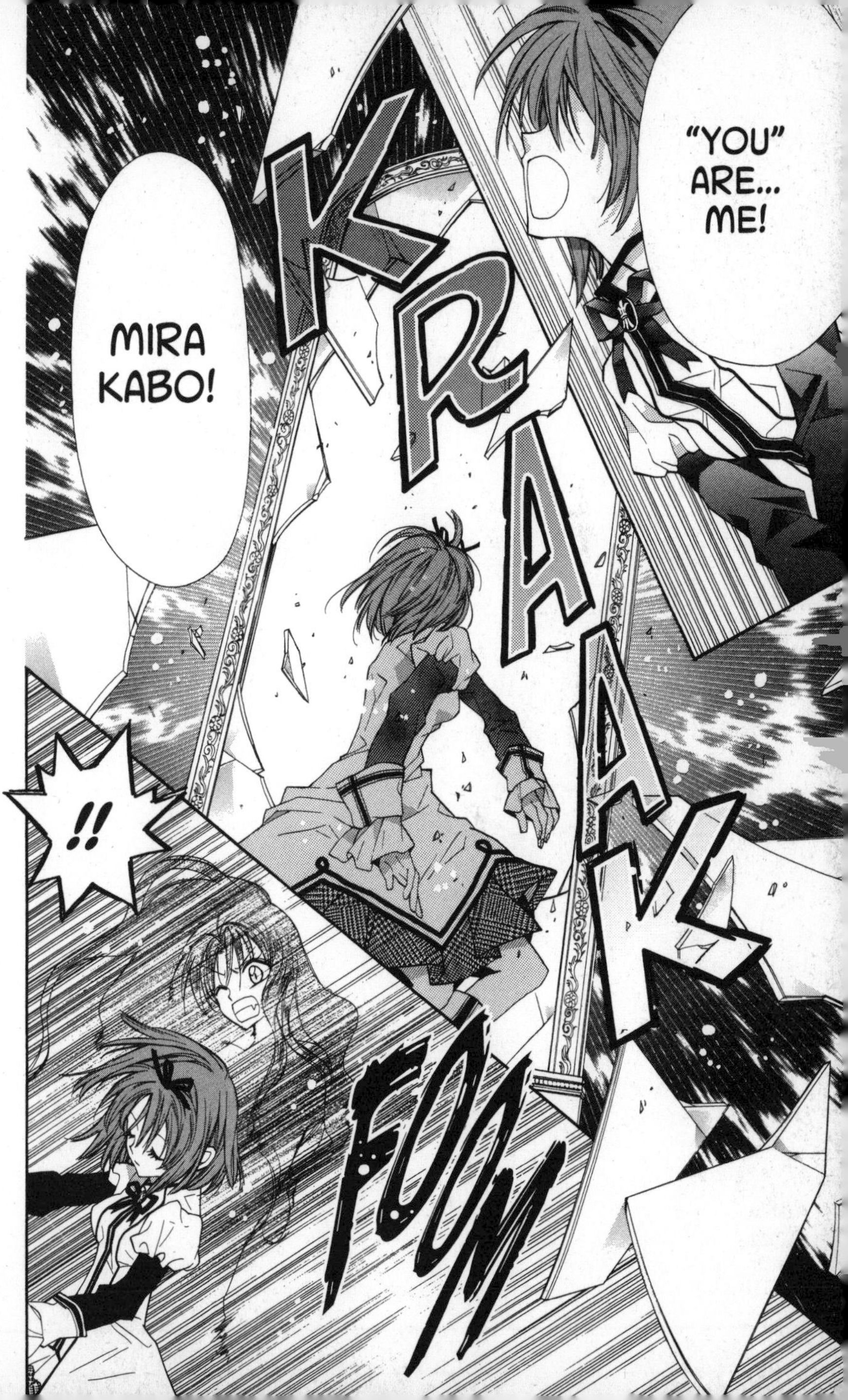
"YOU" ARE... ME!
KRAAAK
MIRA KABO!
!!

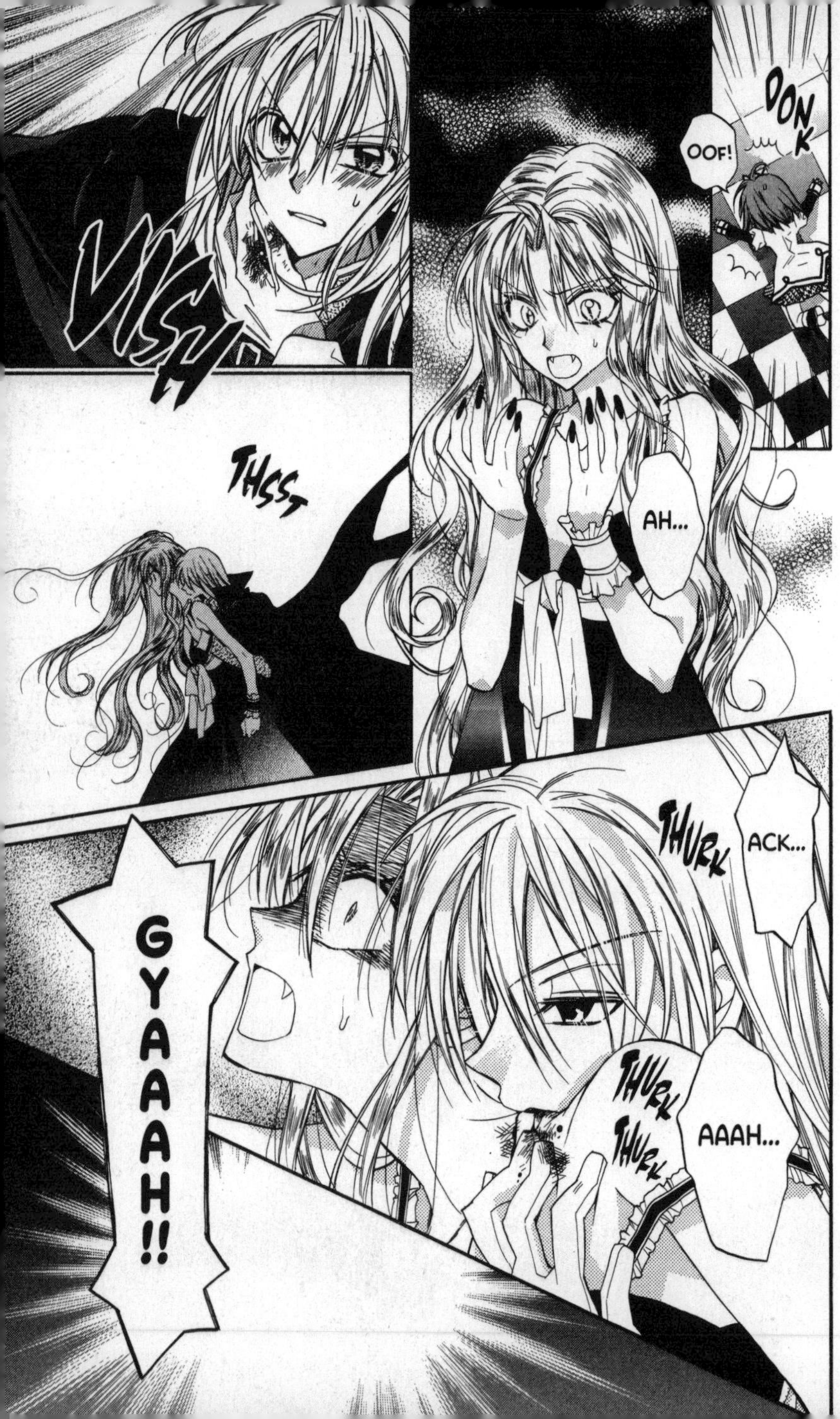
DONK
OOF!
AH...
VISH
THSST
THURK
ACK...
THURK THURK
AAAH...
GYAAAAH!!

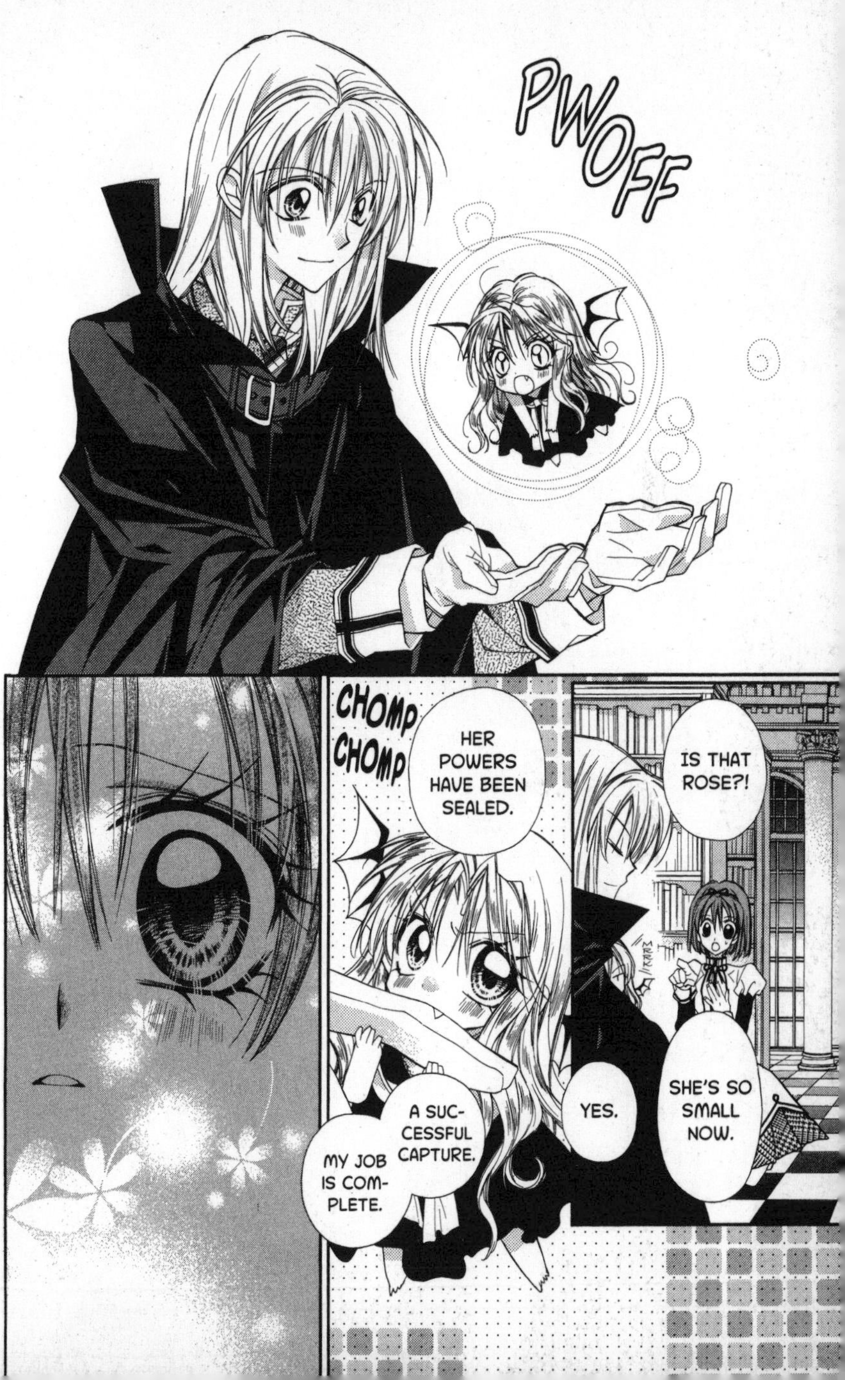
PWOFF
IS THAT ROSE?!
SHE'S SO SMALL NOW.
YES.
CHOMP CHOMP
HER POWERS HAVE BEEN SEALED.
A SUC-CESSFUL CAPTURE.
MY JOB IS COM-PLETE.

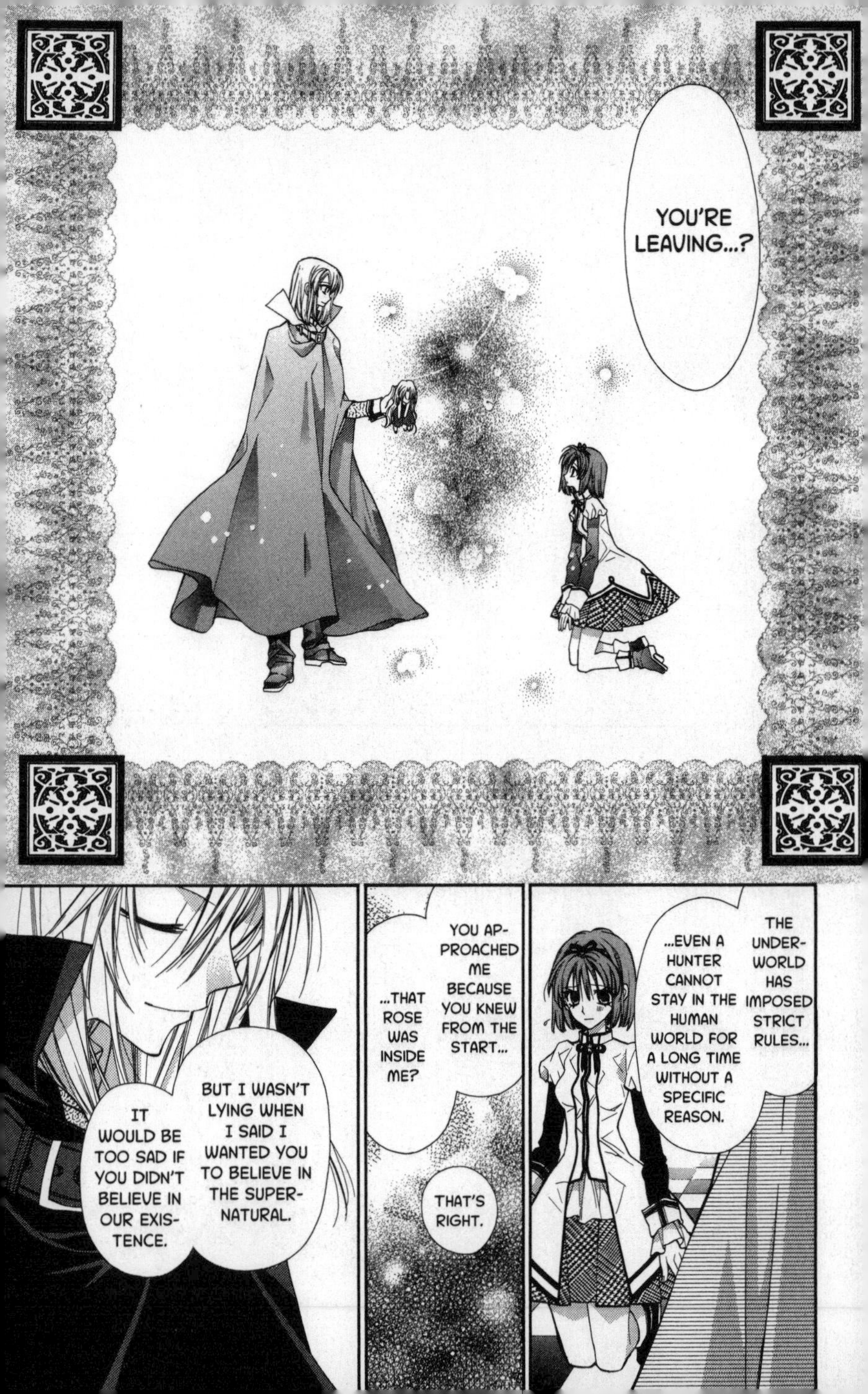
YOU'RE LEAVING...?
THE UNDERWORLD HAS IMPOSED STRICT RULES...
...EVEN A HUNTER CANNOT STAY IN THE HUMAN WORLD FOR A LONG TIME WITHOUT A SPECIFIC REASON.
YOU APPROACHED ME BECAUSE YOU KNEW FROM THE START...
...THAT ROSE WAS INSIDE ME?
THAT'S RIGHT.
BUT I WASN'T LYING WHEN I SAID I WANTED YOU TO BELIEVE IN THE SUPERNATURAL.
IT WOULD BE TOO SAD IF YOU DIDN'T BELIEVE IN OUR EXISTENCE.

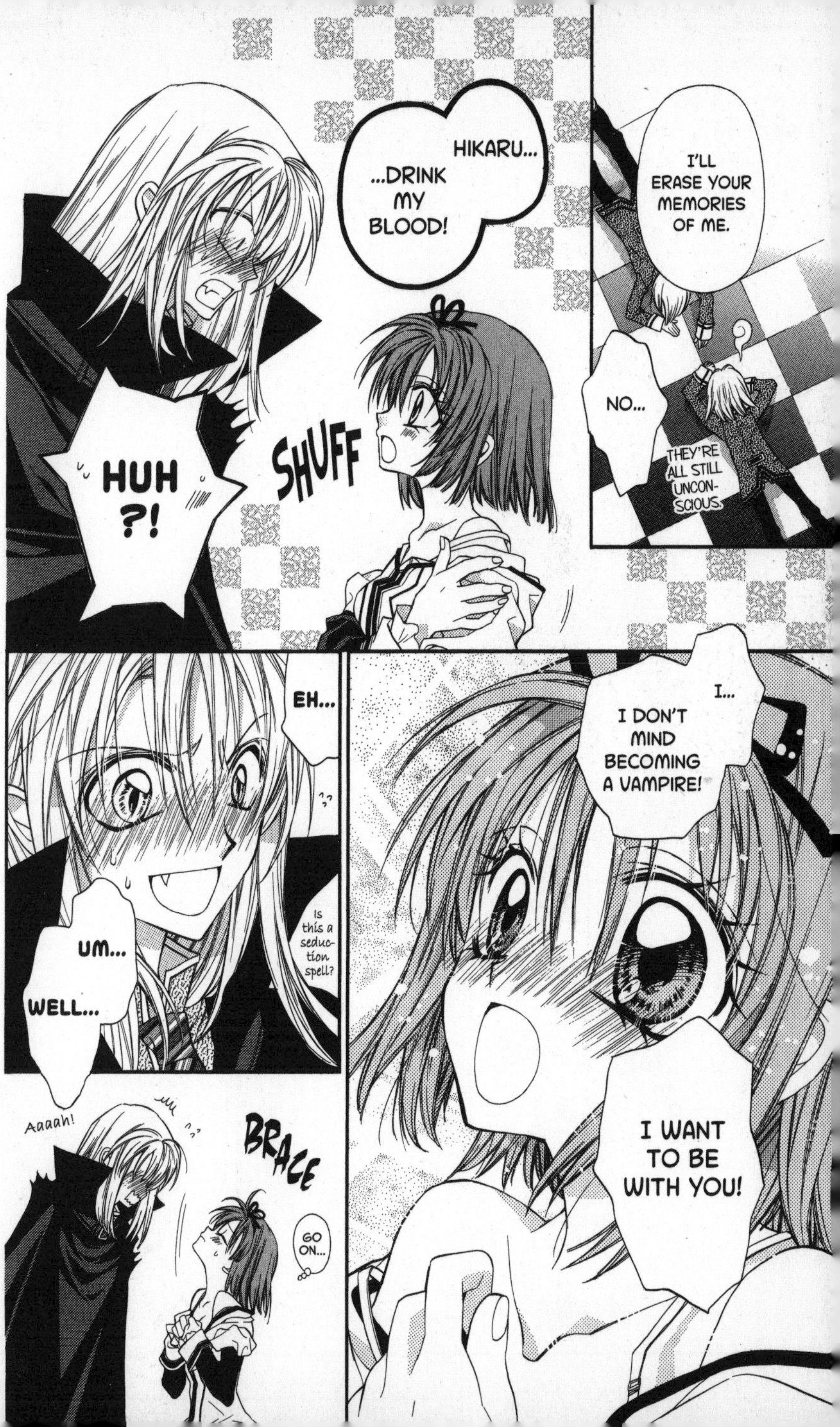
I'LL ERASE YOUR MEMORIES OF ME.
NO...
THEY'RE ALL STILL UNCONSCIOUS.
HIKARU...
...DRINK MY BLOOD!
SHUFF
HUH ?!
I...
I DON'T MIND BECOMING A VAMPIRE!
I WANT TO BE WITH YOU!
EH...
Is this a seduction spell?
UM...
WELL...
BRACE
Aaaah!
GO ON...

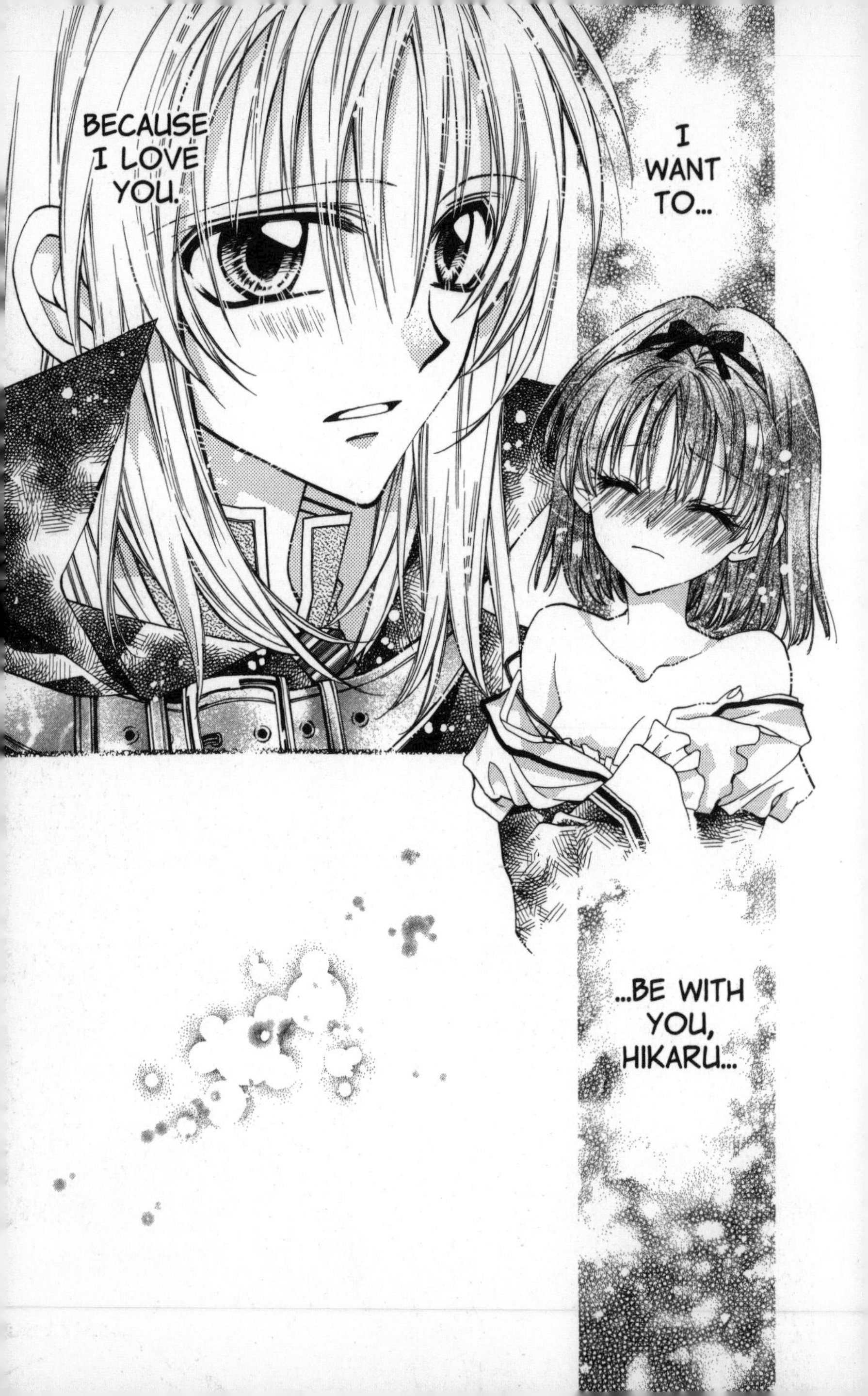
I WANT TO...
BECAUSE I LOVE YOU.
...BE WITH YOU, HIKARU...

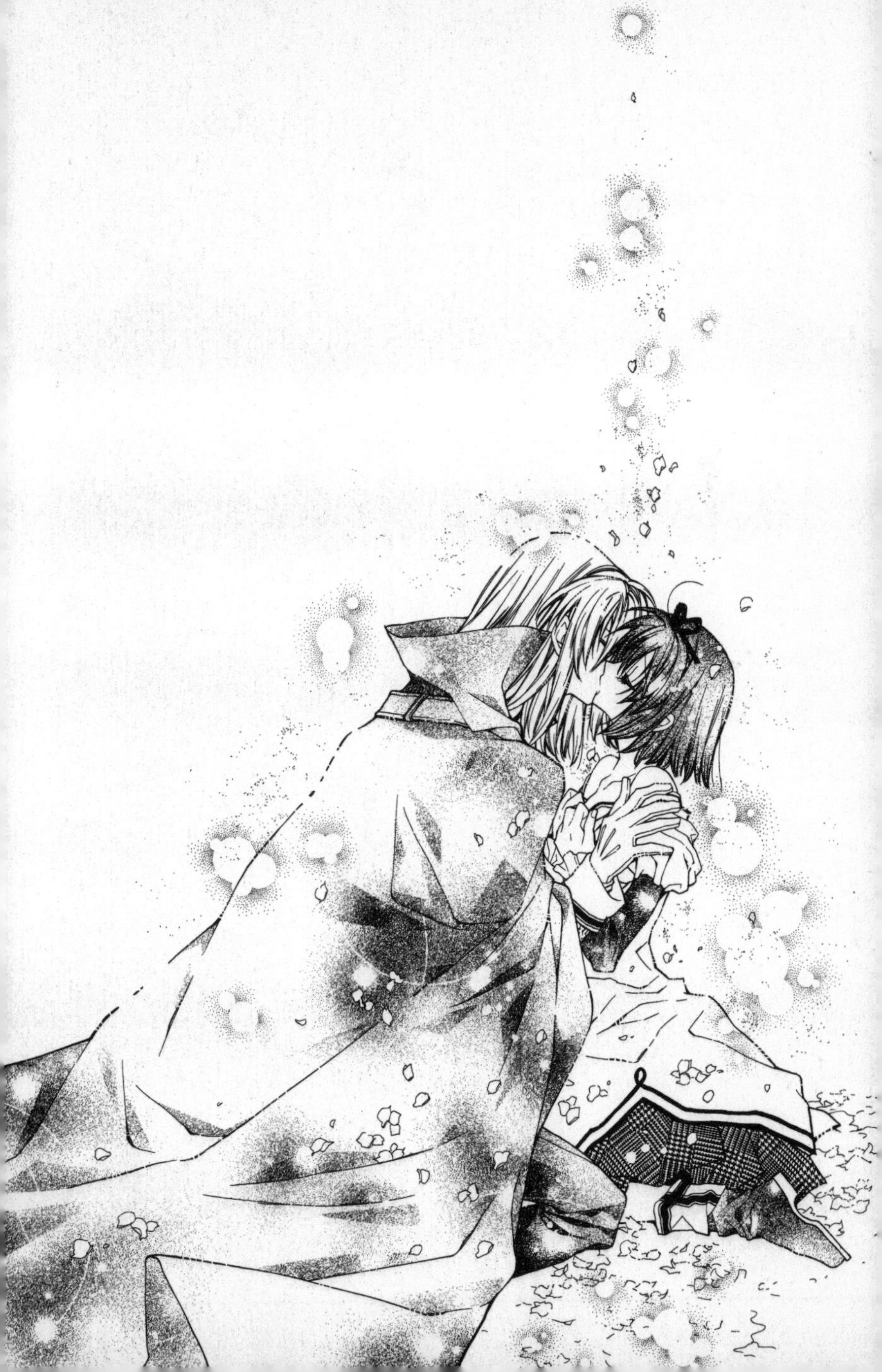

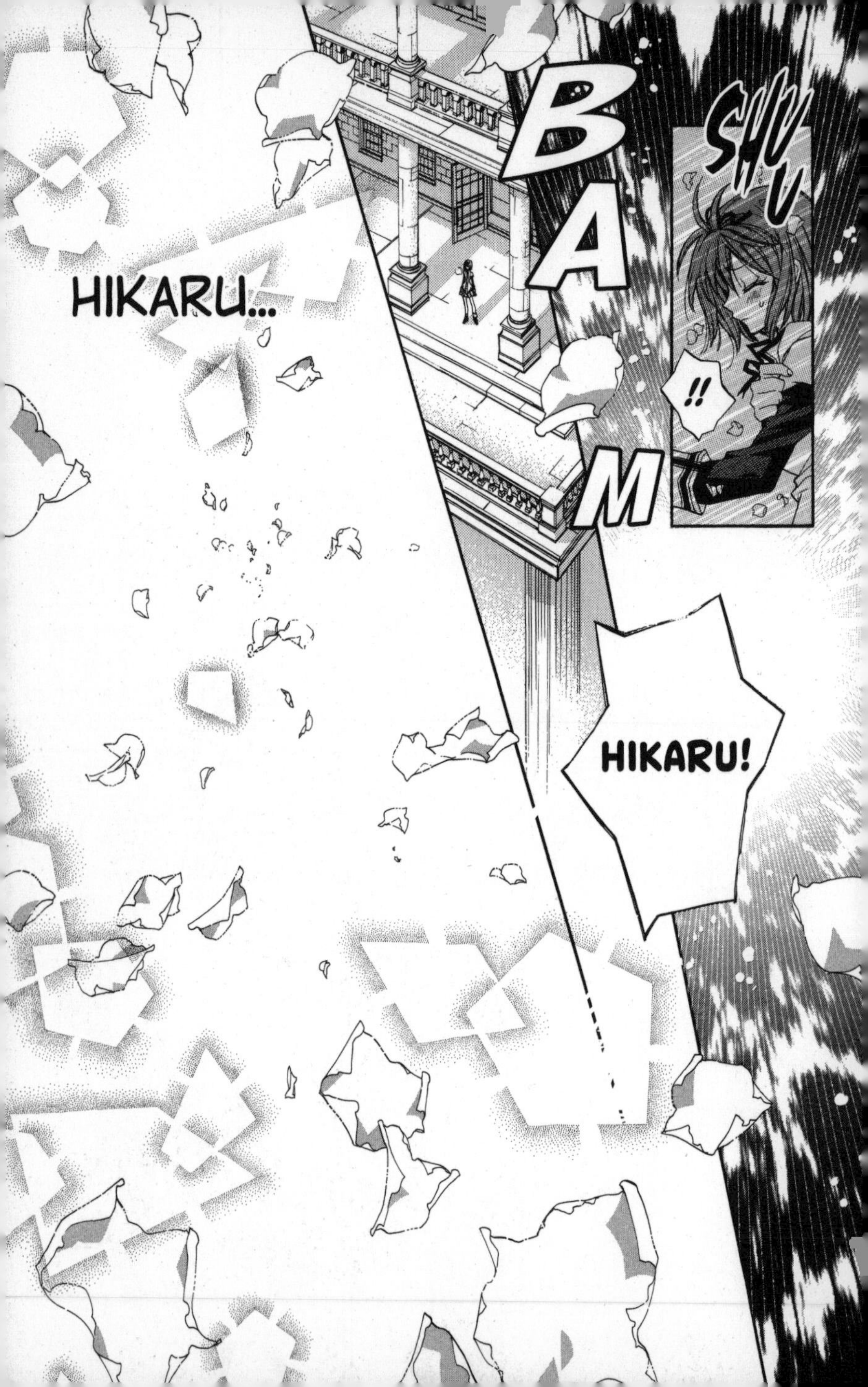
SHUU
!!
BAM
HIKARU!
HIKARU...

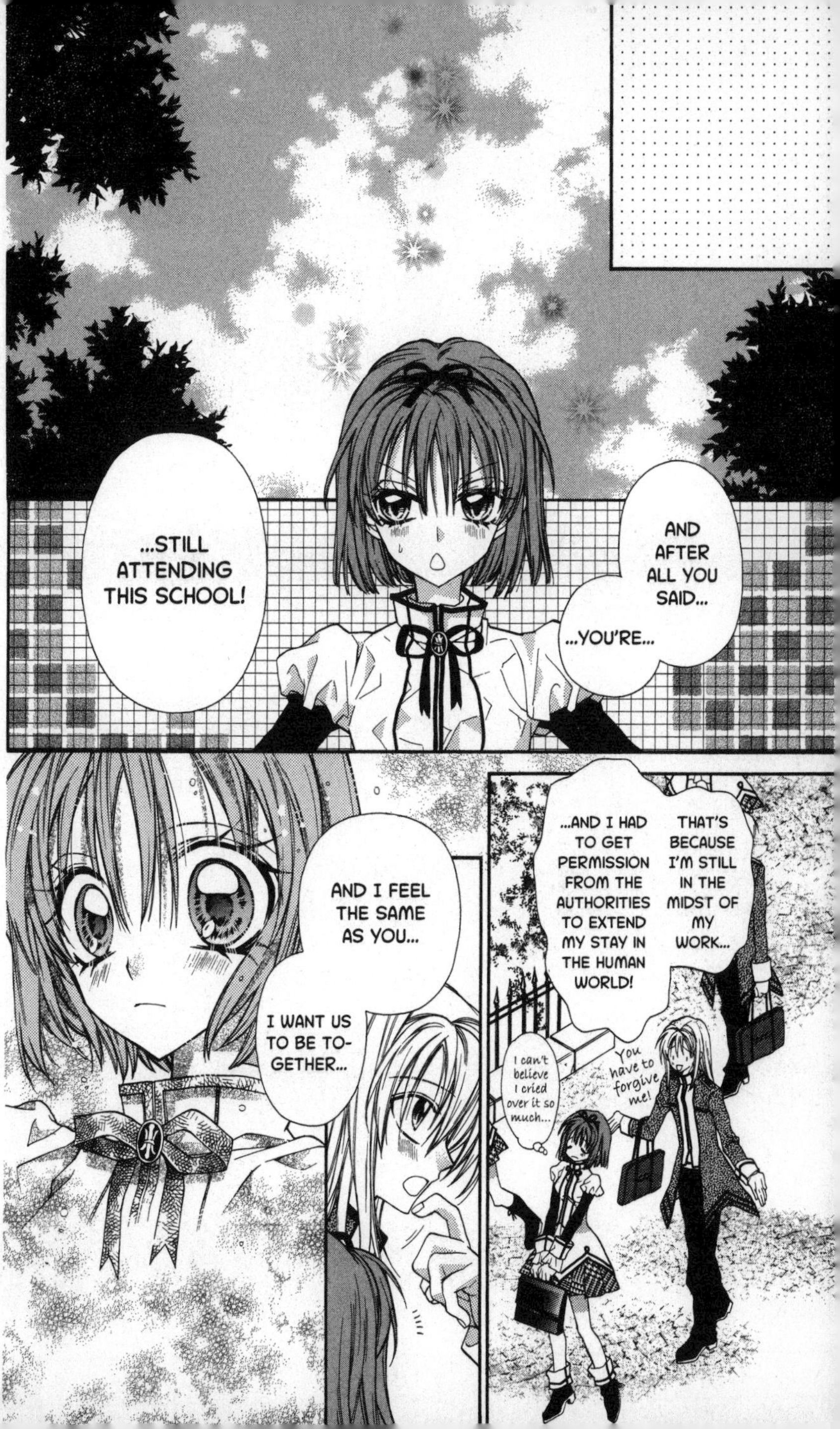
AND AFTER ALL YOU SAID...
...YOU'RE...
...STILL ATTENDING THIS SCHOOL!
THAT'S BECAUSE I'M STILL IN THE MIDST OF MY WORK...
...AND I HAD TO GET PERMISSION FROM THE AUTHORITIES TO EXTEND MY STAY IN THE HUMAN WORLD!
You have to forgive me!
I can't believe I cried over it so much...
AND I FEEL THE SAME AS YOU...
I WANT US TO BE TO-GETHER...

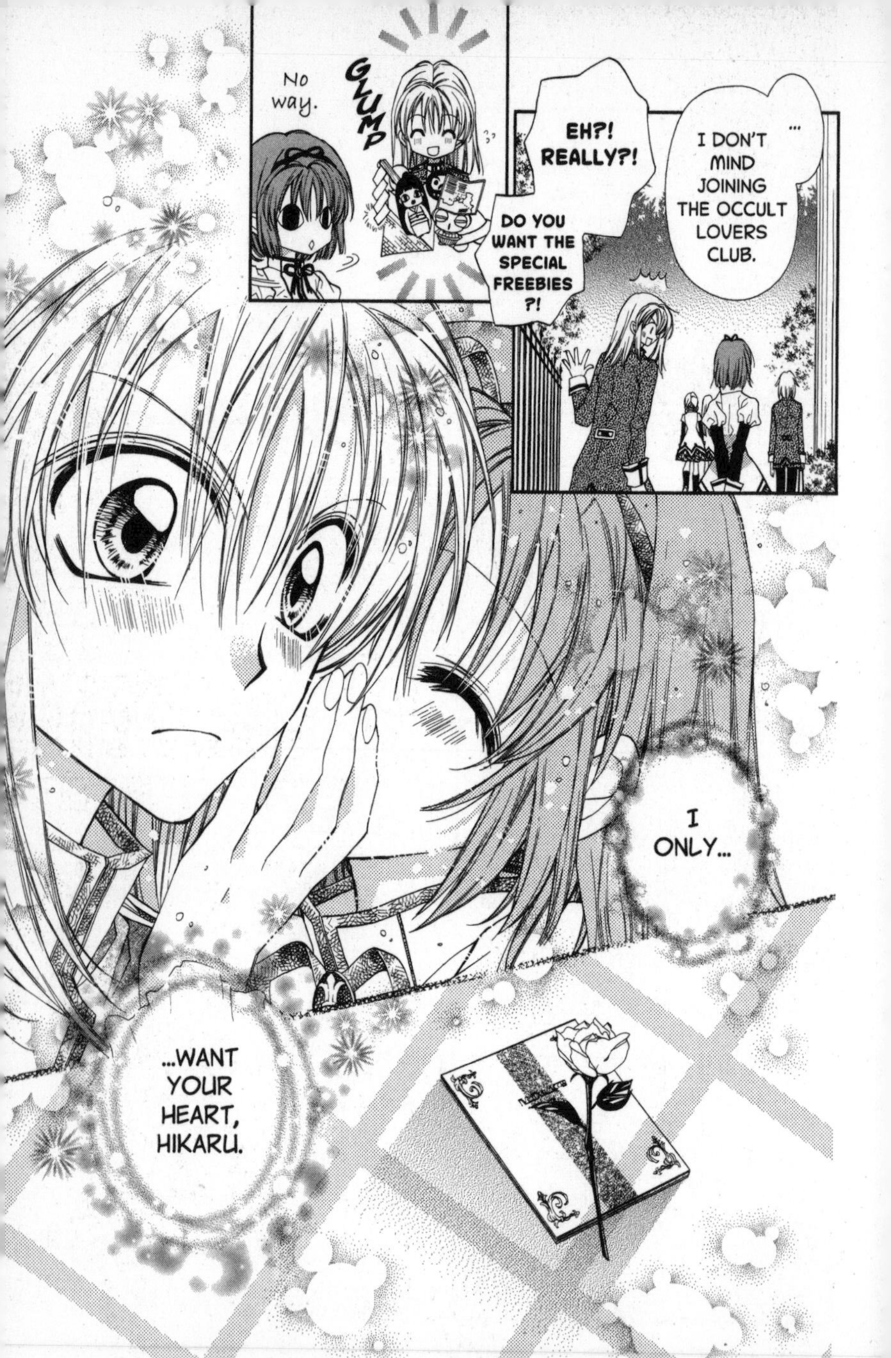
...
I DON'T MIND JOINING THE OCCULT LOVERS CLUB.
EH?! REALLY?!
DO YOU WANT THE SPECIAL FREEBIES ?!
GLUMP
No way.
I ONLY...
...WANT YOUR HEART, HIKARU.

White Rose Academy: Vampire Rose/End

The return of?!

HINACHI GA SHAKIN☆

~ Inside Ammonite?! Assistant Diary ~

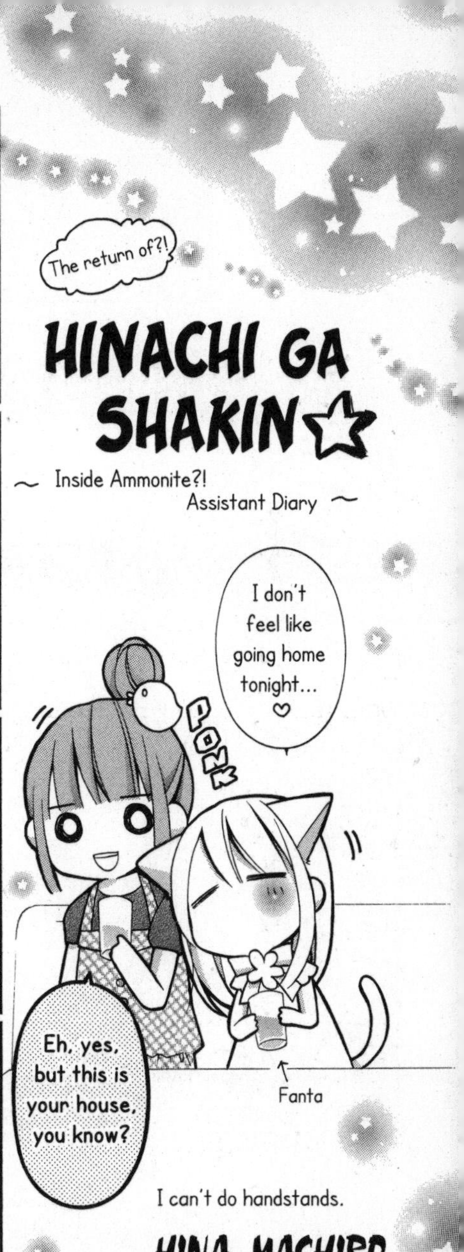
I don't feel like going home tonight... ♡
POMF
Eh, yes, but this is your house, you know?
Fanta

I can't do handstands.

HINA MASHIRO

Yaya Puri volume 1 is on sale in Japan!

Excitement Thief

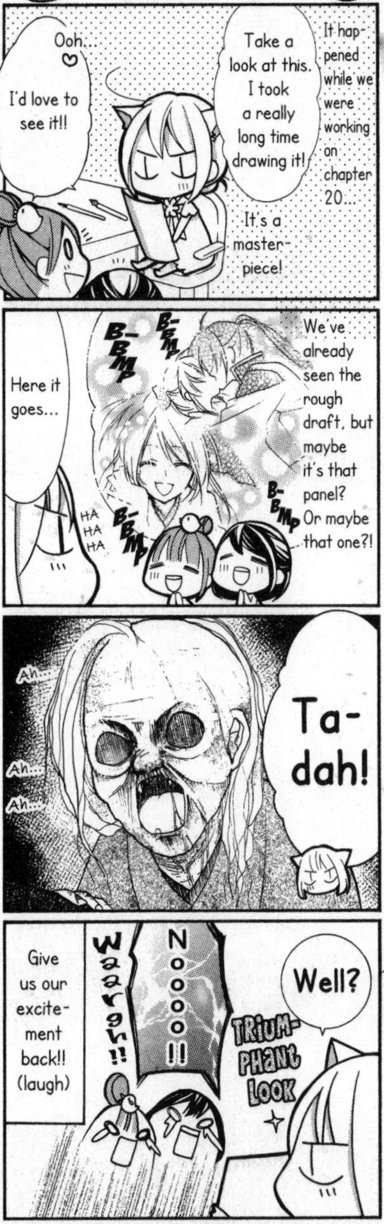
It happened while we were working on chapter 20...
Take a look at this. I took a really long time drawing it!
It's a masterpiece!
Ooh... ♡
I'd love to see it!!
We've already seen the rough draft, but maybe it's that panel? Or maybe that one?!
B-BMP
B-BMP
B-BMP
B-BMP
Here it goes...
HA HA HA
Ta-dah!
Ah...
Ah...
Ah...
Well?
TRIUMPHANT LOOK
Noooo!!
Waaargh!!
Give us our excitement back!! (laugh)

※ Chapter 20 will be included in *Sakura Hime: The Legend of Princess Sakura* volume 6.

Detonation Switch

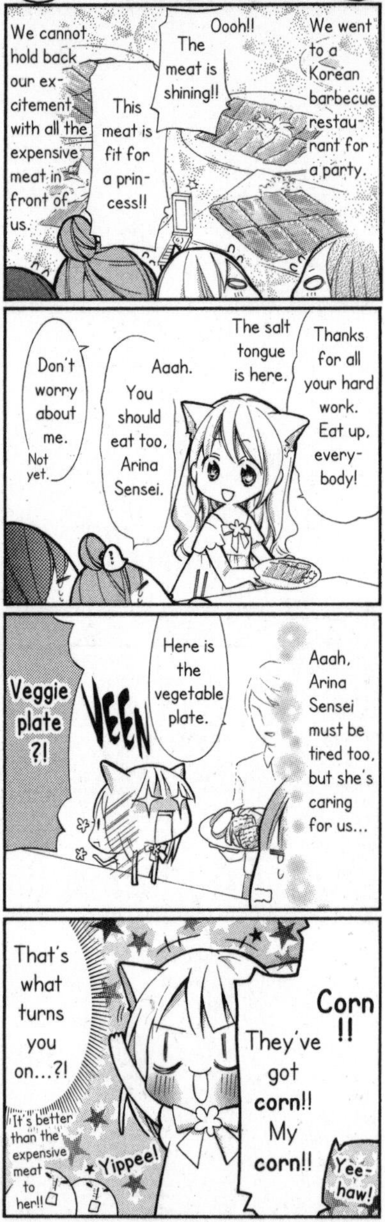
We went to a Korean barbecue restaurant for a party.
Oooh!!
The meat is shining!!
This meat is fit for a princess!!
We cannot hold back our excitement with all the expensive meat in front of us.
Thanks for all your hard work. Eat up, everybody!
The salt tongue is here.
Aaah. You should eat too, Arina Sensei.
Don't worry about me.
Not yet.
Aaah, Arina Sensei must be tired too, but she's caring for us...
Here is the vegetable plate.
VEEN
Veggie plate?!
Corn!!
They've got corn!! My corn!!
Yee-haw!
That's what turns you on...?!
Yippee!
It's better than the expensive meat to her!!

A Very Big Part

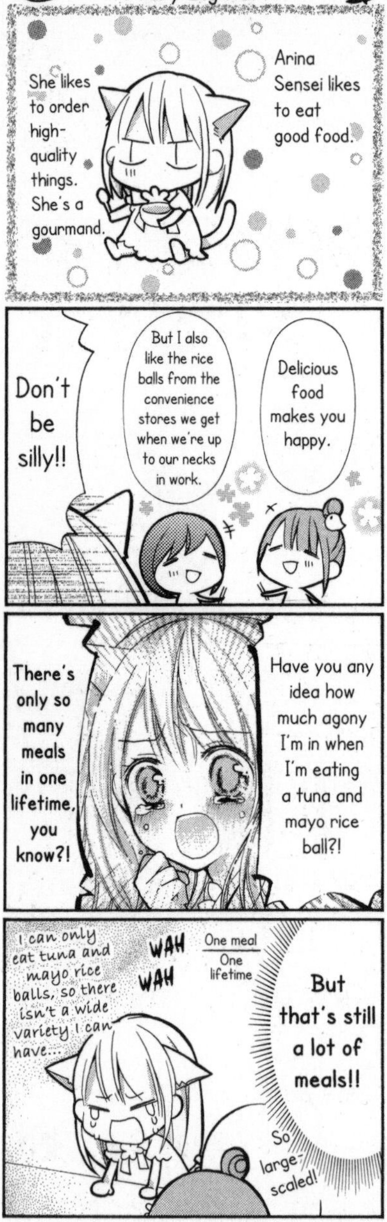
Arina Sensei likes to eat good food.
She likes to order high-quality things. She's a gourmand.
Delicious food makes you happy.
But I also like the rice balls from the convenience stores we get when we're up to our necks in work.
Don't be silly!!
Have you any idea how much agony I'm in when I'm eating a tuna and mayo rice ball?!
There's only so many meals in one lifetime, you know?!
But that's still a lot of meals!!
One meal
One lifetime
WAH WAH
I can only eat tuna and mayo rice balls, so there isn't a wide variety I can have...
So large-scaled!

Failure to Launch

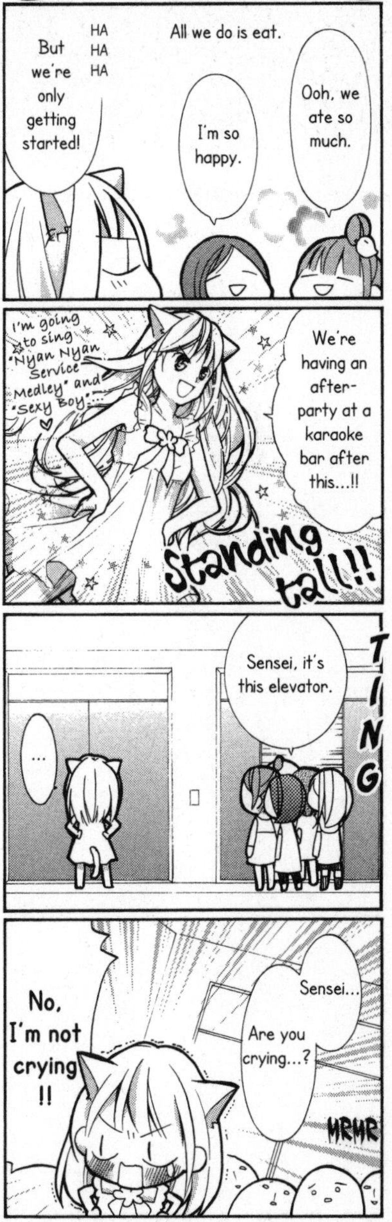

Ooh, we ate so much.
I'm so happy.
All we do is eat.
HA HA HA
But we're only getting started!
We're having an after-party at a karaoke bar after this...!!
I'm going to sing "Nyan Nyan Service Medley" and "Sexy Boy"
Standing tall!!
TING
Sensei, it's this elevator.
...
Sensei... Are you crying...?
HRMR
No, I'm not crying!!

A Fad at Work

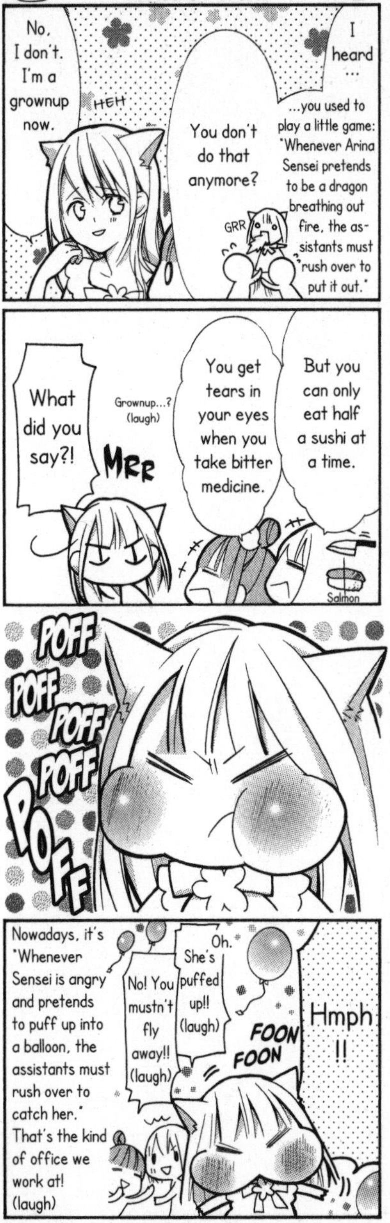

I heard...
...you used to play a little game: "Whenever Arina Sensei pretends to be a dragon breathing out fire, the assistants must rush over to put it out."
GRR
You don't do that anymore?
No, I don't. I'm a grownup now.
HEH
But you can only eat half a sushi at a time.
Salmon
You get tears in your eyes when you take bitter medicine.
Grownup...? (laugh)
What did you say?!
MRR
POFF POFF POFF POFF POFF
Hmph!!
FOON FOON
Oh. She's puffed up!! (laugh)
No! You mustn't fly away!! (laugh)
Nowadays, it's "Whenever Sensei is angry and pretends to puff up into a balloon, the assistants must rush over to catch her." That's the kind of office we work at! (laugh)

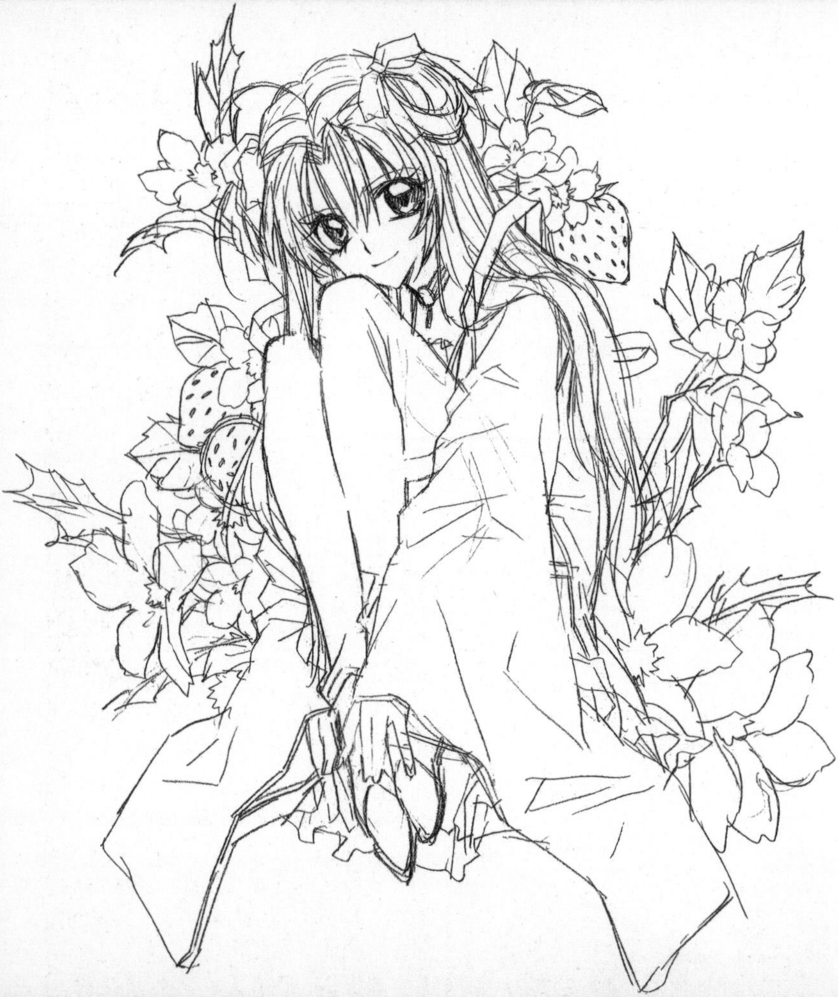

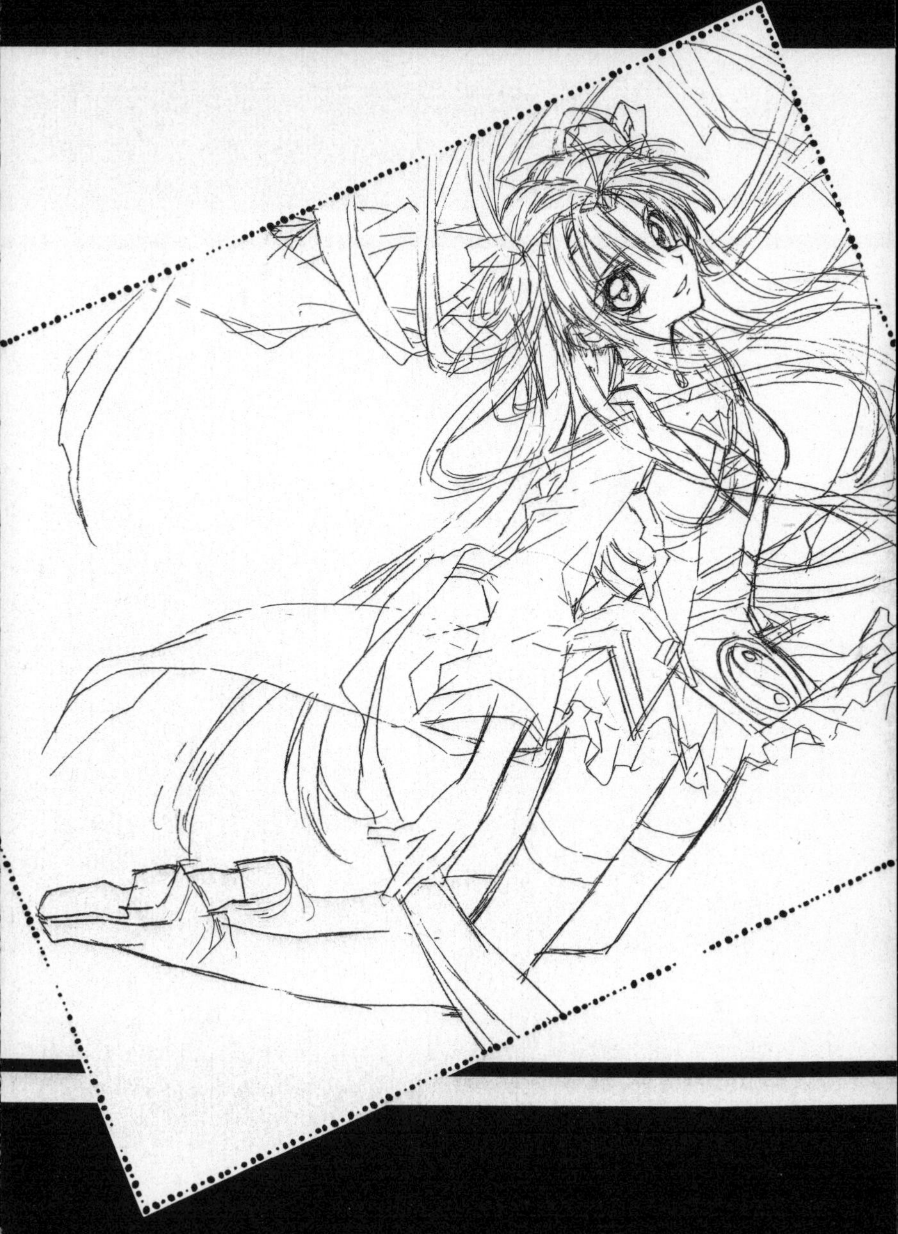

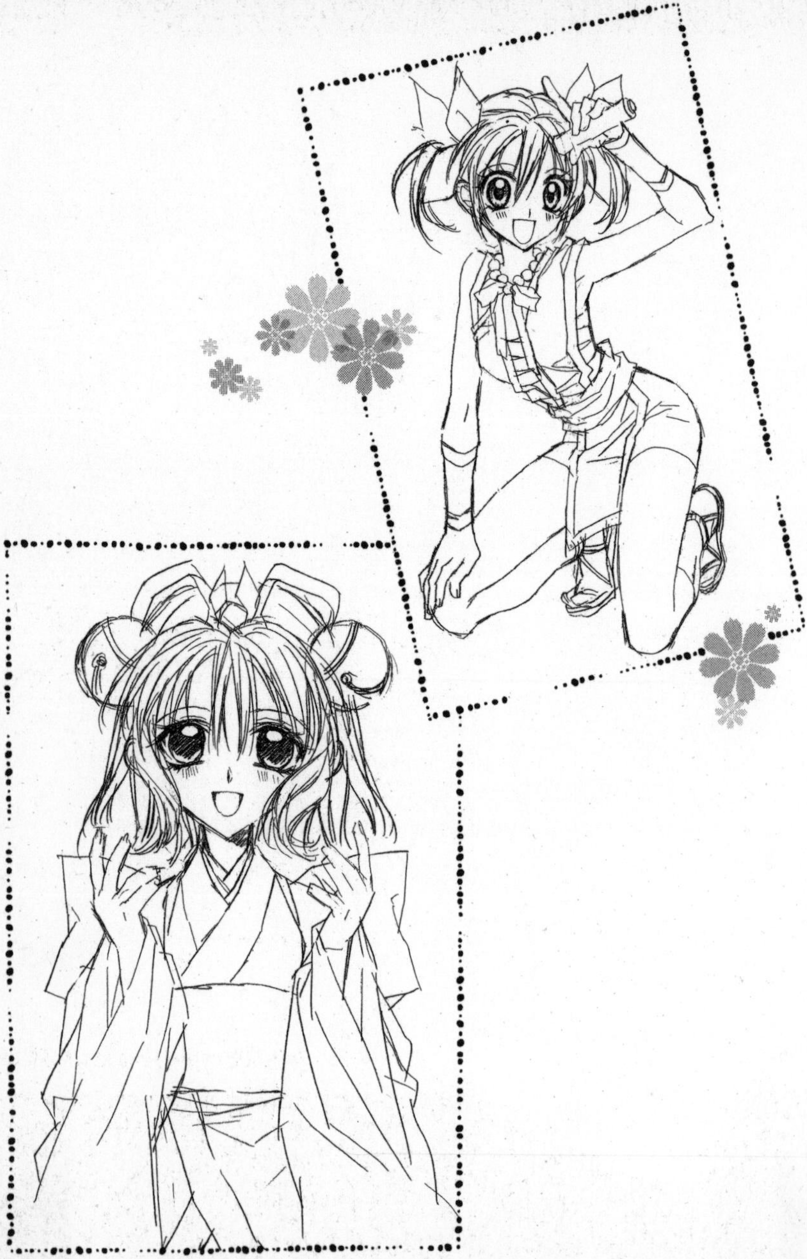

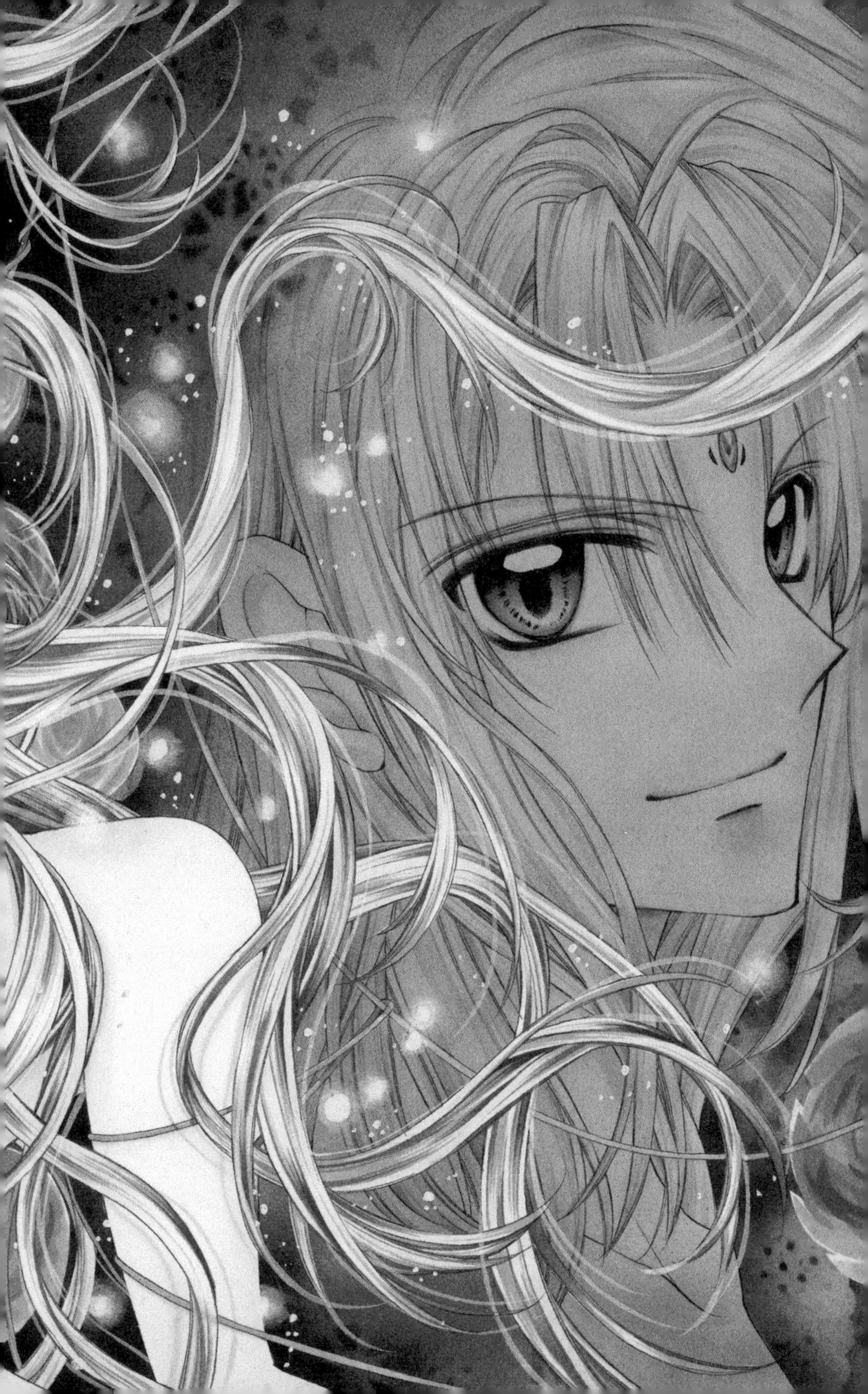